Seven Stages to co-Creating PROSPERITY FROM YOUR SOUL: A Step-By-Step Guide to Reclaiming Your Ideal Life

A Lifestyle of PROSPERITY FROM YOUR SOUL: A Guide to Living a Prosperity-Magnetizing Lifestyle

Coming Soon

Books:

Reiki – The Light of Your Soul: USUI REIKI RYOHO—臼 井 靈 気 療 法 *As Originally Taught by Mikao Usui*

Innovative Modalities:

RezoDance: meditative healing movement imbued with reiki energy and Nature elements to affect complete balance, and harness the freedom of spirit to affect freedom of mind and body.

Rezossage: holistic massage modality that treats the whole person, and affects deep changes in a nurturing way. Deep tissue massage without pain!

Retreat Courses:

Level 1 – Prosperity From Your Soul: Combining the metaphysical understandings of the book Prosperity From Your Soul, with reiki training, and RezoDance empowerment, leading you through the Seven Stages of tuning into your Ideal Lifeplan, and devising a specific plan of action to manifest it. A weeklong retreat.

Level 2 – Soul Communications & Soul Mates: Learn to employ True communications in all of your relationships, from the business place to your Soulmates, and by that, magnetize a higher degree of happiness, health, and True abundance into your life. A weeklong retreat course, which includes Second Degree reiki training, as well as a Kindness Massage training.

Level 3 – Reiki Mastership & RezoDance Facilitators Course: Become empowered as a reiki master, and learn the art of hosting and facilitating RezoDance sessions. A weeklong retreat, which empowers and prepares participants to open their own reiki school and RezoDance studio.

Level 4 – Rezossage Course: A yearlong 650-hour course, which teaches the art of Rezossage.

Prosperity From Your Soul

The Metaphysics of co-Creating Your Ideal Life

Zohar Love

BALBOA
PRESS

A DIVISION OF HAY HOUSE

Balboa Press books may be ordered through booksellers or by contacting:

Balboa Press
A Division of Hay House
1663 Liberty Drive
Bloomington, IN 47403
www.balboapress.com
1 (877) 407-4847

ISBN: 978-1-5043-2669-8 (sc)
ISBN: 978-1-5043-2670-4 (e)

Print information available on the last page.

Balboa Press rev. date: 06/08/2015

Contents

Introduction

Have you ever wished for an easier, more fulfilling way to manifest prosperity for yourself and your family? Don't you just wish that everything you need and want would fall into your lap easily and abundantly? And don't you sometimes wish you could drop all anger and stress, let go of the rat race, and gracefully cruise through life without having to worry about your finances? Do you sometimes feel like your life is in a stuck place that doesn't hold much joy for you? For most of us, the answer to at least some of those questions is "yes". And most of us tend to get caught up in a go-go-go achievement mode, which doesn't necessarily produce good results in terms of prosperity, health, or happiness.

But let me also ask you: have you ever made a choice you thought was right at the time, but trying to follow through mounted every block in your way? Then have you ever changed course and found that everything was suddenly going your way? Gifts and opportunities just fall into your lap abundantly, and everything was just cruising along easily and joyfully? This is something that happens to most of us at one point or another: we choose one path and everything is going difficult; we then choose an alternate path, and everything is just smooth sailing. But the biggest question is: What if there were a way to always walk the path that leads to smooth sailing? How nice would it be if you could always know and *choose* the path in which health, happiness, and prosperity come easily and abundantly? And how wonderful would it be if you could make that your new way of life.

Well, **you can! This is the path of Prosperity From Your Soul!** But let me qualify that: This book is *not* a "get-rich-quick" scheme! It is about co-Creating prosperity into your life harmoniously, joyously, walking the ideal, most auspicious path you can walk through life, from the highest perspective possible.

What Is Prosperity?

But what exactly is Prosperity? Have you ever asked yourself that? Even at first glance, it is obvious that true prosperity encompasses more than just money. *Wikipedia* defines prosperity as: "… the state of flourishing, thriving, success, or good fortune. Prosperity often encompasses wealth but also includes others factors which are independent of wealth to varying degrees, such as happiness and health." The *Miriam Webster* dictionary defines prosperity as "an ample quantity, a relative degree of plentifulness." Notice that there is no mention of money in that definition. Further, Webster's definition of the verb 'to prosper' is: "to succeed in an enterprise or activity; especially economic success; to become strong and flourishing; to cause to succeed or thrive." So while the definition of the verb does encompass economic success, the main emphasis is on success, strength, and a state of thriving and flourishing. So even from these definitions, it becomes obvious that true prosperity is *more than* just an abundance of money, and more than having a good investment portfolio, although it certainly includes an abundant flow of money.

True prosperity comes from the deeper knowing that you are, and always will be, provided for; that everything is going to be all right in the greater sense—a knowing deep within you, which accompanies you throughout your life, that your True Source for prosperity is Infinite, that your natural state of being IS love, joy, happiness, health, freedom, and abundance, and that you are worthy of all that because it is your birthright! And the beauty of it is – the kind of prosperity that we are talking about is quite literally Infinite! It is without limits because it encompasses all that the Universe has to offer you!

Of course true prosperity does include an abundance of money. But it also includes the whole… I gave it a funny acronym BACE LHA LHA FAJG (pronounced like BAKE LA LA FUDGE), which stands for:

Beauty – within, all around you, and in everything/everyone you encounter

peAce – the inner peace of knowing that everything is absolutely going to be alright

Connection – Oneness with Universal resources and with Creation

IntelligencE – Divine guidance and intelligence guiding your life

Light – Divine Light and goodness, lightheartedness and Divinely resourced power to manifest anything you truly wish for

Health – perfect balance and health: spiritually, emotionally, mentally & physically

Abundance – of money, love, success, and all that is good

Love – feeling absolutely beloved, loving your life & manifesting loving relationships

HAppiness – deep happiness within that bursts with the zest of life

Freedom – of choice, freedom from all bondage and freedom of spirit

rAdiance – feeling the Divine radiance protecting you and making your Light truly shine

Grace – enjoying Divine Grace within you and in the circumstances of your life

Joy – feeling true joy in every moment of your life

I know this list sounds a little too good to be true. But it really isn't! It is what you were meant for. And *all you need do in order to receive this kind of prosperity is live authentically from the perspective of your truest Self.* In this book, we will discuss why once the True You is restored, everything else follows, and why *your Original Self was always designed to be abundant in every way!* In the book *Seven Stages to co-Creating Prosperity From Your Soul* (published separately), I will show you how to restore your True Original Self, and thus restore the free flow of Divine Abundance that was always meant to be yours, and in the book *A Lifestyle of Prosperity From Your Soul* (also published separately), I will show you how to bring all of those internal changes into physical manifestation in the reality of your life. You see – the reason why you always strive for health, beauty, love, happiness, joy, radiance, and abundance is because they are of you, and you are of them. Your Original Self was carved directly out of Oneness *completely stress free, perfectly healthy, radiantly joyous, enormously beloved, and absolutely abundant in every way!* And that's why these things resonate with the truest part of you. Like attracts like! To harvest that crop of health, happiness, and prosperity, all you need do is restore your original state of being, and… presto! The rest takes care of itself.

Now, you might ask: "Whom/what is this original-Self that I have to restore myself to?" We will cover that in depth in Chapter 1. And we will spend the first part of the book understanding why it is that your own original-Self is in charge of bringing you the successful manifestations of your desires, and how the manifestation process works, from a metaphysical perspective. In other words, we'll go into the nuts and bolts of how to manifest prosperity. By the end of the first part of the book, you'll be an expert on how manifestation works. But for now, the short answer is: your original-Self is this best version of you. The simplest way of understanding the premise here is: where there is health and happiness, there is lightness and ease in walking through the paths of life – a lightness that makes everything easier to come by. As you'll come to understand in this book, it is this lightness and connectedness with your True Self that leads to the manifestation of abundance in the most auspicious way—a way in which an abundance of blessings (including money) just easily fall into your lap—the way of Prosperity From Your Soul.

The Program

It is not enough to say, "just think positive, and you will magnetize good things into your life." There have been many books and movies that presented that approach. And as the millions of people who have started to follow these programs have ultimately come to find out – that simply isn't enough! In fact, that simplistic approach has failed to work for the majority of people. Despite the fact that you have been co-Creating your reality since birth (and even before), to be a *conscious* co-Creator, that is, to consciously co-Create only that which you Truly want, requires some training. This is what this book will give you: training in becoming *a conscious co-Creator*, and controlling what you magnetize and manifest into your life.

This book delves deeply into understanding the metaphysics of co-Creation of your life. It will give you a solid background of understanding the 'why' and 'how' of the manifestation process. The vantage point of these deep understandings will help you become a more successful co-Creator of your life, because just like with anything else in life, when you learn a skill by rote, it is difficult to be consistently good at it. But once you understand the nitty-gritty of why and how it works, it is much easier to become consistently good at it. The same logic applies to co-Creating your life: Understanding all aspects of the co-Creative process will help you become consistently good at consciously co-Creating the prosperity you seek.

That being said, I acknowledge that some of the metaphysical chapters of this book are loaded with information that may seem pretty esoteric at first. They may not be an easy read for everyone. So I invite you to use your inner wisdom, and skip through any parts that might cause you to get stuck. At first read, it is mostly important for you to get the jest of things. Once you start the meditational practices of the book *Seven Stages to co-Creating Prosperity From Your Soul*, your consciousness will dramatically open up to guidance from your Higher Self, and it will suddenly become easier to understand the parts of this book that you've skipped, because the concepts will then be backed up by experiential, internal knowing. At that point, you may want to go back and re-read the parts that were difficult before, so you can have some more aha moments to strengthen your understanding of the co-Creations in your life.

The second book of this series, *Seven Stages to co-Creating Prosperity From Your Soul*, will lead you through a very detailed seven-stage meditational process of becoming a more conscious co-Creator of prosperity in your life, tuning into *your unique, most ideal lifepath* (discussed in details in Chapter 2) of success, and devising a specific plan of action to merge your current life with your Ideal Lifepath. However, I will not spoon-feed you what to do to make more money, because by definition, *your ideal path of prosperity is your own unique path.* No one can walk that Lifepath for you, and no one can tell you the details of your Ideal Lifepath better than your Higher Self. All anyone can do is carefully guide you to get your own answers and your ultimate plan for success from your very own Higher Self. And that is what I will do in the second book: *Seven Stages to co-Creating Prosperity From Your Soul*.

The third book of this series, *A Lifestyle of Prosperity From Your Soul*, contains sound healthy practices that I have put to the test over the years with great results. Following these healthy practices will help you start to walk the path of a conscious co-Creator of your life, as they will help you start bringing the ethereal understandings that you have acquired in this book, and the internal decisions you've formulated during your *Seven Stages to co-Creating Prosperity From Your Soul* into the physical practices that are conducive to co-Creating prosperity. Your physical body is the host and the foundation for Creative energy to come through. It is the conduit for all the manifestations in your life and the vessel through which your Higher Self acts on the stage of your life. Thus, feeling freer and healthier in your body, will start you on your way to finding a harmony and balance in your daily life, as a first step towards allowing and making room for the new Creative energy of prosperity to come flowing into your physical reality.

As you can see, our path together starts from the very ethereal and becomes more grounded and anchored into reality gradually. The first part—understanding the metaphysics of co-Creation, while important, still has a very ethereal "out there" flavor to it. In *Seven Stages to co-Creating Prosperity From Your Soul*, you will ground these understanding into feelings and personal internal experiences, and allow them to grow roots within you. You will connect with the wisdom of your Highest Self, and allow it to guide you on what the best plan for success is *for you*. But even after *Seven Stages to co-Creating Prosperity From Your Soul*, even though your understanding will have hit home and be experiential, it will still not be anchored into action, although you certainly will have a specific plan of action at the end of *Seven Stages to co-Creating Prosperity From Your Soul*. *A Lifestyle of Prosperity From Your Soul* will help you further ground all of your conclusions, and actually walk the path of a successful co-Creator of prosperity.

Higher Power, Anyone?

Before you close this book with a big bang, let me just tell you that it is not necessary to believe in a higher power in order for you to reap the rewards of this program. The understandings and practices contained in this book will work for you whether you believe in God or not!

In fact, many people pride themselves in believing only what they can see or what can be proven in a laboratory by the "scientific method." On the other end of the spectrum, there are people who are suspicious of anything that doesn't bear the stamp of approval of their particular church. And that's OK. Whether you are an atheist, or believe that God to be the laws of physics, Nature, Jehovah, Jesus, Buddha, Shiva, or anything else, everyone agrees that there are unseen "unmeasurable" energies in the world, such as the energy of love, for example. And even scientists would have to agree that there are also un-provable truths that science pre-supposes (axioms). For example, to begin with, we cannot prove that science is logical because that proof in itself would require the use of logic in order to work, and you cannot use that which is being defined in the body of the definition. We also cannot prove by a scientific method that historical events really happened because the scientific method is about predicting results that are repeatable and measurable, and historical events by definition cannot be repeated or duplicated. We cannot prove morality, and yet somewhere inside all humans is a higher sense of morality, which transcends time, the individual's society, and geographical boundaries.

Another thing you cannot prove is that you are you. True, you can show your driver's license and prove your earthly identity. But who's to say that the way you perceive reality is based on fact? The only way of probing, or getting an impression of reality is through your five senses. But your eyes themselves don't see anything. Any first year medical student will tell you that sight itself happens in the brain, where the electrical impulse coming through your visual nerve get interpreted. The same is true for all of your senses: your ears don't hear anything, your pallet doesn't taste anything, your nose doesn't really smell anything, and your hands can't really sense any touch. All of the sensory inputs are really interpreted and understood in the brain. So it is the brain that sees, smells, tastes, hears, and touches. But there is a glitch: the brain itself is a "black box." No light or sound actually penetrates the brain itself. The brain doesn't actually smell or taste anything. And it has no sense of touch. It is blindly relying on the inputs from your sensory organs. So scientifically speaking, we have no way of proving definitively that you are not just a brain in a jar being manipulated to think that 'reality' is as you see it. You see, we presuppose science is logical; we assume historical events really happened; and we believe that the sensory input into your brain is telling you the truth about reality. So if we assume, presuppose and believe so much, than what's wrong with opening yourself up to entertaining the thought that there may be a higher intelligence and a loving energy out there that Creates this reality and helps you manifest your life? I'm not saying that you have to become devoutly religious in any, way, shape, or form. I'm just saying it wouldn't hurt if you open yourself up to possibilities, such as the possibility that you have a vital role in co-Creating your own life and your reality, a role that if you learn to control, becomes the key to manifesting True and all-inclusive prosperity in your life.

My Path

My own path of coming to know the Infinite actually started with my two atheistic parents who raised me to think logically and to trust only things that could be proven in a laboratory in the scientific method. In my youth, I studied biology, math, chemistry, and physics, which trained me in analytical thinking and in the scientific method. Then in my 20s and 30s, I pursued a career as an airline pilot and eventually became a captain, a career that didn't lend itself to spiritual interpretations. I mean, if for example, your right engine catches on fire shortly after takeoff, there is no time to say, "oh well let me meditate on what to do..." You have to act quickly and skillfully in order to extinguish the fire and bring the airplane back to safety. So I too started my way as a skeptic, or at the very least, an agnostic.

But with all my logical and analytical training, I always thought deeply about the world and about the True nature of our existence. My elementary school principal always used to pinch my cheek and ask me what I was thinking so deeply about. He used to tell my mother that he thought I was going to become a philosopher. You see, at some level deep beneath all the science, I felt that there had to be something more than just this physical existence, and I wanted to get to understand "it." Beyond particles and forces, there had to be a meaning to our existence, which was beyond continuing the human race, for continuing the human race was just the means of our survival, not a purpose in and of itself.

As a young adult, I read Stephen Hawking's *A Brief History of Time* and learned about the Big Bang. Understanding the deep implication of Hawking statement that the sum of all particles and their anti-particles in the universe was zero made me understand that in order to create a universe this vast out of "nothing," a tremendous amount of energy would have to be invested. But if I understood the first law of thermodynamics correctly—if indeed "energy cannot be created or destroyed," than the energy required to create the Big Bang must have always been there. Now it is true that one need not assume this immense always-has-been energy is intelligent or benevolent. But the second law of thermodynamics[1] states that entropy—total chaos—is constantly increasing and is the natural state of the universe. According to scientists[2], the low degree of entropy (i.e., the high degree of order) at the beginning of the universe is so precise that it cannot even be easily expressed with an ordinary mathematical number, let alone be attained by coincidence. This uniquely high degree of order simply cannot be explained unless you assume the presence of an intelligent Establisher-of-Order. Moreover, even the very laws of physics (including the law of entropy) that allow the creation of living systems display a level of order that cannot be explained by coincidence. So how can highly complex and orderly systems such as living cells, and sentient human beings, no less, exist in a universe that favors chaos?

Despite my logical understanding of how all this points to the existence of a supreme higher energy-intelligence, as many scientists do, I kept denying Its existence. I felt comfortable with my previous "purely scientific" understandings, and didn't wish to rock the boat. Of course, a change of paradigm is always uncomfortable. I guess I needed to experience it for myself in order to believe. When I was 23 and living in New York City, one evening I went to see the movie *Moonstruck*. As I stepped out of the theatre, it was snowing, and I was moonstruck by the beauty of the city in the snowflakes. As I crossed the street, a taxicab hit me and then everything went dark. Witnesses later told me that I had flipped twice in the air, hit again by the cab's windshield while I was inverted, and then I fell lifeless on the snow-covered asphalt. But while I was "lifeless," I was far from being unconscious. Being in this darkness was the most alive and sharp I've ever felt. At the same time, I was very aware that I was separate from my body. I was in a dark tunnel, and I kept asking, "Where is my body?" Despite my confusion, I had a deep sense of calm and knew everything was going to be alright. When I came to, the people who surrounded me said: "Wait, wait, we've got her, she's alive!" Although I did not see the "Light" as other near death experiencers report, after that accident I knew beyond doubt that I was more than just my body, and I know that my consciousness lives on even when my body is lifeless.

But it wasn't until many years later, when I became a reiki master, that I truly felt a Divine force working through me. I started experiencing so many "unexplained" healing miracles that the Divine energy performed through me that I could no longer deny that there is a higher power, which is intelligent and benevolent—a God of all-encompassing Love.

The Science Of God

Because of my background in science, I understand what goes on in the mind of a skeptic. And because of my healer's deep love for humanity, I lovingly accept you, your belief system, and where you are in your personal evolution. As a side-note here, there have been many scientists throughout history that believed in God, including Nicolaus Copernicus, Sir Francis Bacon, Johannes Kepler, Galileo Galilei, René Descartes, Blaise Pascal, Sir Isaac Newton, Sir Robert Boyle, Michael Faraday, Gregor Mendel, William Thompson Kelvin, Max Planck, and Albert Einstein, to name a few. Albert Einstein was quoted saying: "I want to know how God created this world. I am not interested in this or that phenomenon, in the spectrum of this or that element. I want to know His thoughts, the rest are details."

Now from a logical perspective, let me ask you – what is the point of maintaining or living by any particular belief system or discipline, if not to derive pleasure, health, happiness, and prosperity from it? What's the point of waking up at four o'clock in the morning and doing your daily yoga or workout routine, if not to make you healthy and happy? What is the point of giving up your favorite thing in Lent, or fasting in Ramadan if not to win Divine favor that would bring you health, happiness, and prosperity? You see, *from a logical standpoint, the validity of any practice is measured by its results!* When scientists devise an experiment, they start from a hypothesis of the predicted results and a hypothetical explanation of the processes they think may lead to those specific results. When the experiment confirms the predicted results, they then conclude that the hypothesis was correct. So from this perspective, does your atheism/skepticism towards a higher power make you happy? Does it empower you? Does it use all facets available to you to promote your health? And does it help you financially thrive?

If, on the other hand, you believe (or your old preacher had convinced you) that we are all sinners and that the wrath of God is coming, does that belief system empower you? Does it make you happy? In other words, does your current belief system support your greatness? Does it foster the manifestation of health, happiness, and prosperity into your life? Or does it keep you limited by pre-programed attitudes of "I can't" and "I'm not worthy?" So if you are not completely satisfied with the way things currently are your life, one question that you should also ask yourself is: Is there anything besides fear that makes you stick to it and resist change? The point is to open up your mind to a reality that is much wider-scoped and more multi-faceted than the one you have perceived until now, as well as to put your belief system to the test: does it help you manifest the life that you want?

Now for those of you who are religious: co-Creating your reality along with God does not negate humility and awe of God. God is the Creator, the process of Creation, and the manifested Creation all at once. God is the intelligence and the spark of life within each of us. That is a fact. She-He is the essence of every living thing. Her-His Infinity flows into each part of Creation to manifest blessings in your life. Therefore, God is the Source of all inspiration and wishes you might have, as well as the power enabling their manifestation. We will talk about the process of co-Creation in depth in the chapters to come. But in a nutshell, the way it works is: you exercise your free will to provide the intent for your desired manifestation, and God provides the power to make it happen. That is why I prefer the term co-Creation to the word manifestation.

Throughout the book, I will be referring to God in many names such as "The Infinite," "The Love," "Divine," "The Light," "Truth," and many others. Words that are capitalized (unless they are names) infer that they are referring to something that is Divine in nature. Similarly, throughout this book, I'll be referring to God as She-He (or Her-His). This is because God and Her-His Creation are One and encompass both male and female aspects of everything as One. However, *I invite you to replace the name of God with any name that puts you at ease.* If you are a Christian, you can replace the name God with "Jesus." If you are a Buddhist, you are totally invited to replace God's name with "Buddha." If you are an orthodox Jew, you can replace the word God with "HaShem." If you are on the fence between believing and not, you may find it helpful to replace it with "The Infinite." And if you are a skeptic or a scientist, you are absolutely welcome to replace the word God with "Consciousness", "the Universe" or simply "Nature," whichever works for you... Heck, you can even call Her-Him "Smith" or invent another personal name for God if that practice puts you more at ease. The point is, don't get stuck on semantics. I'd like you to be as comfortable as possible, so that you can derive the most benefit from the program.

How This Book Came To Be

The information contained in this book is universal Truth, as it was communicated to me. That is to say – I am only a conduit for these wisdoms. But don't get me wrong, I don't presume to "know it all: in any way. Despite having been a kundalini yoga instructor, a spiritual teacher, and a reiki master for many years, when the information first started to come through me I was surprised. I suddenly started waking up at all odd hours of the night scribbling notes in trancelike state, kind of like automatic writing. I usually then went back to sleep, and when I woke up in the mornings, I had no idea what I had written. It was as if it wasn't really me who was doing the writing. Then when I started transcribing all those notes to the computer, I was in awe of it, and the question that I would ask myself over and over was: "Holy s#!t – I wrote this? Really?" But as I continued to go along with the process, it became obvious (as it will to you too) that the things that were being written through me were Universal Truth. And I believe that those Truths came through me directly from Source for your benefit.

Nevertheless, after I was done with the first round of arranging all the pieces of the puzzle into a book, the little scientist in me started to ask questions and wonder about the validity of the writings. And so I started to dig up as much scientific evidence as I could to support the wisdoms. Of course, as esoteric and deeply metaphysical as some of this stuff is, there wasn't always scientific proof that was available to quote. Still, I was in awe of how many resources there were of people who have tuned into the same Truths and were out to prove them using the scientific method. I mean, I have found study after study that proved these wisdoms true. I have summarized some of those studies here, but only to the extent possible without taking away from the authenticity of the core wisdoms as they were communicated to me.

Another thing that was communicated to me is that this information is out there. It is encoded in the ethers that underlie our physical existence, and available for all human beings to tune into on their own. On a certain level, whether we are aware of it or not, we all receive Universal guidance that is a derivative of Universal Divine Truth. It's just a question of how intently we listen to it, or whether we do at all. Religious leaders, thinkers, and philosophers throughout the ages have all tuned into different aspects of the same all-encompassing Truth, and related to humanity the parts of it that were in agreement with their pre-existing human biases and agendas. Metaphorically speaking, it is like we each have sunglasses embedded in the cornea of our eyes that are tinted in many different colors and shades. The same bright sun shines its white light on all of us. But because of the color of our particular lens (bias), we only see a shade (an aspect) of the overall Light (Truth). It is my aim in this book to help you remove your tinted lenses and give you the tools to listen to the Universal guidance that will lead you to an all-inclusive prosperity.

Validating You As The First Rule

Throughout this book, I have taken great care in being a clear channel for the wisdoms given to me. I have kept it as pure and stripped of old religious ideas as possible, leaving you with the ultimate choice on how to harness this information to best benefit *you*. All I want to do is give you the tools to re-examine the colored lenses through which you've been seeing reality, so you can regain the ability to tune into the brightest Light available, and harness It to co-Create the life that you want and the prosperity that was always meant to be yours.

This brings us to the next topic. Since self-validation is a key concept in co-Creating prosperity, don't take *my* word for it either. Empowering and validating your True Self is more important to your success than any one particular concept contained in this book. Regarding everything as a suggestion will help you to develop your ability to tune into the Divine wisdom that is already within you. Deep inside the most precious cell of your heart resides Divine intelligence that has always been with you. So I invite you to measure everything I say with this internal God Meter (for more details on the God Meter, see Chapter 7).

However, do not measure it against preconceived notions that originate from fear, hate, stress, or society-enforced biases. And do not measure it against the very biases that have kept you cut off from Universal prosperity until now. Remember that your resistance to change comes from fear. I call it "the old slipper misery." You know that old slipper is old, and all dirty and torn up; and you know that it doesn't serve your wellbeing any more. And yet you stick to this old slipper and resist change. We will discuss in detail how to replace old habits with new healthy ones throughout this series of books. And the most excellent tool for tuning into higher wisdom is "Zohar Breath Meditation," given in the book *Seven Stages to co-Creating Prosperity From Your Soul*. But for now, I want to ask you to sound everything I say against the innermost cell of your being: does it resonate harmoniously or discordantly? Ultimately, I wish for you to develop your own clear channel for tapping into Infinite wisdom and resources, so you can be blessed with Her-His Love and favor, with every breath that you take. That is my highest wish and prayer for you.

Success Story:

One beautiful example of how the process of this book works is a woman I'll call Dee. Dee came to me to learn to manifest prosperity at a point when she was really desperate. When she first called me, she had been out of work and living without a paycheck for over six month. She had problems collecting unemployment and was facing eviction from her apartment. So I invited her for a free lesson. She had to take three buses from Santa Monica to get to my apartment. To respect the rules of sacred reciprocity, she made me a pot of delicious Spanish rice as payment for the lesson. I taught her some of the meditational processes of *Seven Stages to co-Creating Prosperity From Your Soul*, which were personally tailored for her. At the end of our long lesson, I gave her specific written instructions of the processes I had taught her, and told her to follow the meditational program daily for at least seven weeks.

The program worked like a charm! Dee followed my instructions to the tee, and it paid off. Within two weeks she had several serious job interviews lined up. After two additional weeks, she received her unemployment back-pay, with which she was able to repay her debts; after about the fifth week, she had selected two part-time jobs that best suited her needs, and gave her not only an adequate income, but also enough time off to pursue her long-term manifestation goals. And by the end of the seventh week, she continued to be happy at her new jobs, and was deep into planning her long-term objectives.

Now, did the program work only as a self-fulfilling prophecy? Or were the meditations I gave her truly powerful and potent in magnetizing prosperity? I don't really know. But who cares? The point is that they worked! I have many more examples of these processes being instrumental in people's lives. D is just a classic one because of how adamant she was in following the meditations, and how quickly and powerfully results showed up in her life.

Are you ready to manifest prosperity from your Soul? I'll see you in Chapter 1

Chapter 1

Your Magnificent True Self

You are fabulous!

Did you know that? You are so much more than you ever gave yourself credit for!

Somewhere deep inside you is a powerful co-Creator, who is already empowered by the Universe to manifest all the prosperity you wish for and more. **Your True Self is already an expert at co-Creating endless amounts of prosperity**, because your Source for prosperity is Truly Infinite! *Your True Self was originally Created and* designed to be perfectly healthy and balanced, joyously happy, immensely beloved, *absolutely free, radiantly beautiful, and Infinitely abundant in every positive way!* All it takes to reclaim all of those gifts is to restore your True Self—the way you were designed to be from the get-go.

But wait a minute! What is this True Self, and how can you "squeeze" prosperity out of it? Ah… Restoring your True Self, and deriving easily flowing prosperity from It is what you will learn to do in this book. But before you can learn to derive prosperity from your True Self—your Soul, you need to become intimately familiar with It. For having a full understanding of just how powerful a co-Creator your Soul Self really is, is monumentally important to being able to harness Its Infinite powers to co-Create True prosperity in your life. So our first order of business, and the subject of this first chapter, is to explore the many facets of your magnificent True Self. But first, to illustrate the relationship between your True Self and your current reality, a little story.

You Are The King – A Story

My yoga teacher[1] told me a story about a king (who of course lived once upon a time) who was very beloved, and very pampered with every riches. One night the beloved kind dreamed that he was homeless and poor, sleeping on a straw mattress on the floor, hungry, cold, sick, and alone. But even though this dream seemed real to him, somewhere deep in his consciousness, he still knew that he was the beloved king. It wasn't a cognitive memory but more of a deep feeling that this state of affairs of being poor and sick and alone did not really match how he felt things should be. Because of this contradiction between the reality of his dream and who he felt he was deep at his core, he was very shaken by the dream. He finally woke up frantically calling for his servants and asking them – "I am the kind, aren't I? I am healthy, affluent, and beloved, aren't I?" And of course they reassured him that indeed he was their beloved king, and that all he wished for was his.

This beloved king is a metaphor for each one of us. Just like this king, the Truest existence of each of us is at the Divine realm, in which all Souls are perfect from their inceptions, and are integral parts of the Infinite prosperity of the Divine. As you'll find out in Chapters 5 and 6, our "reality" of sickness, emotional turmoil, imbalance and lack is but a holographic illusion. By virtue of who you Truly are (which we will explore for the rest of this chapter) *it is your birthright to live in perfect health, harmony, and balance. It is your birthright to have perfect vitality and youth. And it is your birthright to have a life that is prosperous in every way!*

If you want to (but only if you want to), you can look at it from a biblical standpoint: God Created you in Her-His image. Therefore, it logically follows that She-He Created you in perfect health, happiness, and abundance. Settling for anything less would be blasphemy, because it isn't that some god that is external to you had created some poor replica of himself. Your Creator IS also every part of Creation, as well as the process of Creation all in the same time. If you think of life as a play, then God is the playwright, the director, producer, stage-set, the music, the audience, and every actor in the play, all at the same time! So the more accurate way to look at it is that *God has really crafted a part of Her-Himself as you, to experience Her-Himself more fully through you* in this lifetime. And since you really are an integral part of your Creator, you were always designed to be carefree, healthy, happy, abundant, and absolutely joyous!

Bear with me here if you are an atheist. But even from a quantum physics perspective, we are all one (the "entanglement principle")—parts of a very organismic universe made of a field of energy (more on that in Chapter 6) in which only "consciousness" creates the illusion of tangibility in this reality. So even from a scientific perspective (as we shall elaborate on in Chapters 5 and 6), it is our conscious intent that creates our reality. And even if you are agnostic, surely you must realize the greatness of life and of the human spirit of which you are part. That is, even scientists and conventional psychologists agree that as human beings – we are all capable of greatness.

From a metaphysical standpoint, as an integral part of your Creator, **you already are co-Creating your own reality as you read these lines. You always have!** In fact, you have magnetized this book into your hands in order to help you becoming a more successful co-Creator of your life. ***Co-Creating a more prosperous life for yourself is just a matter of becoming a more <u>conscious</u> co-Creator, thus co-Creating and magnetizing into your life only that which you truly desire and serves your highest good.*** And that is what this book will teach you to do.

But before you can co-Create all that prosperity that you wish for, first, you need to open up your perception to all that is available for you to manifest… And the first step to that *expanded horizon of wanting* is to understand just how powerful a co-Creator you Truly are. That is, before you set your goals on what it is that you wish to co-Create into your life, it is essential that you understand that nothing is too large or too small for your Creator to give Her-His beloved—you! It is important that you know that all is possible, especially if it is a wish that is anchored in the wisdom of your True Self. To facilitate these understandings, we need to discuss the many facets of your magnificent True Self.

Your Higher Self Versus Your Here-Now self

The first simple distinction of the different aspects of you is between your here-now self and your Higher Self. Your here-now self is the part of you that you dwell in during your everyday life. Most New Age thinkers refer to this part as the "ego." I personally don't like the word "ego," because implies negative characteristics, such as selfishness, egotism, or just being detached from Universal Truth. The truth is that your here-now self is an important part of you. It protects you from harm, and is the part that animates you and opportunes you this physical existence you currently call "you." It enables you to be immersed in this human experience and fully enjoy it. Some healers refer to this quality of being healthily connected to our Earth-mother and to your physical reality as "grounding." This grounding, facilitated by your here-now self, affords you the zesty, youthful "alive" feeling.

However, your here-now self, which most people have come to cherish in this lifetime, is also the part of you that produces the illusion of being segregate, or "cut-off," from the Whole. And this is important to note, because *the Whole is the Source where all prosperity comes from*, and you are *not* separate from it. The totality of who you Truly are is an integral part of that Whole, which is so much more than just your here-now self.

In fact, the majority of who you are lies in the enormity and power of your original True Self. In simple terms, your Higher Self is the best version of you. But as we shall see, it is more than just that... Sometimes called your Soul, your True Self, or your God Self, this is you as God has originally Created you to be, and as God still holds the loving intent for you to reclaim being. It is the part of you that is always connected with the highest Universal wisdom. And in the larger sense, your original-True Self is as vast as God is, because as we shall see in this chapter, it merges with the Divine.

And this Higher Self is always present within you. It is the life-force animating you to live, breathe, and read these lines. Becoming better able to tune into this ever-present wisdom, radiance and power is the real stuff of manifestation! So let's delve deeper into the glorious being that your total-Self Truly is.

Your Soul & Its Composition

As the title of this book is *Prosperity From Your Soul*, if we are going to be "milking" prosperity out of your Soul, than first we need to fully understand what the Soul is, and then we can proceed to understand how to derive prosperity out of it. Sounds like a good plan of action to you?

As we will explore in the coming sections, you are a humungous multifaceted being that extends all the way from your physical self... to the heart of your Creator. Within this multifaceted self, your Soul is the part of your consciousness that is integral with your omnipresent Creator who is still Creating our multiverse each moment anew (more on that in Chapter 6). If you are not apt at visualizing these concepts, it is helpful to think of it as a wheel and spokes or the sun and sunrays – God being the hub or sun, and each one of us as one of its spokes or rays. A better visualization is likening God to the ocean, and each one of us to a wave. Each wave is still part of the ocean, but at the same time has its own agency to decide on its own height, direction, and energetic essence. Metaphysically speaking, God has Crafted your Soul from the very core of Her-His Light-Love energy – perfectly radiant from Its very inception. That is why I write the word Soul with a capital letter – because it is part of the Divine.

For the scientific skeptic among you, let's explore for a moment the very existence of a Soul, which lives beyond the physical body from a logical standpoint. For argument's sake, if you believe in scientific determinism than you believe that given the same conditions, any process would have the same results, which are predictably repeatable. And if you believe that human consciousness is nothing more than the results of the physiological (neurochemical, hormonal, etc.) processes of our bodies, meaning that there is no Soul or consciousness beyond this physiology, than it would logically follow that we are all machines operating in a perfectly predictable way. And since despite our genetic diversity human physiology is remarkably uniform, it would logically follow that we do not really decide anything… that everything is predetermined by our remarkably similar physiology, and we cannot really tell right from wrong or have opinions of our own. If you follow this scientific determinism, given the remarkable similarity of our basic structure and physiology, all human beings should have a consciousness, personality, and opinions that are as similar as a production line. But obviously that is not the case!

Further, scientific determinism cannot explain the countless cases of identical twins, who are genetically identical, grew up at the same household, were nurtured with the same foods and environmental conditions, and yet have completely opposite personalities? And as their parents attest, the twins have different personalities right from the very start. One twin is an extrovert, and the other one is an introvert; one is gifted at baseball, and the other is gifted in the arts; one twin is a pessimist and takes life heavily, and the other is an optimist, who always takes life lightly. What it is that gives these genetically identical kids such different personalities right from the beginning of their lives?

The millions of examples of identical twins who are different from one another are but one phenomenon that forces us to acknowledge that we are more than just our bodies, more than our intelligence, and more than all of our physical characteristics. Then comes the question: what is the essence that is independent of a person's physical body, which gives us each our true identity at such an early age? And that is, of course, our Souls. It is the Soul that really makes us who we are. And as we shall see in this chapter, it is also an aspect of our Souls (the etheric body) which forms the template for the selection of our genetic code, and governs the development and differentiation of cell within our bodies from our conception, through our embryonic and developmental stages, and as adults. As it relates to manifestation of prosperity, it is also our Souls are empowered to decide what we manifest into our lives, why, when, and how.

Another proof of the Soul's independence from the body comes from reading accounts of people who have died and were then resuscitated[2] (called Near Death Experiences or NDE). These people actually died and lived to tell about the heavenly experiences they've had while their Soul was out of the body (OOBE). Jeffery Long, M.D. and Paul Perry wrote a book called "Evidence of the Afterlife,"[3] in which they collected a more than six hundred NDE accounts, and have analyzed their finding statistically and scientifically. Beyond verifiable facts NDEer observe while on their out-of-body experience, which they had no other way of knowing, the book lays nine lines of scientific reasoning, which prove that there is no other medical explanation of this phenomenon but to assume that they are real. To me (and to many researchers who have studied this phenomena in countless other books), this is sufficient proof that although the Soul animates our physical bodies while we are living an earthly life, **it is actually independent of the body, and lives on forever**.

To better understand how powerful and awesome your Soul Truly is, and why it is so empowered to co-Create all the prosperity you deeply desire, let us look at the composition of Soul—the different aspect each Soul includes. In the following discussion, while the names I've given each aspect of Soul corresponds to the Kabalistic names of the Soul's aspects, the description of the essence of each aspect is a very distilled version that was meditationally communicated to me directly by the Divine Source one night at 3am. And again, the purpose here is not to convert you to any religion, to prompt you to study Kabala, or even to have you take my word for any of it. No, the purpose is solely to help you open up to how vast and powerful your total-Self truly is, since tuning into your ability to co-Create your reality would greatly enhance your effectiveness as a conscious co-Creator.

OK. So each Soul has five aspects. As you read through these aspects of Soul, keep in mind two things: First, each Soul is always whole! There are no fragmentations of any kind. All these aspects of Soul flow freely into one another and complete each other. Second, there is no need to memorize any of this in order to become a successful co-Creator. As you read through the descriptions of all the aspects of your total Self, just become aware of how this information resonates with you. And when something resonates with you, just allow your spirit to take wings and your consciousness to open up to all that you Truly are.

The aspects of your Soul are given here in a descending order – from the most Divine to the very mundane.

Yechida – Divine Oneness:

Yechida literally means singular. This is Divine Oneness. At this level of existence, there is no form, no energy and all potentiality at the same time. This is the Divine pure bliss of the unmanifest Creator, before She-He shifts Her-His consciousness into being a Creator. For the physicist among you, this might be understood as what comes before, or underlines the so called "super-string" field.

And why is it important to know about this aspect of your Soul in order to manifest prosperity in your life? Simple, because notice that *this singular Divine Oneness essence is an integral part of your very own Soul*. Thus, Divine empowerment is an integral part of who you already are. Therefore your Soul Self is truly as Infinite as God. And as we will learn throughout this book, your Soul's Oneness at the Yechida level is indeed your Source for co-Creating Infinite abundance.

Chaya – Life Creative Energy:

Chaya literally means alive or animated! This is the pure unmanifest Divine, at the moment that She-He shifts Her-Himself into a Creator, and becomes the Creative energy, or "element," if you will, from which all of Creation stems. I call this "the Divine Element", which is essentially the Source of the same energy called Ki in Japan, Chi in China, prana in India, and Ruach Chaim in the original language of the Bible – the same energy that every aspect in Creation is vibrating with. This Divine Element is not really an element in the chemical sense, but is the Divine life-force energy underlying all energies, all forces, and all particles… in all universes and dimensions. It is the pure potentiality from which the Creation of all worlds stems. This "Alive" energy occupies all the time-space there is, and yet no space-time at all (since space-time is really a holographic illusion—a perceptual convention, which facilitates the Soul's experience as you—a human being living on Earth. More on that in Chapter 6). If you are quantum physics oriented, than this is God as She-He becomes the pure Energy, Potentiality and Intelligence of the so called "super string field." And this life-force, which gives life not only to every living being, but also to all matter and manifestation (i.e., Infinite prosperity), is also an integral part of your very own being. So it logically follows that you are empowered to tap into it, and draw from it all that you Truly desire.

Neshama – soul:

Neshama literally means soul. Notice I didn't capitalize the word soul, because this is only one aspect of the total Soul—the Higher Self aspect of Soul. Your total Soul contains all five aspects listed here, and by definition is integral with God. The Neshama aspect is the highest intelligence of your individual soul. It is not just your cognitive intellect. It is your Soul's essence of wisdom. The Chaya and Yechida aspects of you are not yet individualized consciousness, but are the consciousness of the Whole. Your Neshama is the first part of you that is differentiated into your individual consciousness. Therefore it is through your Neshama that your Soul stays in oneness with God throughout your lifetime. And it is through Neshama that, like the king in the yogic story, each of us actually has a (subconscious) memory of what it feels like to actually be in oneness with the Divine, for it is the part that keeps us in contact with Chaya (undifferentiated Divine Life-force) and Yechida (Divine Oneness). You can say that your Neshama is the bridge between the Heavenly aspects of you and the earthly aspects of you.

However, your Neshama is alive whether you are embodied or not. Your Neshama is actually the part of you that goes back HOME (the HOME of the Soul) at the end of each lifetime. People who have had NDEs report that they were surprised to learn how alive and crystal clear they felt when their bodies (and brains) were clinically dead. They report that their consciousness was clearer than ever before or since, and that they were able to see and feel everything with a much lighter, clearer, calmer and happier perspective. This is a function of the Neshama.

As it relates to co-Creation of prosperity, as you will understand in Chapter 2, the most abundant prosperity that you can manifest comes from living the Ideal life that you were meant to live—the one that makes your heart sing and your best talents shine. And the part of you that has the ability to tune into the details of this Ideal life is the Neshama aspect of your Soul. This is the part we will learn to connect with during Zohar Breath Meditation, detailed in *Seven Stages to co-Creating Prosperity From Your Soul*—the next book, which will help you devise a concrete and specific plan of action to reclaim your most auspicious Lifepath—the built-in prosperity plan that was devised by your Neshama and empowered by Chaya and Yechida.

Ruach – Spirit:

Ruach literally means wind or spirit, referring to the air in our lungs, and the breath of life. The term Ruach is taken from Genesis, which details how God blew the "Ruach Chaim" (the breath of life) into Adam and Eve. It is your living spirit that animates the physical body and also gives it your emotional composition. Ruach is the bridge between the higher Neshama and the lower-Nefesh. But because Ruach is also anchored into Nefesh for the purpose of animating the physical body, the emotions that it gives expression to while embodied, including love, are many times tainted by the primal animalistic instincts of the Nefesh. As it relates to manifestation, the most auspicious manifestation happen when your Ruach (emotions and spiritual vibration) derive their influence from higher Neshama, rather than from the lower Nefesh.

Nefesh – Primal Animal Instinct:

Nefesh is what anchors all of the above more ethereal parts of your Soul to this here-now existence. It is your instinctual animal-spirit, which is so wonderfully apt at surviving in the jungle of this physical existence. Physiologically, Nefesh is closely related to the heart and circulatory system and to the sympathetic and parasympathetic nervous systems that activate the very instinctual "fight or flight response". All these systems relate to the heart, and how fast it's pumping the blood through your body… i.e., how fast it is enlivening your 'animal-spirit' to fight or to flight, and to participate with your here-now reality. Although the Nefesh is still ethereal, it is the part of you that is most closely related to your physical existence.

In stressed situation, as your Nefesh does its utmost to protect your here-now existence, it can drive your consciousness to be too immersed within the physicality of this reality. But as valuable as survival is, getting too immersed in this reality, to the point of forgetting your Divine identity (where Infinite abundance comes from), can taint one's consciousness with primal fear, which the Nefesh is influenced by. And as you may know, fear is a bad boss and a very poor manifestor. This does not mean that the Nefesh is bad. It just means that the proper activation of Nefesh is not as the part that rules you, but as a facilitator through which you ground all the wisdom and abundance of the higher realms into *physical manifestation* in your life.

Plants & Animals:

Animals have Nefesh (animal-instinct) and Ruach (spirit), but not a Neshama (higher consciousness). That is why animals' instincts are very sharp, and very connected to their raw form, since they don't engage in rights and wrongs or in higher philosophical thoughts that are the domain of the Neshama. The Nefesh alone can get saturated by the denser, lower-vibrating energy. But the highest animating aspect of animals is the Ruach (spirit). Thus when an animal is hunting for prey, there is no malice, just a raw survival skill. Animals are predominately governed by their spirits, which in turn ruled by Nature's spirit, as a conduit of Divine Spirit. It's not like animals don't have individual identities, but because of the lack of a higher Neshama, to a degree, animals are like Divine Spirit on autopilot, if you will, like Spirit retains the ability to speak through the actions of various animals. This is why Native American and other shamanic wisdoms believe that animals can be messengers from Great-Spirit (God), if you open yourself up to receive messages from them. We will explore this avenue of tuning into Universal wisdom in the second book— *Seven Stages to co-Creating Prosperity From Your Soul*.

Plants, on the other hand, have Ruach (spirit) but no Nefesh (animal-spirit). That is why they are not animated like animals. But they do breathe, and their life energy is pure and untainted by a lower Nefesh. Therefore they only bring good spirits into any environment. In both a physical sense and spiritual sense, plants convert negative energy into positive one, which we will explore in *Seven Stages to co-Creating Prosperity From Your Soul*.

In comparison, it is only we humans who through our Neshama have this unique connection with Divine Creative energies, which makes us powerful co-Creators.

How Many "Me"s Are There?

So how is it that your Infinitely vast Soul Self can exist as an integral part of God, but also at the level of your very mundane here-now self, and still be one integral and indivisible unit? How does your Soul filter into the various levels of your existence? And more importantly for our purposes – if at the Soul level you are a powerful co-Creator, than how can we harness that power of co-Creation into your here-now reality? We will spend the rest of our journey together answering these questions, and boosting up your ability to tap into the supreme Intelligence and harnessing the awesome co-Creative power of your Soul. And by the end of *Seven Stages to co-Creating Prosperity From Your Soul*, by tapping into the wisdom of your Soul, you will devise a specific plan of action, that's personally catered to you, to bring easily flowing prosperity into your life.

But for now, let us understand the basics: Harnessing the tremendous power of your Soul Self for manifestation of prosperity depends on bringing the various aspects of you into harmony and balance, thereby allowing the supreme intelligence and power of your Soul to pour through you into manifestation in your life. And the first step to restoring this balance is acquiring a deeper understanding of your energetic makeup on the various levels on which you exist, and an exploration of the doorways through which your here-now self transmit its manifestation intent into the Universe, and through which the Universe then obliges and channels these manifestations into your physical reality.

The Aura:

Most people have at least heard of the human aura, which is the protective electromagnetic field that surrounds each human being. In fact, the existence of the human aura is so well known in most cultures throughout history, that in a book called Future Science, John White and parapsychologist Stanley Krippner have listed ninety-seven names that different cultures around the world gave the aura. This attests to the universality of the knowledge of its existence. But beyond cultural naming, there is also compelling evidence of its existence.

Michael Talbot, in his groundbreaking book "The Holographic Universe," forwards quite a few accounts of talented psychics who are able to see the human aura (or "energy field" as he calls it), some of whom are medical doctors. He also forwards some double-blind experiments (which I will summarize) that prove beyond doubt that what these individuals see in the human energy field is real.

The first of these accounts is of psychic reader and healer Barbara Ann Brennan – author of the book "Hands of Light." Brennan's psychic talent actually started as a young child, when she was able to wonder through the woods blindfolded and avoid bumping into the trees, simply because she could internally see their energy field. She describes that as a child, she saw all things (living or non-living) as having colorful energy fields, like a halo, which extend outwards into the space around them and merge with the energy fields of everything else. But as Brennan grew up and concentrated on her science studies, her ability to see energy became dormant, and she became an atmospheric physicist for NASA's Goddard Space Flight Center. She later re-discovered her talent and became a counselor. "Brennan," says Talbot, "not only sees the chakras, layers, and other fine structures of the human energy field with exceptional clarity, but can make startlingly accurate medical diagnoses based on what she sees." In her book, Brennan gives many examples of diagnosis she has given people based on looking at their auras, which later proved to be medically sound, and helped people overcome issues... from uterus problems, to a man's sexual dysfunction which originated from a broken coccyx, and many more examples.

Another psychic aura reader, whom Talbot seemed to have known personally, is Carol Dryer. By looking at a person's aura, Dryer can diagnose illnesses, a person's thoughts, past occurrences in a person's life, and—important to our discussion—some of the manifestations in their life as they first ethereally manifest in their aura before manifesting in their reality (more on that in Chapter 5).

An extensive research, also forwarded by Talbot, was done by neurologist and psychiatrist Shafica Karagulla, who have found many cases of medical doctors who can also see the human aura. Although it took quite a bit of doing for Dr. Karagulla to get these medical doctors to admit their secret talent, she eventually found many doctors who could either "see" or scan the aura with their hands, and consequently describe a person's health and internal medical condition based on the aura scanning. And in all of those cases, the description was correct in every detail when compared with subsequent medical diagnosis. The doctors "invariably described what they were seeing as an 'energy field' or a 'moving web of frequency' around the body and interpenetrating the body. Some saw chakras, but because they were ignorant of the term, they described them as 'vortices of energy at certain points along the spine, connected with or influencing the endocrine system.' And almost without exception they kept their abilities a secret out of fear of damaging their professional reputation," reports Talbot.

Even beyond the reported sightings of the human aura by a few talented individuals, there are actual measurements of the aura's electrical frequency, forwarded by both Michael Talbot, and Richard Gerber MD in his book Vibrational Medicine. One experiment was done by Valerie Hunt, a physical therapist and professor of kinesiology at UCLA. "Hunt has discovered that an electromyography, a device used to measure the electrical activity in the muscles, can also pick up the electrical presence of the human energy field," reports Talbot. "The normal frequency of the electrical activity in the brain is between 0 and 100 cycles per second (cps), with most of the activity occurring between 1 and 30 cps. Muscle frequency goes up to about 225 cps, and the heart goes up to about 250 cps, but this is where electrical activity associated with biological function drop off. In addition to these, Hunt discovered that the electrodes of the electrograph could pick up another field of energy radiating from the body, much subtler and smaller in amplitude than the traditionally recognized body electricties but with frequencies that average between 100 and 1600, and which sometimes went even higher." Hunt also employed a trained psychic, who was able to psychically observe the changes within the test subject's auric field, while denied any feedback from the electromagnetic electrodes' reading. She found that the psychic's independent observations relating to the color of the test subject's energetic field correlated exactly with the electromagnetic electrodes readings.

So even at first examination, we see that your aura is real, and is much more than just a protective shield. New Age thinking explains that beyond your physical body, your auric field actually consists of several energetic bodies of different vibrational frequencies. Listing them from the denser (low vibrational) to the lighter (high vibrational), they are: the physical body (and our reality), the Etheric Body, the Astral Body, the Mental Body, the Casual Cody, and other higher vibrational bodies that merge with the Divine. Even in physics, the Principle of "nondestructive coexistence"[4] states that matter of differing vibrational frequencies can occupy the same space at the same time, nondestructively. So since all of these bodies exist on different vibrational frequencies (and energetic levels), they can all occupy the same space-time, which means they are superimposed on one another. And they all have relationships that affect one another and manifest in your physical reality, including the manifestation of prosperity.

Now as it relates to co-Creating prosperity, here is one reason why it is so important to know your energetic anatomy in such detail: any debris, imbalance or blockage within your energy bodies and chakras apparatus blocks the flow of energy between you and your abundance-giving Source. So having a good understanding your energetic anatomy would obviously help you keep this apparatus cleansed from any obstructions, which in turn would help you allow the Infinite's abundance to flow in, making you a more successful a co-Creator of prosperity. As captain Jack Sparrow (way too much TV…) would put it: "Savvy?" OK, so here we go… Let's delve in a little bit deeper into the energetic anatomy of your magnificent True Self, starting with your Light Bodies.

The Etheric Body:

The Etheric Body is the energetic body that most immediately communicates and feeds life-force energy into the physical body. This feeding happens through the channels of the chakra and meridian systems, all of which exist in the Etheric body as doorways through which it feeds chi, Divine living and Creative energy, into your physical body and reality. According to Dr. Gerber[5], "the etheric body is a holographic energy template that guides the growth and development of the physical body... The physical body is so energetically connected and dependent upon the etheric body for cellular guidance that the physical body cannot exist without the etheric body."

According to Dr. Gerber, who have spent over ten years diligently collecting the data he presents so eloquently in his 600-page book "Vibrational Medicine," there is considerable scientific research that proves the existence of this Etheric Body, done by neuroanatomist Harold S. Burr at Yale University. Burr's experimented with salamanders and plants, and proved that an electrical-energetic field (which he was able to electrically measure and map) forms around seeds and developing embryos from the moment of conception. What is interesting is that even at the very early embryonic stages, this electrical field has the shape of the adult organism, not of the embryo. Newer research in electrographic (Kirlian) photography has been able to actually capture this Etheric Body on film. An interesting phenomenon shown by Kirlian photography is of the "phantom leaf effect:" when amputating part of a leaf and destroying the cut off piece, Kirlian (electrographic) photography of the remaining (living) part of the leaf shows the Etheric Body as still whole. In other words, the etheric body of the plant still contains the whole leaf intact, as it was never amputated. It is Dr. Gerber's conclusion (from this and other experiments) that this Etheric Body actually precedes and guides the formation of the physical body and the differentiation of cells during the embryonic stages. He also concludes that throughout a person's life any changes in health happen in the Etheric Body first, and only then manifest as physiological changes.

I personally have had an experience with phantom-limbs effect in my early career as a massage therapist. I was fresh out of massage school, working at a local clinic. A client came in who had had the fingers of one of his hands cut off in a work accident (he was a gardener). The owner, who was also a spiritualist in her own right, told me that I should massage his missing fingers. I gave her a puzzled look, since this concept sounded very strange, even for me. But I decided that it couldn't hurt to try it. Although I don't have the psychic ability to see the aura or the etheric body with my physical eyes, I pretended that his missing fingers were still there and made the motions of massaging them. And you should have heard the sigh of relief that came out of his mouth. He even commented on how he still had feeling of his missing fingers, and liked having them massaged.

As it relates specifically to the things that we co-Create into our lives, as the physical body is the vessel through which we experience this physical life, the Etheric Body is the body that most immediately facilitates the translation of Creative (abundance) energy into your life. In the remaining part of this chapter, we will examine more closely how the different chakras function as doorways between the various levels of your existence and as centers for processing the various aspects of co-Creation. In other words you'll understand how this energetic Light Bodies and chakra apparatus is responsible for the various manifestations in your life.

The Astral Body:

The next high vibrational (less-dense) energy body is the Astral Body, also called the emotional body, which is responsible for our sensual appetites, desires, longings, and moods. In that sense, the astral body is equivalent to the Ruach (spirit) aspect of Soul. The seven chakras that exist on the Etheric Body also exist on the higher-vibrational Astral Body, such that energy from the Astral Body filters down to the Etheric Body, and then to the physical, through these doorways called chakras. The Astral Body is superimposed on the Etheric and physical bodies most of the time. The times in which it is not superimposed are in situations called "astral projections" in which a person has an "out of body experience" (OOBE).

Dr. Gerber details some interesting experiments that scientifically prove the existence of the Astral Body. One such experiment was done by Dr. Karlis Osis at the American Society for Psychical Research in New York. Dr. Osis used a subject that could have out of body experiences at will. The subject was then to travel to a remote box in which Dr. Osis arranged various figures, and report back his findings. While there are virtually hundreds of out of body experience reports available, the interesting thing in this experiment was that Dr. Osis designed the box such that things would appear differently if viewed form inside, or if viewed from a special peeping hole. When the subject projected his astral body, he later reported the figures in the box from the perspective of viewing it from the peeping hole. Dr. Osis also placed in the box electrical detectors that were able to detect significant energy spikes attesting to the presence of the subject's Astral Body.

Additional similar experiments were done at Stanford Research Institute by physicists Targ and Purhoff. Again, a subject was used who could project his Astral Body at will into the experiment apparatus, which was buried in a vault and shielded by various superconducting shields. During the period that the subject projected himself into this apparatus, a magnetometer recorded a doubled sine-wave and other disturbances to the magnetic field in the apparatus, which attest to the subject's presence there. And after returning to his physical body, the subject was able to describe in great detail the content of this protected apparatus. Dr. Gerber notes that these findings impressed a number of physicists in Stanford Research Institute.

As it relates to our purposes, the Astral Body relates emotional and spiritual energy. It is also the closest body to the physical that can actually leave physical body consciousness, and roam around free in the Universe. And if you think of co-Creation of prosperity as a process of projecting your intents into the Cosmos and then being receptive to the resultant Creative energy pouring in, then the Astral Body plays an important role: It has a vital part in carrying your intent for manifestation out into the Universe, and creating a vibrational resonance with the object of your desires. And as we'll see in Chapter 5, it is this mutual vibrational resonance between you and the object of your desire that then magnetizes it into manifestation in your life.

The Mental Body:

The mental body is the next high-vibrational (less dense) energetic body, which also occupies the same space-time as the astral, etheric and physical body. It carries your higher intelligence responsible for clear and unobstructed thoughts and ideas. In our model of the Soul, this is equivalent to the intellectual aspect of Neshama, but of course Neshama is more than just the intellect.

The mental body also contains the seven energetic doorways called chakras, through which it relates information (your manifestation intents released into the Cosmos, and Divine intelligence feed to you), and feeds Creative Life energy cascading down into the Astral Body, the Etheric Body, and finally to the physical body and reality. The existence of this Mental Body is evidenced in Near Death Experiences, after which people report the crystal-clarity and sharpness of thought they had experienced once they left their physical body—a clarity that they had not been able to experience ever before or since, and which was so supreme that it was difficult to describe in words. This absolute clarity and peaceful sharpness is the gift of the Mental Body, which lives on beyond the physical.

The mental body is less dense, and is also able to free-roam around the universe. Many scientists[5] researching the nature of human consciousness support the idea that our consciousness is not localized to our physical body or the brain, but is in fact free roaming in oneness with Universal consciousness.

It is through your Mental Body that you are able to conceive the clear inspiration from your Soul on how to manifesting your most prosperous Lifepath. But it is through the potency of the denser Astral Body that you would then be able to beef up those thoughts with the vibration of passion for manifesting these ideas, and it is through your Etheric-physical apparatus that these ideas actually come to fruition in real life.

Casual & Higher Bodies:

The Casual Body is described as the energetic body that contains the essence of one's being. It is equivalent to the part of Neshama that is beyond intellect, the part that vibrates as the very essence of your Soul. The Casual Body is also equivalent to Chaya (the Divine Creative element) in that it extends beyond individual consciousness and into the consciousness of the Whole. Higher energetic bodies are ones that approach the essence of Yechida (Divine Oneness).

It is important to understand that information goes both ways in this apparatus of multiple energetic bodies. As you project your manifestation intents from your physical being, the information projection filters upwards through your Etheric, Astral, Mental, Casual, higher bodies, and all the way into the absolute power of the Divine. The stronger your projection and the more uniformly it shifts the energetic vibration of all of your energetic bodies, the more profound its effects are on Yechida (Creative Oneness). And by virtue of your God-given free will, this manifestation intent that you transmit up your energetic bodies automatically shifts the Creative intent of the Divine to oblige your request, which then causes the energy of the new Creation to pour and cascade down your energy bodies… until it shows up ethereally in your auric field, and finally manifests in your physical reality. We will understand exactly how that works in Chapters 5 and 6. But for now, let's understand the basics of co-Creation.

Now, within this apparatus of multiple energetic bodies that extend from your physical being all the way to the Divine, one particular body is unique in that it contains an extensive system of channels that brings all this Divine Creative energy into manifestation in your physical body and life – that is the etheric body. While each one of your energetic bodies contains the system of multidimensional doorways we call chakra, only the Etheric Body contains the channels we call nadis and meridians. So the next step to keeping your energy apparatus clear to receive prosperity is to understand the doorways through which it happens, so that we can know which aspect of our reality manifests through which doorway.

The Chakra-Nadi System

The Chakras are important doorways through which information of your vibrational essence travel from one realm to another, and through which life-force energy and co-Creative energy manifests into the physical. The Sanskrit word 'chakra' literally means "wheel of light." The chakras are energy centers, or vortices if you will, that exist as dynamic doorways in all of your energetic bodies. With regards to the physical body and health, Dr. Gerber concludes that "the chakras appear to be involved with the flow of higher energies via specific subtle energy channels into the cellular structure of the body… they seem to function as energy transformers, stepping down energy of one form and frequency to a lower level energy. This energy, in turn, translates into hormonal, physiologic, and ultimately cellular changes throughout the body." He also notes that each major chakra is anatomically associated with a major nerve plexus, and a major endocrine gland, which I have included as a reference in our discussion of each chakra.

There are seven major chakras, which we will discuss below. Yogic thought considers the eighth chakra to be the aura. Beyond those, there are additional major chakras in the center of each palm, in the arch of each foot, and in the midbrain. There are also numerous minor chakras in all body joints and in other places. And there are interrelationships between all the chakras, as each exists as part of the whole.

As reported by Dr. Gerber, there is extensive experimental data to prove the existence of this chakra system: Dr. Hiroshi Motoyama of Japan created a special lead-lined recording booth, which was electrically shielded from outside electromagnetic disturbances. Within this booth was a movable copper electrode positioned opposite but at a distance from the various chakras of the test subjects. Motoyama's test subjects were advanced meditators who were able to direct energy to awaken specific chakras at will. The results showed the amplitude and frequency of the electrical field of the chakras being awakened to be significantly greater than the energy of the chakras of control subjects. This experiment was repeated many times and replicated the same results. These results, combined with the results of the aforementioned experiments done by Dr. Hunt, convinced Dr. Gerber of the existence of the Chakra system.

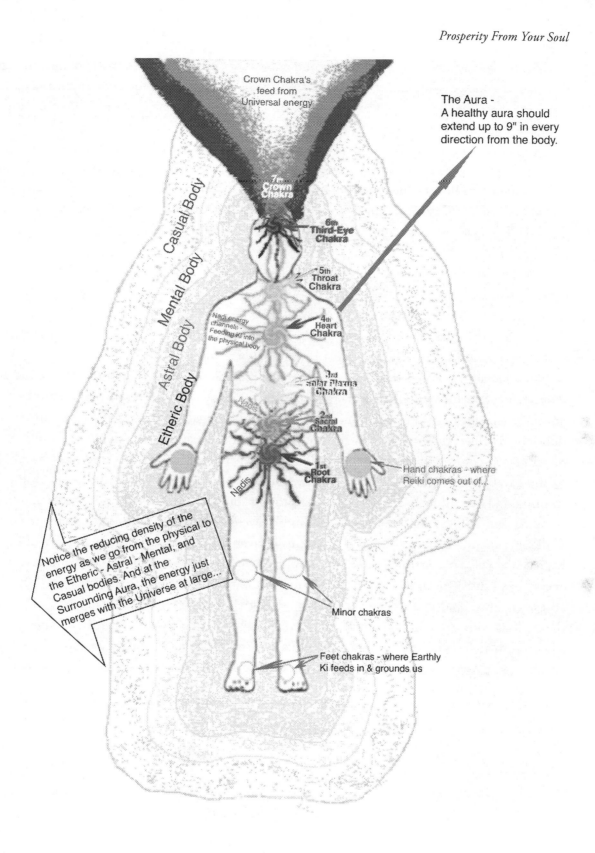

Crown Chakra's feed from Universal energy

The Aura - A healthy aura should extend up to 9" in every direction from the body.

Casual Body

Mental Body

Astral Body

Etheric Body

7th Crown Chakra

6th Third-Eye Chakra

5th Throat Chakra

4th Heart Chakra

Nadi energy channels: Feeding Ki into the physical body

3rd Solar Plexus Chakra

2nd Sacral Chakra

Nadis

1st Root Chakra

Nadis

Hand chakras - where Reiki comes out of...

Notice the reducing density of the energy as we go from the physical to the Etheric - Astral - Mental, and the Casual bodies. And at the Surrounding Aura, the energy just merges with the Universe at large...

Minor chakras

Feet chakras - where Earthly Ki feeds in & grounds us

The life-force energy, which animates and enlivens us, has been given many named in many different languages (Ki, chi, prana, Ruach Chaim, to name a few). For convenience sake, let's adopt the short, Japanese word Ki, shall we? So now let's see exactly how this Ki feeds every aspect of us and every cell in the body.

You realize, of course, that as extensive as the chakra system is, it is still not enough to explain how Ki penetrates each and every cell in your physical body, and how Creative energy comes into all manifestations in your life. In Chapters 5 and 6, we will talk at length about how objects and events that you co-Create filter into physical manifestation in your here-now level of reality. But for now, let's first understand how Ki (life-force) energy penetrates and enlivens every cell and micrometer of your body.

Yogic wisdom[6] explains that in addition to the chakra system, there are also 72,000 nadis— energy channels extending from each chakra like hub and spokes (see illustration above), distributing the life-force energy into every part of the body. Dr. Gerber notes that evidence suggests that these nadis are also interwoven with the physical nervous system and affect nerve transmission within the brain, spinal cord, and peripheral nerves.

Ancient yogis pointed out three major nadis that are of particular importance: the Ida, Pingala, and Shushmana. Ida is an energy channel that leads feminine Ki through the left nostril down the left side of the body into the navel center; and Pingala leads masculine Ki through the right nostril down the right side of the body into the navel center. Together, the feminine and masculine Ki coming through the Ida and Pingala constitute our constant feed of Heavenly Ki. At the navel center (below and inward of the physical navel), this Heavenly Ki, containing the feminine and masculine Ki, mix together with the person's Innate Ki, which is stored/anchored at the navel center. Then the combined Innate and Heavenly Ki proceeds through Shushmana down to the first chakra. Here at the first chakra, this Heavenly Ki, imbued with the imprint of Innate Ki, receives a feed of Earthly Ki coming through the feet chakras and up the legs. The combined energy of all three "flavors" of Ki then flows up the Shushmana, which naturally travels through all the chakras. And if the energy flowing is strong enough, it can clear, balance, and enliven the chakras with fresh Ki on its way to the crown, where it reconnects with the Divine realms. The shushmana, then, is the energy channel that starts at the navel center, descends to your root chakra, and then spirals up around the physical spine as it feeds and connects all chakras.

At the same time, each chakra is still fed with Heavenly Ki directly through the Etheric Body. The circuit of energy that flows through the Ida, Pingala and Shushmana is an energy force that keeps moving, and thus it has the power to cleanse our chakras of debris, balance them, and actively enliven us with fresh Ki. This flow up the shushmana is also the only channel through which Earthly Ki is introduced, which as we'll see in the next section, has an important function. From the double feed that each chakra receives, the very alive Ki distributes to every micro-part of the body through the extensive network of the remaining 71,997 nadis.

Crown Chakra merges
back with the Universe...

Shushmana energy feed to
the **Third Eye Chakra**

Ida -
Universal feed of feminine
Heavenly Ki through the left nostril

Pingala -
Universal feed of musculine
Heavenly Ki through the right nostril

Shushmana energy feed to
the Throat Chakra

Shushmana energy feed to
the **Heart Chakra**

Shushmana

Shushmana energy feed to
the **Solar Plexus Chakra**

The physical navel

Navel Center - the center of **Innate Ki**...
also called:Hara in India, Tanden in Japan
& the lower Dan-Tien in China.

This is where Universal energy coming
through the Ida & Pingala mix... & then
descend & join the Shushmana

Shushmana energy feed
to the **Sacral Chakra**

Hu Yin Point -
The combined energy from the
Navel Center now channeled
through the Shushmana - feeding
the **Root Chakra**, where it also
gets the feed from Earthly Ki

Earthly Ki - feeding
the Shumana through
the Root Chakra

Casual Body

Mental Body

Astral Body

Etheric Body

Feet Chakras

Earthly Ki feed

17

When your energy is free of all debris, and its flow along these channels powerfully awakens each of your chakras with a balanced combination of Heavenly, Innate and Earthly Ki, your kundalini is said to be awakened, and you become a more potent co-Creator and manifestor of your life.

Three Flavors of Life-Force:

It is true that all forms of Ki and Creative energy come from the same Divine Source. And at the moment of Creation, all Energy is the same – pure Divine. Creation of a tangible "physical" world does not happen until the Unmanifest Divine shifts into a Creator—slows down Her-His vibration of Supreme Love-Light-Peace-Intelligence… into all the different flavors, aspects (or if you are into physics, into the energy-strings, forces, and particles), and finally – elements that make up our "physical" world. Within this process of Creation, the One Divine Creative energy differentiates into many different "flavors," if you will. We will talk about the flavors of Energy that manifest into prosperity in Chapters 5 and 6. But for now, the first flavor that's of interest to us is the energy that supports life, which we've called Ki, since without life there is no prosperity. At the moment of Creation, all Ki is the same: extremely high-vibrational, ethereal, and almost imperceptible to humans. It only differentiates into three styles of Ki in order to support physical life in the best way possible.

From the profile drawing above, it may be intuitive to understand that Heavenly Ki is the life-force energy that animates and enlivens us while we are each living in a human body. Indeed, Heavenly Ki is fiery, charging, passionate, vibrant, extremely alive, and has a very yang-like flavor of Light. It contains the Ultimate frequency of energy that gives life and supports perfect health. And as long as you breathe, Heavenly Ki is flowing through you. How freely and powerfully it flow depends on how clear of energetic debris your Ida and Pingala channels are.

It may be also easy to intuit from the drawing that Earthly Ki is our feed of Divine life-force energy reflected to us by our Earth-mother, which is imbued with a very earthly and grounded flavor of aliveness. Earthly Ki is grounding, soothing, nurturing, balancing, and has a very yin-like flavor to it. And as long as you have a heartbeat, Earthly Ki is flowing through you. How freely and powerfully the combined Heavenly-Innate-Earthly Ki flows, depends on how clear of energetic debris your Shushmana channel, as well as your chakras and other nadis are.

What is not so intuitive to understand is: What is Innate Ki? Innate Ki is literally the Soul's innate life-force. Since the Soul is animated with Chaya life-force Sourced directly from the Creator, it is alive and vibrant regardless of whether a person is embodied as a human or not. In fact, both the Latin and Italian roots for the word 'Soul' are 'anima', implying that the Soul is always animated and full of life-force. It is the Soul's integral Oneness with Chaya-Creative life-force at the very core of Existence that gives It Its Innate Ki—the independent life-force that animates It forever. As the Innate Ki is integral to the Soul for all eternity, it not only feeds the Soul with a never-ending flow of Pure Divine energy. It is also imbued with the Soul's blueprint—the particular essence of this individual Neshama, as an aspect of Chaya and Yechida (the Whole).

While the area in the human body that anchors the energy of the Innate Ki is in the navel center, the Soul Itself, as well as Its animating Innate Ki, are non-locale and merge with the Divine. As stated above, the Soul "sits," or connects strongly with the human body at the crown and heart chakras. And It stashes a store of Its Innate Ki at the navel center, which if you look at my drawing of the seats of the Soul (next the crown chakra discussion), is the lower opening of the funnel representing the Soul (the tip of the inverted triangle). But again, the Soul and Its animating Ki are Infinite, and thus not limited to any one locale. Because of its non-locale eternal connection with Divine Creative energy, Innate Ki is never-ending. That explains why the Soul, even after human life has ended and before another one begins, can and does live on for all eternity: because Its resources of life-force draw directly from the Infinite. Certain aspects of information about your Soul are encoded in the ethers as the "Akashic Records" (see Chapter 9), while other aspects—information and life-force energy that relate to your current life—arrive from the Infinite Divine realms into your physical body and reality through your energetic Light-Body-chakras-nadi apparatus.

However, as everlasting and wonderful as this Innate Ki is, its vibration is extremely fast, and thus its flavor is too subtle to enliven the relatively slow-vibrating energy of physical life (more on that in Chapter 6). So Heavenly Ki, combined with Earthly Ki have been specially designed to slow down the pure energy of the Divine into aspects of life-force energy that are capable of resonating with and enlivening us during our physical state—while we are having a human life.

A good analogy to understand the relationship between the Innate Ki and the Heavenly and Earthly Ki is to think of aquarium plants. When you empty the water from the aquarium to clean it, the water-plants falls seemingly lifeless on the gravel. They each still have their unique shape and characteristics, and each plant is still green and alive. But their life energy is very subtle, and not enough to make their physical form perk up. After you clean the aquarium, you'd have to replant the water-plants in the gravel, and refill the aquarium with water in order for the plants to perk up and look alive. Just like the water-plant, Innate Ki is always alive, and always imbued with the Soul's essence. But its life-force is too ethereal resonate with dense energy of the physical body, and thus too subtle to animate it. To animate the physical body, the Innate Ki needs a constant feed of Earthly Ki and Heavenly Ki. The Earthly and Heavenly Ki together constitute a stronger-flavored (less subtle) life-force, which is better suited to move and animate a physical life on earth.

Why are Heavenly Ki and Earthly Ki better suited to support physical life? Simple. Because their vibrations has been slowed down just enough to create a mutual resonance with the physical body, which allows them to support it. Heavenly Ki has been gradually slowed down in its vibration through the energetic step-downs afforded by our Light Bodies, making it more suited to feed physical life. This energy is still very Heavenly, indescribably alive, vivacious, healing, peaceful, Loving, and full of Divine Light. But its flavor-essence is now just a bit closer to being tangible. This is why Dr. Hunt and other researchers were able to measure it electromagnetically. Essentially, when pure Divine energy is slowed down in Its vibration, it becomes slightly denser, and the energy is felt as more powerfully when viewed from our human perspective.

Earthly Ki is life-force energy that has already made contact and created a mutual resonance with the physical aspect of Life, in the form of Earth, its plants, and Nature. But because it is still Divine Ki in its core nature, it can also create a mutual resonance and combine well with Innate and Heavenly Ki. Thus the Earthly Ki can feed the very ethereal Heavenly and Innate Ki with a touch of grounded-flavored-Ki, which enables the combined Ki to anchor and sustain physical life in perfect health.

The Mysterious Kundalini:

Before we move on to describe the role of each chakra in manifestation, let's clear out some of the mist of mystery from the term kundalini. Most people have at least heard of the word 'kundalini', but are a bit puzzled as to what it is. Some people are even a bit scared of it, especially since much of the esoteric literature uses terms like "awaken the serpent" to talk about the kundalini.

OK. So there is actually no snake of any kind in kundalini energy. The word kundalini originates from the Sanskrit word "kundal", which literally means "a curl of the hair of the beloved," the kind that your mom has probably saved from your baby hair. The "kundalini" is no more and no less than the feed of life-force energy that flows through your shushmana channel, as illustrated in the profile drawing above. The energy becomes termed "kundalini," or "curly," since the Shushmana nadi is spiral in its structure.

So as we inbreathe, the feminine and masculine Heavenly Ki come through the Ida and Pingala nadis and travel to the Navel Center, where it mixes with Innate Ki. The Innate Ki, now awakened and enlivened with a fresh supply of Heavenly Ki, descends down to the root chakra, where it receives a fresh feed of Earthly Ki. The combined flow of the three flavors of life-force—now nicknamed "kundalini"—then ascend up the Shushmana, to cleanse, balance, and reinforce fresh Ki into all the chakras, on its way to the crown, where it merges with the Divine.

Notice that by the time that the energy is nicknamed "kundalini"—from the root chakra up—all three flavors of Ki are combined in its flow: the Heavenly comes in at the nostrils on inhalation; the Innate is always there, subtle and ethereal, and therefore perceived by many as dormant; and the Earthly comes in at the root chakra. Thus, the "kundalini" energy should have the subtle flavor of the Soul's innate energy, the powerful Light energy of the Heavenly Ki, and the grounded, soothing, centering force of the Earthly Ki.

So here, no more mystery about the word "kundalini!" Now, the "awakening" that the kundalini is said to need is simply a clearing of all obstruction to the flow of energy within you, and if you wish, a conscious invocation of more Creative life-force energy to flow through you, which we will learn to do in the various meditations of *Seven Stages to co-Creating Prosperity From Your Soul*, and in the lifestyle changes suggested in *A Lifestyle of Prosperity From Your Soul*.

Now that we have demisted some of the mysteries of our energetic apparatus, let's talk about the seven major chakras, and how each of them effects the manifestations in your life...

First—Root Chakra – Muladhara:

Location: perineum, at the base of the spine – the bottom center of the torso

<u>Color</u>: Red   <u>Element</u>: Earth   <u>Organ</u>: elimination organs
<u>Nerve Plexus</u>: sacral-coccygeal   <u>Endocrine Gland</u>: Gonads

<u>Healing issues associated with a blocked first chakra</u>: spinal column, bones, adrenal glands, lower bowel, hemorrhoids, attachment to organizations for security, judgment, attitude towards money and security, greed, lack, fear of death, inability to keep a job, lack of commitment.

As it relates to co-Creation of prosperity, the first chakra is all about brining things into physical existence. Thus, a blocked first chakra can block any co-Creation from manifesting into the physical. How can a first chakra become blocked? Simple. Anything that you perceive as a threat to your physical existence, any circumstance that you perceive as having the potential to compromise your safety and physical 'I am' (real or not), is registered as a first chakra violation. Further, association that you have with a group, and more importantly to group consciousness, which is restrictive, such as "hell fire and fury," or "we are all sinners" concepts, or "our people have always been discriminated against throughout history and were born to suffer the sins of the gentiles," to name a few, can register as a blockage or an entanglement cord at the first chakra, and thus block your ability to bring your co-Creative intents into manifestation. This includes your association with your root family, religion, racial, national, or any other group that at some level compromise your here-now 'I am',

The good news is that there are many ways to clear this and all other chakras. One such profound meditational tool is detailed in *Seven Stages to co-Creating Prosperity From Your Soul.*

Second—Navel Chakra – Svadisthana:

<u>Location</u>: Sexual organ area, below the navel
<u>Color</u>: Orange   <u>Element</u>: water   <u>Organ</u>: sexual organs
<u>Nerve Plexus</u>: Sacral   <u>Endocrine Gland</u>: Leydig

<u>Healing issues associated with a blocked second chakra</u>: lower back, bladder, kidneys, sexual organs, skin disorders, nerve problems, digestive problems, spleen disorders, feeling of abandonment, shame, addictions, mistrust in money and/or in relationships, work issues, sexual problems, imbalanced physical desires.

The second chakra is where issues related to sexuality and relationships are registered. If you've had a dysfunctional relationship, be it with a friend, a family member, spouse, a boyfriend/girlfriend, or even your child, this registers as a second chakra violation. Any emotions you may have buried deep inside you, which relate to intimacy and trust also register in your second chakra, and if those emotions are unconstructive, this may create a block in this chakra. The second chakra is where your creativeness comes through, in the form of creative ideas and birth-giving. So if you have had any abortions, difficulties in child-bearing, or have aborted creative ideas that you might were passionate about, it would behoove you to do some meditational clearing of the second chakra (as we will do together in *Seven Stages to co-Creating Prosperity From Your Soul*).

Incidentally, as it relates to prosperity, this chakra is also the energetic center where issues related to money register. Any bad investments, disappointments, lost jobs, or even lack attitudes about money that your parents might have inadvertently raised you with, can all create blockages in this second chakra. So when you get to *Seven Stages to co-Creating Prosperity From Your Soul*, you'd want to make sure you pay special attention to clearing your second chakra of any blockages or energetic debris. This alone can work wonders in clearing the way for Divine prosperity to come and manifest in your life.

Third—Solar Plexus Chakra – Manipura:

<u>Location</u>: between the physical navel, and solar plexus
<u>Color</u>: yellow   <u>Element</u>: fire   <u>Organs</u>: gal bladder, spleen, digestive, pancreas
<u>Nerve Plexus</u>: Solar   <u>Endocrine Gland</u>: Adrenals

   <u>Healing issues associated with a blocked third chakra</u>: solar plexus, liver, gal bladder, spleen, digestive organs, pancreas, adrenals, lack of willpower, overweight around the middle of the body, loss of energy, inability to accomplish things, victimization, and poor self-esteem.

   This chakra is also monumentally important to becoming a conscious co-Creator of your life. It is in charge of holding your sense of personal power, free will (which by itself is *the* magical key to manifestation), your sense of identity, and control over your life. Unfortunately, many of us have been told by overprotective parents – "you can't do that, you are too little," which then registered as an energetic violation of in our third chakra, and could block our personal power and thus ability to co-Create prosperity. Throughout our lives, we are constantly being told by society that we are but tiny dots in a huge mechanistic universe, and that we have no real power to affect anything. These notions, besides being completely untrue, create a blockage of the third chakra. As you'll understand in Chapter 5, the whole Universe is run by free will—your free will. Your willpower is needed for every step and level of the co-Creative process, including the stage of bringing your will into physical manifestation. The good news is that awareness is the first step to deprograming all of these "I can't" attitudes and clearing their debris from the third chakra.

   This chakra is also the holding space for your human-level emotions—your emotional center. Any heavy emotions that you may have experienced throughout your life, which haven't yet been cleared, would weigh down on your third chakra and dull your sense of self-worth and personal power. And it is this sense of personal power – the knowing that you are a beloved child of your Creator who is worthy of every good thing, which makes you a successful co-Creator of all-inclusive prosperity throughout your life. Many practices will be detailed throughout *Seven Stages to co-Creating Prosperity From Your Soul* to clear and reenergize this important third chakra.

Fourth—Heart Chakra – Anahata:

<u>Location</u>: middle of the chest, between the nipple-line and top of the sternum bone
<u>Color</u>: Green   <u>Element</u>: Air   <u>Organs</u>: heart, lungs
<u>Nerve Plexus</u>: heart plexus   <u>Endocrine Gland</u>: thymus

Healing issues associated with a blocked fourth chakra: blood and heart problems, lungs, chest, middle of back, asthma, inability to love yourself or others unconditionally, mistrust, feeling of betrayal.

It is said that the human side of you is the domains of your first, second and third chakras, and the Heavenly side of you is domains of the upper three chakras – the throat, third eye and crown. But the heart chakra is a special place. It is of both worlds. It is the doorway between your human-self and. Your proverbial heart that experiences human love is hosted here, but also your higher spiritual heart—the part of you that knows God at the very core of your being, and can experience unconditional Love, which is a step beyond human love. This is the energy center that knows real compassion, kindness, and service to others, as a way to connect with All-There-Is, which in turn is the Source for all prosperity. (We'll talk more about how kindness and service to others play an important role in co-Creation of prosperity in Chapter 3). Incidentally, the heart chakra is also the part of you that is privy to the most loving Divine plan for your life, which as we'll see in the next chapter, is monumentally important in the manifestation of prosperity.

The importance of having this chakra open and clear becomes more emphasized when you consider that the energetic projection capability of your heart is about 100,000 times more powerful than that of your mind[7]. You see, it is through your heart chakra that you actually connect with the wisdom of your Soul, and shift your energetic vibration into likeness and resonance with what you Truly want. This is the real stuff of co-Creating prosperity, and we will delve deeply into how it works in Chapter 5.

Fifth—Throat Chakra – Vishuddha:

Location: cleft of the throat   Color: light (cobalt) blue

Element: ether   Organs: trachea, throat, cervical vertebrae

Nerve Plexus: cervical ganglia, medulla   Endocrine Gland: Thyroid

Healing issues associated with a blocked fifth chakra: lungs, ears, vocal apparatus, alimentary canal, bronchioles, voice and throat problems, thyroid, parathyroid, sinuses, shoulders, chin, mouth, need to rule, disagreement between one's head and heart.

Your fifth chakra is your center for self-expression. This is where the resultant outcome of all that you think and feel expresses itself into the Universe. It is where you speak your Truth, and are thus able to inspire and move others. But it is also where you truly listen, and where your ability to discern truth from non-truth spoken by others resides. Of course, this is also the center in charge of telepathic and direct communication, which is the True way in which we all communicate in the heavenly realms.

As it relates to co-Creation of prosperity, when your mind and your heart are in agreement with each other; when the truths spoken has the backing of all the other chakras in a clear and unobstructed way; and when your Truth spoken reflects the True essence of who you are as an expression of your Soul's will, **you gain the ability to speak your words into manifestation!**

Sixth—Third-Eye Chakra – Ajna:

<u>Location</u>: between, and slightly above and in front of the eyebrows
<u>Element</u>: imperceptible to humans   <u>Color</u>: indigo   <u>Organs</u>: brain, eyes
<u>Nerve Plexus</u>: hypothalamus, pituitary   <u>Endocrine Gland</u>: Pituitary

<u>Healing issues associated with a blocked sixth chakra</u>: eyes, head, nose, sinuses, pituitary, hypothalamus, headaches, confusion, being less than fully conscious, living in a fog, unclear mind, lack of spiritual understanding, an overly intellectual approach to spirituality.

The Third-Eye chakra can be perceived as our center for spirituality. This chakra gives you the clairvoyant abilities to see beyond this physical dimension, and to perceive things in the crystal-clear way that your True Self can perceive them. The most common way that this chakra becomes blocked is when we overly rely on perceptions coming from only the "physical" aspect of reality, and doubt or disregard the insights coming through the Third–Eye chakra. This stifles those insights deep inside your unconscious, and can eventually clog the ability of your sixth chakra to receive clear extrasensory perceptions, which by the way we are all capable of to a lesser or greater degree.

And here is an example of interrelationships between chakras: If one's third chakra is blocked, he/she does not feel personally empowered. If this is accompanied by a weak aura that fails to protect them from negative outside influences, it can cause a situation where one tends to be overly influenced by the will of others. It is also associated with cords and energetic obstructions at the first chakra, anchoring the person down to the limiting consciousness of a group. All of this would in turn cause their sixth chakra to be susceptible to accepting archetypal, limiting thought forms from the collective unconscious, rather than grounding clear thought from the realm of their own True Self.

But the good news is that you have a choice: An open and clear sixth chakra that is empowered by a clear flow of energy from all the other chakras can help you connect to Divine intellect and see yourself in the pure Light of your Akashic Records (more on that in Chapter 9).

And this is where things relating to manifestation get serious! As the 6th chakra gives you the power to tune into the realms of the Divine, it allows you to tune into your most auspicious Lifeplan (more on that in the next chapter), which is just waiting for you to reclaim as your life path. And since co-Creating a prosperous life depends on your ability to tune into your Ideal Lifeplan from your Soul's perspective, this chakra, which allows you insight into that plan, plays a very important role in manifestation!

Now here comes the real stuff of manifestation: a clear and open Third-Eye chakra, which has the backing of all the other chakras, also **gives you the ability to *project your thought into reality*!**

Seventh—Crown Chakra – Sahasrara:

<u>Location</u>: the crown of the head
<u>Color</u>: violet   <u>Organ</u>: brain, pineal gland
<u>Nerve Plexus</u>: cerebral cortex, pineal   <u>Endocrine Gland</u>: pineal

<u>Healing problems when this chakra is blocked can affect</u>: pineal gland, brain problems, confusion, loss of free will, inability to make a decision, difficulty in manifestation, lack of inspiration, feeling separateness from God, loneliness

We have seen above how the Universal energy feeds your energetic and physical bodies. With all these spiritual level truth, your physical body is not to be taken lightly (as we shall explore in *A Lifestyle of Prosperity From Your Soul*), since it is the channel through which your co-Creations find their way into manifestation in your life.

Your Infinite Soul
pouring into your
physical being

Crown Chakra -
the 1st seat
of the Soul

Heart Chakra -
the anchor of the
Soul into the
physical

But of equal importance is your connection to your Soul Self. And your center for receiving animating life-force from the Divine is facilitated by your crown chakra. If you will look carefully at the diagram, you'll notice that the key station - monitoring and allowing this feeding of energy is the crown chakra. Indeed it is one of the two doorways connecting you to your Soul (the other one being the heart). And since it is really your Soul Self that is the powerful co-Creator of your life (as we shall discuss in Chapter 5), you can see why being a successful co-Creator requires keeping the crown chakra clear and open.

If you envision your Soul as shaped like an inverted triangle or a funnel pouring Its life-essence into your physical, the crown of your head is the first point at which a wide part of the funnel makes contact with the physical body (which has the power to allow or disallow the connection), and your heart center is the narrow end of the funnel, through which your Soul actually pours its essence into your physical reality. For this reason, both the heart chakra and the crown are considered to be the seats of your Soul through which the Divine pours Her-Himself into your here-now self and manifests blessings in your life.

And these blessings are not just about monetary prosperity. The blessings facilitated by the crown chakra can lead you to transcendence, elevation, and the ability to feel yourself in blissful Oneness with all of Creation, enlightenment, and saintliness. **When you feel oneness with all of Creation, you gain the ability to tap into the Infinite resources.**

Meridian System

The acupuncture meridian system is another system of channels, which feed life-force energy from the etheric body into the physical body. The Chinese believe that there are twelve pairs of meridians, plus the two unpaired channels. The unpaired meridians are called conception vessel, which runs along the front side of the body, and governing vessel, which runs primarily along the back side of the body. The Chinese profess that each imbalance or blockage in this system of energy channels results in a later dysfunction in an organ, and that when the meridians function normally, they feed chi (life-force) energy from the etheric into the physical body. But since the meridian system only exists in the etheric body, they affect only changes in health of the physical body, whereas the chakra system, which exist as doorways through all levels of your existence have a more profound affect on all manifestations in your life. However, since health is an integral part of true prosperity, let's talk for a minute about the meridian system.

Experimental data[4] proving the existence of the meridian system comes from professor Kim Bong Han's experiment in Korea. Dr. Han injected radioactive P^{32} into lab animals' acupuncture meridian points, and was able to trace its uptake in the body. He discovered that the uptake of the phosphorus isotope ran along fine duct-like channels that followed the path of the classic acupuncture meridians. As a control to this experiment, he tried injecting the P^{32} into a vein, and little to none of it was detected in the meridian network. This made him conclude that the acupuncture meridians were independent of the cardiovascular system. More recent experiments, which were done by the French researcher Pierre de Vernejoul on humans (with radioactive technetium 99m), confirmed Dr. Han's results. According to Dr. Gerber, these experiments point to the existence of a deep meridian system, which feed energy primarily into the cardiovascular and lymphatic systems, and a superficial meridian system, which feeds energy into many of our internal organs.

Dr. Han also did this experiment on embryonic chicks, and noticed that the meridian ducts were formed within fifteen hours of conception, which is before the most basic physical organs were formed. He did some experiments in which he experimentally interfered with the energy flow of liver meridian, and noticed that the abnormal changes to the physical liver occurred only three days later. This delayed response between the meridian system and the organs of the physical body is also confirmed through recent Kirlian photographic studies, which have found that changes in brightness of meridian points precede changes in physical health by hours, days, and sometimes weeks. The natural conclusion is that the meridian system as the whole *etheric body form before the physical body does.*

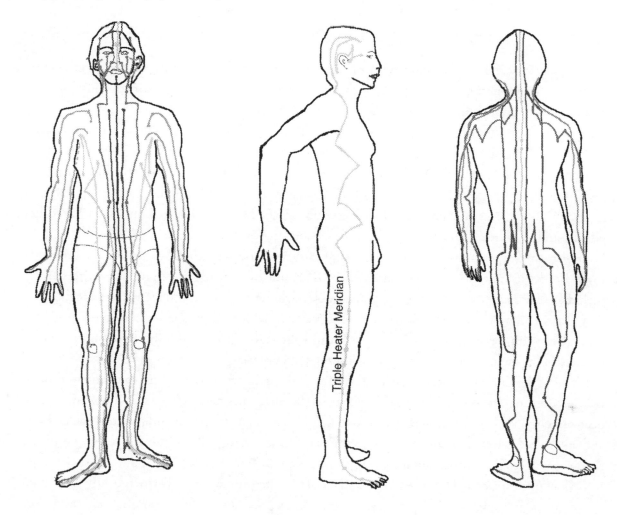

As it relates to co-Creation of prosperity, another concept worth mentioning which comes from Chinese philosophy is the concept of yin and yang. The yin-yang symbolizes the perfect harmony between the seeming opposites – a law that is referred to in yogic philosophy as the law of polarity. Yin is conceptualized as feminine, yielding, earthly, dark, wet, nurturing, calm, soothing, and grounding. Yang is understood as masculine, charging, energetic, light, dry, and heavenly. But yin cannot exist without yang, and yang cannot exist without yin. That is the nature of all things in the Universe.

Even in the Creation of the world, you might say that to birth a universe this awesome, God would have to be a woman—yin energy. But you can also just as easily say that to have the power and Light-energy to carry out the plan, and to actually blow the breath of life into this Creation, God would have to be a man—yang energy. And indeed, as the Creator IS everything in the Universe, She-He is both! That is why I use this She-He expression – to denote the all-encompassing androgyny of God. Chinese philosophy gave us this extra emphasis on how opposites complete each other, and how everything in Creation is a perfect balance. As the symbol indicates, the yin and yang form a complete circle, as if eternally spinning around each other in a perfect harmony.

As we have seen in this chapter, both ancient wisdoms and scientific research point to the same thing: you are more than your physical body, more than your brain, more than your intelligence, and even more than your emotions. You are a spiritual being that extends to highest realms and merges with the Divine. And as spiritual matter filters from your consciousness to the higher realms, and from the Divine realms into your physical reality, it becomes a continuum in which matter, light, and Divine energy (even Relativity understands matter as just frozen energy) are just different aspects of the same flow, a flow in which all your light bodies and energy centers serve as bridges through which the Divine slows down Her-His vibration to manifest as you, other people, and of course also the money and possessions in your life.

But it isn't necessary to memorize the chakra system, the meridian system, or the energetic Light Bodies in order to become a successful co-Creator of your life. The purpose of presenting them here was merely to impress upon you how closely interconnected you are with the reality you co-Create, and more importantly, with the Source from which all prosperity manifests. And this interrelationship between your energetic self and your reality brings to mind two points: first as you reflect on some of the concepts you've just read, it may trigger some personal Ahas about some of the ways in which you already are co-Creating your reality. You may begin to see how some of your predominant thoughts and feelings relate to the different energy centers, and how they have been affecting the co-Creation of your life so far. This leads us to the second point: if the chakras and energetic bodies are doorways through which Divine energy filters into the reality your life, than you can see how important it is to clear and balance them. For once clear and balanced, they can allow unobstructed Divine energy to manifest in the only way unobstructed Divine energy *can* manifest – auspicious! The practices given in *Seven Stages to co-Creating Prosperity From Your Soul* will help you do all that.

At the end of this chapter, I hope you can take with you the understanding of how vast you Truly are, and how Divinely empowered you are to co-Create all that you Truly desire… I like humorously saying that your Soul is in cahoots with God, in terms of Its power and wisdom to co-Create for you all that serves your highest purpose. And I hope you take with you at least the cognitive knowledge that your Soul is an integral part of your all-powerful Creator, and is actively co-Creating all the circumstances and experiences of your life. These understandings lay the foundation for the meditational processes of *Seven Stages to co-Creating Prosperity From Your Soul*, which will enable you to tap into the wisdom and powers of your Soul, and harness it to co-Create a prosperous life.

Besides understanding how wonderful you Truly are, clearing the way for Divine Creative energy to pour into your life is indeed a powerful step towards co-Creating prosperity in your life. And we will take that first step together with the concepts that we will explore in the first part of the next chapter, which will make you feel light, free and wonderful!

However, this clearing of obstructions in order to allow the Creative energy to pour into your manifestations is only the first step. In the next few chapters, we will also learn some more potent steps to actively "suck-in" enhanced amounts of Creative energy for manifestation of prosperity in your life. And of course in *Seven Stages to co-Creating Prosperity From Your Soul*, I will give you specific tools to bring those understandings into action

In the next chapter, we'll answer some of the questions that must be on your mind after this discussion, such as: "if I am so awesome and powerful, why aren't I rich and successful right now?" and we'll delve deeper into how you can shift your co-Creative consciousness to rise above any limitation, and co-Create more auspicious circumstances for yourself.

Chapter 2

From Discord to Harmony

In the last chapter, we have discussed your magnificent True Self and the many aspects that make you such a powerful co-Creator. Now comes the big question: "if I am such a powerful co-Creator and am so beloved by God, than why aren't I healthier, happier and richer right now? Why aren't the circumstances of my life better?" This chapter will address these questions, and pave the way to understanding how to rise above the limitations in your life and co-Create prosperity.

Another question that many people ponder as they begin their path of becoming a more conscious co-Creators is: "How much say do I really have in manifesting what I want in life? Do I really *co-Create* my life?"

Some people believe that everything is preordained by a preset capricious destiny in which we have no say. And if this were so, than you would have had no free choice in how you run your life or how it turns out. I mean, if you believed in the Greek tragedy style "destiny" argument, then there would really be no point in striving for anything, learning anything or being "good," would there? As in argument against scientific determinism, which we have discussed briefly in the Chapter 1 – there would be no point in being moral, nor would we have the ability to decide be or not to be moral. In a deterministic world in which either a capricious "destiny," or the rules of science predetermine everything *for you*, you wouldn't even be able to decide whether you shower or take a bath this morning, or whether to frown or smile through your day. And we all know that that's not the case, so we know that at least at some level, you do decide things. The newsflash here is that your level of "deciding things" does not end with your shower or your breakfast. As we shall prove in Chapters 5 and 6, *you co-Create your life in a very real way*—much realer that you realize.

On the other side of the spectrum are people who argue that there is no rime or reason for how our lives turn out, that as we all are just a genetic "mistake", and that our lives are simply the result of our random choices in an everlasting war against a cold harsh circumstantial reality. But we know that this theory cannot be right either, because synchronistic events (and we've all had them) prove that there is nothing random about how our lives turn out.

As you'll come to understand in this chapter, both of these arguments are really oversimplifications of one broader Truth. You'll see that "destiny" and free will are not mutually exclusive concepts. Simply said, it is the harmonious balance between those two seeming opposites—between living in a harmonious flow with the Universal wisdom of your Soul Self, and being responsible for your own free choices on all levels—that makes you a conscious, and thus successful co-Creator of prosperity.

But before we delve into the real issues of this chapter, let's clear out some conceptual obstacles from your path to co-Creation of prosperity in your life—concepts that have been floating out there in the collective unconscious for many centuries, preventing mankind from reclaiming its God-given radiance and abundance, but which no longer serve neither humanity nor your personal manifestation endeavors.

Cast Out Who?

As you may have intuitively guessed, fear is a bad master that does not serve your new prosperous Lifepath. So let's get rid of one fear that is probably rooted a lot deeper in our subconscious than any of us would care to admit.

There is <u>NO</u> devil! It simply is a man-made invention that is not based on truth! In the physical universe darkness does not exist in and of its own. There is light, or the absence of light. And even in the absence of apparent light and in the void of space, researchers[2] are starting to understand that there is tremendous amount of energy hidden, thus pointing to the fact that even what *appears to be* darkness is an integral part of the Light of Creation. Similarly in our spiritual universe, *evil does not exist* in and of its own! There is Light and there is the lack of light within the polarity necessary to manifest Creation. But there is no such distinct entity as evil or the devil. Those are simply myths, along with all the other myths that people through history have made up out of fear. The was made up by the ancient biblical scholars as a tactics of scaring people into choosing God – basically waving an imaginary stick, so that the child would choose the way that leads to the carrot instead. The Roman Catholic Church and the Spanish Inquisition have made this scare tactics into an art form in their efforts to rule their constituency by fear and obtain absolute power over them. Now that's not to say anything bad about the actual wisdom of the Old Testament, Jesus, or their messages of Love. But whenever wisdom is removed from its source, it becomes hearsay, and that's when things tend to get twisted around.

Much of the symbolism surrounding the beast was derived from things that were taken out of context and distorted to make them look scary in people's eyes. For example, in the days that the temple in Jerusalem existed, the Israelites used to sacrifice goats and sheep in the temple altar to show their devotion to God. The Catholic church needed to paint that tradition in scary colors, so they attached the goat's eyes to the image of their made up devil, when in fact, goats are lovely animals who bring many blessings to humanity, including wool made from their hair, and their healthy and delicious milk. The same twisting of truth was done with some pagan customs and beliefs. Certain European pagan traditions used to sacrifice bulls and read their intestines as a method of divination and to celebrate nature's blessings. The Roman Catholic Church desperately needed to paint those traditions in scary colors in order to drive people away from these traditions and into Catholicism. So they took the bull's horns a symbol of something that is ultimately bad.

But the truth is that such ultimate evil simply does not exist! Interesting, though, how the Church eventually succumbed to these earth-based religions, and integrated their holidays into "Christian holidays," as it turned out to be the only way to make them accept Christianity.

To be fair, the Spanish Inquisition and the Roman Catholic Church were not the only perpetrator in human history who strived to possess absolute power over their constituency and who inflicted countless atrocities in the name of that "power." Throughout history there have been atrocities done by different people, like Bin Laden, Hitler, Mussolini, Queen Isabella of Spain, the Spanish Inquisition, and the Crusades, to name a few, all in the name of a higher power or a self-proclaimed supreme righteousness. Even today people seem to be very magnetized to horror movies. But that doesn't make us evil, and it doesn't prove that "sin crouches in every doorstep" (with all due respect to Genesis). It only proves that we are here having a human experience, exercising our free will in many different ways, and we sometimes forget our Divine nature and the Source for our power and abundance. Sometimes we immerse ourselves so deeply in this "physical" reality that we forget whom we Truly are, and allow fear (which is processed and held at the Nefesh) to rule us. This total immersion can cause us to confuse the adrenaline rush of our fear-driven primal instincts, which can result in cruel actions, with a true sense of power, which is Divine. And if you think about it deeply enough, most of the atrocities of the world were driven by fear... even greed or thirst for power are driven by fear. But again, fear is not evil either. It is simply the absence of Divine Light or more accurately – the perceived separation from It. And the antidote to it is remembering that one ray of light can obliterate total darkness.

Now let us put things in context: Whatever darkness exists in the world, exists as part of a balance that is meant only to give us all free-choice. In other words, if there were only Light and good in the world, you wouldn't really have a free choice, since there wouldn't really be any options to choose from. Without polarity there is no Creation; we would all revert back to an eternal primordial Divine bliss. I know that at first glance, this doesn't sound bad. But this would also mean that we 'freeze-frame' our spiritual evolution – we stop growing. So the only point to the existence of darkness as the polar opposite of Light is to give you free-choice, so that you can fully experience all that you are, and through these experiences of rising above challenges, experiencing things deeply, and learning the lessons that facilitate your Soul's growth, grow to be all that you are meant to become.

But throughout any experience in which you may delve into the depth of discord, know that the True reason for your existence is to experience Love and joy, and to expand the amount of Love and wisdom in the world through your experiences. Remember that the only True Power comes from the Divine, which permeates all levels of reality, and that the energy of the Creator is one of Love. Through the meditations outlined in *Seven Stages to co-Creating Prosperity From Your Soul*, you will get a chance to glimpse at the True Light of your Soul, and you will then experientially understand what true power feels like. I have had some meditational experiences in which I've not only "seen" the Light of my Soul, but also briefly experienced Divine Oneness. And it felt like an almost electrical feeling, which is beyond celestial music and beyond a light. It was an exhilarating vibration and a feeling of absolute power, peace, love and joy all at the same time. The only human experience that comes somewhat close to understanding this feeling is having one of those electrically intense orgasms. Only the Divine "orgasm" is non-sexual, lasts forever (rather than a few seconds), and is Infinitely more exhilarating! It is a feeling of basking in Divine Love, which is unconditional and immeasurably purer than human love. It is the energy from which all Creation, physical or otherwise, is made—pure unseconded Creator energy!

And since the bigger Truth that underlies our reality is that of the Divine power with which our high-Selves are imbued, all sensations of power that we experience through our here-now selves immeasurably fade by comparison. That is why some people tend to get insatiably thirsty for power – because they forget the True power of their higher-Selves. However, while the Divine energy is always pure Love-Light-Joy, if we go a few steps into its filtration into the physical, all physical manifestations of Divine energy depend on which aspect of the Whole we choose to extract from it and refine, which depends on our individual life-mission, but also (unfortunately) on our human biases, emotions, points of view, and scars of disappointment. So while all manifestations originate from the Divine Creative energy, what *you* co-Create into your life is either a reflection of your human biases and scars, or (hopefully) a reflection of your highest mission in life. Sometimes they are a manifestation of something in between.

To help you walk through life knowing that there is nothing to fear and everything to look forward to, let us continue to dust off old myths… At this point, if you are very religious, you might say: "We can't just all drink, eat, and be merry. What about judgment day? Don't we have to account for our actions?" We will talk about accountability later in this chapter. But as far as "judgment day," there is none, at least not in the traditional way in which most religions portray it to be.

Accounts of near death experiencers who have gone into the Light and experienced the famous "life-review"[2] tell us that it's not really a judgment day situation. They describe the life-review as a very fast but extremely vivid three-hundred-and-sixty degree movie, in which you are experientially immersed in a hologram of all the events in your life. The uniqueness of this review is that you are able to intensely feel not only your own emotions in each incident, but also the emotions of the people interacting with you in each event. But the interesting point here is that you—your Soul Self is the one that is doing the judging. Since after your transition you dwell in the ultra-consciousness of your highly moral Soul, as you view the events of your life and experience the emotions of those you've wronged, you feel bad for all of your unkind actions and words. And in the same way, as you watch the good things you've done, you as feel elated as those around you felt as a result of your actions. God, or the Light-being in which you bask, never does any judging! It may point out how you could have handled a particular situation more lovingly, taking a higher road, so to speak. In some cases, people reported that the Light told them that they were judging themselves too harshly. The Light Itself always radiates acceptance, compassion, and unconditional Love.

Some NDEers report seeing in the afterlife Souls (very few and far between) whose earthly personas strayed from the righteous, and performed atrocious acts towards others. These Souls have been seen taken by Angels and Guides to areas where they could bathe in Divine Light-Love more extensively, so that they can heal and restore their original high morality, after which they are able to have a normal life review, and choose corrective incarnations. In extreme cases (if the person's earthly persona was a monster), the process is one of washing away all negativities from the Soul matter of the criminal, and metamorphosis back into undifferentiated Divine matter.

So forget about judgment day, because that too does not exist! Your true essence is that of your Creator. And because your Soul is immortal and an integral part your Creator in a very real way, Her-His Love-Bliss-Light is the Truest essence of who you are. You have the power to shed all layers of density, fear and lower vibrations, and reclaim your true identity—a Soul that is beautiful and radiant beyond measure.

Now that we've dusted off these old myths, let's talk about the real issues of this chapter.

The Nature of Lifting Suffering

Have you ever tried to imagine what Beethoven's music would sound like without any dissonant sounds? In life as in music, discord allows us to experience things more deeply, and builds suspense towards, and appreciation of the harmony that follows. But *discord was never meant to be the main chord of the symphony of your life!* Most of the major challenges in your life were actually orchestrated by your own Soul, to either protect you, redirect you to a better path, or to deepen your human experience for your Soul's growth. And here's a revolutionary concept: it isn't that life gives you lemons, and therefore you must make lemonade. It's the other way around: you needed to drink the refreshing tasty zest of the lemonade; therefore the Universe sends you some lemons (and it also always send you the sugar to make it sweet) to make the lemonade from. However, **these challenges and limiting conditions were never meant to be your permanent state of affairs. Pain and suffering were never meant to be parts of your human experience**! In *Seven Stages to co-Creating Prosperity From Your Soul* and in *A Lifestyle of Prosperity From Your Soul*, we will work intensively on energetically and physically (respectively) removing all limiting conditions from your consciousness and life, so that you can become a more successful co-Creator of your most auspicious Lifepath. But for now, the first step to ridding yourself of pain and suffering is to understand why your Soul had manifested limiting conditions in the first place, as most limiting conditions actually fulfill some purpose in your life. And the sooner you tune into that purpose and achieve the Soul growth that it was meant to afford you, the quicker you'll rise above the limitation. To fully understand this, let's detail the different reasons why difficulty may have shown up in your life, from the perspective of your Soul Self.

Karma:

In one movie called *Little Buddha*, a Buddhist priest tells a story to illustrate karma: Once upon a time, a holy man was preparing a goat to be sacrificed at the altar. Midway through his preparation, the goat started laughing happily. The holy man was puzzled and a little mad, and yelled, "stupid goat, why are you laughing? Don't you understand that you are now going to be my sacrificial goat... that you are now going to die? Why are you laughing?" Of course, he wasn't expecting a reply from the goat, but to his astonishment, the goat opened her mouth and started speaking... "Dear Master," she said, "I am laughing because I am so happy. I have been a goat for a thousand lifetimes, and now that I'm getting the honor of being your sacrificial goat, I'll get to be human again, and have a very auspicious lifetime." This made the holy man ponder the implications of his actions, and the possible err of his ways. No sooner did he start pondering, did the goat start crying deep heartfelt sobs. Of course this made the holy man very confused, and again he yelled at the goat, "Maybe you really are just a stupid goat. You were laughing before. Why are you crying now?" The goat explained: "Dear Master, I am crying for you. Because you kill me, you'll now be a goat for thousand lifetimes now."

But contrary to common belief, karma is not punishment or retribution. Rather, it is a chance for your Soul to learn and grow. For example, if a guy was a "loftier-than-thou" priest that acted with superiority and judgment towards a certain beggar in a previous lifetime, than there is a good chance that in this lifetime he would *choose* to reincarnate as the homeless beggar on the street corner near the other guy's lucrative office. This role reversal is a way for his Soul to learn non-judgment, compassion, and unconditional love for his fellow human being. It gives him a chance to find the Truth of unlimited love and compassion within himself, even when he is immersed in his human experience. And maybe through this karmic choice he has also allowed his now-rich friend to learn the lesson of non-judgment and compassion as he passes his street corner and treats him with generosity and compassion. In this illustration as in all cases, the sooner one learns the lesson afforded by a particular karmic lesson, the sooner the difficulty of that condition would be lifted, even within the framework of one particular incarnation. For example the beggar in the second lifetime might stop judging himself and others, dissolve the fear and negative feelings about his poverty, and begin to feel and radiate love and compassion towards all people who cross his path. And when he can do that, since he has learnt non-judgment, love and compassion for all human beings, there is no longer a need for the limiting condition of his poverty, and this beggar would probably soon see miraculous opportunities and riches befalling him.

Karma is really satisfied as soon as you achieve the Soul growth afforded by its lesson. A good sign that karma of a certain issue or person in your life has been satisfied is if you feel that there is no longer venom inside you from the sting of a certain issue/person. In other words — when it no longer evokes any negative potent feelings, and you find that you can once again feel and act from a higher plain of existence with regards to this issue. This brings us to another misconception about karma: that one must suffer in order to satisfy karma. And that is not true. It is not necessary to suffer in order to complete a karmic lesson. On the contrary: given the function of karma to teach all Souls involved lessons of compassion, love and harmony with all human beings, karma can also be satisfied through harmonious relationship. Because the karmic lesson can only be complete when you've not only uprooted the venom of the sting and healed the wound, but also love the bee that stung you, metaphorically speaking. I always pray that instead of suffering at their hand, I would satisfy any karma by doing good deeds or healing work for the person I am to enact the karmic lesson with. And since the highest purpose of all life is creating more love in the world, this good intent satisfies the purpose of the karma in a much better way than suffering. When I remember to set that prayerful intent, things usually smooth out, as if by miracle.

Another good example to illustrate karma as role-playing is: when you go to school to learn hotel management, once you finish your academics but before you can become a manager of a hotel, you do an internship. During your internship, you work as a janitor, a maid, a dish washer, a cook, a bell-boy, a receptionist... until finally you understand hotel management from the bottom up and can assume the managerial position you were aiming for. For only when you understand all of the roles that can be played, you have the capacity to be a good manager. Another example is an orchestra conductor, who has to learn to play at least a few instruments, so he/she can experience playing different roles in the orchestra, and thus understand the music better and become a better conductor. In the same way, remember the analogy of God being the playwright, the director, the producer, the audience, the stage-set, and every actor in the play? Well, karma is just an opportunity for you to experience this play from different points of view. If you could become good at playing the righteous detective, but also the criminal, than you could see how the shoe feels being on the other foot, and with that experience you become a better actor—more full-ranged.

So that's the story about karma. It is not judgment day. It's not retribution. It's simply a way for Souls to grow to love each other more fully by playing different roles *for* each other. In some sense, karma is really just another words for Soul lesson, or opportunity for Soul growth, which brings us to the next section.

Challenges For Soul's Growth:

To reiterate: in order to know how to lift challenges and limiting conditions, let us now discuss in more detail the different kinds of challenges, and the purposes they fulfill, from the perspective of your Soul Self.

Your Symphonic Version –

Many of the challenges in your life are meant to give you certain human experiences that would enrich who you are, and foster Soul growth. These challenges give you a chance to experience the full array of human emotions and experiences. They also give you an opportunity to get to know yourself in the full array of behaviors, and feelings that your expanded Self is capable of, which reveal a fuller, richer picture of you. For who you really are is God experiencing Her-Himself *as* you. So while God wants to have much fun and enjoy Her-His earthly adventure park, She-He is not necessarily interested only in the whitewashed "loftier-than-thou" version of you, as that would be like listening to a single note continuously played by a single instrument. That would be boring, and would facilitate no growth! No. She-He is interested in the fuller, more symphonic version of you – the one that paints a full range of sounds, colors, emotions, behaviors and thoughts that you are capable of experiencing, all of which serve your Soul's growth! Because your Soul is made of energy—Divine energy. And the full range of experiences, which blends colors of Light and dark into the beautiful balance that only you can achieve, beefs up this energy into a bigger, more glorious you, with a full array of colors that enrich the Divine.

From the perspective of the Creator, experiencing Her-Himself through you can be likened to like having a beautiful rose garden that you love so much that you want to become part of it. Sure, you can experience the beauty of the garden just by looking at it through the window. But that's not a very authentic experience. You can experience it a bit better if you walk through the garden. A fuller experience of the garden would be to bend and cup every rose in your hands, let the softness of its petals rub against your cheeks, and take a full breath of its fragrance. But the truest way to experience the garden, if you could, would be to actually become each rose, every leaf, and even every thorn on that bush. Keep in mind that the thorns are a part of what makes the roses majestic and beautiful.

However, since the objective of this type of difficulty is to simply experience your depth, the sooner you can fully experience each discordant theme and achieve the Soul growth afforded by it, the sooner the Universe will let you move on and shed off the suffering. So for example, if certain sadness is a repeating theme in your life, than instead of avoiding it and stifling it inside, it may behoove you to the bottom of it. So even if you have to let yourself wallow in it for a day or two in a concentrated way in order to tune into its root cause, release it once and for all, bring that theme into closure, and purge out all residual grief; do so knowing that the sun will shine on your life tomorrow as you resurface from your dive refreshed and ready for a new start. Otherwise, these discordant themes will keep reappearing in your life again and again, taking different forms, until you allow yourself to fully experience their depth. For only when you allow yourself to fully experience something, can you tune into the essence of the lesson it opportunes you, and wake up in a new dawn in your life, knowing that you have let that discordant theme go; you have risen above its difficulty once and for all; you have graduated this particular university; and you are now a stronger, fuller-colored, more symphonic version of yourself.

For example, in my own childhood, I was dealt a difficult hand and I felt unloved and detached from God's Grace. This drove me to live my life in search of love. It also taught me to appreciate how important love is to every aspect of existence, which was a monumentally important lesson in life. As a spiritual teacher, I know today that my childhood feelings of detachment from love were not meant to make me suffer. Nor were they intended to last forever. They were only meant to drive me to become a messenger of Light-Love. When I was thirty years old, I broke up from a boyfriend who was one of the few people who truly loved me unconditionally. This drove me to a difficult time of reflecting on my childhood. I remember that I spent a few months listening to Brahms violin concerto and to Mozart Requiem over and over, sitting on the floor sobbing, and begging God to take me to a place where there was Love. This sounds very dark, I know. But the point is that allowing myself to experience this sadness for a short while in a very concentrated way had dissolved the need for it in my life, and thus prevented it from reoccurring. Because by allowing myself to fully experience that particular shade of depth within me, I was purging out those tears. It was that period of allowing myself to experience things so deeply that allowed me to understand that my need for love meant that the resonance with Love was always inside me, and that I deserved love, which then allowed me to accept God's Light and Love into my life. Energetically you might say that it purged out heaviness and debris from my Light Bodies and chakras, which opened my energy fields to receive Divine blessings. And sure enough, shortly after that period of purging, I rose up, and became the most popular and successful flight instructor in the state of Israel. I had several newspaper articles written about me, and interviewed a couple of times on Israeli national television, which then made money flow into my life very easily and abundantly. And not long afterwards, I became a reiki practitioner, and was able to more fully reconnect with God's Love and truly feel beloved. And as a testament, soon after I began to truly feel beloved, I made some close lifelong friends with whom I have bonds of unconditional love and support. And a couple of years later, I became a reiki master, which enabled me to perpetuate God's love and give it to others in a bigger way. But it was my willingness to reconnect with the sadness within, which allowed me to exorcise it and let it go forever, making room for God's Infinite Love, Light, and abundance to come and play in my life.

Universal Redirect –

Some situations in life are really redirects from the Universe to guide you reroutes your life and go follow your bliss – or your highest path through life. Even perceived enemies sometimes serve as messengers teaching us many things, such as concurring our ego, redirecting us towards our highest path, or even helping us get more determined to achieve our goals. Zohar Breath Meditation, detailed in *Seven Stages to co-Creating Prosperity From Your Soul*, will teach you to communicate with your Soul's highest wisdom, which is the best Source of information about the purpose of a certain obstacle, and how to surmount it. Another tool for detecting which is the path that the Universe is trying to direct you away from, and which is the path It's trying to direct you into is: whenever you walk a path in life driven by a certain choice, and find that all difficulties are mounting in your way, than that is the path you are being redirected away from, because the path you are meant to choose is one in which every gift just synchronistically befalls you. Especially when you are at a crossroad in which an important decision is to be made, or when you feel that things just aren't going your way, you might want to take a few deep breaths, tune into your Higher Self, and ask what the lesson here is: Is this a chance to practice kind assertiveness (more on that in Chapter 4)? What is the path that these difficulties are trying to divert you from, and what is the path that these difficulties are directing you towards?

For example, throughout my life I have had dreams in which I was flying like a bird, with my hands as wings. When it was time to choose a profession, I didn't quite know what I wanted to do. The IQ and aptitude tests indicated that I had a high IQ and could study anything I wanted to. But at that time, I hadn't yet awakened to my spiritual True calling. So I chose the goal of becoming an airline pilot. This was a very long and treacherous road, full of many obstacles. It took me fourteen years to become an airline pilot, and another nine years to upgrade to become a captain. But as I started to practice reiki on the side, and was blessed with one healing miracle after another, I began to understand that the airline was not my True calling; I wasn't following my bliss. But like any normal human being, fear and financial uncertainty kept me from taking a step towards living my highest mission in life. And then I started to experience severe frequent migraines, which made it impossible for me to continue to be an airline pilot. But as ridiculous as it may sound, these migraines had allowed me to channel the information of this book from the Divine and onto these pages. In fact, an EEG of my brain, which was done to try and diagnose the cause of my migraines, recorded brain-waves activity that contained such a high frequency and amplitude in the meditative brain waves they were off the chart. So you might say that these migraines were a blessing in disguise, as they gave me a kick in the butt and the inevitable courage to follow my highest calling, which is to share my healing gifts with humanity. However, these migraines were never meant to weigh me down for the rest of my life, and I believe that when the perfect way to bring all this wisdom to you materializes—when I publish this book, and teach the retreat courses, the knowledge of which I also received meditationally, then the Universe will take away the migraines.

I recently met a woman who proved my theory right: She had been a schoolteacher for twenty years when she started suffering form a continuous migraine. Her migraines lasted for about eight years. Then, an inspired idea came to her to become an educational therapist. She spent two years toughing out the pain and getting an additional degree as an educational therapist. Soon after she graduated, she began to work individually with dyslectic kids and kids with learning disabilities. Although inexperienced, she soon found out that she was truly gifted in this area—she was able to get kids to read after many experts have failed and given up. But she also discovered something else: while she was in-session with a child, her migraine pain would seize. As the session would end, and even between sessions while commuting to meet the next child she was to work with, the migraine pain returned, along with trembling hands, photophobia, and confusion, all of which made it difficult for her to drive. But as she persisted, she kept doing an excellent job helping kids, and after a while, she started to have longer and longer periods that were migraine-free even between sessions, until after two years her migraines altogether. At the time that I spoke to her, she had been migraine-free for eight years. But there were two more interesting "side-effects" that this temporary period of suffering produced: First, it had lead her to choose to become an educational therapist, a field that as she found out she deeply enjoyed was obviously her True calling. And since this was her true calling in life, she became instantly good at it, and her counseling sessions quickly became in demand. And you should see her house – all decorated with beautifully written essays of gratitude – written by kids who other therapists had declared would never learn to read or write. This brings us to the second "side-effect:" Since for the first two years being in session with a child was the only time slot in which she was migraine-free, she worked a lot. And while the need for financial gain may not have been what drove her to work a lot, the side effect of working a lot was that it also brought her financial prosperity that she would have never had as a schoolteacher. This is another example of Universal lemons being sent knowing that the sugar to make them into a sweet lemonade was always dormant within this woman. The lemons were just sent in order to give her a push to capitalize on her gift.

Protection ~

Many times difficulties mount in your way as a way to divert you from danger. The Bible tells us that when Moses was a baby growing up in the Pharaoh's palace, the Pharaoh wanted to make sure that Moses was not going to pose a threat to his son as his heir. So the Pharaoh placed Moses in front of two bowls: one with gold and gemstones and the other one with red-hot stones. The Pharaoh reasoned that if Moses instinctually chose gold and gems, than his sights were naturally set on greatness and he might pose a threat to the Pharaoh's son. But if Moses instinctually chose the fire, than he posed no threat. As the pharaoh sat in front of the two bowls with the baby Moses on his lap, the baby's hand naturally started to go for the gold and gems. But an Angel pushed his hand towards the bowl with the red-hot stones. The baby put one of the hot stones in his mouth and the burn made him stutter for the rest of his life. This is a perfect example of a suffering that actually protects you. In our example, going for the fire saved his life, because had he gone for the jewels, the pharaoh would have had him killed! In Moses's case, stuttering was a small price to pay for staying alive and being opportuned an upbringing and education at the pharaoh's palace level, which later allowed him to become a great leader. But even you look at the stuttering as the limitation or "lemon" that God gave Moses to surmount. God also gave Moses his loyal brother Aaron, who interpreted-spoke for him, and who helped him lead the nation throughout his life. So the Universe never gives lemons without also giving you the hidden sugar and ice to make our lemonade sweet and cold.

If you have a task you are trying to achieve, and something is just not letting you go there, this might be your Higher Self (or your guardian Angels) protecting you from a bad situation that your here-now self is just not in a position to see. You can use Zohar Breath Meditation to tune into your Soul's wisdom and ask what the danger is that your Soul Self is trying to protect you from, and what your here-now self can do to avert the danger without experiencing the difficulty of the situation.

Why Do We Need Soul Lessons?

Your Soul is pure from its inception. That is undisputable Divine Truth. Even if you don't believe in reincarnation, the Soul is always bright, pure, and without blemish before it comes to life on Earth. So you may ask, "If my Soul is perfect and pure, why do I need any challenge or difficulty?" To answer by illustration, think of the Universe as a vessel—a perfect clay vase, which at a certain point willfully shatters itself into a gazillion pieces. Then over time, each piece in its search for the Whole, gathers around it more clay and other materials, which make it bigger, stronger, and more beautifully colored. When the vase reassembles to regain its Wholeness, since each piece is now a bigger stronger fuller version of itself, the vase as a whole is a bigger stronger vase with a more beautiful color pattern. In reality, of course God hasn't really broken or reduced Her-Himself in any way, and you and I are not really separate. As you'll understand more fully in Chapters 5 and 6, we are all still One, and God is still Whole. But it works as a metaphor to explain why the Soul needed to keep growing—becoming more of who It is, and in the process, enriching the Whole. For in reality, your Soul is made of energy—the Divine energy of Creation. So if each Soul experiences more love, and therefore manifests around it more "love-energy material," than it becomes bigger, which quite literally expands Creation.

So after and before each earthly lifetime, the Soul takes with It the growth afforded by lessons of past experiences, which become part of the Soul essence. In this Heavenly interim between lifetimes, each Soul then bathes in Divine Light to completely cleanse all suffering and negativity, and becomes completely healed and recharged in Divine Light. However, after the life review, your Soul may decide on another incarnation—a do it over, if you will. It's kind of like if you knew that you were normally very good at monopoly, but on a certain occasion a friend who was bad at monopoly beat you at the game so easily that it put you to shame, you would inevitably ask for a do-over. Wouldn't you? Well in the same way, after each lifetime, when you get to dwell in the ultra-moral consciousness of your Soul, many times you decide on a do-over, to prove to your Self that you can do better. If you decide on another incarnation, when you plan it, you usually take with you certain karmic lesson objectives: certain character flaws and limiting conditions as the challengers of the game, so to speak. These are all meant to deepen the humanness of your experience here, and to give your grand spirit a chance to rise above them and win this game fair and square. As you plan each lifetime carefully, your spirit actually rejoices at the growth opportunity that would be afforded by taking on those challenges into your next lifetime. For to not only surmount the difficulties and limiting conditions of the past, but to truly master their lessons, one must get another chance to face the same challenge. To illustrate this point, let's say that you had previously started taking a very difficult history test at school, with which you had some challenges because you are slightly dyslectic and have difficulty reading the long texts of history books. And let's say you have started taking the difficult test doing the best you can, but never got to finish taking it because there was a fire drill evacuating everyone from the school building. Well, if the school were to automatically give everyone an 'A' in this test, you would never know if you could have aced it or not, and you would never know if you had it in you to rise above your dyslexia and show to the teacher and yourself your true brilliance. The only way to find that out is to actually take the test again, while being subjected to the same limitations you had before. And to emphasize our point here, in our example, after taking a few tests and showing yourself that your brilliant mind can help you overcome dyslexia, you start doing so well in school that you forget you even had dyslexia once. By the way, the case of having a difficulty with history and long texts due to dyslexia is my case. But see, I have surmounted that difficulty so well that I'm actually writing a book! Difficulties in life are similar. The whole purpose of taking with you certain weaknesses, challenges, or limiting condition is to give your spirit a chance to shine so bright, that it helps you surmount all the difficulties even from within your human-immersed position.

All that being said, since your free choice rules at every level of your existence (as we will discuss in Chapter 5), you always have the choice to either fall back on preexisting but limiting behavior patterns, or to rise above the challengers and act according your Soul's directive. As an example, when I was in high school, there was a boy whose presence evoked very strong feelings in me, which at ninth grade I didn't quite know how to interpret, let alone handle. My lower here-now self decided to interpret those feelings as hate. So for the first year and a half in which I knew him, that was the behavior I publically displayed towards him. It took me a year and a half to realize that I actually loved him deeply, and I didn't know what to do with this kind of love at age fifteen. We graduated high school and went our separate ways, with him never knowing how deeply I loved him. It took me another thirty-one years to realize, meditationally (regressing myself to recall a mutual past life that we had), that I had antagonized him in a previous incarnation, and that the lesson in this lifetime was for me to learn to love him unconditionally, so I can learn unconditional love. And I say *unconditionally* love him, because I'm pretty sure that my love for him was not reciprocated, and yet I love him dearly to this day. I realize now, from a slightly-closer-to-enlightened perspective, that in the first year-and-a-half, I simply fell back on the old behavior pattern that was ingrained in me as the challengers of the game, the one that made me antagonize him in the past life. Of course, that was the behavior I needed to learn to overcome. But for my fifteen-year-old-self, it was easier just to hate someone and give in to pre-conditioning than it was to comprehend unconditional love. And it took a long time for my teenage self to remember the intense love between our Souls. It has taken me 31 years to acknowledge that I was meant to carry this unrequited love for him throughout this lifetime, for that was the pre-agreed upon thing that would fully release each of us into our own Godlight. But the point of that lesson was never missed, for I have achieved the benefits of this lesson. I have learnt to embrace the very feeling of love, to rejoice in the openness of my heart, and to send the distant healing that only selfless love can afford. And in that, I am the winner in this situation. The funny thing is that once I have acknowledged that this was the function that this guy had fulfilled in my life, and learnt to be grateful for the very feeling of love, I stopped being tortured by the events, and his image stopped appearing in my dreams… thirty-one years later.

Here is a way to know whether a particular Soul lesson has truly been mastered: A continued bad experience or heavy feeling about a particular issue in life is a telltale that you still haven't mastered the lesson. As explained above, only when you no longer feel the potency of emotions about it sting, have you truly graduated from this lesson. And Truest sign that you have mastered the lesson is when you can not only rise above the challenges or suffering of this lesson, but have also discarded the heavy feelings associated with it and are able to feel joy, love and happiness for the Soul growth you achieved on top of it. This graduation party, even if internal, is what makes you abundant and absolutely grand-spirited!

In *Seven Stages to co-Creating Prosperity From Your Soul,* we will do many meditations to eradicate negativities from your life. But when it comes to a lesson that your Soul keeps manifesting in your life in different forms until you get it, there is no way around it. You need to meditate and get to the bottom of the issue. Doing some Zohar Breath Meditation can help you tune into the Soul lesson of the situation, and find the way of Grace to achieve this lesson. And there is always a way of Grace! For example, let's say that you are playing a computer game of sorts. In this game, why do you raise the challenge level from one to two… to five, knowing full well that it would make the game more difficult for you to win? To show yourself how great you are! In the same way, ultimately all challenges and discordant themes of your life were implanted by your Soul Self not to inflict suffering on you, but to show you that you that you can rise above them, to give your spirit a chance to shine, and to teach you about how great you are! But there is always a way of Grace through each situation, in which you tune into the root cause and the lesson in it meditationally (instead of through suffering), find a more harmonious way to acknowledge and learn the same lesson, and get into the prosperous-winning half of the game quicker.

All That No Longer Serves:

All that being said, not all "challengers of the game" (the ones your Soul decided to take with you into this lifetime) were meant to be in effect throughout your life. For example, two of the character flaws that I know I must have taken with me into this lifetime are impatience and stubbornness. I have suffered much in my youth from my extreme impatience and stubbornness. However, during my twenties and thirties, I have learnt that stubbornness and impatience translated into the perseverance that gave me the oomph to become a captain in a major airline, despite all odds being against me. Thus, I have reaped much benefit from these two character "flaws." But once I reached the position I had set out for myself to achieve, and was ready to fulfill my truest mission of being a spiritual teacher, the need for being impatient and stubborn no longer existed. But since these are still the challengers of my game here on Earth, I still have to deal with them – tame them and rise above them on an everyday basis. And I have to tell you that it is this need to tame these character flaws that drives me to meditate more, do more healing for myself and others, and to do more Nature Meditations (detailed in *Seven Stages to co-Creating Prosperity From Your Soul*) and Nature Walks (detailed in *A Lifestyle of Prosperity From Your Soul*), all of which make me happier, more peaceful, and more harmonious with the perfect flow of my life. The bottom line for here is: many of the challengers of the game that you have taken with you into this lifetime have already fulfilled their purpose. They've done for you what they were supposed to do, and are therefore no longer necessary for your growth and your human experience. Therefore it is time to let them go!

Pain, for example, is one thing that never serves your highest purpose. Most people hold on to it completely unconsciously in order to feel more alive. Pain can be very awakening as it gets you in touch with very primal raw emotions that most of us have come to *mistakenly* associate with feeling alive. But pain's awakening only gets you in touch with one aspect of you: the most primal-instinctual here-now self—the Nefesh. And as previously stated, the Nefesh can get you too immersed in this "physical" reality to the point that you forget whom you Truly are, and start dwelling in the lower-vibrational darkest shade of reality, carrying the shackles of negative limiting conditionings of your past. It is in times that we allow fear and its close cousin stress to take control our lives that the subconscious becomes programed with limiting conditions that can magnetizes more stress, pain, and negativity into our lives. **But there is an alternative!** And it is time to let all those limiting conditions fall away and dissolve.

The proper way to ground and feel alive, on both the ethereal and earthly levels, is to find the balance and harmony between the Higher Self and the earthly here-now self, through proper grounding and connecting to all the elements of Nature in their full radiance. Some tools that can help you do that are: RezoDance (if it is offered in your area), Nature Meditation (*Seven Stages to co-Creating Prosperity From Your Soul*), and Nature Walk (*A Lifestyle of Prosperity From Your Soul*). But of course there could be many other balancing practices that you may feel inspired to engage in. The idea is to ground yourself and get your life to feel real to you by connecting to Nature *as the physical manifestation of the Divine and a reflector of the earthly aspect of Her-His Light*. Once you ground yourself by connecting with Nature, there will be no more need for your subconscious to accept pain or suffering as an existing condition, and you'll soon see them dissolving from your life. From that vantage point of having shed some of your limiting conditions and energetic blocks, which is the first step to co-Creating prosperity (we will go through it together in *Seven*

Stages to co-Creating Prosperity From Your Soul), you'll see that it becomes easier to reclaim your True Self, which is always free, peaceful, healthy, happy, joyous, and Infinitely abundant!

In the sections to follow, you will learn why pain and suffering are not necessary in order to achieve Soul growth or fulfill your life's mission on Earth. But for now let me just say that the Truest alive feeling comes from your Divine essence flowing freely and abundantly into every part of you in perfect balance. As you will experientially find out in *Seven Stages to co-Creating Prosperity From Your Soul*, bliss can be very powerful too. It is more ethereal, less dense, and may be perceived by some as less tangible or real… But anchored into your physical self by Nature, bliss can be very grounding too, but in a Lighter more hopeful way.

Now let's see what energetic forms "all that no longer serves" can take, so that you can learn to eradicate and dissolve those energies from your life.

Mental Blocks –

Sufferings of past lives or even childhood may lead to negative conditioning in your mind, which can unconsciously block you from achieving your goals and living a better life. These include mental blocks that can exist in your personality because of some negative learning of the past. For example, a person whose mother rejected him/her as a baby due to postpartum depression may develop a negative conditioning of not being worthy of receiving love, which can subconsciously prevent him/her from having a healthy intimate relationship. But don't worry. I'm not a big believer in psychotherapy. You are perfectly capable of removing all of these mental blocks from yourself, with just a little meditation. A meditational cleansing and removal of these limiting conditionings can do wonders towards developing a healthy self-love and a feeling of worthiness, both of which are necessary to co-Create prosperity. *Seven Stages to co-Creating Prosperity From Your Soul* also contains a meditation targeted specifically to dissolve these blocks, called Meditation To Remove Childhood Trauma.

Entanglement Cords –

As you already know, at some level, we are all One. And as will be discussed in Chapter 9, we all have people in our lives that we have a deep love connection with. Meditationally, the love connection between Soulmates, or even kindred spirits, look like extensions of Light that connect them.

However, entanglement cords are different than those Light-Love extensions. Entanglement cords are energetic entanglements that meditationally look like entangled dark roots of a tree. These are unhealthy energetic entanglement, which leave you vulnerable to losing your personal chi through them to the person or situation you are entangled with. They keep all people involved in an unhealthy relationship that holds them back. Dissolving these cords doesn't mean that you cut these people out from your life. It just means that you heal your relationship with them to where both of you are free to be the best versions of yourselves, which in turn leads to maximizing their potentials, and allowing blessings to pour into each of your lives (see Cord Cutting Meditation in *Seven Stages to co-Creating Prosperity From Your Soul*).

For example, when I was in China, I experienced a very difficult time. I was sick, found it difficult to breathe, and felt miserable like reality was closing in on me. I realized very quickly that

I had entanglement cords with both China, and with the people I shared previous incarnations with there. So one day, I sat in my hotel room, and did Cutting Cord Meditation. I sat all day long sending reiki distant healing to any people in China that I may have wronged, or who may have wronged me in a past life, as well as to my past self. After that day of intense healing, I woke up the next morning feeling like a new person – healthy and happy. I was able to then enjoy the rest of my trip to China, which attests to the effectiveness of Cutting Cord Meditation in removing entanglement cords. Also, whenever my relationship with a person feels strained, I do a Cord Cutting Meditation. And it is always amazing how much more harmonious and streamlined the relationship feels the next time I see them.

Cellular memory –

Traumatic events or injuries in past lives can register as a cellular memory. These are past difficult experiences that are energetically embedded in the ethereal memory of our energetic bodies, which guide the development of our physical bodies. But while these cellular memories do create a propensity for injury and suffering in a particular area of your body or personality, torturing you is not their objective. The reason you take with you these challenges is, in most cases, to remind you of lessons that your Soul has previously learnt, so that you wouldn't repeat them. Once the wisdom of the lesson resurfaces into your consciousness in one way or another, it's time to let the energy of the suffering dissolve.

For example, one of my clients was convinced that he had fibromyalgia. Every part of his body was achy and stiff, and he was suffering. Despite that fact, this man was determined to reassert freedom within his body. He used to do long walks despite his body pains. And despite his financial difficulties, he used to diligently save up money to come and see me for treatments. Of course, knowing how hard this man worked to find freedom in his body, I only charged him a nominal fee for diligently massaging him for nearly two hours each time. But I knew that he also loved my energy healing work. So one time, I asked if I could do some healing work that was a little outside the box. And although this client was a very simpleminded guy, he was happy for the chance to find a solution. I then tuned into one of his past lives, in which he was imprisoned and chained with metal chains that were nailed into his body at certain places. I tuned into the fact that in that other incarnation, he was wrongly accused of a theft he did not commit, but have assumed the feeling of guilt that others have projected on him, and spent his life with a wing-clipped spirit. Visualizing all chains removed from his body, I used the combined power of his and my free will to remove the energetic imprints of this cellular memory, and the Divine power of reiki energy to bring healing Light into these spaces. In an effort not to freak him out, I did not tell him the full extent of the details of this cellular memory removal. But I did reveal to him messages I had gotten from the Light-beings regarding the lessons learnt in his previous lifetime, which were still pertinent to this one: I asked him if he felt that he sometimes assumes as his own other people's negative expectation and judgment, if he felt that he sometimes takes on other people's burdens, and if he felt like his personal freedom suffers because of it. He said "yes, absolutely." Then I gently suggested ways to set healthy boundaries and reassert his personal freedom. When he rose from my treatment table, he said that he felt like a new man. He couldn't remember when he had never felt such freedom in his body, and he gave me a hug of gratitude. I talked to him several months later, and he said he was still enjoying the new freedom in his body. This goes to show you that it doesn't necessarily have to take much to remove cellular memory of suffering. All it takes is meditationally tuning into the lesson that this cellular memory aims to awaken in you, acknowledging it, and then asserting your free will to remove the energetic imprint of the suffering, all of which we will learn to do in Meditation To Remove Cellular Memory (detailed in *Seven Stages to co-Creating Prosperity From Your Soul).*

Now, cellular memory can affect more than just muscles. There is extensive evidence to the existence of cellular memories in recipients of organ donations, who then start experiencing cravings and personality traits that they never had before.

As it relates to co-Creation of prosperity, cellular memory can affect behaviors, which can either facilitate or block you from achieving what you are meant to achieve in life. Therefore clearing out negative cellular memories is vitally important in manifesting prosperity in your life.

Lineage ~

There are those who believe that some of the suffering of our ancestors transfer to us energetically (not genetically) additional negative conditions. One spiritual healer that I saw believed that I had received the propensity for suffering from my Jewish heritage. I personally am undecided about this issue. I don't know if I can fathom that people who lived hundreds of years before I was born can inflict on me any suffering that I haven't agreed to. They might, if I allow myself to resonate only with their suffering, and if I allow that programing to vibrationally dictate who I become and what I manifest in my life. But remember that no one can inflict on you anything that you do not choose to accept, at one level or another!

However, despite the fact that I don't really believe in suffering from your ancestors' issues, it never hurts to do Lightening Bolt Meditation (detailed in *Seven Stages to co-Creating Prosperity From Your Soul*), as this meditation sends distant healing through time and space to your ancestors, as well as to your own past self. When I first did this meditation, I felt a profound healing, perhaps because it healed any programing I may have subconsciously carried with me, which resonated with the suffering of my heritage. It took several months to see the positive results of this meditation unfold in my life, which was very profound.

Psychic Attacks?

Bad intent from others in your life can only be received and absorbed by you if you let them. By virtue of your God-given free will (which we will talk about in Chapter 5), no one can inflict on you anything that you don't agree to. We will learn to behaviorally deal with the energy thieves in your life in Chapter 4. In *Seven Stages to co-Creating Prosperity From Your Soul,* I have also devoted a large section and how to energetically defend yourself from psychic attacks.

Empathy ~

While being open and empathic towards others is a good thing, it can also lead to unknowingly energetically taking on the pain and suffering of others, and to giving them our personal life-energy (chi). Letting one's own energy drain and assuming other people's suffering through one's energetic connections with them is common, especially amongst healers. But since empathy and compassion are good traits, it is possible to be empathic and compassionate without allowing it to drain our personal energies, and without energetically assuming other people's pain. To do so, the empathy must come from a place of peaceful strength that is anchored in your Soul Light. Metaphorically, if you are to pull someone out of a pit, than you must be strong yourself, so that you can pull the other person up, and not of allow him/her to drag you down. We will talk more about how to find the balance of being empathic without allowing it to drain yourself in Chapter 4.

In *Seven Stages to co-Creating Prosperity From Your Soul*, we will talk at length about how to eradicate, uproot and dissolve all of these negativities from your life with meditational processes that will leave you feeling light, empowered, peaceful, and joyous. But for now, just know that you, and *only you have the power* to uproot any negativity, let go of all suffering, and prevent any future occurrence of it.

Sweet Sweet Lemonade

The big question becomes: How do you know which suffering was laid out by your Soul, and which suffering is self-imposed by limiting conditions that no longer serve your highest good? Of course this becomes a mute point when you realize that suffering in general was never meant to be a part of your human experience. Even at the level of your here-now reality, you'd be in awe of how many conditions that you thought were "permanent" in your life are just miraculously lifted once you have mastered their lessons. But even if a condition is permanent in your life, like a paralysis for example, the meditational practices given in *Seven Stages to co-Creating Prosperity From Your Soul* will help you deal with it more gracefully and find the hidden blessings in your condition. Flowing harmoniously with and being guided by the wisdom of your Soul allows your spirit to shine, and magnetizes more blessings into your life.

For example, Itzhak Perlman is a world-renowned violinist. When he plays, his radiant Soul shines through the music in such a palpable way, that I have to close my eyes and fully let myself bathe in the music every time I listen to him play. His playing is so touched by Divine beauty that it often brings tears of joy to my eyes. Mr. Perlman describes[3] his childhood experience with polio, and how he couldn't play outside like all the other kids. So instead, he applied himself to his violin studies. Whenever I comment on his incredible talent, he always replies that talent is really ninety percent hard work and ten percent talent. Today I realize that his answer was probably partially motivated by his modesty, and partially motivated by my father pushing him to say something that would make me practice playing the piano more. At any rate, if I was to take Mr. Perlman at his word—that it was the long practice hours that made him who he is today—than paralysis turned out to be the blessing that helped solidify his decision to become a violin soloist, a blessing that still benefits and enriches all of humanity today. Although I personally believe that Mr. Perlman's radiant Soul would have shined for us regardless of his circumstances, it is possible that had it not been for his childhood polio, his here-now self would not have chosen this higher path of being a channel that delivers such Divine beauty for us through music. As it relates to co-Creating prosperity, it is true that Mr. Perlman's motivation for playing the violin was inspirational, and that he enjoys the playing, performing and uplifting people. But his sweet "lemonade" doesn't end with just being able to benefit others. As a byproduct of living his bliss, Mr. Perlman has also manifested real prosperity for himself and his family: he earns about $50,000 for each concert that he plays, and is bucked three years in advance (you do the math). He also has a great sense of humor, indicating to me that he is generally a happy person. Of course, regardless of what he says about practice and hard work, a huge part of Mr. Perlman's success is due to his incredible talent and bright Soul. But if you think about the role that his paralysis played in his life, it has pushed him to accentuate his talent, and in that, facilitated his manifestation of True and all-inclusive prosperity in his life.

Another example is Ludwig Van Beethoven, who started becoming deaf while writing his third symphony. Beethoven went on to write nine symphonies and many other musical compositions, all of which are deep with the majestic beauty of God Her-Himself. I often wonder if Beethoven's music would have had the depth that it does without the discord in his life. But if you think of Beethoven in terms of prosperity, while Beethoven might not have been a very happy camper (to put it lightly), he was not poor. Ludwig Van Beethoven and his music were very beloved and popular even during his lifetime. And he had many rich baronesses who sponsored him very abundantly. One thing I am absolutely sure of: Beethoven's "limiting condition"—his deafness— was only allowing him to hear God's music more clearly.

Now, in each of these two examples, it is obvious that there was a limiting condition that was physical and permanent in the person's life, which the person has transformed into a profound blessing. But keep in mind that most of the limitations that you'll face in the course of your life are not permanent. That is, they are only there so you can rise above them as you achieve Soul growth. And in most cases, they are there as hidden blessings. For example, Albert Einstein was a rebellious teen who could not accept what his science teachers were teaching as true. And it was, no doubt, this very freethinking inability that caused his high school teacher to tell him that he would never amount to anything, and made him drop out of high school (his father later paid for him to have private schooling to continue his education). So you might say that thinking "outside the box" was Albert Einstein's limiting condition. That was the "lemon" that his Soul gave him, which was undoubtedly difficult to deal with as a kid. But it was exactly his inability to accept the science of his time as true that led him to later develop his theory of Relativity. So given his incredible contribution to science and the success he enjoyed in his life including a Nobel prize winning, you understand how ridiculous it would be to think of Einstein's freethinking ability as a limiting condition, right?

In the same way, I know that you (each of us) have a gift hidden inside you. It could even be something that you currently regard as a detriment, which is actually meant to help you thrive. One of the points to this program is to help you find this hidden treasure inside you, and learn how this gift can pave your way to your greatest success ever.

This brings us to our next discussion: what is it that sets one free from the shackles of all of these Soul lessons, and enables one to have an easy, happy, abundant and *liberated* life? And what exactly does this liberation mean?

Liberation While Alive – The Ticket To Prosperity

Although Judaism, Christianity, and Islam differ in their concept of reincarnation, and although they may not call it liberation, they all agree on the idea of liberation as a state of being reunited with the Creator for an eternity of bliss. Buddhism, according to the Dalai Lama, does not believe in God, but believes in an eternal cycle of reincarnations in which liberation manifests as a favorable lifetime, free of all the shackles of karmic lessons. Yogic philosophy (Sikh and Hindu) understands liberation as the ticket out of suffering through endless cycles of death and rebirth, and a reunification with God in blissful Oneness.

One interesting possibility that Sikh philosophy talks about, which relates to co-Creating True prosperity, is the concept of "Jivan Mukht"—*being liberated while alive!* According to this concept of Jivan Mukht, when one lives a life of Dharma (which we will talk about here in a bit) guided by the Light and wisdom of one's Soul, one earns the right to live a totally carefree life that blessed with – health, bliss, abundance, and liberation from all bondage. And that's a huge thing! Think about it: even if you've always felt unlucky, or felt that your life is all messed up, there is more than a good chance that your life would turn around and become easy flowing and extremely lucky! Because as we have been discussing throughout the last two chapters, you were always designed to live a liberated life—a life that is carefree and abundant in every way. And as the vibration of all of life on this planet continues to accelerate, you no longer have to wait until your reunification with the Divine in order to live this carefree blissful and liberated life. You can reclaim it now! This is the way of Prosperity From Your Soul—it is what you will learn to do in this book. But how does one achieve liberation, and what is this dharmic lifepath that you'd have to follow? Don't get too concerned. It's not such a tall order at all.

In yogic terms, liberation occurs through non-reaction, and through living a life of Dharma, which I know can sound daunting. But non-reaction doesn't mean that you suddenly become spineless, or allow others to walk all over you. It simply means that you stay heart-centered but firm on your highest Truth, which we will discuss how to do in chapter 4. Living a life of Dharma doesn't necessarily mean that you join some kind of a cult, or impose strict religious limitations on yourself. It simply means that you follow a life of devotion *to the path you deeply believe in and feel is right*. And the only path I recommend adhering to is the one that makes your heart sings with the celestial music that only your Soul Light can bring. So all the meditations and practices that I will give you in *Seven Stages to co-Creating Prosperity From Your Soul* and in *A Lifestyle of Prosperity From Your Soul* are really just meant to guide you to reclaim the uniquely auspicious path that was meant *for you*—the one that not only brings you prosperity, but also makes your heart rejoice.

Non-Reaction:

Since the concept of non-reaction affects how you co-Create your life, let us expand just a little bit on it. As we've seen, liberation from the karmic cycle of death and rebirth, happens naturally when Soul lessons are learnt and appreciated.

Psychologists and spiritual gurus alike agree that it is never a good idea to make decisions based on stress, anger, or fear. Even business people agree that your actions should be measured and well thought through, and not instant knee-jerk reactions. From the perspective of ancient Eastern traditions (Sikh, Hindu, Buddhist, and even Taoist), the word "re-act" implies a knee-jerk reaction, in which one is neither heart-centered nor connected to their Higher Self. Reacting to someone's rudeness, hatred, or stressed out actions keep you both in a karmic cycle of "who's going to have the last word" quarrel. So knee-jerk reactions keep us in an eternal bad cycle of reaction:

Knee-jerk unkind reaction → bad karma registered in one's universal bank account of karmic lessons that still need to be learnt (the Akashic Records) → more life-lessons and incarnations to satisfy the karma, only this time with more entanglement cords, negative cellular memories, and other negative energetic "baggage" → more chances of re-acting in a non-loving way (it's harder to be heart-centered when weighed down with all that baggage) → more bad karma… This cycle can go on forever, until you find a away to connect and stay connected to your Soul, and to live your life in a state of heart centered, loving, joyous non-reaction. This will not only break the bad cycle. It will allow you to start a new cycle of harmonious happy life, perhaps even a life of liberation while alive.

But the main point I wanted to reiterate is: non-reaction *does not* imply yielding to someone else's wishes, or even agreeing with them. For example, if someone yells at you because you double parked and blocked him from getting out of parking, you yell back, and he yells even louder… and there is no telling where this quarrel would end. In contrast, imagine the same situation where you've double-parked and blocked someone who is stressed to get somewhere on time. You come back and offer a heartfelt apology to the other driver, and offer him/her an extra cup of herbal tea and some cookies you happen to be carrying. In the second example, you didn't agree with any of the things the other driver said. You didn't agree that you are an asshole or an inconsiderate bitch; you didn't agree that you have no regard for other people's time; you didn't even attempt to justify or explain that you just stopped by for a minute, and that you didn't know it was going to inconvenience anyone. You just stayed heart-centered and replied with kindness, which in nine times out of ten instantly disarms the other person and turns their day around too. In my case, and this was actually a personal example, the other driver did not accept my offer for herbal tea or cookies. But he instantly stopped cursing, and simply grunted one last softer grunt, which told me that I've made him think about his level of stress, and that he was a lot calmer. In a small subtle way, I believe that my kind response shifted his day for the better too. So in this incident, instead of getting sucked into a stressful situation and turning it into an ever intensifying down spiral, I instantly put an end to the situation and uplifted both of us. Now I'm not claiming that I can always behave in such a heart-centered manner. But if I could, than that is exactly the non-reaction that leads to being liberated while alive!

Liberation Through Grace:

The best way to become liberated is through Grace. That is, through the manifestation of mercy and favor by God. Because when your memory of being blissfully united with your Creator is so vivid that you long for Her-Him from the depth of your heart and with everything that you are, than you have proven that you have risen above all the trials and tribulations of your Soul lessons with joy… you have proven that despite all the sorrows, you still love God and all of Her-His Creation deeply. And that makes you worthy of standing in Her-His Light and enjoying Her-His Infinite abundance during this life, and forever.

Your Ideal Lifeplan – Your Soul's Blueprint

OK, so here is where all of these concepts tie into your ability to co-Create prosperity in your life, and in fact, co-Create your entire life. This is where we zero in on the question on who actually decides your fate. The short answer is: You! You decide your fate, but not in a random way. As you'll understand more fully in Chapter 5, your crafting of your own fate happens both at the level of your here-now self, and at the level of your Soul. First, let's see how you decide your fate before you come into a human lifetime.

Before taking on a human incarnation, your Soul "sits" with God and your Angels and decides on the experiences that would best serve Its growth in the coming lifetime. This is the expression of your God-given free will at its highest level—the level of your Soul. It is a mutual loving understanding between your Soul and God as a unity that has given you the gift of this human lifetime, and has arranged this perfect "play" of your human existence. And in this play, each human experience has been lovingly chosen to serve the growth of your Soul. This is what I call "your Ideal Lifeplan:" the plan that your Soul has made, composed of all the themes, events and people you would cross paths with, which would best serve your Soul's growth in this particular stage of your personal evolution.

Some people call this lifeplan "destiny" or "highest Destiny." But there are several problems with the term "destiny." I personally don't like the word "destiny," because it implies something that is externally and arbitrarily decided for you, and has a connotation of something that is unchangeable. And noting could be further than the Truth. The Truth is that nobody other than yourSelf had dictated your lifeplan for you. Your Ideal Lifeplan is the ideal blueprint for this lifetime that *your* Soul *has chosen* for you, which still leaves room for decision-making at the level of your here-now self. So the resultant path that you walk is your actual life-path. When we walk a life-path that brings into manifestation the Ideal plan that your Soul has charted for you, this path is the path I call your Ideal Lifepath.

And here is the big difference between the terms: You see, the word destiny has the same root as the word destination. And the True destination of all people is the same – to rejoin the eternal bliss of Love-Light's embrace as an expanded Soul, leaving behind all residual energy of any suffering, and bringing with us the positive learning and growth that we have achieved in this lifetime – to bring with you into Oneness all that you have become. So whether you know it or not, your ultimate Destiny (Destination) and the Destiny of all of us is to live in eternal bliss in Divine embrace! It's just that we each have different paths of getting there, and different aspects of Soul growth that we had each set up to achieve enroute to that destination. Therefore the word "destiny" is not appropriate to describe the actual Lifepath that you live enroute to that destination. A better term is your Ideal Lifepath.

As we shall see in Chapters 5 and 6, you have many possible lifepaths – many possible routes to the destination, all floating out there in countless parallel existences, each waiting for you to choose to bring them into manifestation, depending upon the choices that you make in life. But only one of those possible lifepaths is your Ideal Lifepath – the shortest (not necessarily in terms of a short life, but rather in terms of the minimum number of trials, tribulations and reincarnations that it takes to achieve the particular growth desired), most effective, and most auspicious way to get to the destination of liberation and eternal bliss.

Your life mission, then, is the specific task that you are meant to do for your Soul to achieve the growth that It has set out to achieve by means of this human lifetime.

In terms of co-Creation of prosperity, there are three things to remember: First, your Ideal Lifeplan was designed and chosen *by you*, and not by anyone else. It was carefully chosen and crafted by the highest aspect of your Self – as an extension of God. Secondly, as the word "plan" suggests, it is indeed just a plan—a blueprint that still needs to be cemented and beefed up with actual human experiences, driven by the free choices that you make at the level of your here-now self (hopefully in tune with your Soul wisdom) at every step of the way.

The third thing to keep in mind is that the purpose of life is not necessarily to achieve financial success, a position of power at work, become a hotshot, or even accumulate possessions, which you of course do not take with you when you go HOME. It is true that you may leave behind things that you created, which enrich mankind; and it is certainly true that if you follow your highest Lifepath, you will indeed co-Create financial prosperity while you are here having a human life. But all the prosperity and material comfort are byproducts of living your Ideal Lifepath. They are precipitated upon you as means for achieving the life-purpose. They are not the purpose itself. The purpose itself is to become all that you are destined to become, which as we'll see in the next chapter, is best served by experiencing love and joy. We will also talk in Chapter 7 about how to know whether or not a particular decision or vision is indeed in accordance with your Ideal Lifeplan. But the thing to remember right now is the right order of things: You don't strive for financial success like a horse with blinders on in order to achieve your life purpose. You'll never achieve true long-lasting success when money is the only thing in front of your eyes. No. The correct order of things is: First you need to align your life with your Ideal Lifeplan and concentrate on grounding the radiant Light of your Soul into this existence; then financial prosperity will inevitably befall you. And I promise you that once you align your life with your Ideal Lifeplan, financial prosperity and happiness *absolutely will* chase you.

Now let's talk about discordant themes or any suffering you may have experienced in your life. So when you think about situations that your Soul has laid out for your growth, first keep in mind that the choices are not arbitrarily precipitated on you from an almighty that is external to you. You were fully present in the process. In fact, each and every discordant experience in your life was delightfully planned by your very own Soul. In *Seven Stages to co-Creating Prosperity From*

Your Soul, you will learn how to tune into your Ideal Lifeplan, and how to co-Create its most prosperous implementation and integration into your current life.

But the most important thing to remember about your Ideal Lifeplan is that while it may present some challenges along the way—just to make the game interesting, we are not in any way talking about a path that has you sitting on a mountaintop in a brown robe contemplating chastity and poverty. Not by a long shot! Ideal really means ideal! This Ideal Lifeplan is the one that brings all of the earnest-most dreams and desires you've ever had into the most auspicious manifestation! It brings into play your Truest talents and gifts. And it usually also benefit those around you in a way that is harmonious for everyone involved. When you walk the path of this Ideal Lifeplan, you feel deeply satisfied and happy to the very core of your being. **Your Ideal Lifepath is also the path that allows you to co-Create all the Divine blessings of health, happiness, freedom, love, joy, and prosperity in the most natural and easily flowing way – without effort, while laughing all the way to the bank!**

☯   ☯

☯

With all the points that could be counted for the Soul growth that could be earned by difficult experiences, I would like to end this chapter with positive food for thought: Some people believe that in order to retain the conscience and morality of lessons leant, one must hold on to the pain of discordant experiences, and that marveling in their scars gives one good moral character. And I'm here to tell you that this is not true.

As we have discussed, *the Soul growth afforded by each difficult experience becomes part of your Soul essence, while the suffering does not.* As you graduate each karmic lesson, it is this separation of your True essence from the heavy energies of the experience that helps you move on to greener pastures and become a more successful co-Creator of your life. You'll find the meditations detailed in *Seven Stages to co-Creating Prosperity From Your Soul* very helpful in producing this separation.

But one thing to remember is that your True moral character is part of your Soul essence. Therefore it is not driven by any earthly experience, good or bad, that you might have had. Who you Truly are has nothing to do with what you have done or achieved in this physical realm. Who you are is the eternally radiant spark of your Creator, complete with a built-in moral compass that has, and always will, point to Divine Truth and Justice. And it is dwelling in your Divine Truth that will *always* lead you to co-Create the most auspicious Lifepath, complete with health, happiness, joy, and the abundance that serves your highest purpose.

In this chapter, we have walked the path of removing some of the conceptual barriers that have thus far stood in your way of becoming a more conscious co-Creator of your life. Indeed, shedding layers of density and removing blocks of negativity is the first step to being able to consciously co-Create prosperity. But now that we have moved beyond the perceived limitations of the challengers in your life, at least conceptually (we will do so meditationally in *Seven Stages to co-Creating Prosperity From Your Soul,* and physically in *A Lifestyle of Prosperity From Your Soul*), we are ready to erect the four pillars on which True and Infinite prosperity stands—the subject of the next chapter.

Chapter 3

The Four Pillars of Prosperity: Self-Validation, Gratitude, Kindness & Love

Before you build your tower of prosperity, and before you erect walls, and a top it with a beautiful roof, you must make sure that it is built on the only four pillars that can ever serve as a solid foundation to support a long lasting flow of prosperity: a healthy self-worth, gratitude, kindness, and love-joy. In this chapter, we will see that these concepts are not just loftier-than-thou ideas. We will see how they come into play in vibrationally connecting you with the True Source from which all prosperity comes.

But first, before we delve into the real issues of tuning into the high vibration of self-validation, gratitude, kindness and love, let's conceptually set you free from the deepest root of harsh self-judgment that humanity has ever known.

Non-Religion

The original purpose of religion throughout history was to help individuals as well as for peoples find a path to living a healthy, happy, and harmonious life. Unfortunately, as each religion got further and further away from its founder, it calcified more and more, until it has become difficult to see the core Truth that underlies it. And the Truth is that of Love, of a true brotherhood of mankind, of peace, of a Divine spark at the core of each being, and of the uniqueness of each of us allowing us to complete each other like pieces of a beautiful mosaic, making us whole *together*.

About five thousand years ago, a prince named Siddhartha was born in India. He was so beloved by his parents that for many years they had sheltered him from the world outside the palace, in an effort to prevent him from seeing the world's miseries and atrocities. One day, the young prince slipped out of his palace and saw poor people, sickness, hunger, old age, and many of the miseries of life for the first time. This shook Siddhartha to the core. He packed a bag, left the palace, and pursued a life of solitude, poverty and meditation in the woods. One day while meditating, Siddhartha was blessed with a Divine epiphany. He suddenly awakened to the higher Universal Truth. Thus, he was named "The Awakened one," or Gautama Buddha. He spent the remaining years of his life teaching these higher truths to all who would listen, and lived on donations of food and shelter. But the **Buddha never meant to be worshipped himself as a god**. He simply believed that he was a vehicle to share the truths that he had become privy to. Yet today, Buddhists around the world worship him like a god. I have seen Buddhists do a hundred and eight salutations a day to a wooden (or sometimes even a plastic) statute. Was that what "the awakened one" wanted to teach us? More than that, throughout history, Buddhists have segregated themselves from other religions and even amongst different sects of Buddhism, to the point that China—a predominately Buddhist country, cruelly concurred Tibet—another Buddhist country, all in the name of the "righteousness" of their path. Was that the gift that the "enlightened one" came to teach humanity? Really?!

About thirty-four hundred years ago, Moses accepted the mission of uniting the twelve tribes of Israel into one people, and to lead them out of slavery and into freedom. As he climbed Mount Sinai, his mission was to bring Ten Commandments that would be wise directives, which lay a good foundation for living a healthy and peaceful life, trusting the Divine as the Source providing all of our needs. However, **creating a new religion that would segregate its people from all others was never Moses or God's intent**. Do you really think that creating a people that would be persecuted throughout the ages (and led to the gas chambers) because of their strangeness was the intention of our loving Creator? Really?!!! And do you think that separating meat from dairy dishes was at the top of the agenda of a God that is interested only in generating more love in the world? I think not!

A little over two thousand years ago, a blessed baby was born in Nazareth to a woman named Miriam. His name was Yehoshua (Hebrew for Joshua). He had special healing gifts, and a wisdom that seemed to be divine. This child grew up to channel through him many healing miracles for the people around him. He channeled God's wisdom to all who would listen. But while the name Yehoshua does translate to "savior" or "he who God has saves," Yehoshua was a very common Hebrew name, especially in biblical times. Yehoshua wanted to make people understand that he was the son of God, and his intent was that we all are sons and daughters of God, and that we should regard our Creator as a loving Father. He showed us great many truths. Sure, he wanted to save his people in the same way that any true leader wants to bring salvation to his people. But he himself never claimed that he was the messiah. It was his followers that started this rumor. Yehoshua, whose name was later changed to **Jesus** (through its translation to Latin)**,** may have intended to breathe new life into the understandings of his old religion (Judaism), but he **never intended to create a new religion**. And the main point, which you would agree with me on, is – he never would have dreamed that so many millions of people throughout history would be killed in his "honor." What part of "love thy neighbor" do you think was promoted during the atrocities of the crusades? What part of "do unto others as you would have them do unto you" do you think was honored during the Spanish inquisition? And what part of "Blessed are the peacemakers, for they shall be called the children of God" do you think is served by hating everyone who believes differently than you?

Most of the atrocities of the world were driven, at least in part, by religion, despite their original peaceful intent. And while I understand the human need to belong, and to have a program to follow, organized religion has done us a disservice. It has segregated us and taught us to regard members of other religions as members of an enemy's camp. Further, many religions, in their long path of branching out from Source, have come to revolve around "sin" and punishment. The original intent was to teach people that every action has a consequence, and to be responsible and kind to our fellow human being. I can understand the need for that. But so many of us have been taught in churches to be suspicious, to fear, and subsequently to hate all who doesn't follow our preacher's advice.

And here is where I get to the point that we need to acknowledge before we can manifest prosperity: religious have taught us to hate not only all who are different from us, but also ourselves. Many church sermons revolve around the "hell, fire and fury" theme, preaching that if we are bad boys and gals, we will be punished. And since very few of us live completely righteous lives, this has planted a seed of guilt and self-punishment so deep inside our unconscious, that it's been preventing each of us from living up to our Soul's potential of being happy in your human experience.

Contrary to all of this "hell, fire and fury" preaching, if you think about it deeply enough, the original intent of any religion was supposed to be to teach us love, kindness, and gratitude as tools to connect us with our higher-Selves. But it is said that God never gives you more than you can chew on. Perhaps these ancient traditions included the threat of "fury" because that threat was a necessary motivator at the level of consciousness that humanity had evolved to in those ancient times. But since these ancient times the spiritual vibration of mankind as a whole has evolved much. So scare tactics that were necessary two thousand years ago are not necessary today. We no longer burn people at the stake. We already know that it's wrong to cheat on your spouse, so there is no more need to stone adulteresses to death. Those are all proof that humanity has come a long way in its spiritual understanding. So it is time to put aside some of those old judgments (especially self-judgment) that no longer serve, and take a fresh look at what the objective of life is.

For example, do you really think that giving up your favorite thing for the month of Lent establishes a closer relationship with Jesus? With all due respect to Catholicism, wouldn't he'd rather you built your relationship with him based on love, instead of through religious enforced self-deprivation? In the same way, if you are Muslim, do you really think that fasting for the entire month of Ramadan brings you closer to Allah? Wouldn't Allah rather you keep him in your heart instead of fasting? And in the same way, does the constant preoccupation with harshly judging yourself for every little thing you think you may have done wrong serve your highest purpose? Does it make you happy? What I'm saying is: you need to trust deep within your heart that whichever version of God you believe in would want you to follow the path makes you most joyous and whole. As we shall see, *one of the first pre-requisites for co-Creating prosperity is validating yourself as a beloved child of God (in whichever form God takes for you)*, and establishing a personal relationship of trust and love with your own Soul.

All that being said, if you are a devout member of any particular religion, *and you feel that it truly empowers you as an individual, keeps your heart open to love all of Creation, and keeps you connected to God's Infinite funnel of abundance*, than I salute your path in deep respect. But if your belief system is based on fear and limiting conditions, and leads you to lack and misery, than you and only you have the power to change that belief system into one that it is anchored in Truth — a truth that resonates deeply at the core of your being. Remember - you, and only you, have the power to change your life so that it does honor to radiant child of God that you Truly are.

Feeling Worthy

We live in a society that attempts to judge, qualify and quantify everything in an effort to order our reality into a logic we can understand. Quantum physicist David Bohm, a protégé of Einstein, notes[1] that everything in our reality, including language, has been fragmented from its true nature of Wholeness in order for us to understand the physicality of our existence in a universe that is really composed of what he calls "the implicate order"—an energy field that encompasses All, as one big Whole. It is possible that as Bohm suggests, this fragmentation is the origin of our judgment and qualification of others and ourselves? As it relates to co-Creating prosperity, with all this judging, we have gotten so used to being judged and put down by others, that we all tend to forget our True divine origin, from which Infinite abundance comes.

An important point to remember and imprint deep in your consciousness is: your highest goal in life is just being whom you are—becoming more of all that you can be, enroute to your destination of eternal Divine bliss. Yes, there is a specific mission that would best facilitate your Soul growth; and there is an Ideal Lifepath that would most effectively achieve that mission while immersing you in the most auspicious circumstances *for you*. But remember the original goal of choosing a human life: achieving Soul growth and to co-Create more love in the world, which in turn enlarges Creation and the Divine Her-Himself! Soul growth is not achieved by the amount of money you have in the bank, your credentials, or your materialistic objectives. To achieve Soul growth, you must first live in the Light of your Soul now. Then, and only then, your Soul can grow with your life experiences, your interactions with people, and the amount of love and joy that you dwell in in every second of your life. Financial prosperity is just a byproduct of that. But within this process of growth, your first mission is just being who you Truly are.

Because the simple truth is that you already are a beloved child of God; that She-He accepts and loves you unconditionally for just who you are. All paths lead to God. Now obviously, because we all exercise our God-given free will in different ways, and because our choices vary in their vibrational essence (i.e., low road/high road), some paths take longer than others to reach HOME. But that's OK, because throughout all the trials and Soul lessons of our lives, God's essence of Light, Love, and wisdom is always within each of us. And here is an important tidbit, in case you have ever wondered about the meaning of life: the whole reason of being alive is to expand the amount of Love in the world, through experiencing love and joy in our human life. So while you have a specific mission to fulfill on your earthly Ideal Lifepath, the main purpose for you being here is to be happy and experience love and joy! And of course, being happy includes having the financial prosperity you need to sustain your physical existence comfortably. So stop judging yourself, and start being kind and loving to yourself.

To be fair, harsh self-judgment is not the fault of religion alone. Many of us had parents that conveniently waved at us the notion that if we are bad boys or girls, there would be punishment, and that if we continue our mischief, we would be unworthy of receiving goodies and treats. And in most people, this disciplinary tool have gotten ingrained so deeply within our subconscious, that we have unknowingly allowed it to become a definitive notion that we are not really worthy to receive love, health, prosperity, and joy, unless we work hard to justify our existence, suffer some, and achieve something "real" to show for ourselves. But we forget that we are each worthy even before we work hard, even if we do not "justify our existence," and even if we don't suffer. We are each worthy for just whom we are in this very moment. But in some people, this notion of not being worthy is so deeply ingrained within their subconscious that they get alarmed when great things happen in their lives, and internally say to themselves, "wait a minute, this is too good, something bad is no-doubt going to happen now to burst my bubble." It is exactly those thought patterns that we need to eradicate, because the things that you co-Create into your life are dependent on your thought patterns and resultant feelings and energetic vibration. So if you are to become a conscious co-Creator of prosperity, these non-serving thought patterns cannot continue to be guiding your feelings about life and your energetic vibration.

To start shifting your thought patterns into more successful ones, there are two things that you should remind yourself, which would help you instantly feel worthy of every good thing: First, remember who you are and Whom you represent. Whom you really are is a part of God, experiencing Her-Himself *as you* and the circumstances of your life. And since God is Love, Light, joy, and every abundance there is, it is almost blasphemous of the name of God to say that you are unworthy of receiving love and abundance. Don't deny Her-Him the chance to experience health, abundant, and joy through you.

But the second reason to self-validate and feel worthy is because it magnetizes success and abundance into your life! Because ultimately, your Source for all abundance, health, and happiness comes from the Divine Infinite! We will discuss in Chapters 5 and 6 the exact mechanism by which Divine energy materializes into your life, and how you already are co-Creating your reality. But for now, you can visualize your connection with the Divine as a funnel through which the Infinite pours Her-His Abundance into you and your life. The trick is that you must believe that you are worthy in order to keep your connection with this Infinite funnel of Abundance open, nurturing your kinship with the Infinite in order to keep the relationship alive. Believing and truly feeling that you are worthy will help strengthen your vibrational likeness and resonance with your Infinite Source from Whom all abundance to come.

Now, when I say validate yourself, I'm not talking about rationalizing away low-vibrational behavior, or overindulging in the temptations of the lowest possible aspect of yourself. As we shall see, kindness is a three-faceted thing. So a part of kindness-to-self is to push yourself forward to be all that you can be. On the other hand pushing yourself to be the best version of yourself doesn't mean putting yourself down when you haven't yet achieved a particular goal. It doesn't take the place of a healthy self-love, and of knowing that you are absolutely worthy of receiving every good thing. The healthy balance here is giving yourself an honest but loving self-assessment—a self-assessment that leaves room for growth, knowing that you were always designed to become the highest version of yourself, but on the other hand acknowledges that you are absolutely worthy of living a happy, healthy and abundant life.

On an everyday basis, there are many ways to validate yourself. Many practices of self-love and self-validation will be given throughout Parts 2 and 3 of this book. But in general, wake up every morning and recite to yourself the mantra: "I am beloved. I am worthy of every good thing." As you go to the bathroom to do your morning routine, look at yourself in the mirror and reiterate: "I am a beautiful radiant child of the Divine. I am validated for just who I am at this moment." Of course, I encourage you to make up your own mantra or even your own process to help you feel validated.

Gratitude

Gratitude is a huge concept of manifestation!

You already know that on a here-now level, positive thinking makes you resourceful and efficient in making good decisions. And let's state the obvious: you can't be miserable and be grateful all at the same time, since gratitude is a product of happiness. But on a spiritual-energetic level, gratitude for what-is helps you joyously connect the internal reality of what you want (things that bring you joy and are dear to your heart), with the external reality of your life. And there is a reason you want the things that you want: They remind you of your Divine essence—the part of you that is integral to God's Infinite funnel of abundance. And if your desire is a deep yearning of the heart, then its fulfillment is probably part of your Ideal Lifeplan. In other words, your most passionate desires were implanted there by your Soul. That is why getting the things that you deeply desire causes you so much joy – because they awaken within you the vibration of your Soul, and help you dwell within Its Love, peace, joy, and radiant Light.

In order to co-Create prosperity in your life, you must operate out of a feeling of gratitude, because gratitude, just like self-validation, brings you into vibrational likeness and resonance with the prosperity you seek, which magnetizes it into your life (this concept will be explained in greater detail in Chapter 6). And since most of us are driven to feelings in relation to the present reality of our lives, than in order to get yourself into the high vibration of gratitude, you should find things that are already present in your life to be grateful for. And I know that is not always easy to do. For example, you may wish for a bigger home, but it is the feeling of gratitude for the home you have, along with the vision of the one that you want, the deep knowing that you are empowered to magnetize it into your life, and feeling worthy of receiving it that pave the way to the manifestation of the bigger home that you want. If you wish for better health, start by being grateful for the health that you do have. This connects you with the vibration of Infinite health in the Divine realm. If you wish for a better job, or a better professional position, start by being grateful for the one you have.

Adding gratitude to an otherwise mundane situation not only fosters the knowing that you are absolutely capable of manifesting what you want. It also awakens within you the vibrational essence that resonates with what you want, and allows you to tap into the well where Infinite amounts of it exist in the Divine realm. This in turn magnetizes the object of your desire and brings it forth from the Divine-Source into manifestation in your life. In the same exact way, if you wish for more money to flow into your life, you must first establish a connection of gratitude with the money that you do have, as this gratitude fosters a feeling of wealth in you, which shifts your energetic vibration into likeness and resonance with the Infinite Divine Source for all wealth, thereby magnetizing more money to manifest in your life. How and why this process truly works will be explained in detail Chapters 5 and 6. But for now, know that feeling grateful for what is present currently in your life is key to co-Creating more of it from the Divine-Source.

To be clear, we are not feeling gratitude for the shitty things in our lives. When I say be grateful for the money that you do have, I do not mean that you settle for only the amount that you have now, or that you be grateful for lack of more. I mean, be grateful for the money that you do have, from the perspective of knowing deep inside you that because you are worthy, much more of it is not only coming, but it's already on its way to you. Be grateful for the shitty old studio apartment that you live in, knowing full well that you absolutely are about to move into the big beautiful house that you dream of, as soon as you start walking your highest Lifepath. It is this deep knowing that more is coming, which allows you to be grateful even for what you cannot see because it hasn't yet come into full physical manifestation in your life.

Now I know that it's easy to be grateful when everything is peachy, but not as easy in the face of challenge and difficulty. Finding things to be grateful for at any given moment in your life is an art form that, I admit, can take a lifetime to perfect. For example, it's not easy to feel grateful while lying down in your dark quiet room suffering from a bad migraine. That I know personally.

One thought that might help you tune into gratitude when you are finding it hard to find something to be grateful for, is remembering that God is in on each breath that you take. You can start by deepening your breath (drawing in more life-force), and being grateful for the breath of life. Think of your body as a beautiful suit that a very beloved friend has loaned you for this lifetime, and be grateful for it. Be grateful for its wonderful ability to heal. Remember that one single ray of light can illumine a totally dark room. Remember that even in your darkest hour, your human spirit has the capacity to rise above the difficulty and shine. And as Scarlet O'Hara (Gone With The Wind) used to say, "After all, tomorrow is another day." Once you start being grateful for the most basic things, I'm sure you'll find many more reasons to be grateful, and you'll start noticing that your previously dark perspective is starting to shift into a lighter one. This lighter perspective is the crack in the door that would allow more Light (hope) in, as it opens wider to allow more and more positive manifestations through your Infinite funnel of Abundance.

Now this expression of gratitude, even in the face of difficulty is not an expression of gratitude for the suffering inflicted on you by a situation. Rather, it is a feeling and a vibration of gratitude for the lessons learnt and Soul growth afforded by it. This is important because being grateful, especially for lessons learnt through difficult experiences, automatically helps you rise above the negativity and suffering aspect of those experiences, and keep only the positive essence of the growth it afforded. In the same way that you always become extra proficient in the exercise you initially got wrong in class, discarding the negativity of tough experiences, but being grateful for the lessons learnt through them allows you to move forward to the next phase of your life, strengthened by the lessons of the experience and not weighed down by it. It also, by definition, allows your Soul to put a little √ mark next to that particular karmic lesson, which ensures that the lessons will not have to be repeated in this or any other form, which in and of itself is reason enough to feel grateful. For once you are able to not only go through an experience successfully, but also learn and grow from it, and be grateful for it on top… you have truly mastered the lesson. And that means that you are liberated, at least as far as that particular lesson is concerned! So in a sense, gratitude is one of the keys to liberation. And when you become liberated, your life automatically becomes lighter, freer, more joyous, and Infinitely more abundant.

Remember that the path through life that is in accordance with your highest, most empowered Lifeplan is inevitably one of joy, love, health, and abundance. This brings us back to the discussion of your Higher Self. When you harbor positive thoughts, feelings and actions, and you let those be the driving force for positive manifestations in your life, you bring yourself a step closer to reclaiming your Soul Self, which is inevitably in state of Grace, blissful liberation, and of course - all-inclusive prosperity.

Metaphysically speaking, gratitude reaffirms the special bond between you and the Divine, for your prayers and positive intents are the sweet to God. And it is that bond that keeps Her-His funnel of Infinite abundance pouring into your life. Because when you are blissful and grateful, you inevitably tap into the Divine realm. And when you tap into Divine realm, you inevitably draw from it Infinite blessings of abundance into manifestation in your physical reality.

Kindness

Kindness is also a key concept in the co-Creative process. And kindness begins at home—with yourself!

Psychologically speaking, as we grow up, we get used to our parents putting us down in their efforts to discipline us, which in most cases molds people to be overly self-conscious or overly critical of themselves. This can create a pattern of subconsciously self-sabotaging our conscious efforts for happiness and success. So even from a purely psychological standpoint – letting go of this self-sabotaging mechanism, and creating new pleasant experiences of kindness to yourself will help build a healthy self-confidence and self-love, which are crucial to being healthy and happy.

Practicing kindness-to-self is beneficial also on a physiological level. In a fascinating movie called "What The Bleep, Down The Rabbit Hole[2]," a Nobel Prize winning scientist explains that our feelings are created by chemicals called peptides, the absorption of which depends on peptide receptors located on the membrane of each cell in the body. Each type of peptide generates a certain feeling, the experiencing of which depends on the existence of the particular peptide receptors it needs to bind with. Thus, she explain, having predominately a specific kind of peptide receptors makes the body crave, and therefore perpetuate the manufacturing of, the particular peptide that binds with it. In other words, the predominate feelings we are used to having depends on what kind of peptide receptors are predominately built into our cells. So if that's true, then we are all addicted to these predominant feelings by means of our own peptide receptors. And because of our physiological affinity to keep manufacturing the same feelings (peptides) that we are used to having, we crave them just like we crave a hamburger, french-fries, and chocolate milkshake. The interesting thing explained in the movie is that if you consciously make yourself feel a different way for a period of time, you can actively re-wires nerve circuitry in your brain, and correspondingly, within a few weeks, get your body cells to produce more peptide-receptors for the new feelings, thus making the new feelings the predominate ones. The implications of this scientific finding are very liberating: It means that if you are used to feeling unworthy or depressed, you can make it a point to start bulldozing yourself into feeling worthy, grateful and happy, which over the next few weeks will cause your body to restructure itself (manufacture more peptide receptors) to make worthiness, gratitude and happiness your new predominate feelings. And this, of course, has a tremendous effect on shifting your energetic vibration into one that magnetizes all-inclusive prosperity.

From a metaphysical standpoint, kindness to yourself and to others is an important part of the process of co-Creating your most auspicious Lifeplan. Tuning into, and truly feeling and being in a vibration of kindness, automatically connects the kindness and love that are already within you to Divine kindness and Love at large, which vibrationally connects you to the Divine realm from which all prosperity comes. This magnetizes the Infinite's funnel of Abundance to manifest in your life. We will discuss the exact mechanism of how and why works in Chapters 5 and 6.

The Balance of Kindness:

However, kindness is a three-faceted thing, the balance amongst need to be found in every moment anew.

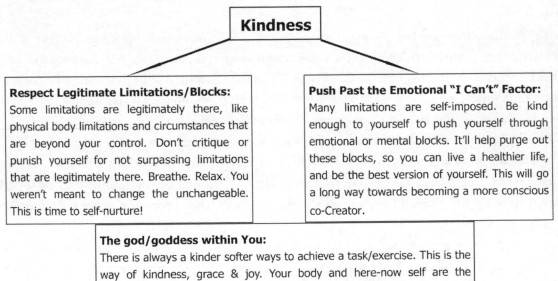

Kindness

Respect Legitimate Limitations/Blocks:
Some limitations are legitimately there, like physical body limitations and circumstances that are beyond your control. Don't critique or punish yourself for not surpassing limitations that are legitimately there. Breathe. Relax. You weren't meant to change the unchangeable. This is time to self-nurture!

Push Past the Emotional "I Can't" Factor:
Many limitations are self-imposed. Be kind enough to yourself to push yourself through emotional or mental blocks. It'll help purge out these blocks, so you can live a healthier life, and be the best version of yourself. This will go a long way towards becoming a more conscious co-Creator.

The god/goddess within You:
There is always a kinder softer ways to achieve a task/exercise. This is the way of kindness, grace & joy. Your body and here-now self are the vehicles for your Soul to experience itself in this lifetime. Nurture them during a challenge. There might be some purging happening as energy blockages are lifted. Take precautions to ensure that this process is harmonious and joyous! In the same way, there is always the way of Grace through (or around) most Soul lessons——the way of Prosperity Form Your Soul.

Let's elaborate on this little diagram a little bit. There is a very delicate balance to kindness: Some blocks are legitimately there, like if you have to lift a three hundred pound block in order to go a certain path, than maybe this is not the path you were meant to walk. Or does this block only look like it weighs three hundred pounds, but really weighs 10 oz. because it is hollow? Can this block be circumnavigated to the same destination? Could this block be telling you to take a deep breath and relax for a minute before you figure out how to surmount it? Or is it perhaps instructing you to go a different route and set an entirely different objective? Those are questions that only you can answer, by tuning into your Soul Self (which we will learn to do in the second book—*Seven Stages to co-Creating Prosperity From Your Soul*).

So for example, when it comes to your physical body, it is important to honor it and be kind to the Nefesh, because despite the fact that they represent only the lower aspect of your being, your physical body and the Nefesh still carry the important task of protecting you and facilitating your survival in this reality. So in the case of physical exercise for example, sometimes kindness means allowing yourself to rest because your body is legitimately deprived of sleep, proper nutrition, or downtime. Other times being kind to yourself actually means pushing yourself through the exercise, so you can feel lighter and more energetic afterwards. Where is the thin line? That's the beauty of it is: the only one that can really answer that is you, because when you are being totally honest with yourSelf, going deep within gives you the ability to communicate and tap into the wisdom of your Soul—let's call it your inner kindness meter.

And just as there is a kindness balance in terms of your physical body, that balance also extends to all areas of life. There is always a perfect balance between cutting yourself some slack and pushing yourself to realize your highest potential. That balance also extends to which aspect of yourself should be dominant in experiencing reality: Not too lofty or aloof to the point of losing contact with reality, but not to roll in the mud of despair (we will talk about how to achieve that perfect balance in Chapter 7). Kindness to yourself allows you to live a happy life that is balanced between the guidance of your Soul, and the execution of Its will by your here-now self in a perfect harmonious flow with all that is. Having your consciousness balanced between your Higher Self and your very physical "I Am" allows you to live in this physical existence, while still being guided by your Soul. It allows your Soul the gift of growth, and especially so when you experience joy. Some people say that living a physical incarnation is kind of like a having guilty pleasure, so you may as well enjoy it!

The Serenity Prayer can provide an important understanding of the delicate balance between the two sides of kindness that are on the top of our diagram: "God, please give me the courage to change the things I can change, the serenity to accept the things I cannot change, and the wisdom to know the difference." When should you strive to become serenely accept legitimate blocks that cannot be changed? And when is the time to challenge yourself to surmount the blocks or redirect your lifepath to one that is better aligned with your Ideal one? When your enjoyment of too many cream puffs and lazy TV days is infringing upon your enjoyment of freedom and lightness in your body; or when your addiction to feeling sorry for yourself is interfering with your joy of the very nectar of life. That is: when your enjoyment of a lower-vibrational theme interferes with your enjoyment of a higher-vibrational theme that is more in accordance with your Ideal Lifeplan…

then it is time to be kind enough to yourself to change. The empowering thing here is that only you can decide which theme is more important *for you*, since you are the only one that can be privy the details of your Ideal Lifeplan, and know which themes are most important within it. I will guide you to tune into your Ideal Lifeplan, and how to devise a plan to co-Create it in *Seven Stages to co-Creating Prosperity From Your Soul.*

Now, an honest self-assessment is an integral part of kindness to self. An honest self-assessment doesn't mean putting yourself down in the overly developed self-critique that is typical of type-A personality overachievers. On the other hand, it doesn't always mean tooting your own horn to mask inadequacies where no credit is due. But it does mean *privately* assessing yourself lovingly and from a heart-centered place, giving yourself credit when one is due, and leaving yourself room to evolve and grow in areas in which your Soul wants to grow. This is part of the second wing of kindness. An honest self-assessment can motivate you to move forward, so you can ground more of your Soul Self into this existence, and so that you can, in turn, reap the rewards of living a healthier, happier, open, honest, free, and abundant life.

And of course, let us not forget the third facet of kindness: there is a softer kinder way to achieve any task. This is the way of grace. As an example, it is not always necessary to run on the treadmill at an uphill speed of ten miles-per-hour, as you may achieve even greater results from walking on the beach, smelling the fresh scent of the ocean, enjoying the sights. It may not be the greatest course of action to stay up all night working on a project that's due tomorrow. You may achieve better results if you treat yourself to a nice dinner and a good night sleep, and wake up an hour earlier in the morning to finish it with a fresh mind. Those are just two examples. There are many more. Even in yoga, you don't have to do emphatic spinal flexes to find freedom in your spine. In fact, doing the same exact spinal flexes with the mindset of finding softness and kindness-to-self within will achieve far greater results in terms of the flexibility and health of your spine. And of course the softer-kinder spinal flexes open up your kundalini energy channels in a much more profound way than the emphatic ones. In life, even when you have already decided whether to cut yourself some slack or to push yourself forward in a particular direction, that course of action that you've decided on can be achieved in a kinder-to-self more graceful way, that will allow you to enjoy it more. And if you listen carefully to your own kindness meter, you'll find the way of grace through most challenges in life. There is a thread of kindness, beauty, and softness to this reality that lead to Divine-given prosperity. And when you tune into this kindness facet in every situation, you are again tuning into the Source from which the Infinite pours Her-His abundance into you and your life.

Kindness to Others

We have seen why kindness-to-self is one of the important pillars of co-Creating prosperity. But there are also many reasons to be kind to others that relate to your manifestation of prosperity.

The lowest level of motivations to be kind to others is to release yourself from the karmic repercussions of being unkind. If you think about it deeply enough, most of the miseries of the world—greed-lack wealth imbalances, poverty, prejudice, and war—are all caused by fear. And

I dare say that fear is the opposite of God-likeness. We hate because we are afraid of it and don't understand it; we become greedy or needy because fear blocks the free flow of the Divine energy into us, thus driving us to further fear of lack; we go to war to gain territory, money, power, and influence because we fear that we do not naturally posses enough of them, and that we are going to need the safety and the surplus they afford. All of those happen because we have long forgotten the nature of our True Selves—that of basking in Divine light, power and abundance. Holding onto ill feelings for someone who have wronged you is not only taxing you—the bearer of the grudge, but also keeps you energetically entangled with the person who have wronged you, until neither one of you has any room for growth. Of course, there are times in which you absolutely have to stand up for yourself and what you believe in. As we shall see in Chapter 4, being kind to others absolutely does *not* mean being weak or yielding your position in a disagreement. It means being firm but kind.

But there is a simpler reason to let go of grudges and be kind to others: because harboring bad feelings keep *you* (the bearer of these feelings) in a low vibration that resonates with everything that you *do not* want to magnetize into your life. It's like holding on to toxins in your body. You need to let those negative feelings and thoughts go in the same way that you need to let your throat expectorate access mucus when you have a throat infection; or in the same way that you need to allow your body to eliminate freely during a food poisoning. If you were to allow yourself to harbor these negative feelings as a result of what has been perpetrated on you, you would shift your energetic vibration into likeness and resonance with more of that unkindness, which would magnetize it to keep manifesting in your life. So no matter what was perpetrated on you, by harboring ill feelings, you are in effect cutting yourself off from the Divine funnel of abundance. So the bottom line is: it doesn't really matter how much someone has wronged you. You need to let those negative feelings go *for your own sake*! Realize that any attack or injustice done to you are the karmic problem of your aggressor, not yours. So give them responsibility for their own action. Don't take their negative energy onto yourself. Of course, we are not talking about throwing all those toxic feelings and thoughts at your opponent's face. We are talking about speaking your higher-level Truth firmly but kindly, and then doing whatever meditation or activity necessary (go punch a punching bag in the gym if you need to) to dissolve any remnant thoughts, feelings and energy of the negativity. We will discuss in more detail how to deal with perpetrator in your life in Chapter 4, and I will of course give you some powerful meditational tools in *Seven Stages to co-Creating Prosperity From Your Soul*.

But the point here is to understand that letting go of all grudges, and being kind to your opponent on top of it, dissolves the negative vibrations of the discord, and allows you to reconnect with the natural Light of who you Truly are. Kindness is the middle grounds, the glue, if you will, between loving yourself, and loving all people as your brothers and sisters to the human race. Metaphysically speaking, it is what harmoniously connects the kindest inner cell within your heart (as the seat of your Soul) to the reality of your life, and helps energetically anchor into your reality the Divine abundance that comes through your funnel.

And this kindness does not have to be huge. It could be a simple but profound act of kindness. Many a times, as I have traveled through America's busiest airports, I have stumbled across people who were frowning upon their day. They could be anyone from the girl that works at the bagel shop, to gate agents. My first thought at the time was, "this bitch! Why is she being so mean to me?!" And then I usually took a few deep Zohar Breaths (see *Seven Stages to co-Creating Prosperity From Your Soul*), and reconnected with my Higher Self, which helped me understand that these people didn't really mean to be mean to me or anyone else. They were just stressed, unhappy, tired, worried, or whatever the case may be. I started making it a point to be extra kind to them, even if they were bitchy to me (turning the other cheek). It could be just a kind smile that I was giving a person, or I would ask the person how they were feeling and if they've had a long day, or tip them an extra dollar or two. And you would be amazed at the results. Seeing the good in others, and taking the time to express simple kindness to them, especially if they were frowning or bitchy, reminded them of the good in themselves and helped them see their own beauty. It showed them that someone cares about them, which always yielded a radiant and kind smile in return.

Although my intent in extending kindness was benevolent, I later found that the results always benefited me somehow. Sometimes the benefit was just making my day more pleasant, as I was now surrounded with happier people. Other times people completely turned around and extended kindness to me back. The point is that when you are kind to others, you are in a vibration of Divine Love, from which only good things can come.

This brings us to the next level of why you should be kind to others. On a here-now level, you never know who, of all the people that cross your path, is the one that's meant to open your door to success. There are many examples on how people who are seemingly unimportant in your life can trigger a chain of events that lead to your co-Creating your highest Lifepath. One example is the many bad massage therapists I have encountered that have led to my insightful invention of the Rezossage—a deep but nurturing holistic massage modality. Another example is: some years ago, I was helping a friend through some difficult times in her life. And since I was getting ready to initiate her to be a reiki practitioner, I was telling her and her ten-year-old daughter about reiki, and in the process, I was pontificating about my ideas to co-Create a safe-haven retreat that would help people find their higher-Selves and co-Create better lives for themselves. At the time, I couldn't think of what I wanted to call this retreat. The little girl, still mulling over the meaning of the word reiki (Divinely guided life-force), then started to say something, when her mother shushed her. I couldn't stand this shushing of the girl and said, "Wait, I want to hear what she has to say." And the girl then said, "Why don't you call the place 'Sole of Energy?'" It was the tossing of this little girl's idea in my mind that eventually yielded the name "Soul Path Retreat," which energetically opened up a Niagara Falls worth of creative ideas, leading to the retreat's manifestation and success. In this case it was the little kindness I extended to a ten-year-old girl and to her mother that opened one door to my success.

On a higher level, since our reality is a reflection of our consciousness (a notion that will be expanded on in Chapter 6) and we each co-Create our own realities, it is also true that each person that crosses your path is there because at some level of your consciousness, you have magnetized him/her to cross your path. This means that if, for example, you cross path with a bitchy person, then there must be at least a tiny little bit of that bitchiness in you. Maybe you wish you could be as outspoken as him/her; or maybe there is a part of you that would have liked to serve yourself just a little more. Whatever your connection with the bitchy person, seeing the good in them reminds them of the goodness in themselves, and drives them to magnify that goodness. Acknowledging that these imperfections, however small, are also within you, and being kind to both yourself and the bitchy person will help you smooth out these sharp edges within yourself, and come into further harmony with the flow of life. How many times have you had a day in which everyone just seems to be cross and unkind; and then you took a good look at yourself and you realized that the underlying condition that makes everyone react to you in that way was your own stress? And as I'm sure you've found out, in many cases taking a few deep breaths can remind you to be kind to you, and change your vibration into a radiant one, which then leads to a new, more positive chain of events. On the other hand, I'm sure you have had many days in which you just feel good, go through your day radiating kindness and happiness, and in return it seems like the world is just smiling upon you, your luck is shining, and everyone is kind to you. Being kind to yourself and others fosters the true feeling of self-validation that is required to co-Creation of a prosperous life.

Indeed, living a life of kindness and service to others is a testament that you have moved beyond survival mode, and onto a mode of connecting with your Universal greatness, which is the basis of all good manifestations. And of course, the highest motivation to be kind and respectful of others is because you can't help but be kind to them. It is a state of being that comes out of whom you Truly are, and a recognition of your Oneness with all of mankind. It is this recognition of oneness that connects you to all-there-is harmoniously, and connects you vibrationally to the Infinite funnel of abundance. And you will find that the most auspicious synchronicities in your life always come from asking not what others can do for you, but what you can do for others.

However, there is more to kindness and generosity than meets the eye. It's not all just about being "oh so lofty." There are real energetic workings that are at play, which make the extension of kindness an active force that pulls the prosperity into your life, as we will discuss in the next section.

Generosity Breeds Abundance

Being generous to others goes hand in hand with being kind to others, but goes beyond it energetically. It is a concept that can be backed up by many ancient traditions as well as by modern concepts. As explored in Chapter 2, Buddhism, Sikh, and Hindu traditions all talk about Karma. And from that perspective alone, it is good to be generous with others as a way of remaining on a heart-centered path leading to liberation. There are many Judeo-Christian biblical concepts related to generosity to others: "Do onto others as you would have then do onto you," "Turn the other cheek," and "love thy enemy," to name a few.

From an energy healing perspective, when you become a reiki healer (when you take Level 1 Prosperity From Your Soul Course), you feel a higher level of Oneness with the person for whom you channel the healing energy, and are able to really tune into the highest feeling Oneness.

Even from a here-now perspective, there are several auspicious outcomes to generosity: The immediate feeling of satisfaction you get when you are generous to others actually comes from the fact that at some level of your consciousness (even if you are not yet aware of it), you already feel your Oneness with the receiver of your generosity. This is easier to feel when giving gifts to your kids and seeing them tear open the wrapping with excited smiles. Since you have a higher degree of Oneness with your own kids, it is easier in this case to truly feel the happiness they feel when they excitedly tear open their gifts. But this feeling is more than just satisfaction, or even happiness that stems from your love for them. In that moment, a part of you feels excited as if you were the kid receiving the gifts, because at that moment you are in oneness with your kids (or the receiver of your gifts).

Indeed, feeling the joy of oneness with the receiver of your generosity brings you to connect to him/her through the core of Oneness between you and the Divine Source, which in turn strengthens your oneness with all of Creation. On a higher level, when you are generous to others, you are really being generous to another aspect of your-Self in the larger sense.

Metaphysically speaking, giving to others creates a unity and an energetic Love connection with them, which opens up your heart chakra to activate the highest Divine essence within you, and allows you to palpably feel it. This activation allows the Divine energy to pour out of your heart chakra, which creates a vacuum that activates your crown chakra to actively pull (suck in by the vacuum) more blessings through its connection with the Infinite funnel of Abundance, which in turn manifest as abundance in your life. To understand this, let's think of it for a moment of water flowing through a hose. If you block one end of the hose thinking you need to create a little reservoir, then after a while no additional water could flow in. But if, on the other hand, you open up the hose on both ends, knowing that the faucet would always deliver as much water as you need and want, then infinite water could abundantly flow through the hose. Let us continue the metaphor and say that this particular hose is an elastic one, so that the more water you allow to flow through it, the wider the hose will become, which will, in turn, allow even more water to flow through at a faster rate… until you become able to channel water from that hose to anything you see fit, and eventually, the hose becomes a funnel that delivers fresh living water from a source that is endless, unto you and your life. This analogy may help you understand that although the Divine energy is already scintillating within each of us and through every corner of Creation (just like there is water in the hose/funnel even when its end is blocked), it flows more freely *for* you when it flows *through* you—when you are being generous to others. Thus, through acts of kindness and generosity—through giving the Divine energy of Abundance that flows through you openly, you create a vacuum that sucks in more of that energy to flow both *through* you and *for* you.

Now this does not mean that you give your last dollar to the homeless person every day. It just means opening up your heart to feel generous with yourself and others. On some occasions it might mean buying a cup of coffee or a meal for a homeless person. And in other occasions it may just mean giving a kind smile to a stressed individual who crosses your path in traffic. If you listen to your Higher Self, It will guide you wisely on which avenue your kindness and generosity should take. And as I've explained in the previous section, you'll be amazed at the results, and at the positive ripple effect that one simple act of kindness can have on brightening your day.

Love

As we have discussed, the chief reason for you to be here is to experience love and joy, and through your experience, expand the amount of love in the Universe. You are an amplifier and a resonator of Divine Love. But the Love that I'm talking about is even more than just love. Love is the energy that creates the Universe, and that is not an overstatement! Physics may call it energy-strings, quarks, forces, or the "unified super string field." The Chinese call it Chi, the Japanese, Ki, the Indians (Sanskrit), Prana, and the Bible calls it "RUACH CHAIM"—the breath of life that God blew into Adam and Eve. But all of these energies are one and the same: the Love energy that is the very building block which Creates entire universes.

Although quantum physics may call it "consciousness" or "the observer" instead of God (Science will catch up one day, we can be patient), the physics of love is simply that Love is the Divine Essence that then becomes the super-energy and super-intelligence of the so called "unified string field," out of which all energy, forces (quarks), and particles stem to create ours and other universes and dimensions (we'll definitely talk more about this in Chapter 6). But the long and short of it is: Love is the very essence from which everything is made.

Just to clarify, when it comes to relationships, loving others freely does not advocate, sixties-style free love. It means being kind to yourself and others, and communicating through your True Self (which will be discussed in Chapter 9). It can mean being compassionate towards others. On an even higher level, it can mean seeing others as an extension of yourself, as I do when I perform reiki healings for others. Loving others can take many forms and all forms, even if sometimes it has to mean respecting that they are different from you—that they are on a different path, and holding space for them in your prayers to evolve and be all they can be. In the next chapter, we will discuss relationships with others in greater details, from the perspective of co-Creating a more abundance in your life.

But as it relates to erecting the pillars of prosperity, know that Divine Love shines at the core of each of us. It is what animates us to be alive. And it is also the Source for all prosperity. It is only through remembering the Love essence of whom we Truly are—our Soul essence—that can we reap the rewards of co-Creating abundance in our lives. Remember: since you are an integral part of God, you are already connected to Her-His Infinite Funnel of Abundance, where an Infinite amount of resources exist for the manifestation of all that you wish for. So there is no such thing as overspending your love. Love, and therefore all resources for manifestation, will never run out! It's just a question of: do you choose to block yourself from feeling love and therefore block your connection to Infinite resources? Or do you choose to allow yourself to feel love, thereby activating and strengthening your connection with the Infinite funnel of Abundance and allowing its resources to flow freely and easily into your life?

<u>To give it to you straight up</u>: dwelling and living from a vibration of Love shifts your vibrational essence to powerfully connect you with the Source from which all prosperity comes. And the more tuned in you are to Divine Love, the more readily Its abundant resources will flow into your life and empower you to co-Create everything you want.

☯   ☯

☯

As we have seen in this chapter, a healthy self worth, kindness, generosity, and love connect us vibrationally and energetically to the Infinite Source from which all prosperity comes, as well as connects us to the reality of our lives through bonds of love, so that the Infinite's resources can not only be ethereally magnetized to us, but come into manifestation in our lives. I will explain in greater detail why these pillars are so important in co-Creating prosperity, and exactly how the process works in Chapters 5 and 6. In the second book—*Seven Stages to co-Creating Prosperity From Your Soul*, I will give you many meditational tools to start erecting your own unique prosperity tower.

In the next chapter, we will go deeper into what effect that people around you have on your co-Creation of prosperity, the mechanism by which peace and harmony on both a personal and the global level affect your successful co-Creation of prosperity, and how to practice kindness to self and to others while being true to yourSelf and to your Ideal Lifepath. I mean, let's face it: the course of one's everyday life is not always ideal. Every day, we meet distractions and people who may display aggression or even attempt to block our highest path to success. So in the next chapter, we will deal with the question of how to fend off these attacks and low-vibrational energies, while at the same time staying heart-centered, dwelling in a state of connectedness to one's Soul Self and the Infinite Source of prosperity, walking the Ideal Lifepath.

Chapter 4

The Prosperity In Peace

In the last chapter, we have established that living and dwelling in self-validation, gratitude, kindness, and love strengthens your connection to the Divine Source of Infinite abundance, and therefore help you manifest prosperity in your life. However, in the everyday reality of our lives, no one lives in a vacuum. Therefore one of the keys to staying centered on your Ideal Lifepath is knowing how to practice kindness, but at the same time not allow other people's low vibration to weigh you down. Because in the reality of our lives, it is not always easy to maintain your heart-centered, knowing there are adversities and wars in the world. It's not easy to stay loving and kind when you are surrounded by stressed out, or even self-serving people. And it can be even harder to maintain your belief in the righteousness of your path when faced with the naysayers and antagonistic people in your life. For example, how many times have you waken up in the morning excited about your new path, only to face the antagonist in your life who knows just how to push your buttons and take all the wind out of your sail? And how many times have you started seeing success from your new auspicious Lifepath, only to get a phone call from the person that always weighs you down? When you can find harmony with other people in your life and a perfect flow with your surrounding, while still keeping a deeply peaceful center within you, it becomes easier to tap into the Infinite funnel of Abundance, and bring forth from it all the prosperity that your Ideal Lifeplan has designed for you to have.

So you can see the value in having some tools to help you reach a level of peace that would allow you to neutralize those distraction, and stay heart-centered on your Ideal Lifepath. For peace is an important key that allows you to restore and retain your Original Self. In the first part of this chapter, I will give you some conceptual tools to dealing with antagonizers and naysayers in your life, so that you can reach that level of peace that would allow you to tune into your Higher Self and your Ideal Lifeplan. But peace extends much beyond just your close personal environment. The obvious connection between world peace and prosperity, from a here-now reality perspective, is that peace economy is always much more prosperous for everyone than war economy.

Even from a laws-of-nature's perspective, unity and world peace are not just loftier-than-thou ideas. Have you ever seen a school of fish containing hundreds, maybe thousands of fish all changing their direction at the same instant? And have you ever seen (perhaps on a TV nature show) an entire colony of ants all engaged in performing the same task, say carrying little grains of sand to build a nest? Even at the basic intelligence level of ants, there is a high degree of cooperation that makes every ant know the direction to go in perfect unity with the rest of the colony. The same instantaneous changes in the direction of an entire group can be seen in most animals that man has been able to observe, such as a herd of antelopes or a flock of birds. And they are so instantaneous and perfectly coordinated among all the members of the group, that it suggests a mechanism of coordination that involves something other than reading each other's gills or wing signals as responsible for the unity—a unity that is directly feeding information from a higher energetic unity of consciousness. And cooperation and unity in Nature don't end there. Very few animals in nature live in separation. Ducks live in rafts; lions live and hunt in prides; even wolves, which have earned themselves the expression "a lonely wolf," actually live in packs! In other words, despite the fact that there is a certain amount of competition over natural resources, competition is not the rule but the exception. The most fundamental governing rule of Nature is cooperation and unity.

And mankind, although it thinks of itself as separate, is no different. We as people were never meant to live in segregation from each other or from nature. And just as it is in Nature, competition was never meant to be the rule, but the exception. Cooperation, Oneness and peace were meant to be the principle by which we live, and which would carry mankind to thrive on this planet. Some seers say that we have been engaging in competition, separation and war only because humanity is in its infancy, but is moving into its adolescent more mature stage, in which peace and Oneness will govern our way of life.

This brings us into the more spiritual perspective of why a more global peace is also important to your personal manifestation of prosperity. At first spiritual glance, while the absence of world peace is not *directly* standing in your way to successful manifestation of your Earthly mission, certainly, a more harmonious global consciousness would give everyone more peace of mind, and help everyone's earthly mission be achieved in a more auspicious way. But going just one step deeper into the metaphysics of the matter, to a certain degree, we all co-Create our mutual reality together, by our mutual consciousness and free will. For example, if your will is to become president of the company you work for, but the will of fifty other people is that you do not, then chances are that you will not become the president of that company, unless of course their will is governed by their lowest here-now selves and yours governed by your Infinitely powerful Soul, in which case you would absolutely become president. But if everyone around you starts exercising their free will harmoniously in accordance with the will of their Soul, then they would not block the highest expression of your free will, and at the same time, everyone's best interest would be served—everyone would be co-Creating exactly what they want on all levels, and living their respective Ideal Lifepaths. And this is possible for two reasons: One is that the resources for co-Creating love, health, and prosperity are truly unlimited, since they all come from the same Infinite Source, bound only by our God-given free will. And secondly, consider that the will of the Soul is directly connected to Divine Will. Thus, it always encompasses the highest perspective possible, which is always loving and kind to everyone involved. So a global free-flowing facilitation of each other's Ideal Lifepaths also translates to the personal level of manifestation of prosperity.

Of course peace, at the deepest personal level, really means deeply knowing-feeling that all is (and always will be) provided for you, by virtue of your Divine origin. But when world peace prevails to the point that everyone is rooting for each other to succeed, it becomes easier to deeply embody the feeling that anything is possible for you, and there is no limit to what you can co-Create.

A more metaphysical understanding of this concept is that energetically, every choice that we make, every thought, and every action creates an energetic vibe that resonates throughout Creation—a wave of energy that is either harmonious or discordant. The more lovingly and harmoniously we each exercise our individual free will, the brighter and less inhibited our collective Light is. And because every action and moment in your life is so intricately connected with everyone else's life (more on this in Chapter 5), harmony and world peace would enable the Divine Energy of Creation to flow more abundantly for all of us, and enable the collective manifestation of each of our most auspicious Lifepaths. So in the second part of this chapter, I have included a discussion on achieving a global consciousness of peace, which would bring forth a grander kind of prosperity for all of us.

Love Thy Enemy, But Be True To Thyself

Loving your enemies doesn't mean that you have to roll over and play dead, or let your enemy walk all over you. Certainly, every person has the right *and the obligation* to defend themselves, and stand up for what they truly believe in. On the other hand, this doesn't mean that you should bunker in your lower vibrational limiting behavior patterns either. Your obligation here is to your higher-level Truth—the Truth of your Soul. Your Soul's Truth will give you the wisdom and peaceful strength to be strong and graceful at the same time. It is a strength that comes out of a position of heart-centeredness and compassion rather than fear, for your Soul is always kind to both you and to others. Even according to the three facets of kindness, sometimes the best interest of your opponent is also served by your telling them the truth. If your opponent is unkind to you, than maybe your telling him/her your Truth in a firm but kind way would help remind them to connect to a more tender and kind side of themselves. For example, a dispute with a neighbor may force you to set boundaries and let the neighbor know (firmly but kindly) that he/she is harassing you. This may force the neighbor to take a deeper look at him/herself, to find the root of this unkind behavior within him/herself, which in turn would drive him/her to strive for a more loving relationship within him/herself. So in this case, your standing up for yourself gives the neighbor the "kick in the butt" that eventually caused them to become a happier person.

In other times, the highest Love that is within you may instruct you to soften up and get to a higher vibration within you, so you can deal with this enemy with compassion. An example, let's say that you've had a disagreement with a friend, and within that quarrel, your friend told you that you have been needy lately. After careful consideration and meditation, you may recognize that you have been neglecting your personal meditational practices lately, which have caused you to feel detached from Source. You may also realize that you have unknowingly been trying to get the "missing" energy from your friend in the form of sympathy and requests for help. Recognizing that would give you a chance to correct it and resume the meditational and physical practices (given in *Seven Stages to co-Creating Prosperity From Your Soul* and in *A Lifestyle of Prosperity From Your Soul*) that would restore your health and happiness. So in this example, the argument with the friend helped put a mirror in front of your face and consequently get you back into a more balanced, happier, and abundant state of being.

Of course, not every low-vibrational encounter is worth your time and your energy. Some situations are just better off ignored, like people who are stuck in a lower vibration, but who have no importance in the bigger picture of your life. Simply put, in some of these annoying situations, you are better off just moving on, and not letting them get to you. For example, the person who cuts you off or even flips you in traffic has absolutely no significance in the bigger picture of your life. So you can either allow him/her to ruin your day (which could start a chain of events that veer you off your path), or you can stay heart-centered and feel compassion for that poor stressed out individual (which would only serve to perpetuate your own high vibration), and let the incident go.

Another type of low-vibrational situation that is in your highest interest to ignore is the people in your life who are always naysayers, or the people who always see doom and gloom. Keep in mind that the people in your life who always try to discourage you are just stuck in their own low-vibration and its resulting limiting conditions. They are unhappy. They foresee only limitations for you simply because that is the only reality they see themselves manifesting, because they haven't yet opened up to the bigger reality of their higher-Selves. You, on the other hand, if you are reading this book and following its processes, have already begun opening up to the infinite possibilities afforded by your magnificent True Self. And you know you have your own Ideal Lifepath, waiting for you to reclaim. It is one that nobody else can walk for you or even tune into. The only one that can truly know whether or not your dreams are the true vision of your Soul is you, because *your Ideal Lifeplan is for your eyes only!* So don't listen to anyone who tries to discourage you from your True path, in which you're guaranteed success. But at the same time- have compassion for the limited view of these naysayers. Knowing which situations are better off ignored, and which need dealing with is at art form that can take time and maturity to develop. But on that distinction too, the only one who can guide you on the most auspicious solution for each situation is the inner wisdom of your Higher Self.

Now when it comes to relationships with people who are here to stay in your life, when I say, "dealing with," what exactly do I mean? To answer that, I have listed several types of relationships, in which the give and take of energy is unbalanced or discordant. This is by no means a complete list of all types of human relationships. Rather, it is a narrative of a few types of relationships that is meant to open your awareness to all other types of subtle energy imbalances that might exist between you and others in your life, and some suggestions on and how to correct these imbalances. These imbalances can be a considerable draining force on your personal life-force energy (chi), which in turn can slow down your manifestation of prosperity.

But keep in mind that none of these less-than-harmonious relationship constitutes judgment. Nobody is perfect, because the very fact that we are here having a human life means we still have some learning and growth to do. Identifying people in your life who drain your personal energy could just help you either balance the relationship, or disentangle yourself from this relationship and its limitations more easily. So in this section, I have detailed some specific styles of energy exchanges between people that can be taxing on you. As you read through these subsections, try and identify the people in your life that fit each of these categories, and let the section inspire you into some soul searching on what to do about each unbalanced relationship.

As you start thinking about all the people trying to claim your energy for themselves you may wonder why they are really in your life. But before you get angry, let me stop you and remind you of the importance of forgiveness, compassion, and kindness, not to mention love. Because all evidence (from NDEs, past-life-regressions, and other profound channelings) suggests that souls reincarnate again and again to be in loving relationships with each other, forgetting the horrible things they may have done to each other in previous lifetimes. This indicates that even from within the framework of any one particular lifetime, if you strip away the memory of the wrongdoing, if you forgive, remove cords, and release each other into one's own God-Light (see Cutting Cords Meditation in *Seven Stages to co-Creating Prosperity From Your Soul*), there is *always* love between the Souls. So every relationship can be healed, and has the potential to be harmonious and loving, even if sometimes the most loving thing you can do for each other is to release the other person, and hold space for them to evolve at their own rate.

Many people are so deeply immersed in the physicality of their reality, that they forget who they Truly are, and let the scars of disappointment, injury, and lack to build limiting conditions in their personalities. Now this doesn't mean that the Divine spark of has left them or has turned off. They would not be living and breathing if it did. It just means that their Light has become obscured the dark crust of these limiting condition. And it is this dark crust that is preventing you from seeing the Light inside these people, and obstructing them from seeing the bright world around them, almost like they are seeing the world from within a dark cage. Despite the difficulty in interacting with these people, remember that the spark of God-likeness is what breathes life into both you and your perpetrator, and that every Soul is beautiful and radiant *at its core*. Your enemy, be it someone whose bossing you around at work, someone who cut you off in traffic, a distant family member who drains your energy, a political rival, or even a nation that's at war with yours, is a person (or a nation of people) with a Divine spark inside them.

In most cases, a person who takes away your personal energy (chi) is doing it quite unknowingly, as he/she is so totally immersed within his/her own drama that perhaps they even perceive themselves acting out of self-righteousness. While there may be many shades and categories of people who try to claim your personal chi for themselves, the following examples are few of their categories, and some guidance on how to channel those relationships into a more harmonious ones.

The Miserable Me Chi Beggar:

The miserable me type is a person who always tells you a sob story in an attempt to get your pity and perhaps even physical/financial help. This is a person who is not necessarily faking it, as they mostly try to convince themselves that the drama going on in their life is real and is not self-imposed. These people are usually so immersed within the drama of their circumstances, that they start expecting negative things to happen to them, which of course magnetizes more difficulty and drama into their lives. The more aggressive within this type are the people who are needy and who express their expectation for your physical help (action, money), rather than just the expectation for your listening and compassion.

When encountering this person you must remember that love begins at home, with yourself. Being compassionate to other people is a wonderful gift and a true testament of your humanity. But the energy that you give must be the access energy within you, after the Divine Love-Light-Joy fills you to overflowing, and you are ready to give others your attention, your compassion, your love, and perhaps even physical resources. You cannot allow yourself to give them what you don't have enough of—your personal chi and your personal resources, financial, physical, emotional, mental, spiritual, or otherwise. And sadly, this is what usually ends up happening, especially to those of us who are natural givers. What I'm saying is: don't be guilted into giving your heart and soul to the needy, while depleting your own self, and suffering for it later.

Now let's differentiate a little: Miserable Me Chi Beggars are *not* true charity cases. The people who really are in a tight bind are usually very appreciative of your help. And they usually show their appreciation by picking themselves up the rest of the way, and consequently re-establishing their own connection with the Infinite funnel of abundance. So the people who are truly worthy of your help are the one that are positive, hard working and hopeful, and who after you pick them up are able to walk and even run with life in a way that honors their highest Lifepath. The Miserable Me Chi Beggars, on the other hand, are people who are always needy, and regardless of how many times you've helped them, they seem to be unable to stand on their own two feet, or use your help to change the direction of their lives into a more positive one. It is almost as though it is easier for them to get compassion, pity, and help from you than it is for them to help themselves. And so they keep coming back for more and more help, giving you new sob stories, a cycle that repeats itself.

But consider that when you keep giving without limit, you keep enabling this person's dysfunction, which causes them to stay in a loop of not being able to tap into their own Divine resources. And as long as you keep enabling their dysfunction, you are not helping them find True happiness and abundance. Conversely when you set healthy boundaries, you are effectively forcing your friend to tap into his/her own resources and connect with their own Infinite funnel of Abundance. So the truer way to handle these people is to set healthy boundaries, guide them to the True Source of power in the Creator's abundant energy, and hold the vision in your heart for them to evolve into a happier and more complete individuals.

A good example is an acquaintance of mine, whom I've known for many years and who has always been needy. She has never assumed responsibility for her own life, and always looks for others to care for her. Her pattern was: she would meet a guy, immediately invite herself to move in with him, and immediately give him all the financial and emotional responsibilities burdens. This would eventually (usually after about six months) drive the boyfriend to break up with her and kick her out, at which point she would expect someone to rescue her and provide for her. And for many years that someone was I. After many of her breakups, I would drive up (usually in the middle of the night) to pick her up, let her stay on my sofa, and mother her for a few days while she figures out her next move. This always took everything out of me, and when she would leave I would always feel so drained that I was vegetative for a week. But I kept telling myself that if I only help her one more time, she would rise up and her Light would shine in the way that honors her True Self. It took me years to realize that as long as I was rescuing her, she would never learn to stand on her own. As I started to set boundaries, she realized the need to stand on her own two feet. As the years went by, she started holding onto jobs a bit longer, and started to have short periods of time in which she was supporting herself. At the time of this writing, she is still learning slowly how to be more responsible. Now, it is true that she may have other friends who occasionally save her after each one of her breakups, but I believe that my setting healthy boundaries has driven her to the realization that standing on her own feet is actually in her best interest. So as you see in this example, giving needy people everything they request of you may not even serve *their* best interest.

But as we are all connected, in some way, we are each other's teachers. Wherever you set the boundary, your relationship with the Miserable-Me Chi Beggar inevitably drives you to tap into your own Divine resources of wisdom, compassion, Love, and Abundance. For the true wisdom is to find the perfect balance – knowing when to give, and when to set boundaries and send this person to stand on their own (kind of like letting your baby experiment with taking their first step without your help). Compassion is a noble endeavor. And the compassion to extend kindness to this person can only come from your pure and open heart – anchored in Divine Love. So if your highest guidance tells you to continue to give to this person, your financial and other resource for giving to this individual should only come out of the overflowing abundance flowing through you from the Divine. On the one hand, do not be afraid to say "no" if you feel that continuing to help this person is not serving your or their highest path. And having the heart-centered power to be firm but kind at the same time, as well as the wisdom to know which side of the balance to embrace, can only come from tuning into your Soul Self.

The Indifferent Chi Thief:

Another type of person with a claim to your personal chi is the indifferent-detached person. This is usually a person that you care about, and want to interact with more openly, but who is always too detached and aloof to have any deeper interactions with you. Be kind and patient with this person. He/she doesn't mean to suck all your energy away, and in most cases doesn't even know he/she is doing it. It's just that this person is naturally an introvert, possibly because they have been hurt badly, either earlier in this lifetime or in another incarnation. Being "indifferent" or an introvert is their defense mechanism. Therefore the only way they know to interact with the world is from within the protected calmness of the wall they put around themselves.

Consider this: if the indifference of this person bugs you tremendously, then it may behoove you to do some soul searching of your own: why does their detachment bother you so much? Are you the antagonist/interrogator in their life? Is drama in your life your perpetual claim to other people's energy? This is not a judgment, but a tool to help you recognize your own shortcomings, which may have been blocking you from the Divine Funnel of Abundance and Love—a tool to help you lift those blocks, so you could enjoy all the blessings that are always meant to be yours.

Back to the Indifferent Chi Thief, the only way to open a crack through the wall of the indifferent one, and allow the Light in, is through kindness. And in this case, your kindness should be specially wrapped together with patience and compassion. Sometimes the very act of giving this introvert her/his space, and co-existing with them, is the very kindness that would make him/her comfortable in your presence, and perhaps even make them open up to you. It is this co-existence in peaceful kindness that stops any unbalanced energy transfers from you to them. For example, my brother is one of those indifferent introverts, to the point that I don't remember my brother ever telling me his inner thoughts or feelings. But I don't regard this as my problem. I trust that deep down he does care for me, so I don't need to poke him or provoke him to get attention. I fully give him his space, and I peacefully respect his need for privacy. And it is exactly this letting go that ensures that he is *not* an energy-taker in my life, and I'm not an energy taker in his life. When we get together, we respect each other's boundaries, and we rejoice in each other's company, even if we don't talk about deep thoughts or feelings.

The Interrogator Chi Thief:

Another type of person, who takes your personal energy a little more aggressively, is the interrogator. Interrogators are somewhere between the indifferent and the antagonizer in terms of how proactive they are in stealing your personal chi. The Miserable Me Chi Thief is the most passive: They arrange the situation so that they don't really take your energy, but are eliciting you *give* them your energy. In comparison, most Indifferent chi claimers, are a little more, shall we say, passive-aggressive? The interrogator is the most proactive chi-thief we've yet talked about.

Interrogators usually originate from a place of the fear of revealing themselves and of opening up their hearts, which of course blocks further inflow of Divine energy into them. But they still need approval, love, and attention. So they have a strong drive to communicate and attempt to get energy, attention and approval from others the only way they know how—through interrogation. Most of the time they don't mean to interrogate you, as they don't even know they are doing it. Since most Interrogator Chi Thieves are benevolent, they may even believe in their own minds that they are simply showing interest in you. The way to tell the difference between people who show genuine interest in you and Interrogator Energy Thieves is the way you feel. When you feel like you are on the spot, and are forced to justify yourself in the conversation, that is the first clue that the conversation is unbalanced. The second clue is that you feel (perhaps sometime into the interaction or even after it is done) tired and drained. These clues mean that indeed, your energy is being drained, and the poking, questioning and prodding are tools through which it is being drained.

In some situations the interrogators are more aware and more aggressive, and their interrogation comes out of their need to either validate themselves by invalidating you, or even out of a need to take their pent up frustration out on you. But even in the case of the interrogator who is more aware, questions may take the disguise of real interest in you. But it is the undertone of their non-acceptance of who you are, and their attempts to invalidate you and everything you say that reveals their underlying intensions of robbing you of your personal chi.

As an example of how to act in these situations, I'll tell you about a time in which I was confronted with the master-chief interrogator in my life. On this particular evening, we were having dinner at a restaurant with some friends of the family. During the conversation, I described our friends how I knew beyond the shadow of doubt that God would take away my migraines when I've found my True bliss. My Interrogator immediately jumped up and asked in a very demanding suspicious voice and said: "How do you know? How can you know something like that for sure?" Now that sounds like a reasonable question. But it was her tone that revealed that all she cared about at that moment was to prove me wrong! I took a deep breath, envisioned a huge bubble of Divine white Light around me, and then answered calmly: "I will not answer this question right now. If you were asking this question because you wanted to learn how to meditatively connect with your all knowing Soul Self, I would teach you and take you step by step through the meditations. But since you are only trying to invalidate me right now, I will not answer. If and when you ever do want to get in touch with your Soul Self, just let me know, and I will be there for you." She completely shut up, and for the rest of the evening (and for several months later), she did not continue to interrogate me. I was secretly proud of myself for way I acted in this situation, since that was the very first time that I was able to stay polite, even graceful, but still stand my grounds firmly, in the face of her interrogation. While I can only wish that I were always this heart-centered, I believe that this exemplifies how one should act when being interrogated by a chi-thief. Because what all of us tend to do, especially those amongst us who are pleasers, is we tend to get sucked into justifying ourselves, which takes away from the Truth of our convictions.

Maybe the thing that will help you through this interrogation, beyond taking a deep breath, is remembering Whom you represent. Because when you say or do something out of your most heart centered Self—when your thoughts, words, feelings, and actions are lit by the Light and wisdom of your Soul, you represent God. Now I'm not talking about stubbornly bunkering yourself in old habit patterns and lower vibrational thoughts. I am talking about your core inner Truth that originates from the Truest place inside you. That Truth represents an aspect of the total Divine Truth that God has chosen to express uniquely through you. Therefore those Truths that are anchored deep within your heart should never be compromised, because the Divine in you never needs any defending or justification of any kind. It just IS. Period.

An old yogic saying is that the argument between two siddhis (holy men) is always a silent one, even if their opinions are diametrically opposed. Since they are holy men, each of them has lived her/his life being a clear channel for Divine Truth. And so they each feel their aspect of Divine Truth resonating through every fiber of their being. They thus know that this deeper truth cannot be swayed by anyone. But because of their knowledge of the Oneness of us all, they also each know that the other siddhi has also received an aspect Divine Truth that compliments their own, as part of the Whole. So in this "argument," the two holy-men sit in silence, deeply pleased that someone else has received a different aspect of the total Divine Truth that compliments and completes their own. And they each bow to the other in deep respect. Now, wouldn't it be nice if all of our disagreements could be resolved this way?

The Antagonizer Chi Thief:

Perhaps the most forceful of the energy takers is the antagonizer. A rival at work who antagonizes you is often someone whose life circumstances are extremely unhappy. The Pink Floyd illustrated this point very graphically in the animation of the song *We Don't Need No Education*, in the movie *The Wall*. The animation showed a teacher spanking a student. But then the teacher himself was a puppet controlled and spanked by a large figure of a woman (his wife? mother?). I think this was a brilliant way to drive this point home, because if you think about it, most people who are bitchy, overly demanding, and never satisfied with anything you do for them, are people who have forgotten about the True Source of beauty and power within. They have forgotten their true identity as the child of a loving God. They have turned their back on their connection to the Infinite funnel. And they have forgotten that True validation comes from the Divine spark within. So they are unhappy, and they dump it all on you.

The antagonizer is usually strongly willed, and stubbornly believes in his/her own paradigm of reality. So much so, that he/she finds the need to impose his/her belief on others to validate him/herself. This behavior is a result of fear that if their paradigm, and their perception of what is true and what isn't, shift, the ground beneath their feet will shake and no longer be able to sustain them, metaphorically speaking. This fear, of course, is not a rational one, since we know that changing their belief system, and opening up to happiness would only serve their highest good. The rigidity in which these people hold on to their paradigm of belief puts them in a prison of their own making—one in which the stress levels are enormous. And so they throw darts at you in order to dump some of that stress on you. It is this stress that drains their own personal chi, and it is their rigidity that keeps them closed off to receiving fresh chi from the ever flowing Infinite funnel of life-force. Their war-like barking and interrogation is but a cry for help, and their way of forcefully taking your personal chi.

Although challenging, the best way to treat this antagonizer is actually to stand up to them and speak your truth firmly but kindly. Because when you yield by verbally agreeing with them even though you internally disagree, you give your personal power away, since you are acting contrary to your inner Truth; when you yield by taking action in accordance with their belief contrary to your own inner wisdom, you give them even more of your power away; even when you stand on your back feet and kick… that is – when you take action to spite, you are re-acting to the antagonizer and straying from the higher wisdom of your Soul, thus still yielding your personal power away. So don't devote twenty-one years of your life to pursuing the wrong career (like I did), just to prove your antagonizer wrong and spite him/her.

Most of these antagonizers are so immersed in the drama of their lives that they are not fully aware of what they are doing to you. Others are not so innocent. Some people are hungry for the power that putting you down gives them, and know they are doing it at least on some level. And with those, you just have to set some boundaries (walk away if you can), remain in your heart center, and pray for them from a distance. But don't spend too much of your personal energy, and don't get too invested in trying to please them and uplift them. Realize that until they tap into their own Divine Light and Love, and until they open their hearts to the ultimate Source of joy, nothing you say or do, and in fact nothing earthly can ever please them. Even though it may not be the will of their Soul that they suffer so – even though it is only their here-now self that is imprisoning them within this darkness, it is still an expression of their free will. As ridiculous as this may sound, you can't rob them of their free will to be miserable, for there may be a Soul lesson that this misery is supposed to drive them to.

All you are responsible for is you: how you're going to think, feel, and act in relation to the situation. Are going to re-act? Or are you going to stay in your heart center? So in those moments in which they antagonize you, whatever you do, DO NOT re-act automatically! In order to liberate yourself from the cycle of karma, you must remember to take a few deep breaths and tune into your highest most compassionate Self. Envision yourself surrounded by the brightest bubble of Angelic protective light (more about this in *Seven Stages to co-Creating Prosperity From Your Soul*). This will help you be calm and kind, but stand your ground firmly. From within your protective bubble of Light, you may think compassionately on how unhappy in his/her own lives your attacker is. You can be grateful that you are not in their shoes. You may also take the time to remember that persistent antagonizers in your life might just be your teachers, orchestrated by both of your Higher Selves to drive you to be the best that you can become, and to evolve to the lighter, most loving, happiest version of yourselves. From the perspective of your Ideal Lifeplan, an antagonizing boss, for example, may be there to drive you to learn to stand up for yourself firmly but kindly while physically staying at that job; or he/she may be there to drive you to find a job that is more in line with your highest calling. Which is it? The only one who can know the answer to that is your Soul. And we will learn how to tune into that in *Seven Stages to co-Creating Prosperity From Your Soul*.

All you really *can* do is protect yourself energetically (more on how to do that in *Seven Stages to co-Creating Prosperity From Your Soul*), stay within your heart-centered God-Light, hold space for your opponent to break free of their self-imposed prison of darkness, and radiate the Light for them when they are ready to change.

To be clear: holding space does not mean living in illusion. It means actively seeing this person for who they are in this here-now reality and taking the precautions needed to secure yourself and your position; but at the same time *not expecting them to keep behaving in the lower vibrational manner* in which they have been displaying. Holding space also means envisioning within your prayers this person stepping out of the darkness and into the Light, leaving room for them in your consciousness to become happy, healthy, and all that they are meant to become. In teaching and helping others, holding space can be extended to mean holding protective energetic boundaries for self and others, in order to facilitate your student's feeling of safety and security during their process. But at any rate, to stay centered within the core of your True Self, and properly hold space for another, requires a high vibrational level of neutrality, which is the domain of the Soul.

This process of protecting yourself, removing yourself from the situation, but at the same time holding space for your opponent to evolve at his/her own pace does a few things: Firstly, it removes you from being the target of their attacks. Secondly, it removes the negative energetic entanglement you have with this person and allows you to stay centered on your prosperous Ideal Lifepath. And lastly, it creates a space in Universal consciousness in which this person becomes the best version of him/herself, which allows them to then step into that Light whenever they are ready. And being the Divine radiant child that you are, you can do all that, while maintaining your distance, protection, and neutrality, or whatever the situation calls for.

Fear-Not:

In some situations, the antagonizer is so aggressive that you actually fear them. Remember that fear originates from your Nefesh – your lower primal instinctual self whose aim it is to protect you. Now I know that I have spent considerable part of the previous chapter helping you see that fear keeps you away from prosperity. But sometimes, when the threat is real, fear is there because your Nefesh (animal-spirit) is picking up subtle clues of imminent danger and is trying to alert you and protect you. And in those cases, you need to pay attention, so you can remove yourself from danger. I once allowed myself to get mugged in a dark narrow ally in Beijing, because I ignored the signs. I took a rickshaw tricycle ride from my hotel to the entrance of the Forbidden City. As the ride went on, I noticed that the guy was going against traffic, and taking shortcuts. I also noticed that another guy with an empty rickshaw was riding along us, waving to my driver, winking and smiling secretive smiles. But as I was in a strange country in which I didn't know the customs, I excused this suspicious behavior as, "well, maybe in China people always disregard traffic and do as they please, and maybe the other guy is his brother and it is customary for family members to keep each other company and make each other laugh." My suspicion rose even more when a couple of police officers passed us and honked waiving their hands at my driver. But I still thought I was being too paranoid, and contented staying in that rickshaw and hoping for the best. I knew something was wrong when the guy passed the main entrance to the Forbidden City and took a turn into a deserted narrow ally. At that point I tried to ask him in English to stop, but he either didn't understand English or pretended to not understand. When we got to the deep part of the ally, his "brother" suddenly showed up out of nowhere, and they both motioned for me to give them all the cash I had in my wallet. I tried to argue, but that didn't help. One passerby came and went, but my cries for help only made him avoid us more. At that point, the two rickshaw drivers got physically close to me, and their body language told me that I either give them my cash, or I get hurt. I gave them all of my money and they ran away. So this incident was not the end of the world, but was enough to be considered a threatening situation. But the signs of danger were there. And somewhere in my consciousness I must have known that I was ignoring the signs. My Nefesh was giving me a dreaded feeling, which being the fearless and independent woman that I perceived myself to be, I chose to ignore. The point is: sometimes fear is justified, and is warning you to stay out of trouble. Once you listen to it and remove yourself from danger (or a bad situation), the feeling of fear will be gone, and you will be your happy self again.

Other times, however, fear is based on conditioning that had served to protect you either at some point earlier in this lifetime or in another life. But if the threat of the situation no longer exists, than this conditioning is irrelevant to your present situation, and no longer serves your wellbeing. This is when fear stops being a protector, and starts being a poor co-Creator of circumstances. And I dare say that for most of us, most of our fears fall in this category of fears that have already served their purpose in the past, but do not serve our highest purpose in the present or future. And it is those fears that if you hold on to, have the potential of keeping you in a low vibration of magnetizing everything that you don't want into your life. So in order to co-Create a more prosperous life for yourself, it is imperative that you learn to distinguish which fears protect you, and which no longer serve your highest purpose, so you can let them go.

By now you must be asking, "How do I know whether the fear is foretelling of real imminent danger, or is based on past conditioning that no longer serves?" And the simple answer is: while you are in the presence of the person you fear, you don't! It is hard to tap into the wisdom of your Soul while you are in the heat of thing. So the safest thing for you to do is to remove/excuse yourself from the situation. There is always time to stand your grounds firmly but kindly later. You don't have to put yourself in harm's way. And you certainly don't have to be a Jedi. Even Luke Skywalker removed himself from the situation and went to regroup on a far planet, before confronting Darth Veda. Removing yourself from a situation is not cowardice, since you haven't said your last words on the issue yet. For example, if a rival at work attacks you and you fear for your position, you would not allow yourself to react instantly. In business situations, most people know that the best response is a measured, well thought out plan, and not a knee-jerk reaction. Just remember that when you devise this best thought out plan, your Soul Self should be consulted, because It is in on the biggest picture of all—the one that God sees. Food for thought here is: if you already know it is advisable to sleep on it before you react in business, why would you even consider not employing the same tactics in the other areas of your life? This removal can be just an emotional spiritual detachment, or it may necessitate a physical removal of yourself from the situation. Trust your highest intuition on which one it is.

Once you have removed yourself from the situation, the next step is to meditationally re-center yourself to once again dwell within your own God-Light. In *Seven Stages to co-Creating Prosperity From Your Soul*, we will discuss how to regain your peaceful center, heal yourself with the Light of your Soul, and meditate deeply on what the lesson of this fear is: is it indeed still protecting you from danger, physical or otherwise? Or is it a conditioning of the past that no longer serves? You see: a person in your life whose always yelling or being confrontational towards you, may or may not actually have intent to harm you. Your fear may very well originate from a pattern that no longer serves you. For example, it may be a projective mechanism you've developed in childhood when your father yelled at you before beating you up. In this example, yelling has subconsciously become a trigger for fear of being beaten, when in fact, this person may not actually have any intention of doing so. Another possible reason for your fear may be a subtle pattern that originates from a previous lifetime in which this person indeed *was* your perpetrator. In this case, this person may have learnt their Soul lesson, so they may not actually have any intent to harm you in this present lifetime. On the contrary: if this person was your perpetrator in a past life, than their mission in *this* life is usually to help you and develop a harmonious relationship with you. They may temporarily be falling back on their old behavioral programing, which they have taken with them into this lifetime as challenges of the game. But in this case, your relationship with this person in this life, as well as your present situation, serve to bring this conflict up to the surface, in order to rebalance the energy between the two of you, to give your perpetrator an opportunity to learn to become kinder and more compassionate, to dissolve your feelings of fear and victimization, and restore a position of True peaceful power in both of you. A huge tool in restoring your personal power is knowing that you have the power to not allow any person to hurt you. As we'll discuss in Chapter 5, nothing can be perpetrated on you that you haven't at some level agreed to. Another tool is meditationally dissolving the energetic potency of the fear, by doing Cord Cutting Meditation, and Dissolving Fear Meditation (see *Seven Stages to co-Creating Prosperity From Your Soul*).

After you have removed yourself from danger, is the time to figure out whether your fear still serves any purpose, or whether it needs to be dissolved. And the only one who really is in a position to know the True nature of the situation is your Higher Self. The wisdom of your Higher Self can shed Light on the best-measured response that is for everyone's best interest. Learning how to clearly communicate with your own Soul is an art form. I will give you some initial tools for assessing decisions in your life in Chapter 7. But the biggest tool that I can give you is Zohar Breath Meditation, detailed in *Seven Stages to co-Creating Prosperity From Your Soul*. Use these (or other) tools to meditate and find out your highest Truth. And heal yourself sufficiently to restore the peaceful strength and the assurance that the Universe will always take care of you if you stick to your highest Truth.

The final step is to stand up to the person that you used to fear, and speak your truth, calmly, collectedly, kindly, but with the conviction of your righteousness. If your dynamics with this person is such that you always yield to him/her out of fear, this will most likely startle him/her. At the very least, it will make this person think twice before they attack you again. And if your response really was deeply anchored in the wisdom of Soul, there is an excellent chance (subject to your opponent's free will, of course) that it will present a solution that is pleasing to both you and your opponent at the same time. Trust that the solution given by your Higher Self is indeed for everyone's highest good, even if the benefit to your opponent may not be immediately apparent, as was the case with my earlier example of an antagonizing neighbor. It may take some time for your relationship with your attacker to become harmonious. And that's OK. Once you have stood up to this person out of the graceful strength of your Soul Self, it changes the dynamics of your relationship into one of mutual respect. And mutual respect is a big step towards creating more love in the world, which in turn is key to co-Creating prosperity.

Give And Take Between Friends:

Even in the dearest friendships, there always comes a time when one friend is leaning more on the other, as everyone gets to be needy sometimes. But the thing to do for your friends, as well as for yourself, is to lovingly tell them that they are being needy lately, so that they may take a deeper look at the cause of this neediness and resolve it. This telling is not a criticism if told from within the Truth of your heart, as you are doing it out of love for your friend, because you want him/her to evolve to the next level of their personal evolution, and be happier. And then again, ask yourself if you are the one who's being too needy. If so, go out into nature, meditate, engage in some of the meditational practices detailed in *Seven Stages to co-Creating Prosperity From Your Soul*, or any practice of your own that you know to be helpful in replenishing your energies. It could be getting a hug from your friend, buying yourself a massage or a spa day, or anything else that you know usually restores your energies and nurtures you when you are in need of it. We should all know ourselves well enough to know what makes us tick. We just need to re-learn to give ourselves the kindness and love that we each deserve as children of God, so we may one day learn to truly love one another in a way that helps each of us co-Create all of our Ideal Lifepaths.

The Balance:

As you can see, in all of those categories of Chi Thieves, we are not talking about the love connection that always subtly underlies all relationships, since love between the Souls is a given. And we are not talking about a relationship with perfectly balanced of energy exchange of giving and receiving. We are talking about an unbalanced situation where one person sucks the energy out of the other, which causes discord and suffering. Thus, all of those ways of getting energy from others are extremely wasteful of energy and involve carrying heavy burdens of unhappiness on the part of both the taker and the unconscious giver. Moreover, this taking of another personal's chi is a poor temporary solution to a deficit in one's personal energy. Opening one's crown and heart, and allowing the Divine funnel of Light to flow in, is the only solution that keeps one permanently connected and tapped into the Divine funnel of all that is good. You probably already have at least some tools of your own to connect with your Higher Self that you may not even be aware of. The meditations and practices included in *Seven Stages to co-Creating Prosperity From Your Soul* and in *A Lifestyle of Prosperity From Your Soul* will greatly enhance your natural ability to tune into Light, Love and Abundance from your Soul.

Remember that above all the antagonisms and hostile energies, there is always love between the Souls, since Love is the essence of the Universe. But of course, the ultimate choice on whether to embrace the Divine Light and let It guide one's life or not is up to each individual. Rejecting the Divine Love-Light and Its guidance leads to a life of selfishness, loneliness, and unhappiness. It also leads to cutting one off from the Infinite funnel of abundance, and to a life in which one must work hard for every possession and achievement. On the other side of the scale, fully opening to the guidance of Divine Light leads to a life of health, happiness, freedom, easily flowing abundance, Grace, and feeling connected and beloved. The choice seems like a no-brainer!

Forgiveness Paves the Road To Inner Strength

Forgiveness has a direct connection to co-Creating prosperity in your life! On a here-now level, resentment, anger, and hatred are heavy burdens to carry. They make you unhappy, and turn against you—the carrier of those feelings, even if there is a very just cause why you should resent the perpetrator in your life. But on an etheric-spiritual level, the negative feelings that you carry connect you to energies that are not of God, and therefore cut you off from the Infinite Funnel of Abundance. If the bad feelings are severe, they can also magnetize into your life all the lower vibrational circumstances that you don't want to manifest. So when you forgive, you're not really doing it for the object of your forgiveness. You are doing it for yourself, as a way of unburdening yourself from these heavy loads of energies and feelings that do not serve your highest good. And the sooner you can unburden yourself, the freer, and more successful at co-Creating prosperity you become. Because all the prosperity, Love, Light, and blessings are awaiting you as soon as you allow yourself to realize the Divine Light within you own Self.

Mikao Usui, the founder of the healing method of Reiki, lived by five principles that he used to chant with his students daily:

Today only –

> Do not anger
> Do not worry
> Be grateful
> Work diligently
> Be kind to others

As you can see, all of these principles have to do with unburdening yourself from negative emotions, and fostering within yourself feelings of kindness, generosity, and bliss. Forgiveness frees you from the energetic repercussions of the perpetrations acted against you. And if you think about it, that is a very powerful tool towards freedom, enlightenment, liberation, and the magnetizing of prosperity (in the full sense of the word) into your life.

At this point, one of the main questions that you might be asking is: "OK, acting from my Angelic Self all the time is difficult. How can I unburden myself of negative feelings that result from pain that other people have inflicted upon me?" And that would be a very good question.

Forgiveness does not mean that you should bend over backwards or even yield to your perpetrator. It does not in any way mean that you allow them to wrong you again and again (that would not even be beneficial for them). Forgiveness simply means that you let go of the responsibility for the negative acts that they did, untie yourself from the bonds of your entangled connection with the person who's wronged you, and energetically give him/her the responsibility for their own actions. Know that it is their karma, not yours. Forgiveness is really just a way to shake off the feelings of helplessness and victimization, and restore your natural position of personal power. Therefore it needs to come from a place of strength, not a place of weakness.

But I know that forgiveness is not always easy. Understanding the process of forgiveness, and how it strengthens you—the person who is doing the forgiving, may make it easier for you to unburden yourself and get light enough to walk upon greener pastures in life.

Step 1 – The Light Within:

The first step of forgiveness is realizing the Divine radiant child within you. You already know that you are a radiant child and a direct emanation of God's Light-Love. But in most of us, this realization is mostly cognitive. We know in our minds that we are extensions of God's Light. But of course, the next step is to be able to really feel it. Despite whatever injustice or violence was perpetrated on you, you need to stop feeling like a victim, and start feeling worthy and validated, for you need to honor the Divine Light within you. This is a strength that is not fed by emotions of violence or revenge. It is a strength that originates from your inner Light—a peaceful and

Graceful power that can never really be taken away from you. Tuning into and dwelling in this fabulous inner strength can be a lifelong process.

There are many practices that help this shift: Self Nurturing Meditation, Nature Walk, Nature Healing, Nature Meditation, and other the meditations in *Seven Stages to co-Creating Prosperity From Your Soul*. In addition, it is helpful to develop a habit of doing kind things for yourself. For example, one of the things my father used to say to me when I was growing up was, "You are not smart. You are not pretty. You're not the kind of girl that a boy would turn his head to look at. So you are going to have to work hard for everything in life." As an adult, I understand that he said that only in order to motivate me to be hardworking. But at the same time, I also know how important it is to undo the damage he did. So I make it a point to give myself credit for my cognitive abilities, especially when I am able to act out of true wisdom. And I make it a point to appreciate and nurture my natural beauty. In the same way, if someone were physically violent towards you, for example, than you would need to make it a point to be soft and gentle with yourself; if someone were always in your face, disturbing your peace, and antagonizing you, then you would need to make it a point and give yourself extra quiet time to take meditational walks on the beach (or in any quiet nature environment). We all need to give ourselves endless unconditional love, in whatever form it needs to take. Step 1 is really about taking the time-out to heal and strengthen yourself.

These acts of kindness and nurturing for yourself will open a crack, and allow the Light to come flooding into even the darkest place inside you. And from that point, it becomes easier to feel at peace with the realization that, "I'm a beloved radiant child of God. How dare this person wrong me in that way?!" But this realization is not one of a false self-righteousness, but *one of peaceful strength*, which is needed in the next step.

Step 2 – Give Your Perpetrator Responsibility For His/Her Actions:

From this new place of Graceful strength, it becomes easier to let go of any attachment towards the actions of the person who have wronged you. For example, think of a scenario in which you are sitting in a restaurant with someone who has wronged you in the past. And since this person invited you to come, you fully expect him/her to offer an apology. But you soon realize that the more beers this person downs, the more profane his hand gestures and language becomes. In this scenario, if you get sucked into an argument at his/her level of expression, than besides the fact that you're both making fools of yourselves, you are belittling the radiance of the Divine child within… that is- you are behaving in a way that is unbecoming of whom you Truly are. If, on the other hand, you listen to this person and stay in your neutral Divine radiance, than you're not the loser here, and your opponent is the only one making a fool of himself. He/she is the only one whose light is obstructed and clouded by the ugliness of the low vibration he/she's in. And in the grand scheme of things, he/she is the only one suffering from carrying the burden of their anger and unhappiness. I had a situation just like that a couple of years back. As soon as I saw the true colors of my former perpetrator, I said a little prayer, which helped me visualize myself in a protective bubble of Divine Light. He went on and on all evening long with his bad language and obscene hand gestures, and anger, and I stayed neutral and listened. I opened my heart, and tried to beam Divine healing light and love towards him, for I understood just how unhappy this guy really was. And by the end of the evening, I didn't feel violated or weak. Quite the contrary: I felt empowered with Divine Grace. I felt a profound peace that came from knowing that I became all that I could be, at least in that evening.

On a deeper level, if you behave and live by the guidance of your Soul Light and someone wrongs you, the karmic burden is on them and not on you. It is them who have failed to learn their Soul lesson, and have missed the opportunity to create more love in the world. It is them who have failed to grow from the situation, and it is you who, if you remain heart-centered, have absolutely achieved the Soul growth you were designed to achieve from the situation. Just this realization that rising above and taking the highroad earns you brownie points in the cosmic bank account of karma should be enough to give you the strength to do it. But there is another process going on here, which is exponentially more powerful than saving brownie points.

Our thoughts, feelings and actions all have deep and wide ripple effects that reverberate throughout fabric of the Universe. Anyone's Soul Light will never give them guidance to be unkind to themself or others, for the highest Truth of existence on every level is Love. I have already mentioned that at the highest level that overlies all of reality, there is always Love between the Souls, and that this love helps Souls reincarnate again and again in different roles with each other, forgiving terrible wrongdoings. But normally, when the role-shifts happen from lifetime to lifetime, the forgiveness is facilitated by the life-review, which straightens out the lines of communication, and ensures that the next encounter will be more harmonious. NDEers report that when they've reached the Light, they experience a life review in which they re-experienced all the events of their lives (sometimes even past and future lives too) as a holographic 360° movie, in which they were able to feel not only what they felt during the event, but also what the other people involved in each situation were feeling. So that if you had called a girl in your school "fat" or "ugly," than in your life-review, you would be feeling how devastated she felt when you called her that; if you had beaten someone up, you'd be feeling the pain of being beat up. And since during the afterlife you dwell in Divine Light and Unconditional Love, you become anxious to right the wrongs, and to prove to yourSelf that you can live in a harmonious loving relationship with all Souls. So the honest self-assessment of the life-review does us each a great service in assuming responsibility for our mistakes, and correcting the wrongs. However, from within one particular incarnation, we are not often afforded the opportunity to feel the consequences of our actions, and to know where we've missed the opportunity to expand Creation through love.

So on a here-now level, some situations lend themselves to your feeling peace and forgiveness without facing your opponent. But if the opportunity permits, it is extremely beneficial (for both you and your opponent) to stand your grounds and make the other person aware of the suffering that he/she has caused you, and let them know that enough is enough! This must be done not from the position of a victim, but from a position of peaceful heart-centered strength. Standing up for yourself reasserts your Graceful strength, and frees you from the energetic cords through which your perpetrator may still be sucking away your personal energy even years after the incident. In effect, if you are able to peacefully but firmly demonstrate to your perpetrator how they've made you suffer, you are helping them hugely, since now he/she doesn't have to wait until his/her afterlife life-review, and possibly the next incarnation to learn this particular lesson. This way he/she can learn to act more lovingly right now, thereby liberating themselves from the karma of this lesson.

Here is one example of just how powerful giving responsibility can be: A friend of a friend was a very vibrant young woman who was in a long-term relationship with a guy. They were living together for about a year when this woman found out that her boyfriend was cheating on her. Although my first reaction was to say, "dump him, she began a long and treacherous road of writing him letters, pouring her heart out, and begging him not to leave. At that point, I felt insulted that a radiant woman like her should wheel over her personal powers and belittle herself in this way. But I guess she had to walk her own path… It took several months for her to get to the point of letting go. And when she did, she started seeing other guys too. Because of the housing situation in the area where they lived, they were still living together when she started dating other men. But in effect, this created a situation where she was now cheating on him. Deep down, she still had a deep love for this guy. But on the surface, she was giving him a taste of his own medicine. So while I do not condone cheating in any way, this was how this woman chose to make her beloved feel what it feels like to be cheated on by the one you love. And it worked! He corrected his ways very quickly. He apologized many times over, and is now very devoted to her. So while this story may not exemplify the highest vibrational way to let your the person who has wronged you know how the shoe feels on the other foot, it is a very clear example that illustrates our point.

However, giving someone responsibility for his/her actions does not have to be dramatic. It could be peaceful and harmonious. For example, a number of years ago, I joined my brother's family in a vacation in Cancun, Mexico. Throughout the vacation, while my sister-in-law and dear friend was very respectful towards my blessing of the food and my spiritual practices, my brother cracked all kinds of jokes relating to my spiritual beliefs, which his kids quickly followed. After each of these ridicules, I would go into my room and cry. So after receiving much emotional support form my sister-in-law, I took the time to meditate to connect with my Soul, to re-center and heal and myself. Then on a peaceful afternoon walk to dinner, I let my brother know how I felt. Peacefully, calmly, quietly, but firmly, I said, "You know, I appreciate your atheism and scientific skepticism. I respect that you believe differently than I do. But after every time you ridicule my spiritual practices I go into my room and cry." He said, "really? I had no idea. I am so sorry. I won't do it again." But it wasn't so much his verbal apology that resolved the issue. You should have seen the looked in his eyes. It was like it hurt him to the bottom of his soul to know that he had caused me any kind of pain. And it was his action that spoke the loudest. From that moment on, he showed so much respect for my spiritual practices, that he was the first one to explain to his kids that one needs to respect other people's beliefs when they tried to laugh about my food blessings. And after that, the issue no longer had any potency. It was resolved, and forgotten about.

Step 3 – Freeing Each Other Into Our Respective Divine Light:

Once you have gotten through steps 1 and 2, and you have given your perpetrator the responsibility for his/her actions, either meditational, verbally, or by your actions, the potency of your hurt feelings and the sting of poison should start to drain almost automatically.

But the potency of your hurt feelings from the situation does not always dissipate immediately as it did between my brother and I. So Step 3 is about releasing each other meditationally into your respective God-Lights, as a way to finish draining the sting from your internal wound, and as a way of healing both yourself, and your relationship with the person who wronged you. This process can be helped by doing Cord Cutting Meditation (*Seven Stages to co-Creating Prosperity From Your Soul*), by praying (sending distant healing if you are a Level 2 reiki practitioner) or by invoking Angelic-Divine help for healing process. It is especially helpful to invoke the help of Archangel Michael—the Divine aspect of protection, cord-cutting, and helping people live up to their highest Lifeplans, and Archangel Rafael—the Divine healer (more on Archangels in *Seven Stages to co-Creating Prosperity From Your Soul*).

As you meditate to completely drain all the potency of any emotions from the situation, and as you continue to send healing intent to yourself and your opponent, you will start to feel empowered, light, and free from your entanglement with this person, free to express all that you are in an unobstructed way, free to co-Create harmonious and loving relationships in your life, and of course, free to manifest abundance from the highest expression of whom you Truly are. And the more forgiveness you impart on others, the more you liberate *yourself* from all cords that are weighing you down, the more empowered you become as a conscious co-Creator of a healthy, liberated, and abundant life.

A Heaven Of Your Own Making

So far, we have discussed that fear, anger, stress, resentment, and hatred only turn against holder of those feelings, and get him/her stuck in a loop of negativity that prevents him/her from moving towards happiness, health and abundance. And we have discussed how to deal with the naysayers, energy thieves, and perpetrators in your life. But the benefits that forgiveness, letting go, and being kind to others holding space for them to evolve hold for you are far greater than that.

Consider a scenario in which someone who is permanently in your life, such as a family member for example, is continuously barking at you or being difficult. You already know that replying with loving-kindness would fix the problem. Because in nine times out of ten, all the person really want is to be heard. They want to matter to someone, and their barking is just a (misdirected) cry for love! So attentively listening to your opponent is very important. It makes them feel that they matter. It disarms them as it makes them understand that they don't need to be verbally and energetically abusive in order to matter and be heard.

But remember that listening is not doing. Attentively listening to your opponent does not mean you agree with them, or that you would do anything as a reaction to their words. It just means you respect that that's their opinion. For when you react and get upset, you are giving their unkind or antagonistic words power. So for example, let's say that someone says to you, "you are an ass-hole!" If you react and yell back at them and use profanities, then you behave like an ass-hole and prove them right! By staying centered, taking a deep breath, smiling, and radiating loving-kindness, you elevate your own vibration, and plant the seed for your opponent to evolve. This doesn't require you to do or say anything in particular. Just stay in your radiance and wait for them to change.

But at this point, you may ask: "What if I tune into dwell in all that Divine Love and Light, and I radiate it towards this difficult person, and they still don't come around? And what if ten years later, the other person is still grouchy and difficult?" And to that I have to reply with a story. During one particular meditation, I was Graced into "seeing" my Soul Self—the very essence of my being for the first time. This was a perfectly angelic, radiant beautiful being. At first, I was reluctant to own up to this image, for I couldn't believe that this being of pure love, radiant light, joy, and peace was really I. From a here-now self's perspective, I didn't feel worthy of this angelic being. But as I felt so drawn to this being, the innermost voice of my heart helped me recognize that this was indeed my True essence. Tears of joy started rolling down my cheeks, as I felt like I was floating, and totally warmed by the peaceful loving radiance of my Soul. After a while, my thoughts wondered back to my everyday reality and to situations in my life when I've reacted out of fear and stress, and situations in which I allowed myself to get sucked into other people's stress and negativities. From the perspective of this beautiful Soul Self, those reactions looked like the behavior of a scared lab-rabbit. I then asked my Soul Self: "How should I behave when interacting with the antagonist in my life?" The answer came in the form of another vision: I "saw" my Soul in Its glowing angelic presence as the one in charge of the interaction with the antagonist. This vision gave me a chance to passively observe and see what my Higher Self would do in this situation. My Higher Self simply continued to be centered and peaceful, and continued to radiate Love and Light for the stressful antagonist of my life, all the while being unaffected and untainted by the negativity of the antagonist. Then I (my here-now self) asked my Soul Self: "What happens if the stressful antagonist is not open to receive? What happens if twenty years later, this person is still in my life to antagonize me?" This time the answer came as a combination of vision and clairaudient message: I saw twenty-years-later-me as happily merged with my Soul Self, living in her own paradise, and the stressful antagonist as living in a hell of their own making. Then I understood in the deepest way, that by being heart-centered and kind to others, we have nothing to lose and everything to gain… even from a here-now perspective!

So the answer to your question is: if you've spent ten years being Soul-centered, and the person in question kept being antagonistic, than he/she has just spent ten years in the hell of their own making, while and you on the other hand have just spent ten years dwelling in Divine Love, Light, and heart-centeredness. You are not the loser in this situation, since you have spent those ten years co-Creating for yourself a heaven of your own making: You have connected yourself to your Divine Funnel of Infinite Abundance, manifested from it all the prosperity you wished for, and consequently co-Created Heaven on Earth for yourself! Many meditational tools will be given in *Seven Stages to co-Creating Prosperity From Your Soul* to help you achieve this Heaven of your own making.

A Critical Mass for Peace On Earth

Up to now, we've covered tactics and processes that are beneficial to bringing you to peace and harmony into your personal relationships, so that you may harmoniously walk the highest path of your new prosperous life. But let's talk about liberation and harmony on a worldwide level – what about world peace? We already know that **world peace would help accelerate the energy of co-Creation to such a higher level that we could each co-Create a far greater level of wealth than the one we are currently co-Creating**. But how do we achieve it?

Let me start by saying that true peace on earth must be driven by the hearts of the people. While I acknowledge the profoundness of the influence of our leaders' decisions and actions, it has been made clear to me long ago that peace on Earth can never be achieved by politicians. Firstly, to be a politician you must have a certain thirst for power that ignores the natural Divine power that is already within each of us! And this statement is not meant to offend any politician. On the metaphysical level, peace on earth can *only* be achieved by people, if we all start living by the Light and wisdom of our Souls, acting as gracefully and lovingly as this Light would always lead us to act. So if peace on Earth can only be achieved by the hearts of the people shifting into oneness, than it is time that we (all the people of this planet) go back to caring about "We, the people." It's time to shift the power back into the hands of the people of this world. On the spiritual level of our collective consciousness, it is time that "we, the people" get ready to lead ourselves into the New Earth, in which world peace, economic flourishing, and kindness to each other and to Mother Earth are prominent. But how do we get ready to achieve this peace on Earth? By awakening the hearts of its people to the spark of God-likeness within us, and to the kinship we all share. The bottom line is: we just have to wake up every morning and decide to love one another! And let's talk a little bit about how.

I am not a politician. But from a spiritual standpoint, the first step is to realize some of the underlying causes of turmoil in the world today that are causing many people to act violently. Planet earth is going through huge astrological and energetic shifts right now. The polarities in the earth's magnetic poles are shifting, which energetically influences everyone on a subtle level. And that in and of itself affects huge energetic changes in the vibration that we as a planet reverberate throughout the cosmos. But beside that, astrologically, we have also just transitioned into the Age of Aquarius after nearly 2,300 years of being ruled by the darkness of the Piscean Age. And as much as the Age of Aquarius is going to be the age of enlightenment, it is still up to us – the people of the earth – to claim the peace, and reaffirm our resonance with the Light. So as all profound changes happen, this switch too is not automatic or immediate. It takes time, especially in bringing the energetic changes of our promising future into the physical reality of our earthly lives. As a result of all these energetic and astrological changes, there is much turmoil and many extremist groups in our world today.

Since you are reading these lines, I know that you are not one of those extremists, but are in fact well on your way to ascending to a vibration of harmony with all of Creation, as you step into being a more conscious co-Creator. And from the vantage point of your compassionate self, understand that hatred and violence do not exist in and of their own, since every Soul is a spark of God's Love. It is only through forgetting the Original Self that people begin to feel detached from their Source of life, and all that is good. It is those feelings of detachment and lack that brew fear. And when one gets to the level of lack and fear experienced by the poor members of some of the extremist groups today, one reverts back to their basic animalistic instincts of survival—kill or be killed. This is how fear turns into rage and hatred, which is often directed at anything that is different from oneself—anything we don't understand and we fear could harm us. And along this process, we forget how to simply stand in God's Light, rejoice in our differences, and have compassion towards those less fortunate.

Think for a moment on the circumstances of individuals within some of the extremist groups in the world today. As an example, (and without making excuses for anyone) most members of Islamic extremist groups are very poor, hungry, and ignorant, none of which is of their own volition. And this extreme lack and hunger activates the most primal animal instincts that shifts those people's vibration into fear. And at that point, it only takes one strong ill-indented leader (who had himself forgotten his Divine Light and is thus hungering for power at the expense of his people) to tell those hungry poor masses that America or Israel is to blame for their lot in life, and to twist their minds into hatred and violence. To be fair, there are also many extremist groups right here in America today, in the form of extreme right wing, white supremacy groups, church groups, and even extreme liberals. And their hatred also stems from fear. But take any of the individuals from any extremist hate-group, and provide them with safety, food, life's fundamental necessities, surround them with love, and teach them not to take the brainwashing that their extreme leaders programed them with at face value; teach them to meditationally find out the Truth from their own Higher Selves, and pretty soon you'll start seeing a normal person with a spark of God-likeness inside them—a person just like you!

You can prove this point even on yourself: we all have days in which we hate the world and feel like it is all against us. Well, on one of those difficult stressful days, take yourself out to the best celebratory dinner of your life: I mean, indulge in a huge rib-eye steak, potatoes with cream sauce, good bread, butter on top, and chocolate mousse for desert. Pretty soon, you'll start feeling all the anger and frustration leave you, and by the time you finish your chocolate mousse, you may find yourself saying, "All is right with the world right now." So on a physical level, if you think about it, if we (I don't necessarily mean we-the US) started supplying steak and potatoes to the world's hungry masses, we would have world peace, or at least be a heck of a lot closer to it.

Now, I know that some of you are probably shaking your heads right now and saying that I am too naïve. But achieving world peace by just deciding to love each other is not as farfetched as it sounds. People all over our planet are awakening to their Divine nature. They may call it a different name. But a huge spiritual shift is happening on our planet right now. An exponentially growing number of people are awakening to the fact that there is more to life than waking up in the morning, going to work, eating your meals, hating your enemies, and going to sleep at night (how?)! There is something higher that brings more happiness and meaning to life. And most people in the world today are either in search of it, or well on their way to finding it. There are also many pure Light workers, healers and teachers all across the globe, that have begun to receive Divine teachings (similar to this one) to help show the way to freedom, enlightenment, and happiness.

And you might be wondering how loving thy neighbors as well as thy enemy can bring us world peace? A lot simpler than what politicians might be thinking: by achieving a Critical Mass! Many New Age thinkers and Light workers have long talked about the critical mass as being the smallest number of people (percentage of the world's population) that need to become enlightened to spread the Light and raise everyone else's vibration enough to create world peace, love and harmony. It's kind of like if you are in a small rowing boat with your teenage kids, than if you are strong enough, the kids don't necessarily have to row to. It would be nice if your grown teenage boys offer to help you row to shore. But you have the power by yourself to row the boat to the shore where you'll eat a nice dinner and be warmed by a bonfire. In the same way that it would be nice for your teenage boys to offer to help you, when it comes to enlightened people, the more the merrier. But in the same way that you yourself have the power to row the boat to shore, we only need a certain number of enlightened people in the world to pull everyone else up. The question, though, is how many enlightened people are enough to achieve world peace and help us to the shore of the New Earth. And to that, there are many opinions.

Pure logic dictates that if 51% of the population awakens to the Divine light within and live by it, then the balance would tilt. However, since light is stronger than darkness, and it only takes one ray of light to illumine a completely dark room, some seers and wise-ones have received wisdom that the critical number is a third of the world's population. But I'm here to tell you that it is even easier than that.

It has been proven by yogis for thousands of years that the radiant auric field of a truly radiant person can heal people on a subtle level, up to a radius of twenty-five miles in every direction. This is a fact. For example, every time I do yoga and meditation on the beach and reclaim my radiance, I find that people just move their beach towels to sit next to me. People I encounter just seem happier and more peaceful. Dogs come close sniffing my energy and just laying by my feet. And even birds don't fear me. Now that's not to say that I'm a saint. I'm not. I am an ordinary person who occasionally gets angry and low-vibrational, just like you. But yet in those moments (hours, days) when I am able to reclaim my radiance, this yogic principle proves itself over and over.

Here are two more examples that prove that this radiant body theory really works: Snatam Kaur is a woman who sings devotional yogic songs, who has published many CDs. Beyond being a personal favorite of mine, Snatam Kaur is one of those people who are just a very pure channels for Divine peace, love and grace. In 2010, she was giving a concert in Los Angeles, to which I was waiting to go like a kid whose waiting to go to Disneyland. I went to sleep the night before the concert at my normal hour, taking my usual amount of melatonin. Yet on the morning of the concert, despite the melatonin, I woke up at 3:45am jumping up with joy! While I don't know Snatam Kaur personally, I know that in the yogic tradition, she would have wakened up to start her yoga, prayer and meditation at 3:45am. So while Snatam kaur was many miles away from my physical location, the radiance and Divine essence she channeled through her meditation and prayer woke me up out of sound sleep and kept me energized like a 5-year-old throughout that day and evening. Further, all the people I encountered in her concert were peaceful, happy, and high vibrational. And when the concert started that night, more than her beautiful sweet voice,

I felt that her benevolent devotion and radiance channeled the Divine essence to transform me and everyone else in the concert hall. And this is just one example.

You may think that it was just because Snatam Kaur is someone I was in tune with, and that it was only the adrenalin of the anticipation of the concert that healed me. But the next example negates this rationale: Some time during 2009, there was one week in which I felt like there was a different kind of peace in the air. It was as though the whole week, everything and everyone around me were peaceful. Despite the fact that I personally was at the time of the month in which I usually am somewhat bitchy (PMS), it was like a new dawn had come. This lasted several days… but eventually, things went back to normal. Several weeks later, I was talking to a friend who told me that during the week in question, the Dalai Lama was visiting in Los Angeles, and was giving a talk that thousands of people attended. So in this example, I and all the people who crossed my path that week, were uplifted by the Dalai Lama's peace and radiance (and perhaps the radiance and spiritual vibration of his followers), despite the fact that none of us are Buddhists, or were even aware of his presence. We were all affected by the radiance of his being without even knowing it.

There are many saintly people walking the earth plane among us, who channel Divine Light and Love just like Snatam Kaur, and just like the Dalai Lama. A person need not be a saint in order to be heart-centered and radiant and uplift others. They just have to be true to their Soul Self in order to shine this peace-generating Divine Light for themselves and others.

And why is this resonance radiance so important? Because here is a little interesting calculation for you: if each radiant person can heal and transform people on a subtle level (that means: without doing anything other than being present in their full radiance) up to a 25 mile radius, than each of these radiant people uplifts all people in the sphere of roughly ($\prod r^2$ = 3.14x25x25=) 1952.5 square miles around them. Now let's see how many of those radiant people we would need in the world in order to tilt the balance into world peace: The surface of world's seven continents and islands on which population dwells is about 58 million square miles. So if you take 58 million square miles and divide it by the 1952.5 square miles (the sphere of influence around each radiant person), you get the answer of 29,706. This means that since every radiant person uplifts people in 1952.5 square miles, if disbursed evenly and strategically, we would only need 29,706 enlightened-radiant people in the world to transform the rest of the world's population towards harmony, happiness, peace, and needless to say, abundance! So according to this calculation, we only need 0.00043% of the population to be radiant and enlightened to achieve world peace, which is not such a tall order at all!

So even if we don't do anything politically, if we just recognize the beauty and potential of our brothers and sisters to the human race, however different from us they may be, and if we just hold space for them to evolve and feel beloved, than gradually we will start seeing the extremist of all ends calm down and awaken to our Oneness with each other! And then world peace and kindness to our Earth-mother cannot fall that much behind. And let us not forget that miracles do happen, and it would only take *one* truly saintly person of the caliber of Buddha, Moses or Jesus (and many others throughout history) to magically transform the entire world population towards world peace!

Our Differences Make Us Whole

Many religions, like Jewish religion for example, are adamant about praying only to Source-God, and not to Angels. But to understand the irrelevancy of this critique, we need to understand that Angels are not separate from God. In fact, all Archangels, Angels, messengers of Light, deities, and even the masculine (yang) and feminine (yin) aspects, are just the many aspects of the same Creator. In Truth, nothing is really separate from God, as God is omnipresent! That means that there is nothing but God. All that permeates and surrounds everything that is in the physical and non-physical Universe is God. Angels and Archangels are really just the many faces of God, and Her-His way of appearing to us in some form that we as humans can understand. It is Her-His way of multitasking for our understanding. Angels and Archangels are necessary Creations to help us understand our "physical" existence in a universe that is holographic and made of energy. This is possibly the only way our human mind could perceive Creation, as a force that is separate from us that is doing the creation, or as a God that has given up Her-His enormous Wholeness in order to fragment Her-Himself into the gazillions of pieces that make up our observable universe. But as we shall see in the coming two chapters, God collapses Her-His Infinity *only in our human perceptions*. Appearing to us as something other than Infinity-Radiance-Love-Light is only so that we could understand and relate to Her-Him from our temporary human perspective. The bigger Truth is that God is still Whole, and we are still One with Her-His Wholeness. Although it may not be apparent, and although we may not feel it while we are immersed in our seemingly small human life, at a certain level of our existence, we are still all One with the Divine. It is this oneness that provides the Infinite Source for all that is good, and all that we wish to co-Create in our lives: health, love, happiness, wealth, and much more.

But besides the unseen aspects of God, Her-His glory really shines through Her-His Creation. For all of us are indeed not only a part of Creation, but also each person and each flower petal within Creation really is an integral part of God Her-Himself. And within all the faces and aspects of Creation are the many religions and life philosophies that seemingly set us apart. So your belief system – be it paganism, Christianity, Judaism, Buddhism, Sikhism, Hinduism, Shinto or any other religion, is an integral part of God, was always intended to be a gift for humanity. It is a part of the Wholeness that IS God. But more than that: it is our differences as peoples, cultures, races, religions, and even our distinction as human beings, that make us Whole – *together!* Just as body tissue is differentiated to fulfill different functions within the body as a whole, so do we—as people—differentiate to bring forth the many wisdoms that correlate to the many aspects through which God experiences Her-Himself as each one of us, each leaf, and each spark of Creation. You see, accepting the truth embedded in other religions is not necessarily a cognitive process. It is a matter of *feeling* Oneness with someone else despite their different belief, knowing in your heart of hearts that their heart is also in the right place. This resonant feeling allows you to *feel* the other person's truth even if you don't cognitively agree with it. So let us all rejoice in the beauty of our differences, cherish nature, which was Created for our enjoyment, and know that it takes all of us to make God whole.

In this chapter, we have seen how to achieve harmony both in your personal relationships and globally, and why this harmony is so important to co-Creating prosperity. There is one type of relationship that is the most empowering you can ever have, in terms of always supporting your greatness, and reminding your True Self to come out, and thus helping you co-Create your Ideal Lifepath. We will discuss that relationship in Chapter 9.

In all the chapters until now, we have laid the foundation for understanding the metaphysics of the co-Creative process. In the next two chapters, we will delve deeply into understanding the actual process you already engage in as a co-Creator of your own reality, which will help you become profoundly more conscious and successful in co-Creating True prosperity in your life.

Chapter 5

The Essence of the co-Creative Process

In the previous chapters, we have covered many concepts, which lay the foundation for understanding the process you already engage in as you co-Create your life. In this chapter, we'll go into the very essence of the creative process, the understanding of which will help you become a more conscious co-Creator of your life. For once you are fully conscious of the process, it becomes much easier to invite into your life only that which you Truly want—the abundance, health, love and happiness that were always meant to be yours.

Free Will

Free will is the foundation of Creation! And the reason the Universe is driven by free will is that this is the condition of God "fragmenting" Her-Himself into the spark that is you, and me, and every other part of Creation: that each spark would retain a respective aspect of the free will of the Whole. But as we'll understand more deeply in Chapter 6, God has not really fragmented Her-Himself. She-He is still Whole, and you are an integral part of that Wholeness. It is as an integral part of the Wholeness of your Creator that you were given a mandate to co-Create your own life according to your free will. However, when we talk about *your* free will, whose free will are we really talking about? Ah… Although your free will extends to every level of your existence, in order to understand which level of your free will swings the balance of your co-Creations, a clarification of the various levels of your free will is needed.

As we have discussed in Chapter 2, on a Soul level, before each of us came into this human life, we have each chosen an Ideal Lifeplan that incorporates all the opportunities and experiences needed for the next level of our growth. But as ideal as this plan is, it is only a plan – kind of like a blueprint for a building. And the Lifepath built on this blueprint still needs to be beefed up with actual life experiences… according to the free will of the various aspects of you.

The free will of the Soul does not end at the planning process that precedes your birth. At every moment of your life, your Soul is still rooting for you to follow the most auspicious Lifepath, and is actively directing you towards it. And since your Soul also remains connected to the highest Divine wisdom throughout your lifetimes, It may choose to make small adjustments in the original Ideal Lifeplan to accommodate choices that your here-now self has made. That is, if you've strayed from your Ideal Lifeplan, your Soul may reroute you through a different intersection to still merge with your Ideal Lifepath (that is why the Ideal Lifepath is in most cases somewhat different from the Ideal Lifeplan), all of which is aimed to continue to direct you towards your Soul growth objectives and the overall success of your life-mission.

Your free will, however, does not end at the Soul level. Your here-now self does not just blindly follow the will of your Soul Self. Even within each lifetime, it is necessary for your here-now self to also have free will, because it is the one enacting the choices on the stage of your life. So your here-now self still chooses much for you: First, it chooses which *thoughts* you discard ("oh my life is so difficult, it'll never get better"), and which thoughts you embrace ("I'm going to grab life by the balls and I just know that everything is going to turn out fine"). Your here-now self also chooses how you *feel* about things at every given moment—are you caught in the stress and worry of your hectic everyday life? Or do you allow the naturally joyous feelings of your Soul Self to come flooding in? And of course, it is also your here-now self that decides which *actions* to take: are your actions really just angry knee-jerk re-actions? Or do you only take actions that feel absolutely right to the core of your being – actions that are inspired by the Will of your Soul? These are the three levels of choices (thoughts, feelings, and actions) that your here-now self still makes on an everyday basis.

Now, some situations in life are of little consequence in your overall Lifepath, while others are crossroads. Challenging situations in life are usually Triggering Events—events in which your choice triggers a whole chain of events, influencing your overall Lifepath. Triggering Events are usually set up by your Soul. Those are the re-routing intersections that your Soul has set up, to give your here-now self a chance to make choices that profoundly effect where your life ends up… which hopefully will lead you to merge with your Ideal Lifepath. But these triggering events do not necessarily have to be major life dramas. They could be subtle decisions that are seemingly small at the time… such as – do you allow yourself to wallow and feel lousy? Or do you rise to the challenge with high spirit? From a metaphysical standpoint, *continuously* allowing yourself to wallow means that you are not resonating with what you deeply want, and therefore cannot magnetize True prosperity into your life. At a more mundane level, it may lead you to missed opportunities that were supposed to lead you to merge with your Ideal Lifepath. So rising to the challenge with high spirits basically wins you brownie points on every level.

Beyond Triggering Events, there are many days and moments in life that may or may not be major life intersections, but weigh in the day-to-day balance of how strongly you resonate with, and therefore attract, the desired prosperity into your life. For example – when confronted with a person who is always sour-faced, is it better to just avoid him/her? Or should you say a cheerful "hello" to try and lift him/her up? When faced with a difficulty at work, should you continue to tackle it in the same way and allow yourself to continue to get frustrated? Should you find a different way of doing things, or maybe just a different way of looking at things? Or was this difficulty set up by your Soul Self as a redirect—to drive you to find a different job that is more in alignment with your bliss? I'm not saying that every difficulty at work is there to lead you to leave your job. And even when it is, I know that leaving a secure job is scary for your here-now self. But you should ask yourself: if this job makes you feel deeply unhappy like you are not maximizing your potential, and if major difficulties keep mounting your way, could this indeed be a hint from your Soul Self to drive you to search for something that is more in line with whom you Truly are?

For all of us, there are times when our here-now selves are conflicted with our Higher Selves. These times, in which your here-now self has made choices that were not in accordance with the Free Will of your Soul, are the times in which you co-Create the opposite of prosperity. In fact, the negative outcome of actions-feelings-thoughts, which contradict the Will of your Soul, is our first indication of the dynamics of powers between your here-now self and your Soul Self.

Your Soul is a beautiful radiant giant of Divine Light and power, compared to which your here-now self is as tiny as a spec of dust. And because of the mandate of Divine empowerment that was given to your Soul, It has a greater influence on your reality than does your here-now self. Your Soul Self actually has a bigger influence on your reality than even your physical circumstances do. For example, the Bible tells us the story of David and Goliath, in which David won the battle even though his body size and strength were considerably smaller than that of Goliath. In this example, it was really David's spirit (Higher Self) that was bigger and stronger than that of Goliath. Goliath's spirit was weak and small, and David's Soul Self was empowered by God to win the battle and become a king that would be beloved by his people for thousands of years to come. That was his Ideal Lifeplan. And no giant or obstacle could stand in the way of that. A more modern-day illustration of the power of one's Soul to change physical circumstances can be drawn from martial arts, when you see a tiny-little Japanese guy break a huge pile of eleven bricks in one swift karate move. In that case, the tiny Japanese guy is drawing his power from the energy of his spirit—his Higher Self, stored in his Navel Center, fed through his apparatus of Light-Bodies, chakras, nadis and meridians. According to Eastern philosophy, it is the spirit of a great warrior that must be strong, not necessarily her/his body.

Another way to understand how your Soul, which to us is conceptually ethereal, can influence and move physical matter is to draw on the relationship between energy and matter from a physics point of view (if you want). Dr. Gerber notes that mathematical interpretations of Einstein's $E=MC^2$ imply that matter is just frozen energy—energy that is vibrating in such a slow rate that it appears to be "frozen" solid. And there are tremendous metaphysical implications to this understanding. First, it makes it easier to see why from our perspective, things that are already manifested in the "physical" seem harder and slower to change. Second – since energy and matter are interchangeable, the energy of your Soul Self can and does translate into physical matter and into the reality of your life. And as we have seen in Chapter 1, your whole Self, which includes your physical self, is wholly composed of energy, vibrating at different rates. The third metaphysical implication relates to free will: to move ethereal energy that is vibrating at a high rate, takes only a gentle force. But in order to move the "frozen solid" (low vibratory) energy of your "physical" reality, a much stronger push is required.

Then the next question becomes: "how can I make my will strong enough to manifest everything I want?" And the simple truth is: it isn't really your here-now self that has the immense power of will to literally move mountains. It's your Soul Self! Unless you possess some magical powers of concentration or telekinesis, the only part of you that is powerful enough to move, change and manifest your physical reality is your Soul Self! Your here-now self does, however, have the power to align itself (thoughts, feelings, actions) with the Will of the Soul. And the good news is that your Soul is already as strong, powerful and radiant as it could be. It is an energetic giant that can manifest for you everything that you Truly desire. All you need to do is align the will of your here-now self with that of your Soul, and presto—prosperity comes flooding in.

It's true that as a beloved child of your Creator, you were given free choice at the level of your here-now self too. But in our multi-faceted reality, as smart, beautiful, and successful a person as you may be, your here-now self still contains only a tiny bit of the total Light of your Soul. In comparison, your Soul Self is a direct emanation of the Creator's Light and Power. And It is the main part of you that has been given the mandate to manifest Its free will, as an extension of Divine Will.

So here is the thing: if there is ever a debate between your powerful Soul and your tiny (by comparison) here-now self, who do you think would win, the giant or the dwarf? That's right: the giant wins every time! The bottom line is: if your here-now self desires something that is opposite to your Soul's will, your Soul would win every time. Even if the will of your here-now self is extremely strong, the most it could achieve against the powerful Will of your Soul is a standstill. That is why it is so important to align your will with that of your Soul when it comes to co-Creating a successful and prosperous life for yourself. You can think of it in simple terms as aligning what you think you want with what You (your Soul) really want in the larger sense. The importance of this alignment in the manifestation of an all-inclusive prosperity cannot be overemphasized! This is the reason so many of the meditations of *Seven Stages to co-Creating Prosperity From Your Soul* are devoted to tuning into your Soul's consciousness, and devising a plan of action for manifestation of prosperity that is aligned with the Will of your Soul.

Now, aligning with the will of your Soul is not in any way like bowing to an arbitrary and capricious ruler. Aligning with the Will of your Soul is simply aligning with the highest version of yourself. Also, remember that your Soul is in Oneness with the highest degree of Love, Light, compassion, and prosperity of the Infinite. Beyond that, your Soul Self also has the highest perspective on how certain choices and actions are going to play out in the bigger picture. It is like the Soul has already watched the entire ball game. More than that – It has carefully orchestrated your main moves and the style of your game, and has coordinated them with the moves of all the other players in the game. And It already knows your team is going to win. But in our little parable, despite the fact that your actual life is like somewhat like a re-run for your Higher Self, your here-now self feels like it's playing the game for the first time. So of course you are stressed out about your choices and actions because you haven't been privy to the results yet. It wouldn't be fun if you knew in advance how every move is going to play out, because then you may not try your best - you may adopt a nonchalant detached attitude about the game, and you wouldn't learn or achieve anything from the experience. On the other hand, if you knew that your team is generally programed to win, but didn't exactly know how the victory was going to come about, or how each move was going to play out, you wouldn't be so stressed about the results, but at the same time – you would still enjoy every moment of the game. If you think of this game as a computer game, and think of your here-now self ball player as your programmed-to-win avatar in the game, you know there are going to be times when you would want to have your avatar do the play from the left, for example. But the program keeps directing your avatar to do the play to the right. Well, if you knew that the computer is defaulted to have you win the game, than you wouldn't mind taking its recommended "default" choice, because you'd know it was directing you towards a victory, right?

The same is true about the Will of your Soul: your Soul is in cahoots with God. It's in on the biggest picture of all. And It is rooting for you to win—from the highest perspective possible. So while the victory may look differently from how your here-now self is it imagining right now, you will always be provided for and beloved, and the victory that your Soul is setting you up for is so much bigger than the one you can imagine right now. For example, let's say that from a here-now perspective, you want to marry a rich person. Your Soul Self may be leading you to marry a person of average means, who happens to be your true soulmate, with whom you can co-Create greater amounts of prosperity than you could ever imagine – together, by following your highest Lifepaths! In that case, your degree of happiness will be greater because by the end of the story, you would not only have co-Created greater financial prosperity. You would have also found true love, which is priceless!

Of course, once you have meditationally caught a glimpse of your Soul Self, Its presence feels so wonderful, that you wouldn't want to come back and live life strictly from the perspective of your lowest here-now self. You would want to keep tuning and dwelling in the high vibration of your Soul Self. Once you have fully tuned into how indulgent, nurturing and blissful your Soul's presence feels, and you start craving it, it becomes a mute point whose free will are you following, because at that point you have merged the free will of your here-now self with that of your Soul (I will give you tools to do that in *Seven Stages to co-Creating Prosperity From Your Soul*), a merge from which only blessings can come.

How To Exercise Your Free Will For Best co-Creating Results:

Going back to the free will of your here-now self, which still has some clout, even within the Lifeplan that your Soul has laid out for you, it is still possible to experience each lesson through a vibration of lack and discord, or through a vibration of joy, abundance, and harmony. Dwelling on what you don't want, going along with negative conditioning, or setting up negative expectations for yourself and others (even unknowingly) all hold you back from experiencing the true growth your Soul had set up for you to achieve in this lifetime. On the other hand, living in hope, seeing the positive aspect (or outcome) of each situation, and allowing your Soul to shine Its Light, all help you dwell in a high vibration, which leads to the fulfillment of your True life-mission and the manifestation of True prosperity in your life.

That being said, it is ok to occasionally do some soul searching and to think about what went wrong in a particular situation, in order to draw conclusions and learn how to do (or feel or think) things differently to avoid the difficulty and breeze through similar situations in the future. That is part of the learning that your Soul wants you to do in this lifetime. And it is this learning (and conclusion drawing) that would lead you to rise above the challenges and into the bliss. For example, a while back a friend of mine was going to see a great psychic healer. To honor the rules of sacred reciprocity, since this healer does not accept monetary compensation, she baked him a cake. However, since she was very excited about the opportunity to see this healer (who was very hard to get an appointment with), things did not go well in the kitchen. The first cake she baked, she realized after baking that she had put two cups of salt instead of sugar. So she dumped the cake, and baked another one. Only this time, the cake didn't rise. She set that one aside, deciding to give it to her children later, and baked a third cake. This time, she left it too long in the oven and the cake came out too dry. She then baked a fourth cake, and it rose and then crashed. As time was running short, she just picked the best one, and took it to see the healer, whom she had never met before. As the famous healer opened the door, he took one look at her aura, and then at the cake in her hand and said: "didn't you get my message? I don't like cake!" In this case, after the second cake, it might have behooved her to try and tune into higher consciousness to figure out what the lesson there was. Had she done that, she might have tuned into the fact that it was inappropriate to bring this man cake. What the bigger lesson here was is not for me to know. It may have been doing for others what is best for them instead of what you think you would enjoy; or it might have been a lesson about being able to receive without always needing to be the giver—receiving the healing without feeling the urge to give anything in return. Whichever the lesson, it is only for her to know. The point is, if you are doing something over and over without success, don't get frustrated. Tune into your Higher Self, find out what the message is that your Soul is sending you, and implement the advise in the decisions of your here-now self.

However, there is a difference between doing some reckoning, and dwelling in the negative feelings and vibration of a difficult experience. Sure, if you've been through a difficult experience, especially if you've been wronged in any way, you have the right to feel angry, lost, unhappy, hurt, or whatever the case may be. Those feelings are all legitimate, but what purpose would dwelling in them serve? Does it serve your higher purpose in life? Does it lead to happiness, health and prosperity? Or does dwelling in these negative feelings actually prevent you from experiencing love and joy? As far as manifestation of prosperity, you already know that dwelling in the negativity of bad experiences prevent you from graduating their lessons, and keeps you from tapping into the Divine funnel of Abundance. As we have discussed in Chapter 2, once you have navigated your way out of a difficult experience according to the wisdom of your Soul, the suffering is over, and you now have a lot to feel joyous about: you can feel proud of the way you dealt with the situation and who you have become as a result of it; or you can feel deeply satisfied if during the challenge you have let your Light shine. The most important thing to feel happy about is the new brighter reality you found yourself in once you've moved past the lesson of this challenge, as most challenges do navigate your Lifepath onto greener pastures.

And there is a simple reasoning to why you need to dwell in what you *do* want in order to manifest it in your life. When you dwell on what you *do* want, you shift your energetic vibration to match that of what you want, which sends an energetic signal that echo throughout the Universe… creating a vibrational resonance between you and the object of your desire. Because what you want already exists in the Universe at large (a concept that will be better explained in Chapter 6), you just need to resonate with it vibrationally-energetically in order to magnetize it to you. The simplistic way of understanding this is – making yourself feel like a million dollars actually helps magnetize that money to you. Making yourself feel and energetically vibrate as a person who's beloved and happy helps co-Create that happiness and loving relationship into your life.

But I know that making yourself feel prosperity that you cannot yet see in your physical reality is not easy to do. Most of us are creatures of habit. And at some level, we all fear the unknown, even if it holds the key to our happiness. As explained in Chapter 3, even on a physiological level we are all addicted to our predominant past feelings by means of our own peptide receptors, which we are capable of changing if we consciously change our predominant feelings. On a spiritual level, we have the power to change how we feel, think, and act, as our Divinely given free will gives us the power to change any thought and habit patterns that no longer serve our wellbeing. And by doing so, we vibrationally change the reality that we are co-Creating.

Another factor that plays an important part in the reality that you co-Create is faith. We've talked about the faith that you are worthy of the highest blessings; that your original Self is a radiant, most beloved child of God; and that the Universe is programed to abide by your free will. But if you think of this faith in terms of how you assert your free will, what it really mean is: don't sell yourself short! When you set goals for manifestation, make sure that you are setting them not on the lowest bar of what your here-now self thinks is possible, but on what your all-powerful Creator can help you achieve. For example, why have your eyes set on a promotion at a job you hate, when your true passion is to open up a business that would allow you to live your bliss? Why aim to get a C in a test, when you can aim for an A? Why would you want to assert your free will on staying with a romantic partner who keeps disappointing you, when God wants to send you a true soulmate, who will cherish you and be your true match? Why set as your goal getting by, or enduring, when your True Self wants to help you manifest perfect health, radiant happiness and infinite abundance?

When it comes to asserting your free will by asking the Divine or Her-His Angels for help, there is one important point to remember: all of Creation is moved by free will. This means that no Angelic or Divine power is permitted to manifest anything for you unless you ask for (authorize) it. Even if your belief system precludes you from calling upon Angelic help, still, in order to co-Create prosperity, health, love, and joy, you must ask for it, and assert your free will to manifest them.

And the first step to properly asserting your free will to co-Create prosperity is becoming aware of what you are currently asking for: take a look at some of the thoughts that are constantly going around in your mind. Be aware that your thoughts provoke feelings, and that thoughts+feelings shift your energetic vibration to reverberate throughout Creation, and magnetize to you all that resonates (and is of likeness) with your energetic vibration. So if you constantly worry about everything, imagining the worse that could happen, you are actively magnetizing occurrences of that vibratory essence to come to you. If on the other hand, you dwell in the realistic optimism of knowing that your deepest desires were implanted there by your Soul Self, being ready to take Soul inspired action to help co-Create your Ideal Lifepath, and feeling peacefully confident that with Divine help you can do it, than you are constantly transmitting that high-vibratory signal into the Universe, which in turn magnetize your wishes into manifestation.

Remember – your Soul is angelic. So if you have negative/worrisome thoughts going round and round in your mind, they are not coming from your Soul Self, but most likely from your lower Nefesh, influenced by some aspect of survival fear. Therefore, it is safe to discard those worries, and work on re-tuning into the bliss of your Soul. Even difficult life lessons or deep darker feelings, when touched by your Soul's Light, become less of a Picasso and more of a Monet, as you begin to see the harmony and beauty of the situation (or feeling), and how it is meant to inspire your Soul's growth and drive your life into a magnificent place. Thus, your Soul's perspective, even on the darkest themes, is always brighter, more hopeful, and shows you the bigger picture, which is inevitably a beautiful one. Developing this awareness of your current thoughts and feelings is the first step to re-aligning yourself with the will of your Soul. And it is this alignment that co-Creates a life that is harmonious, beloved, healthy, happy, vital, joyous, and abundant in every way.

In fact, once you are aligned with the Will of your Soul, you not only become free to co-Create what you want. But the very act of wanting expands whom you are, and expands the universe (more about this in Chapter 6). It allows your Soul to grow, learn and experience new things. To illustrate, think of a kid in a playground. You don't want your kid to be an apathetic "yes, mommy dearest" kind of a kid. Every loving parent wants to see their child run in an excited way all over the playground, because they know that's when the kid is happy and getting plenty of stimuli for her/his growth. And if the kid asks you for a bunch of snacks after the playground visit, you know she/he is growing and that makes you as a parent happy. In the same way, when you ask the Universe for the things you desire, Heaven is always happy to rearrange itself to oblige you, because your earnest desires help God expand Her-Himself through your expression of free will, as long as this fulfillment still afford you the experiences you are meant to have in this lifetime for your Soul's growth. This alignment of your will with the Will of your Soul is so monumentally important to co-Creating prosperity, that we will spend all of *Seven Stages to co-Creating Prosperity From Your Soul* going through some detailed steps, in order to help you tune into the details of your Soul's plan for you, and devise a plan for executing that plan.

Now, while superficial and capricious wishes of your here-now self may not be parts of your Ideal Lifeplan, your innermost yearnings and desires are integral parts of your Ideal Lifeplan, and were implanted there by your very own Soul. And remember that when it comes to your Ideal Lifeplan, Ideal means ideal! No "I can't," "this is too good for me," or "I don't have the resources" excuse could keep the door to your Ideal Lifepath locked before God. And God wants to give you all that You (your Soul) could ever wish for.

So the bottom-line when it comes to how to how to best exercise your free will to co-Create prosperity in your life is: Go ahead! Make God's day! Assert your free will by making the boldest wishes you can make – the thought of which makes your heart jump for joy!

Freedom

Freedom goes beyond freedom of choice, and speaks to the very essence of who you are in the greater sense. Of course your spirit is ultimately free from the very inception of your Soul.

However, as the spirit of God filters into the "physical" layers of reality, there are several layers of freedom.

The <u>first layer of freedom</u> is the one that's obvious to most people—freedom within one's life circumstances, such as financial freedom, free time to do what you want, and freedom from obligation to others to name a few. But when you take a deep enough look at each of those, it becomes obvious that most of those are very subjective, to the point that some of the limitations that might be obstructing those freedoms are self-imposed. For example, your obligation to your friends and family are self-imposed, since it is your own inner commitment to them that is making you do things for them, not an obligation that is imposed by anyone else. Now putting those obligations ahead of the one you have to yourself is also a matter of choice. As we shall see in *A Lifestyle of Prosperity From Your Soul* (the third book of this series), the free time that you have is also a subjective matter, which depends on how much free time *you make* for yourself.

$$\frac{\text{What you have}}{\text{What you want}} = \text{Wealth}$$

Even the level of your financial freedom depends on how much you want. For example, a multi-millionaire can be considered very poor if this person has, say ten million dollars, but he/she wants fifty million dollars. So if you look at the formula above, then the wealth factor of this multi-millionaire is only a ⅕! In comparison, if a person who only makes $4,000 a month and has no savings, only desires $2,000 per month, her/his wealth factor is 2, and he/she can be considered ten times richer than the multi-millionaire in our example. So wealth too is relative. Now by that, I'm not suggesting wanting less, for as we've discussed, it is good to aim bold – in accordance with the highest Will of your Soul. I am merely saying that your concept of freedom that your circumstances afford you is a subjective matter – it is what you make of it. And of course, as you are learning to do in this book, all of your life circumstances are subject to change/upgrade, by the correct assertion of your free will.

Beyond circumstantial freedom, <u>the second layer of freedom is freedom of mind</u>, which comes from the conceptual rational understanding that you are free to choose… that you can change any of your life circumstances. Now, it is true that everything has consequences, good or bad. But the freedom of mind here comes from fully realizing that the choice is still yours to make. It is your free choice to drive through a red light, as long as you know it is going to limit your financial freedom when the fine comes, and as long as you've weighed those two choices and have decided which one asserts more freedom for you in the bigger picture. In the same way, it is your free choice to commit a crime, as long as you know that it's going to limit your freedom to roam around when the prison term comes, and you've weighed the choices to see which one asserts more freedom in the bigger picture. You see, it isn't the government that is limiting your freedom. It is you who are choosing not to exercise these lower options, because you don't like the consequences. You choose to be a law-abiding citizen not because someone is imposing that choice on you, but because that is the choice that allows you the most amount of freedom in the greater sense. I'd like to believe that we each choose the higher-vibrational options, not only because we are afraid of bad consequences, but perhaps also because at some level, we tune into our Souls' wisdom, consider the discomfort we would cause someone else if we exercised low-vibrational choices, and consequently adopt the highly moral choices of our Souls, sort of like an inbuilt moral conscience. Whichever the motivation—selfish or benevolent—this level of understanding freedom extends to all other areas of life. It is you who is choosing to give of your time and resources to your family; it is you who are choosing to stay at a job you don't like; and it is you who has the power to free yourself from all circumstances that do not serve your highest purpose. But even this realization is still just a mental freedom. In order to shift your energetic vibration into the likeness and resonance that would magnetize what you want to you, you need to *feel* free.

So the third layer of freedom is truly *feeling* free, knowing deep inside you and with everything that you are that you are ultimately free to go anywhere, do anything, and be all that you want to be. It is easy to *feel free* once you've chosen a higher path that is more inline with your Higher Self, and much harder when faced with a less than ideal circumstance, especially if you perceive yourself to be imprisoned by the circumstances of your life. But you need to realize that feeling too is a matter of choice: you can choose to feel weighed down by life's burdens, or you can choose to feel lighthearted about it and say to yourself- "OK, this situation is temporary. I will soon find a way to co-Create a different situation that is more reflective of the lightness and freedom of my True Self." This feeling of freedom is more than just a comforting thought. It really is a freedom of spirit that shines through. For example, not long ago, I was watching a difficult episode of "Dr. Quinn Medicine Woman," the historic background of which were the pioneers that came to live in the West in the 1800s. In this episode, the Cheyenne shaman "Cloud Dancing" was a sole survivor after his entire family and tribe were killed in the infamous massacre of Washita. (The massacre of Washita is a historical fact. The story of Cloud Dancing, I'm guessing, is fictitious.) And to add insult to injury, the army was now demanding his surrender into degrading captivity in a small reservation shared with survivors from his enemy tribes. The shaman had thought long and hard about this, knowing that refusing the captivity would make him a fugitive and risk his life, but accepting it would be insufferable. It was deep meditation that made the shaman see a way of winning even through surrendering to the captivity. The insight that "the spirits" gave him was that although physically he would be in captivity, by surviving *and keeping his spirit free*—allowing his True Light to shine through even despite his situation, he would be honoring the memory of his people. Although the particular story of Cloud Dancing and Dr. Quinn are fictional, it touched me as it reminded me that the spirit of a great person (in this case medicine-man) can always be free, even despite extremely limiting physical circumstances. And in reality (as opposed to in a fictional TV series), when one finds a way to truly *feel* this freedom of spirit within the depth of her/his heart, the freedom itself usually finds expression in the manifested circumstances of one's life.

However, I know that this *feeling* of optimism and faith may not always be easy to come by. Acknowledging that it is You (your Higher Self) who have co-Created all of your circumstances for your own Soul growth is a good place to start tuning into the feeling of freedom. This acknowledgment may help you go deeper and finally find the feeling of freedom within you. And it is this feeling of absolute freedom that empowers you to break free of whatever your particular prison is. To be clear: we're not talking about leaving behind your wife and baby, or becoming a bank-robber, as the wisdom of your Soul Self would never lead you to such low-vibrational choices. We are talking about a liberation of the spirit, fully tuning into its freedom and powers of co-Creation. It is this deep knowing-feeling of your ultimate freedom that is going to help you co-Create real freedom (including financial freedom) in the circumstances of your life.

To illustrate how important the feeling aspect is, have you ever heard about a millionaire-gone-bankrupt, who after a few years became a millionaire again? Consider that the financial debt and despair of a millionaire-gone-bankrupt is much deeper than yours. How is it, than, that this deeply in-debt person can go on to become a millionaire? It isn't due to financial know-how, because his financial "know-how" didn't really get him anywhere good the first time; and it isn't even this person's connections in the financial world, since if he/she person is bankrupt, than by definition he/she has burnt some financial bridges by declaring a bankruptcy and not honoring his/her financial obligations. So what is it that gives this person the ability to become a millionaire again? Simple – he/she has already had a real life experience of what it *feels like* to be wealthy. So it is easier for him/her to tune into the *feeling* of being wealthy. It is this *feeling* that shifts his/her energetic vibration to resonate and therefore attract wealth again. So if feeling is such an important part of asserting your freedom and co-Creating your desires, you can do it too. And you don't need an actual life experience to tune into that feeling of freedom.

One way to illustrate this feeling of freedom that I'm talking about is movies. Have you ever watched a drama in which the main characters lose their jobs, their house, and pretty much everything they own, but their lives were spared? And don't you always feel incredibly relieved at the end, knowing that as long as the characters have their health, as long as they have joy in their hearts, and as long as they have each other, they'll always be able to find another job and co-Create new prosperity for themselves? And after the movie but while still immersed in your identification with the character, don't you usually feel empowered knowing that the new life that these characters will co-Create would be even better than the one that was destroyed? So as you reflect on how you *felt* after seeing those movies, let me ask you: why can't you feel that liberation and empowerment about *your own* life? Your life, most likely, is already without the drama of the movie: in the "now" of your life, you are not facing the dangerous situations that the character was facing; you have a roof over your head *now*; you still have a source of income *now*; you have your health *now*; and you *already are beloved* by your friends and family *now*! And given that you have all of your basic needs met, you already are at a better starting point to co-Create all kinds of prosperity into your life. Once you understand that point, you don't need to keep watching drama movies to feel free and lucky. You can just remind yourself to feel free and be the best version of yourself daily.

This brings us to <u>the fourth layer of freedom</u>—the freedom to harness your God-given free will to co-Create the most auspicious circumstances in your life. And as we have discussed in the previous section, this involves bringing the will of your here-now self into alignment with the Will of your Soul, so you can enjoy your most Ideal Lifepath in this here-now reality.

Now, adhering to the will of your Soul doesn't always make sense in the present physical circumstances of your life. For example, in 2002, I had to make a decision whether to stay in Florida or move to California. At the time, staying in Florida made more sense for my career, since the airline that I was working for had turboprop airplanes based in Miami, which would have allowed me quicker upgrade into a captain's position, doubling my salary. Moving to California meant that I had to fly a jet airplane, but remain a first officer for a few more years before I could upgrade to captain. Career and money wise, the move to California did not make any sense at all. But to my heart, California has always felt like home. And I knew with every fiber of my being that I just wanted to be in California. Now in retrospect, moving to California was the best choice I could have made. California inspired me to go to massage therapy school; gave me the opportunity to spread the Divine Light and healing energy through the use of reiki healing in my massage work; and fostered the grounds for me to become a kundalini yoga teacher and a doctor of divinity (all of which, by the way, I did above and beyond my airline job, just because healing people and teaching them about their greatness were my passions). But most importantly, being here has inspired me to get to know my True Self, and my highest life-mission. And how could a choice like that be anything but the right one?

So I'm not saying that you should quit a well paying job tomorrow, just on a whim. I'm not saying that cutting the branch on which you stand is a good choice. But if speaking up your Truth firmly but kindly makes you feel free, than perhaps standing up to your boss out of peaceful strength will not get you fired. Perhaps it would only make your boss respect you more. In any given situation, there are an infinite number of choices that could be made. And you have the freedom to make them, knowing that one of those choices is the right one that is in accordance with highest Lifeplan. And it is usually the choice that makes your heart sing... the one that empowers you and makes you feel lightness, freedom, joy, and love. Finding out what that highest choice is, and asserting your free will accordingly, will always lead you to success and happiness.

<u>The fifth</u> and highest <u>layer of freedom</u> is the liberation that happens when you finish your journey on Earth. But there are many freedoms that you need to reclaim between now and then, while you are here enjoying this earthly life. For example, going back to the first level—freedom of circumstances: Now, knowing the hierarchy of freedoms that build up to being able to freely co-Create your circumstances, there are things that you can do to catalyze the feeling of freedom and tune into your Soul's power to co-Create Its free will. You may manipulate your circumstances to give you the opportunity to learn to feel free. Moses had to lead the Israelites round and round in the desert for forty years before coming into the promised land, because he had to let the old generation, who had slaves mentality, die. But you don't have to wait until liberation from the physical in order to learn to be free. You don't even have to wait forty years.

Another example from my own life is: when I was young, I used to have flying dreams in which I would soar like an eagle. When I was 21 and it was time to choose a profession, since I still didn't know what my flying dreams meant, I chose to become an airline pilot. It took me twelve years to make that dream come true, and then another eight years to become a captain, a total of twenty years. But it wasn't until I became a reiki master that I realized that the True way in which my Soul wanted me to fly was in spirit, and that my true calling was to be a messenger of Light. In retrospect, I asked myself: were the twenty years that I devoted to the airline dream wasted? And that's when I realized they weren't. Those twenty years were about learning how to be free. In my particular case, I learnt how to be a good world traveler... I learnt the simple skill of communicating with people even when I don't speak their language. And I learnt to feel free and at home anywhere on God's earth. So in my case, those were the skills I needed to learn to break free from the limiting circumstances of my childhood, before I could truly tune into the freedom feelings that would allow me to co-Create auspicious life-circumstances for myself. But for you it doesn't have to take twenty years. Once you realize that much of your earthly "play" is about asserting your freedom, it doesn't have to take you twenty years to teach yourself to tune into the feeling of freedom. You can do little things to create opportunities that would re-acquaint you with the natural feeling of freedom that you were always meant to have.

One of the things that I have found very helpful for tuning into that feeling of freedom is writing what I call a "Freedom Journal." I usually start my day doing a little reiki healing on myself so I could feel really positive about the day. But I know that once I am fully out of bed and start breakfast, I'll get into a go-go-go productive mode, and the opportunity to communicate with my Soul Self would be lost, at least until the evening. I guess we all have those moments of shifting gears from our morning daydream into a productive mode. So before I make this shift, I open up my special Freedom Journal and I log in one or two paragraphs, "if I were living my life out of total freedom today, I would…" This simple process takes less than 5 minutes to do, and goes a long way to set my spirit free. Because even though I may then spend the day running errands or doing chores, envisioning what I would do with that day if were living completely free—without fear or encumbrance of any kind, vibrationally and energetically connects me with the aspect of me that *is* riding a horse as free as the wind on a sparkling beach. And writing it down brings that freedom from vibration into some physical form, planting seeds for that freedom to manifest in my life one day soon. Freedom Journal is a fantastic tool. I invite you to try it. I promise that you'd be amazed at how an ordinary day can turn into a sparkling one, once you have vibrationally connected with the freedom of your spirit.

Manifestation – Yogic Style

The ancient yogis were very in tune with the energetic nature of Creation. And as you'll understand in the next chapter, there is indeed a real link between co-Creating something ethereally, and manifesting it in our "physical" reality. So let's harness some of that yogic wisdom to deepen our understanding of the co-Creative process.

According to yogic (Sikh) tradition, in any manifestation, whether thought, matter, action or event, it is almost irrelevant whether it has reached the "physical," or is still an ethereal manifestation. Right from the instant of its Creation, every manifestation has five aspects that give it its unique "flavor:" It has a certain vibrational essence (antar); its dimensional properties (jantar), or its potential dimensional properties if the object has not yet manifested in the physical; it has the particular structure, senses and qualities that (would) supports it (bantar); it has specific sound vibration (mantar or mantra) that correspond with its vibrational essence; and it has a specific visual form (yantar). So for example – the thought of having a million dollars, when it comes to its full manifested form, may actually have the dimensional properties of 4"x9"x21" (the dimensions of the briefcase holding the money); the structure that supports it is either a bank or a briefcase; its sound vibration would be the swooshing of the paper bills; its visual form is green in color; and its essence is that of joy (laughing all the way to the bank).

Ancient yogic tradition notes that whenever you can act in alignment with the True essence of a thought (before it becomes clouded by your human biases), you gain power to either manifest or to block the manifestation of those thoughts. In our understanding, acting in alignment with a thought's True essence really means acting in alignment with the angelic Will of your Soul, which is always anchored in a higher vision, and is therefore empowered to manifest. So in the example of a million dollars, if the thought of having it is not coming out of greed or fear of lack, but from the True Will of your Soul, meaning that those million dollars actually have real purpose in your Ideal Lifeplan (such as a project that serves the highest good of yourself and others), than the minute you perceived of the idea or project associated with it out of a pure and crystal-clear thought, if that thought reverberates harmoniously through all of whom you are, than at that moment you actually co-Create it—instantly. We will talk in the next chapter about why you don't yet see your co-Creation immediately in your physical reality, and how to actually pull it into physical manifestation in your life. But for now, it is important to understand that thoughts that are in alignment with your True Self and are accompanied by passionate feelings do shift your entire energetic vibration and therefore manifest the things that are of like resonance into your reality.

According to yogic tradition, Creation originates from the Oneness of the unmanifest Creator. The Divine consciousness then becomes sound vibration (naad), which then differentiates into the energetic-creative force of Shakti, and the destroying force of Shiva, in an everlasting balance, which could be understood to hint that the universe is actually destroyed and reCreated every moment anew (as we'll explore in the next chapter). At that stage, Creation introduces Maya—the illusion that makes us believe that this reality is physical and tangible. Maya has three different aspects or forces of nature, each of a distinct nature: Tamas, which are heavy, confused, concealed, slow, persistent; Rajas, which are fiery, active, initiative, transformative; and Sattva, which are subtle, sublime, clear, neutral and pure. Each of these forces of Nature are then associated with a distinct quality of mind, each of which are an aspect of Universal Mind: Tamas are associated with Manas—the lower sensory mind, which also includes all subconscious mental attitudes and programing usually dealt with in psychotherapy; Rajas are associated with Ahangkar—the here-now self aspect of the self, which gives us a sense of self identity (ego), attachment, boundary, commitment; and Sattvas are associated with Buddhi, which perceives reality from an heavenly intuitive perspective. What manifests our physical reality, according to this theory, is the blending of these three forces in various proportions together with the five elements of Creation: ether, air, fire, water, and earth, which can be perceived as five levels of density of reality.

Now if we discard all the Sanskrit names, this can all be simplified: God becomes a Creator as She-He intends to Create and speaks the world into existence. This means that She-He shifts Her-Himself into a Creative vibration that can be understood as sound (celestial music?). Her-His Creation is ethereal at this point, but is constant—always destroying what no longer serves in order to regenerate and Create new Light (this is the concept of Shiva and Shakti). In the next stage, the Creative process flows into differentiated individualities by Creating different combinations of 3 aspects of each Soul: the Heavenly Neshama (equivalent to Boddhi), the lower instinctual Nefesh (equivalent to tamas/manas), and the firy-windy aspect of Ruach (equivalent to Rajas/

Ahangkar), which gives each individual the energy to breathe life, charge forward, and facilitate the mixing of all the other aspects. It is this differentiation that starts the *perceived* separation of our individual identities. Finally, our "physical" reality is manifested by shifting the energy of our consciousness (holding within it different aspects of the Divine consciousness) into many different combinations of the different densities of Creation, which the yogis metaphorically called ether, air, fire, water and earth. As you can tell from this simplification, each manifestation originates in the Heavenly aspect of our consciousness, but is anchored into the very earthly reality.

So let's harness these yogic ideas into understanding how to co-Create prosperity in your life. Recall from Chapter 1 our discussion of the energetic bodies. Your higher energetic bodies bring the energy and consciousness of your Soul into your Casual Body (the undifferentiated Chaya aspect of your Soul). At the next state, your manifestation intent filters from your Casual Body down to your Mental Body, at which point you become consciously aware of the manifestation as an idea. At this point, if your Mental Body is unblocked and clear of energetic debris, than the thought remains very pure and untainted by any distortions or human biases. Then the manifestation intent spreads from your Mental Body down into your Astral Body, and you begin to feel it. This feeling translates in several ways: one is that you begin to feel that your ideas actually can come into fruition, and you begin to be excited about your new path. Secondly, if you are energetically sensitive, than your sixth sense is probably also picking up the subtle energy shift in the fabric of your reality, as your desired manifestation is about to bubble down into physical manifestation. It is also in the transition from the Mental Body to the Astral Body that the pure thought begins to translate into specific ideas for manifestation. But again, all of this sensing, feeling and translating is only possible if your Astral Body is free of obstruction and energetic debris. Next, the energy of this manifestation filters down into your Etheric Body and finally into your physical body and reality. And as your feelings drive you towards taking actions inspired by your Soul Self, auspicious synchronistic events bring into your life the manifestations you've pulled into this physical reality from the Divine realm through your connection to Soul, as if to show you that the Universe is meeting you more than half way. So manifestation happens in the midst between the Will of your Soul at the highest vibration, and your inspired actions.

It is interesting thing to note, though, that when yogis talk about the mind, they are not talking about the brain. They are talking about what quantum physics would call "consciousness," or "the observer," or what we call your Neshama—the aspect of your Soul that is your Higher Self, which is still differentiated into an individual identity. Recall from Chapter 1 that as you go upwards in components of your Soul, two integral aspects of your Soul are Chaya (the Divine life-force) and Yechida (Divine Oneness). As you filter down into the here-now level, the first aspect that becomes differentiated to individual consciousness is Neshama. Recall, however, that this part of yourself is not necessarily localized to the human body, but is free roaming through the Universe, and lives on after the physical life ends. Your Neshama, than, is part of Divine Intelligence, as is beginning to be understood by researchers today who are researching the quantum nature of consciousness[1].

The most important thing to understand from this yogic theory *is the part where you can exercise control over this process.* As your higher consciousness is a driving force in manifestation, let's understand the nature of thought from a yogic perspective. Yogic tradition believes that each thought actually originates from Divine Intelligence. The thought then becomes the domain of the individual's higher intellect, which is the Neshama aspect of your Soul Self. At this point, the thought is still crystal clear and radiant with its highest Divine essence. But from this point on, as the thought filters down into the Ruach, and eventually into the lower instinctual Nefesh level of your here-now consciousness, it becomes fogged by your past traumas, your emotional baggage, the scars of disappointments of life, and unresolved karmic issues. And there is no judgment or shame in this statement. We all see the world through stained glasses of one color or another. It's all part of the human experience. Now here is the first of the points at which your here-now self can exercise its free will and influence your co-Creations: Once you become a skilled meditator, you can meditationally tune into the pure intent of your Soul that's behind a particular thought, so you can perceive what that thought was at its pure state, before it became obscured and fogged by your human shortcomings. To effect a more permanent change—to minimize the fogging and distortion of thoughts in general in your life, and maximize your ability to retain the pure guidance of your Soul, daily meditation can help you use your intent (free will) to clear your energetic bodies of psychic debris, emotional scars and mental blocks, so that when the thought filters into your emotional and then physical reality, it manifests in accordance with the True intent of your Soul. Now just why would you need to meditate daily in order to cleanse your energetic apparatus well enough to be a conscious co-Creator of your life? Because it isn't that you do this cleansing once, and they you'd be Houdini from then on. We live in an energetically dense reality in which stress and disappointment reoccur daily to one degree or another. So in order to keep your energetic apparatus clear of obstructions and conducive to the high-vibrational manifestations that your Soul wishes for you, you need to not only clear your energetic apparatus, but also *keep* it clear on a daily basis. I actually do this clearing several times a day. I will give you some fantastic tools to do that in *Seven Stages to co-Creating Prosperity From Your Soul*.

But since most of us are not saints, we have human shortcomings, which keep us from always being crystal clear energetically, there is another point, at which your here-now self can exercise its will even after a thought is already clouded by your human imperfections. After a thought gets to the domain of the here-now self and mixes with your unconscious programing, it generates human level emotions. But even at that point, you can decide to attach to this thought-emotion, or stay non-attached. If you attach to this thought-emotion, it becomes a stronger desire involving physical action of your glands and nervous system, which will usually lead you to either action or re-action. Then, if your re-action is low vibrational and contradicts the angelic will of your Soul, it will accumulate more karma (a need for a corrective Soul lesson). If, on the other hand, your action is anchored in the true vision of your Soul (dharma), than it can actually help erase negative karma and bring you closer to liberation, since acts of dharma show that you've learnt the Soul lessons and have grown with them. However, before you allow the thought-emotion to beef up into desires and action (or re-action), you have another choice: you also have the choice not to attach to it, to just dismiss it and not to take action.

The concept of non-attachment is huge when it comes to clearing your energetic bodies and becoming a conscious co-Creator. As you realize you have the choice to not attach to negative thoughts and feelings, the practice of non-attachment can become an important tool to cleanse your mind, so that you can co-Create only that which you Truly want. And the concept is really simple to understand (although not always so simple to do): if a thought evokes a negative feeling, you can rest assured that it did not originate from your Soul, at least not this particular twist of the theme.

Now, I'm not saying that you should blindly wipe off your mind all annoying thoughts that come up. Some here-now level recurring thoughts may actually be clues from your Higher Self. If, for example, you're having a recurrent thought like, "Damn, I just can't seem to get away from this annoyingly huge cable bill!" it doesn't mean that you should throw away the cable bill and not pay it, or that you should put the issue out of your mind forever. At some point when you are calm and centered, it may behoove you to do some thinking and deal with this matter… maybe you don't need all those movie channels and pay-per-views that you've ordered, especially not if you're going to spend all that time getting excited about your new prosperous Lifepath. But in this example, although your Soul Self may be directing your attention to an area of your life that needs attention, it sure didn't initiate the frustration tone of the thought. So the "damn," the "annoying," and the negation ("can't seem to…") tone of your thought absolutely did <u>not</u> come from your Soul Self, but from your here-now self's interpretation of it! In the purity of your Higher Self, the thought might have been something like: "My beloved self, watching so many hours of TV does not do justice to the radiant being that you are, or to your new path of becoming a conscious co-Creator," or it could have even been something like: "Watch out, the cable company is ripping you off and you need to stand up for yourself out of peaceful strength." Do you see the difference between the clouded thought and the original clear thought that came from your Higher Self in this example? That is a perfect example of the difference between the clear and loving message from your Soul Self, and the fogged/distorted message once it gets to your here-now level of consciousness. So you can always discard any negative thoughts and feelings, and assume they are either your human distortion of the pure message that originated from your Soul, or even psychic debris that you are picking up from the collective unconscious or from other people in your immediate sphere. The bottom line is that these low vibrational thoughts did not originate from your True Self, because your Soul is always blissful, radiant, and Angelic. And since the more aligned you get with the True will of your Soul, the more successful a co-Creator you become, it makes sense to discard those low vibrational thoughts and feelings. And meditation can help you do that. We'll work on developing your meditational skills throughout *Seven Stages to co-Creating Prosperity From Your Soul*.

The Infinite Funnel Of Abundance

Putting the yogic perspective aside, let's fine-tune our understanding of just what it is that gives you the power to co-Create your life.

The short of it is: your God-given free will is what gives you the power to co-Create your reality. That is, God expresses Her-His Will through you. At the same time, you glorify God when you experience life joyfully. While some of the experiences and trials we go through here on Earth seem discordant, it is never God's intent to make you suffer, but rather to give you a chance to fully experience the beauty and capacity of the human spirit. Each discordant theme in your life gives your beautiful spirit a chance to rise above the challenge and turn the situation into a perfect victory. That is why all this manifestation stuff really works! Because God wants you to rise above the chaos, the misery, the stress, the illness, and the lack, and reclaim your highest potential! She-He wants you to co-Create your most Ideal Lifeplan, in which you thrive and let your Soul shine with all of its glory. And as explained in chapter 2, your Ideal Lifeplan is the best possibility of a life in which you hold the stick in both ends—you get the lessons your Soul needs for Its growth, and you go through them most harmoniously, living a healthy, happy, abundant life.

And there is a simple reason why God is rooting for your success: She-He *is* you, and you are Her-Him! Who you really are is an expression of God, through whom God is experiencing an aspect of Her-Himself—as you. Each of us and every rose along your path is another form through which God is experiencing Her-Himself. So God ultimately wants to have a good time on Her-His adventure park called Earth. It's true that She-He may enjoy some suspense, in the same way that some of us enjoy watching a suspense drama, or a thriller movie. But ultimately it's about *enjoying* the experience, and co-Creating more Love in the world in the process. That is the whole purpose of our existence. Why else venture out of the stillness of blissful Infinity but to experience your greatness, and to expand the amount of Love, Light and joy in the world?

Now the reason why I call the process of manifestation "co-Creation" is because God is really who is manifesting your wishes for you. That is, you provide the free will through your conscious intent to manifest something in your life, and God provides Her-His power to manifest it. It's kind of like when you were a little kid working with your dad to create a school project. You had the idea of how you want to create the project; you drew the picture of your concept with your crayons, and dad went into the garage (or store), got all the necessary materials, and helped you put your project into manifestation. Now granted, you may have helped your dad put it together, and you sure took full credit for it at school. But your dad was really the one that manifested the project for you. The same is true with God. You provide the idea—the vision of what you truly desire, and God is providing the materials and the mojo to make it happen. More esoterically, you can think of it as you building a funnel, and God pouring Her-His Light into it. In a very real way, God is allowing and providing the mojo for every breath you take, every choice you make and every action you take. But it is the sum of all levels of your free will and intent that drive the manifestation trolley in a particular direction. You provide the blueprint, and God provides the bricks and cement to turn it into a building. But of course, this illustration is an oversimplification, since you and God are not really separate.

In case you are wondering about competing with others over resources, remember that God's resources for giving you (and everyone else) abundance are <u>unlimited</u>! And since She-He IS everything that exists, manifesting a huge house for you is just as easy for God as manifesting a small studio apartment. And in the same way, for God, manifesting millions of dollars is just as easy as manifesting $1, provided these are the true wishes of your Soul Self. So when you allow the Light of your Soul to guide your life, since your Soul is an integral part of God, you are then automatically connected to an Infinite Source through which to manifest an abundance of… everything you Truly want. That is why I call it the Infinite Funnel of Abundance.

To tap into your most potent powers of co-Creation and into the Infinite funnel of Abundance, all you basically need to do is dwell in, live by, and merge with the essence of your Soul, and bring Its consciousness into your here-now reality. To do that you need to get all parts of you – all chakras, energetic bodies, meridians, and all aspects of your Soul into perfect harmony and balance with one another. So in *Seven Stages to co-Creating Prosperity From Your Soul* and *A Lifestyle of Prosperity From Your Soul*, I give some tools for tuning into your Ideal Lifeplan, and bringing about the auspicious alignment with your Soul Self that would bring about the health, happiness and prosperity you were meant to have.

The Roles Belief Systems Play in co-Creation

Having a religious belief, or even believing in this concept that co-Create your life are not necessary for empowering you to co-Create your life. You already are co-Creating the circumstances of your life. But what I want to look at in this section are your pre-existing beliefs as filters through which your manifestations must pass. And let me start by saying that they exist as filters *because* you empower them with your belief.

Despite the comfort that they may give you, religious rituals in and of themselves do not hold the key to successful co-Creation of an auspicious life or afterlife. It is your belief in them that give them the power to influence your life. So for example, if you deeply believe that you must eat only kosher food in order to win God's favor, than you absolutely must follow through on that belief in order to co-Create a favorable life! This is because your belief shifts your paradigm of reality and co-Creates the precondition of eating kosher foods as manifestation filter through which favorable co-Creations must pass before they manifests. It's kind of like a self-fulfilling prophecy. On the other hand, if you believe you must eat pork dipped in cheese every day in order to win God's favor (the opposite of kosher), than that shifts your paradigm of co-Creation the other way in the same manner. In that case eating these non-kosher foods becomes the restrictor before favorable life would manifest. Both shifts are valid, and create preconditions that act as limiting filters to your God-given powers of co-Creation, if you deeply believe in them. Other examples are: if you wholeheartedly believe that you must be saved by Jesus in order to live Heaven on earth, than that shifts your paradigm and manifests a reality in which you absolutely do have to be saved by Jesus; and if you believe you must pray to Lakshmi and Ganesh, or Buddha, or even hold a certain crystal in your hand in order to manifest prosperity in your life, than that shifts your reality paradigm, and becomes the filters through which co-Creation must pass in order to manifest. It's kind of like brewing a pot of hot coco with marshmallows, and then pouring the drink over a filtering strainer. The strainer blocks the marshmallows from pouring into your cup. This may be intentional, as you may be on a diet. But when it comes to co-Creating blessings in your life, do you really want to block God's marshmallows (blessings) from pouring into the cup of your life?

However, the purpose of the section is not to sway you in any way, but to help you develop a higher perspective on what is in your best interest and what is not. If your current belief system already works for you; and if it empowers you to co-Create health, love, and abundance in a way that makes you absolutely happy, than don't change it! But if it doesn't, realize that you yourself have empowered this belief system to limit the manifestation of favor in your life. Many of the old belief systems revolved around crime and punishment. And how many times do preachers devote their entire Sunday sermons to making it clear to their congregation that we are all sinners and instill fear of the "consequences?" The Truth is that God loves you whether you give up your favorite thing in Lent or not; She-He loves you whether you fast in the month of Ramadan or not; and She-He loves you whether you eat pork or kosher food. There is no sacrifice or abstinence required for manifestation of prosperity. The only condition is that you co-Create only that which makes you happy on the highest level—the level of your Soul. That's it. So whether you believe in Her-Him or not, God believes in you, and wants to give you all the abundance you are willing to receive, freely, effortlessly, unobstructed by any filters, and bound only by your highest free will!

Internal Experience – Alternate Points for Viewing

So far, we have understood how important free will is in the process of co-Creation, what gives you the power to co-Create your life, and the role that your belief system plays in the process. But let us take our understanding into the meat and bone of the process of co-Creation: what do you have to do to bring your thoughts and ideas into manifestation in your life?

The notion that visualizing what you want manifests it, as some movies and books have suggested, is a near-truth. Even the notion that just feeling happy manifests good things is a bit of an oversimplification of the process. The Truth is that in order to co-Create something, you have to vibrationally become like it. That is, your vibrational essence has to become identical to the vibrational essence of what you want in order to create the mutual resonance that attracts it into your life. Two water droplets on a windshield attract because they are alike—their chemical polarity is the same, and their vibrational energy is the same. And so they attract, as if magically, to form one bigger drop of water. If, on the other hand, one drop was of vinegar and the other drop was of oil, they would not attract. In fact, they would not mix homogeneously even if you try to shake them in a bottle. Now as you might have guessed, this does not mean that you actually have to have a million dollars to feel like a million dollars, hence the expression: "I feel like a million dollars." It just means that if a million dollars is your co-Creation goal, you have to get yourself to internally feel as you would when you get your million dollars—before it happens. It's kind of like a "fake it till you make it" type of deal.

Now the only successful way to truly vibrate in an identical frequency as what you want is to have a complete Internal Experience of it. What gets your energetic vibration into likeness and resonance with the energetic vibration of what you want is when get your inner self to fully experience reality from the perspective of having (or being) what you want. The internal experience can be better understood when you think of dreams. Have you ever had one of those dreams that you felt were so very real that it took you a while to wake up? And when you were having this dream, everything seemed so real that you woke up sweating with your heart beating fast, like you've actually run a perfect marathon, or you woke up feeling completely satisfied like you've actually had a real orgasm (excuse the down-south example here, but it's a good one). Having a complete internal experience is reminiscent of these real dreams. For example, you may have a limited budget with which to shop for necessities on a particular day. But having written your Freedom Journal that morning, you have tuned into your internal reality in which you shop freely for everything you want. So even though you may be shopping at Food For Less instead of at Whole Paycheck Market, you buy yourself some of the things that make you feel abundant and free in that moment, and more importantly – you do it with the joy of knowing that in the grand scheme of things, you are abundant.

A complete internal experience is more than just visualizing what you want, although clearly visualizing what you want does help. So do fostering positive thoughts and feelings. But what bring your energetic vibration into likeness and resonance with that abundance, and eventually magnetize it into manifestation in physical form in your life, is experiencing life from an internal reality in which you can almost smell, taste, hear, see, and touch the abundance you envision yourself in. That is why, for example, you always get plenty of dating opportunities when you already are seeing someone and are in love… because beyond pheromones, when you are in love, you are radiating a vibration of love, which attracts more love in the form of other potential mates to your new energetic vibration. That is also why the best gifts from the Universe always land in your lap when you already feel abundant. The thing is to feel abundant even if in the current physical reality of your life you can't make ends meet; to feel beloved, even if in the current reality of your life you are alone; and to feel like you are in great shape, even if in the reality of your life you are eighty pounds overweight. Now, this doesn't mean that you should stop honoring your physical limitations, for honoring physical limitations is an integral part of being kind to yourself, and perhaps also having a little 'life-smarts'. But it does mean internally living in a reality where what you want is already manifested. As an example: have you ever seen an ugly looking woman walk into a bar with an air of… "I'm the most desirable woman in here" about her? You must have noticed that every man in the bar turns to look at her, and most men find her attractive. It isn't so much because the men in this example think she is an easy lay that they find her attractive. It is because this woman projects her internal reality of beauty out into the world, and her external reality shifts to oblige her.

Now I know how hard it is to internally really feel abundant, beautiful and in shape when the external reality of things is far from it. But here is another way that meditation can come to the rescue. Meditationally dwelling in the Internal Reality of your Ideal Lifepath is a tremendous tool to help shift your energetic vibration into likeness and resonance with all that you want, and is therefore a powerful manifestation tool. We will learn to do that in *Seven Stages to co-Creating Prosperity From Your Soul*. Another tool is RezoDance, if it is offered in your area. I have had many wonderful synchronicity events happen right after RezoDance sessions, because RezoDance helps me internally experience reality from the perspective of having what I want. Auspicious synchronic events always result when one is able to have an Internal Experience of what they want so realistic that they can dwell in its joy, and project that joy vibration into the world. We have all had days in which we get out of bed in the morning on the wrong side. And on those days it seems like everything is going wrong and every stumbling block mounts our way. On the other hand, we all have days in which we just feel radiant and happy. And miraculously, on those days, it seems like the world follows suit: the cashier in the supermarket beams a kind smile to us, the postman brings us checks instead of bills, and the flowers just bloom our way. These are just some examples of how we constantly project who we are into the cosmos, and how that projection influences what resonates with our essence, and thus manifests in our lives. And here is why this makes sense:

Checks & Balances From Your Higher Free Will

Have you ever heard the expression 'God never gives you more than you can chew on'? Well, it's true. Once you are able to experience reality from the perspective of having what you want it, at least internally, it serves as a system of checks and balances, to help verify that what you think you want (what your here-now self wants) is indeed what You (your Higher Self) really want. Sometimes you experience things differently when you are immersed in them. For example, when I was nineteen years old, one of my dreams was to drive a white sporty BMW. Through the years, I have almost completely forgotten about it. But apparently the Universe did not forget the request I had put in… A couple of years back, I was doing a deep Internal Experience Meditation (see *Seven Stages to co-Creating Prosperity From Your Soul*) in which suddenly the image and feeling of driving a sporty white BMW popped into my mind amongst all the other things I wished to co-Create. For some reason, this old forgotten dream just became part of my Internal Experience vision. I dismissed the BMW vision and didn't think much of it at the time. But about a week later, I had a minor car accident that necessitated some bodywork for which I had to leave my car at the shop. As it turned out, a rental car was paid by my insurance. But that's not all… When I came into the car rental company, they had no cars to give me. So they called the BMW dealer with which they had an agreement. Twenty minutes later, I was driving a brand new white sporty BMW, for which I received a free upgrade. I drove the white sporty BMW for about a week, and the whole time, I was very uncomfortable. The car was smaller than I was comfortable with, and sat so low on the road that I could feel every bump. I was counting the days and hours until I could get my Acura back. In this case, during my Internal Experience Meditation that preceded this incident, I was concentrating on more important themes I wished to manifest in my life, and less on what it would feel like to drive the white sporty BMW. But as it was, my Soul gave me the opportunity to "test drive" it before I contemplated buying one. The point is that not everything you think you want is what You Truly want.

If what your here-now self thinks it want differs from what your Soul Self Truly wants for you (given Its perspective of the biggest picture), than the first thing you'll notice is that it is difficult to bring forth the vision into your mind, and difficult to have a complete internal experience of it. That is the first telltale that perhaps what you think you want is not really what You want. But even if you are successful having an internal experience of something that you only think you want, the meditation will allow you to fully experience it internally, and decide if the experience is pleasant or not. Don't be disappointed if the experience isn't pleasant, for it will have done you a great service by allowing you to understand that it isn't really what you want, thereby preventing you from pursuing the wrong ambition. It is totally ok to have many Internal Experience Meditations (see *Seven Stages to co-Creating Prosperity From Your Soul*), until you have one that is pleasant, and blissfully rings every bell inside you. When you get a meditational internal experience that resonates blissfully, than you know that its based on the True vision of your Soul. It is how the process was Created to be… because God wants you to be happy, healthy and abundant on all levels. She-He does not want to give you *what you only think you want*—on a whim. She-He wants to give you what you Truly want—what makes you happy on *all* levels.

As we will discuss in Chapter 6, everything that you want already exists in the Universe, at least in some realm. *Once your internal experience of what you want is real enough that you dwell in it, and dwelling in it evokes feelings of love and joy, it shifts you into a higher vibration, creating a frequency resonance between you and what you want, which in turn magnetizes it into manifestation in your physical reality. This is the key to manifestation.* Since Love is the energy from which whole universes are Created, and since love and joy are what we all come here to co-Create, they act as catalysts that amplify the volume (strength) with which your energetic vibration resonates with what you want, thereby speeding up the process of manifestation. That is the name of the game. Love is the very fabric of the Universe, and is synonymous with the essence of our Creator. Even biblical scholars knew that, since both the original Hebrew and the English translation of the Bible have instances in which God is referred to as "The Love". The more love and joy you generate from your internal experience, the stronger the energetic-vibrational resonance between you and what you want, the quicker and more powerfully it will manifest in your life.

Being able to internally experience reality from the point of having what you want also means that once your desires are co-Created and fully manifested in your life, you would be able to hold onto them, perpetuate them, and integrate them into your life. They are *of* you. You flow into them, and they flows into you… in oneness.

So for example, let's say that what you want is to have a successful new business or project. Than when you write your business plan, you will have the time to not only visualize the concepts of the business, but also think about whether the activities required by the new business suit your talents. A good idea at that point would be to meditationally ascertain for yourself how being a new business owner would make you feel. When you envision yourself having the new endeavor of your dreams, and you truly allow yourself to internally experience things from that perspective, are you stressed out, or are you joyous? Are you too busy to even sleep? Of do you have plenty of leisure time? When you meditate to have this Internal Experience, it is important that you experience joy and harmony even in the development stages of your dream endeavor, as well as success in its maturity stage. Keep asking yourself, how do I feel when this happens? What aspect of me does this endeavor bring out? Engage your senses to experience some of the sounds, smells, tastes, and physical states you would be experiencing once this new idea takes off. Do they make you blissful? Do they accentuate your Truest talents? What would help this project bring more joy to you and to others? Hopefully your Internal Experience of all stages of your dream is joyous, as this gives a green light to the Universe to grant your wish, so to speak.

In *Seven Stages to co-Creating Prosperity From Your Soul*, we will meditationally explore the different aspects of the Internal Experience as a way to tune into your Ideal Lifeplan that leads to a successful manifestation of your dreams. And of course the most nurturing step-by-step guidance on the manifestation process will be given in Level 1 Prosperity From Your Soul Course, if you choose to take it. For now, know that as you are able to internally dwell more and more in the vitality, joy, love, freshness, and hope of co-Creating what you want, and as you are able to live your life radiating these positive vibes, the physical circumstances of your life will start to change slowly but profoundly. It will feel like the Universe is conspiring to help you, for even little synchronicity events can be read as signs attesting that you are indeed radiating from the Light of your Soul, and that your internal reality is resonating powerfully with what you Truly want. It is indeed a sign that your dreams are on their way to you.

Built-In Time Delay

The sun shines on California and Japan *at the same instant*, but at different angles. We understand this difference in the angle of the sun as a difference in time – it is afternoon in California when it's morning in Japan. The arbitrary International Date Line makes it so that at the same day and moment that California is experiencing as afternoon, Japan is experiencing as the next day. It's true that once the globe continues to turn on its axis, the sun will strike California at the same exact angle that it does Japan. But if you think about it, there is no real difference in time, since it is the same sunrays that just strike both locations at different angles. This is just a little illustration to understand that time doesn't really exist. Time is a man-made invention to help us understand change and physical processes and the natural flow of things. Even quantum physicists agree that time is reversible and is just a mean for understanding change. Still, it is a dimension that is difficult for us humans to grasp.

As we will discuss in Chapter 6, in the section "Universal Travel Of Choice" in greater detail, all of your possible pasts, presents, and futures already exist. It is up to you to navigate the path of your life to the best possible future.

All that being said, in co-Creation there is a matter of timing. From the Divine perspective, the perfect timing facilitates the perfect flow of things that is harmonious for everyone. What is the right time for you, from your Soul's perspective, to co-Create a particular desire? It might be easier to understand this in the example of a new project, or a business you wish to open. Since this matter concerns others, the right timing is the time that is right not only for you, but also for society to receive the service (or goods) that you are planning to provide. In the same way, what is the right timing for your soulmate to meet you? Although your here-now self may be pushing its impatient agenda of 'right now', the most auspicious timing for all of these events to take place can only be ascertained when you have the bigger picture. And as you know, the only one who is privy to the biggest picture of all is your Soul, who is in cahoots with God. There is a Universally auspicious timing for every manifestation. And within that perfect timing, there may be a (slight or large) gap in time, between the time that you tune into your Ideal Lifeplan and internally experience its reality, and the time of its manifestation. However, this time lag was built-in there for your own highest good. And here is why:

The treasure hunt of your life is a mosaic that fits perfectly with the mosaic of everyone else in your life and in the Universe. It is a perfect harmony. No one lives in a vacuum. Think of one of the most beautiful pieces of music ever written, for example, Beethoven third symphony. Have you ever tried to listen when the musicians practice their parts on stage before the concert starts? During this practice, everyone just plays whenever they want to, with no coordination. And it doesn't sound at all like any kind of symphony. It sounds unbearable. It is only when the conductor walks in and the concert starts—when everyone plays together in the coordinated perfect timing, that the symphony sounds so heavenly beautiful. In the same way, even the smallest occurrence in the life of a person who bagged your groceries could potentially have a large affect in your life. This could be a direct result, a very indirect result, or an energetic ripple effect. For example, a couple of years ago, when I started to receive esoteric Truths as a clairaudience dictation, I was never prepared to write it let alone write a book. As a result, I usually took notes on any scrap of paper I could find, or even on a napkin at a restaurant to capture the ideas that were given to me. One time, I was sitting in a restaurant in an off-hour, and information started coming through me. So I converted the paper placemat into writing paper and started to write. As I was writing in a trans-like state, the waiter (who was also a spiritual person) asked me what it was. I told him about the information that has started to come through me, and read to him the paragraphs that I had just written, and he was in awe of it. He was the first person that said to me, "you should write a book. People would read it. I know I would!" So as "unimportant" as a waiter seems in your life, you never know when something somebody says can trigger a great idea that helps your life reach its destination. Every occurrence in your life is planned for its perfect timing, in accordance with your Ideal Lifeplan. This brings to mind the understanding that maybe your conscious wishes and positive internal experience are the ones that brought about the manifestation of your wishes; or maybe it's the other way around—maybe the very desire to co-Create a better life for yourself was planted in you by your Soul Self, like seed that's programed to sprout and bloom at a particular time that fits perfectly with the mosaic of occurrences of yours and everyone else's lives. But understand that these two concepts are not mutually exclusive. Both truths are happening simultaneously, because every occurrence in the Universe is in Oneness with all others.

On a somewhat practical level, time delays function to give you time to adjust and prepare yourself for the changes. As an example, in my efforts to lose weight, various thoughts of lap band, liposuction and the like were floating through my mind. One day as I researched this matter, it dawned on me that if I go through any of those invasive procedures, the extra skin would sag like an old lady, and my appetite would not have a chance to adjust, which may make me regain the weight in no time. I suddenly understood that the time lag between experiencing myself internally as a thin person and actually being skinny serves some important medical purposes of allowing the skin, metabolism, stomach capacity and lifestyle to change gradually. This particular example is of physiological changes. But even the happiest life circumstances take time to adjust to. As much as I want to be married to my twin-flame, I wouldn't want to just jump to the point in the future of just being married to him, because I wouldn't want to miss out on the courtship and romance that happen when two soulmates meet. Even financially, there are many examples of lottery winners who became very unhappy, because they did not get a chance to truly tune into the vision of their Soul… the way to harness that money in order to facilitate their highest Lifepath of prosperity *and* happiness. There are many more examples. But in all of them, the time delay in manifestation of your desires is for you and serves to give you time to adjust to the new reality.

If you are experiencing extensive delays in manifestation of your desired wish, you might want to do some Soul searching, quite literally. The time delays could be happening because you've tuned into the True wishes of your Soul way too far in advance of their set time for manifestation, or it could be happening because your here-now self is trying to co-Create something that is not in accordance with what your Soul wants. We will do many meditations throughout *Seven Stages to co-Creating Prosperity From Your Soul* to help you ask yourself the right questions, and tune into the answer from the perspective of your Soul Self: do you really want what you think you want? Is this desire in alignment with your Higher Self? Or is it a wish that originates from lower vibrational energies (ego, to spite, revenge, fear, or the "I'll show them" factor)? Is there another version of the same dream that could be more aligned with the will of your Soul?

Another aspect of the time delay in manifestation is that although God wants to give you everything you wish for, She-He will never give us more than we can handle—more than you are ready for. It could be likened to a light bulb: you wouldn't send two hundred watts of electricity through a light bulb that can only handle one hundred watts, because it would blow up. That is why changes in life are usually gradual, and why we have to vibrate at the same level as the things that we desire in life. Because if there is no vibrational match (resonance) between you and the things you want, than those things are not true extensions of you, which means that even if you get them, it'll be temporary and you won't be able to hold on to them. And that is another reason why it is so important to shift into likeness and create a true resonance with what you want.

Once you have adjusted internally and your vibration matches what you want, than it is *of* you. You have transcended into the reality in which this object is absolutely magnetized to come to you by your free will and by Divine Grace. And now, it is only a question of finding the perfect balance between taking inspired actions according to your Soul's vision, and allowing your life to flow with Universal guidance, awaiting the most auspicious timing for the blessings and gifts to come to you.

The Treasure Hunt of Your Life

Your life is an exciting treasure hunt in which the gifts and hidden treasures of wisdom, growth, pleasure, and abundance await you behind every experience. Although your immortal Soul is perfect from Its inception, and is an integral part of Divine, it is still through your earthly vessel that your Soul actually gathers experiences and wisdom that facilitate Its growth, create more love in the world, and therefore glorify the Divine. There is a subtle but important difference between letting the circumstances of your life rule you, and allowing your Lifeplan unfold by the guiding Light of your Soul. Learning to consciously co-Create your life involves a delicate balance between allowing your life to unfold according to your Ideal Lifeplan, and transmitting your free will into the Universe.

The Four Levels of Gifts & Wisdoms:

By Divine design, there are four levels of gifts and wisdoms given to us by the Universe. The knowledge of this distinction is important, because it gives you further insight into the different levels of manifestations that are available to you as a co-Creator, so you can become a more conscious co-Creator of your life.

NA'ALA (Sublime) –

Na'ala is the level of Divine oneness. These are the secrets of the universe – the secrets of life and death, which are revealed only after relinquishing your physical existence and returning to the True HOME of your Soul. *This level of wisdom should never be attempted during the course of one's human life.*

RAZ (clandestine, undisclosed) –

Raz are wisdoms and gifts that are hidden. And they are hidden from us for our own good. One needs to attain certain spiritual growth and understanding before learning Raz. This is so you wouldn't waste the trip to earth, because if you learnt all the hidden wisdoms of RAZ before it's time, you would skip some earthly experiences that are important for your Soul's growth.

SOD (secret) –

Sod are things that are meant for you to discover and attain through your exploration. These are gifts that are given through the treasure hunt of our life.

YESOD (foundation) –

Yesod are the everyday experiences and learnings of your instinctual earthly existence, which make you so very alive and potent in the physical existence.

There is an indivisible chain linking all four levels, through which wisdom drizzles down like a Divine cascading waterfall. We may not always recognize that a wisdom or a gift that are at the level of SOD (secret) are actually a drizzle down, or a fraction of a bigger RAZ (undisclosed); and that RAZ may be a drizzle down or a fraction of a larger Truth deeply embedded at the level of NA'ALA (sublime). But as you turn each stone in life, and explore each treasure hidden behind it, the key to knowing whether it's just a consolation prize that pleases you only in that moment, or if it is indeed a keystone that marks a new path for your most Ideal Lifepath, is the level at which it pleases you and the depth to which it resonates with you (more on that distinction in Chapter 7).

The gifts of Yesod (foundation) facilitate living in this physical reality, and ground all other gifts into your earthly existence. Sod (secret), the next higher level of gifts, are gifts that are either tangible such as prosperity, or intangible such as wisdom, which are laid out along your way to fulfilling your life's highest life mission. These gifts are meant to take you out of the mode of enduring something you hate (relationship, job, etc.) and show you a new path that is more aligned with your highest Lifeplan. But as we have discussed in Chapter 2, these Universal redirects do not have to come at a price of pain or suffering. They are simply experiences that you have to have before the gifts of Sod would manifest. This is an arrangement that best facilitates your Soul's growth. For example, how would you know that a guy you've met on a nature hike is the right person to invest in the business endeavor of your dreams, unless you shared your dried fruit and your water with him on the hike? In this example, the Universe has opportuned you a way to meet the investor on a more personal note, so that you may assess his/her energetic sincerity, and so that he/she may learn the authenticity of your intent, before you entrust your life's dream in their hand. In the same way, how would you know that a certain old lady is a phenomenal shamanic healer that can teach you much, unless you approached her in the farmers' market, and perhaps helped carry her groceries? In this example, setting up the need for you to help her carry groceries, as a prerequisite for discovering her shamanic wisdoms is how your Soul can ensure that by the time you meet your teacher, you would have acquired the compassion and spiritual capacity for understanding the wisdoms. So the knowledge is hidden from you until a certain point, for your own good.

The gifts of God could usually be discovered by going after a shimmering light and picking up the glowing crystal (metaphorically speaking) that was "calling you" at a distance—going for what you desire without fear. It is following through on your inspirations, and taking action that is guided by them. Whenever you settle for a mundane life or circumstances that are displeasing to you, and are not exploring the treasures of Sod laid out for you by your Soul. For when you set out to walk your highest path in life, your wishes will always be guided by little gifts of Sod and auspicious synchronicity events.

If your Ideal Lifeplan involves helping others, then when you walk (or rejoin) your highest Lifepath, and for the rest of your life, the jewels of RAZ (clandestine) will be given to you. They are meant to help you help others. This is how the knowledge of this book came to you through me: because it is my life's mission to help others. Therefore I was given this knowledge (as a Divine servant) to help me to do so.

One should not pursue the secrets of NA'ALA (sublime) while living a human life. Rest assured that the objectives of sublime wisdom would be served as they filter through to Raz, then Sod, and finally Yesod. And this is indeed the chain of events of manifestation: wisdom/gifts from your Soul and from the heart of God originate as Na'ala (sublime). The energy of those wisdoms filters into Raz (clandestine). At the level of Raz, the energy is still pretty etheric, but is beginning to take some form as thoughts, feelings, sixth sense intuition, or even written words. In some cases, when physical gifts are meant to help a person help others, Raz gifts can manifest as physical blessings of abundance. At any rate, after Raz, the next level of filtration into the physical is when the energy manifests as gifts of Sod—hidden blessings in the form of occurrences, wisdoms, and manifested gifts awaiting you on your exploration, when you decide to look for your highest Lifepath. Ultimately, all gifts take physical manifested form when they filter down and reach the physical level of Yesod (foundation). But notice that in order to manifest something as Yesod—manifested physical prosperity, you must walk the treasure hunt of life and explore the Sod; you must be prepared to receive Raz (clandestine) if it is meant for you; and all of those energies and wisdoms must come from Na'ala (sublime). This means that in order to harvest easy prosperity, you must walk the highest Lifepath that was meant for you. And this is not such a tall order. Because ultimately, while immersed in the human experience, the objective of all these gifts and wisdoms is for the Divine to experience their auspicious manifestation in the here-now realm, so that She-He can fully experience Her-Himself *as you* in your fully immersed human existence. Thus, the Divine objective is to integrate all the gifts into the foundation level of your being—YESOD.

And you may ask: "how do I know which gift or wisdom belongs to each level? How do I know which stone to turn?" And the answer to this one is actually quite simple. When stumbling across a potential gift, ask yourself:

- ☯ Does it give you only instant gratification? Is it a decision or a path that you may regret later? Then it relates to Yesod. It then benefits mostly the here-now level of you, but may or may not relate to higher level of actualization. Remember that there is nothing wrong with the here-now gratification, as long as this it is not contradictory to your Soul mission. The Yesod (foundation) physical level of your reality is the stage on which your life plays out. But in order for True prosperity to manifest for you, the objective is not to let this Yesod level be just the stage on which only the primal Nefesh gratifies itself. In order for prosperity to flow into your life easily and abundantly, the Yesod physical levels of your existence has to be the stage on which the highest aspects of yourself act their part. This brings us to the next level of questions:

- ☯ Does this decision enhance who you are in the bigger sense? Does this choice/path satisfy you deeply? Does it resonate harmoniously with your very core? Does it make your heart sing? Does it ring every bell within your being to play a celestial melody? Then it relates to Sod, and is a gift that is given to lead you to your highest Lifepath. Exploring this path, turning these stones, and enjoying the synchronistic gifts that the Universe gives you along this path are the gifts of Sod that lead to the co-Creation of the easiest most abundantly flowing prosperity.

- ☯ Will this gift help you help others? And does it give you hidden or metaphysical wisdoms that could shift your world, your perspective of reality, or even liberate you? Then it is truly a treasure, because you have received a Raz, which will definitely serve a higher purpose in your life and in the lives of others. Now, when you start receiving Raz, that is, when your highest life mission is to help others, the level of Universal assistance you receive tends to be much higher than when you just want to help yourself... to the point that it feels like you're being Graced into many unexpected gifts. And it makes sense. It's not really a matter of "if you're good, you'll receive a carrot." What's happening is that when your earnest-most desire is to help others, you are tuning into Universal consciousness in a bigger way, and you are Truly feeling and vibrating in oneness with all that is. And isn't All-That-Is the very Source for all abundance?

As we are all connected and are all in oneness with our Divine Creator, all wisdom and gifts are floating out there in the primordial ethers of the collective consciousness that underlies our reality. Which level of gifts we tune into, ground and acknowledge at each step depends on what we can handle at that moment of our individual personal evolution. But if you are reading these lines, chances are that you have already walked through the preliminary steps of your personal evolution, and are ready for more. You are ready to tune into the secrets of Sod, and perhaps even into the gifts of Raz, which will lead you to co-Create the life you were always meant to live—your most auspicious and prosperous Lifepath.

Being Present in the Moment

Being present in the reality of your life is not about being narrow mindedly stuck on only the observable part of your current reality. It's not about ignoring the existence of the higher aspects of your Soul. It is about allowing the Light of your Soul to shine on and manifest gifts in your here-now reality. Being present in the moment allows you to harness all that you Truly are to support your everyday reality. It means clearing your mind of the clutters of everyday stress, worry, sorrow, and other negativities, so that so that each of your moments in life is dipped in joy, which would empower you to be a powerful co-Creator of your life.

Being present in the moment means achieving a balance that allows you to be positive, joyful, resourceful, and look at every situation as an opportunity. It is a kind of neutrality that keeps you in a perfect flow with synchronistic blessings sent by your Soul through the Infinite Funnel of Abundance, to manifest in your earthly reality.

The way to achieve this "presentness" and perfect flow is to find perfect balance between the blissed-out state of your meditations and being grounded into your reality in a healthy way, through your connection to our Earth-mother (more on that in *Seven Stages to co-Creating Prosperity From Your Soul*). When you find that perfect balance, it becomes easy to appreciate every sound of a birdsong, every beautiful sunset, each fragrance in the air, and experience each moment with joy, and thus resonate at a vibration that cannot help but magnetize heaven on earth for you (True prosperity).

Savor the Journey

When it comes to co-Creating your desires, there is a balance between your efforts to bring it about, and trusting that the Universe is aligning itself to bring it to you effortlessly. And in that balance, there is a perfect flow that brings you the object of your desire at the most auspicious time for everyone involved—not a moment too soon, and not a moment too late. Within that equation, your actions and efforts to co-Create the manifestation of your prayers must be dipped in joy and in perfect faith that it is not only coming, but it is already on its way to you. This is the concept of letting go.

Letting go does not mean that you give up on your dreams. It does not mean that you stop taking action (in accordance with your Soul's wisdom) towards their manifestation. It means that you have fully tuned into your life's highest mission and the Ideal Lifeplan laid out by your Soul; you have already had the Internal Experience meditations necessary to verify that your vision is indeed aligned with the highest vision of your Soul; you have already vibrationally shifted yourself to restore your True Self that is of the same energetic vibration as your deepest wishes; and you have walked the first few steps of your plan. And this path resonates so profoundly with every fiber of your being, that it evokes in you a high level of trust—trust that your Ideal Lifepath and within it your desired manifestations are real, trust that it will come into your life at the most appropriate moment as assessed your Soul Self, and most importantly, trust that you are worthy of it. It is a level of trust that is so profound that you'd be willing to stake your life on it. And it is dwelling in the peaceful vibration of this trust that allows you to perpetuate your vibrational resonance with your desires, which causes heaven and earth to rearrange themselves to oblige you. This is kind of like a kid who really really wants a shiny new bike for Christmas. And yes, he's anxious to get to the moment of riding his new bike. But if he knows he's been a good boy this year, and he's certain that Santa (or his parents) would reward him for being a good boy, then rather than angst, the boy is going to be filled with excitement of the arrival of the new bike. In his mind, he considers it a done deal. The parents, seeing how excited the boy is in anticipation of the new bike, cannot find it in their heart to disappoint him, and so they save up the money, borrow it, or do whatever is necessary to oblige his request. And lo and behold, from the kid's perspective, come Christmas morning, magic happens: he trusted that the bike is coming, and Santa has obliged his request! And if you think of God (or the Universe) as the parent, and you as the kid, this is exactly how it works! You trust and live in the joy of knowing that your wish is already on its way to you, and the Universe cannot help but oblige you.

But here is what letting go boils down to in terms of everyday life behavior: It means that you are so certain that this vision is your True Ideal Lifepath, that you are able to let go of the pain of yearning for it and of the stress of the "how am I going to get it," and savor the waiting to fully enjoy every moment of your journey to the destination. It's kind of like a trip from Los Angeles to Carmel-By-The-Sea. You can surely take the I-5 or even the 101 Freeway, and you can stress out about traffic along the way and about when you're going to get there. And sadly, that is the way many people are programed to live their lives – stressing out even on their way to vacation. On the other hand, you can take your time driving to Carmel through the Pacifica Highway 1, taking lots of pictures of the sun glistening on the ocean on your way, stopping at plenty of picturesque little cafes along your way, buying souvenirs, smelling the fragrance of the ocean air, and have a splendid journey on your way to your destination.

Savoring the journey to your desired manifestation is about letting go of the suspense and the worry, living in the peace of deeply knowing that your earnest-most desires are already on their way to manifest in your life at the most auspicious time according to your Soul's perspective. It is about allowing yourself to feel joy and love at every moment of your life while you await the full manifestation of your desires. And since everything comes full circle, it is this peaceful joyful enjoyment of your journey that in turn help shift your energetic vibration into full resonance with your desires, and thus manifests them in the physical reality of your life.

☯   ☯

In this chapter, we have come a long way towards understanding the mechanism you already engage in to co-Create your life. This is a first step towards becoming a more *conscious* co-Creator. You and I are still going to walk a path together to guide you through some detailed step-by-step processes (*Seven Stages to co-Creating Prosperity From Your Soul* and *A Lifestyle of Prosperity From Your Soul*), designed to help you become a successful co-Creator of prosperity in your life. But before we do, it is necessary to first thoroughly understand the metaphysical nature of the co-Creative process, which is the objective of Part 1. And in this chapter, we have made big strides towards that understanding. In the next chapter, we will delve even deeper into understanding the energetic-vibrational nature of reality as the basis for all manifestations, in order to help you truly grasp the fact that anything and everything really is possible for you!

Chapter 6

What's Real In Our Reality of co-Creation

In Chapter 5, we have laid the groundwork for understanding the metaphysical process we each already engage in as we co-Create our reality. But I know that for some people, all this co-Creation stuff can seem a little "out there." Besides the "out there" factor, there is the matter of trusting in the Divine plan. In the last section of the last chapter, I detailed the process of letting go, in which one of the key ingredients was trusting that once you have aligned your vision/desire with your Ideal Lifeplan, and have begun taking some steps towards it, you won't have to go it alone, because the Universe is already aligning itself to manifest it for you. In fact, once you are in a vibration of trust in your Divine Lifeplan, its manifestation in this physical earth-plane is already on its way to you. But as important as this "letting go" step is, it is this trust in what you cannot see and in what you have no *logical* basis to assume is possible for you, that is the hardest part of co-Creating your desires, at least it was for me.

And if we analyze for a moment what trust is, it is not necessarily a logical thing but a feeling. Particularly the trust that we are talking about—in the Divine plan—is a deep feeling inside that becomes your vibrational resonance with the object of your desire. However, because of the influence of the Mental Body on the Astral (emotional) Body (recall from Chapter 1), intelligent understanding of any subject can potentially influence your ability to fully experience the feeling associated with that understanding. Then once you are able to feel that trust, it shifts your vibrational essence to resonate and attract your desires into manifestation. A more simplistic way of saying it would be – logical understanding of something can influence the way you feel and act, which in turn influence the way other people and the Universe act towards you. Either way you choose to look at it, the objective here is to help you feel trust in your Ideal Lifeplan (once you've tuned into it), so you can shift your energetic vibration into likeness and resonance with it, and consequently co-Create its most auspicious manifestation in your life.

So in this chapter, we'll work on the logic of expecting the Universe to oblige you, from the perspective of understanding the plasticity of our multidimensional reality, and just how real your ability to co-Create is within it. So we'll dig just a little bit deeper into the nature of our reality, in order to help you truly wrap your mind around the fact that everything you deeply wish for or even imagine already exists in some realm within this multidimensional reality, and to reiterate the fact that this process of co-Creation is something you already are doing. In fact, you—your Eternal Self—have been a co-Creator of our reality from the very dawn of time. Co-Creating prosperity is simply a matter of becoming more conscious of how and what you co-Create. I have also mentioned in Chapter 5 that the key to co-Creation is shifting your energetic vibration into likeness and resonance with what you want, thereby magnetizing it into manifestation in your physical reality. And I realize that this statement can seem a little vague. So in digging deeper into the true nature of reality and how it manifests from moment-to-moment, I hope to help you gain the additional understanding that would help you become a more successful co-Creator.

Stream Of Consciousness Flowing Into Many Levels Of Reality

First, let us understand the True nature of reality, so that we may understand where we stand in it—a much more powerful co-Creator than you might have thought.

There are many levels of reality. Despite the fact that we see and feel reality as tangible and solid, nothing could be further from the truth. According to scientists (but don't get all wrapped up in the physics here), as you go from the macro to the micro and observe things at increasingly smaller scales, it becomes apparent that all seemingly solid matter in the universe is in fact composed of tiny structures called molecules, and that those in turn are made of smaller units called atoms. As we dissect things further, we find that at smaller scales, those atoms are composed of even smaller particles called electrons, protons and neutrons. So far, this is all traditional seventh grade physics, right? But the reason it is important for our metaphysical discussion is that even from a traditional physics point of view, the space between those subatomic particles is hundreds of thousands of times bigger than their size. In the groundbreaking movie *What The Bleep—Down The Rabbit Hole (Quantum Edition)*, Dr. Hameroff makes the analogy that if the nucleus of an atom were blown up to the size of a needlepoint, then the first electron in the cloud of electrons surrounding the nucleus would be no closer than a mountain he points to, which looks to be a few miles away. So even at the mere subatomic scale, it becomes obvious that our reality is made of mostly empty space. But the story doesn't end here.

To add fuel to this fire, quantum physicists tell us that looking at reality in even a tinier scale—the Planck scale—reveals that the universe is not composed of particles at all, but of wavy strings of energy (which is by no means news to spiritually aware people and Light-workers. It is just interesting that physics is starting to catch up). According to String Theory, those strings of energy make up all forces and particles that make up our known universe. Going even beyond that scale, quantum physics and mathematics have proven that the underlying reality of all universes is actually made up of what they call the "unified field," or the "super string field." This is a "field" of pure energy, pure intelligence, and pure potentiality, reminiscent of the primordial soup of Creation. Still according to quantum physics, it is only "the observer," or "consciousness" that collapses the infinity of the unified field into the 11 dimensions and countless parallel universes that have been mathematically proven to exist. In other words, it is only our conscious observation and *intent* that make these energy-strings behave (only partially) like tangible particles.

In his fascinating book "The Holographic Universe" Michael Talbot relates some of the findings University of London physicist David Bohm, a protégé of Einstein and one of the world's most respected quantum physicists, and of Stanford neurophysiologist Karl Pribram, an architect of our modern understanding of the brain, both of whom believe that the universe is a giant hologram created, at least in part, by the human mind. Bohm explains reality as unfolding out of what he calls the "implicate order," essentially the same "super string field" that modern quantum physicists talk about. In a private conversation with Talbot, Bohm explains that: "Every action starts from an intention in the implicate order. The imagination is already the creation of the form; it already has the intention and the germs of all the movement needed to carry it out. And it affects the body and so on, so that as creations takes place in that way from the subtler levels of the implicate order it goes through them until it manifests in the explicate." As Talbot explains, "Bohm believes that consciousness and matter are just different aspects of the same fundamental something, a something that has its origins in the implicate order." So it is nice to know that the information contained in this book, most of which I have received from Source meditationally, is also supported by some of the world's most prominent scientists.

Of course in this discussion, it is not so important for you to understand the physics of it all. What is important is for you to wrap you mind around the idea that science and metaphysics both agree that it is your *conscious intent (free will)* that co-Creates and brings those co-Creations into full manifestation in the reality that you regard as physical!

But what is consciousness? That is a huge question. As we have hinted in Chapter 1, some experiments as well as reports from people who have had near death experiences point to the fact that human consciousness is not in the "physical" brain, but the Soul, which expresses itself through our energetic bodies. The physical body and reality is just the final effect of it, not the cause of consciousness. I mean, when you're floating ten feet above your motionless physical body, and at the same time you notice that your thinking is clearer than it's ever been and you are feeling more vivacious than you've ever felt, in those moments, there is not a doubt that your ability to think clearly and conceive of creative ideas do not come from your brain, but from your Soul. There are also numerous prominent scientists[1] that study the correlation between quantum physics and human consciousness (a new field called "quantum consciousness"). And so far they have found that our consciousness is not localized to or even stem from our central nervous system (brain and spinal cord), but is in fact an energetic stream of consciousness that is free roaming in the universe.

Talbot relates an interesting experiment done by UCLA professor Valery Hunt, who I've mentioned in Chapter 1, which proves that consciousness is not in the brain but in the human energy field (which she simply calls 'the field'): "She has discovered that the human energy field responds to stimuli even before the brain does. She has taken EMG readings [which we have explained in Chapter 1] of the energy field and EEG readings of the brain simultaneously and discovered that when she makes a loud sound or flashes a bright light, the EMG of the energy field registers the stimulus before it ever shows up on the EEG. What does this mean?" asks Talbot. "'I think we have way overrated the brain as the active ingredient in the relationship of a human to the world,' says Hunt. 'It's just a real good computer. But the aspects of the mind that have to do with creativity, imagination, spirituality, and all those things, I don't see them in the brain at all. The mind's not in the brain. It's in the darn field.'"

Of course, quantum physicists would not call the boy its name—they would not call the "unified field" and its intelligence God. And what scientists cannot tell you is that the stream of consciousness that collapses the formless "unified field" into energy strings, forces, particles and finally our "tangible" reality, is the Super-Consciousness of the Divine, which takes the shape of the Divine element threading through every emanation of Creation.

In his book, Talbot has collected many levels of evidence, supporting the idea that the universe is a giant hologram in which *our consciousness co-Creates* our reality. He relates many phenomena and miracles that could only be explained as projections of a powerful consciousness into a universe that is holographic in its nature, starting from accounts of people who have miraculously healed from incurable terminal cancers only because they deeply believed they were going to be healed, experiments done to test the effects of the placebo effect (the effect of belief on healing despite the fact that the "drug" given was really just a sugar pill), which yielded miraculous results, stigmata cases which were investigated and found to be caused by the psychic abilities of their sufferers, and many more.

One story, which is enough to make you at least question the solidity of reality and entertain the holographic nature of reality and the profound role that human consciousness has in it, is actually an event that Talbot had personally witnessed. On the date of the event, Talbot's father had hired a hypnotherapist to entertain some friends. "… The hypnotist chose a friend of my father's named Tom as his subject. This was the first time Tom had ever met the hypnotist. Tom proved to be a very good subject, and within seconds the hypnotist had him in a deep trance. He then proceeded with the usual tricks performed by stage hypnotists… But the highlight of the evening was when he told Tom that when he came out of the trance, his teenage daughter, Laura, would be completely invisible to him. Then after having Laura stand directly in front of the chair in which Tome was sitting, the hypnotist awakened him and asked him if he could see her. Tom looked around the room and his gaze appeared to pass right through his giggling daughter. 'No,' he replied. The hypnotists asked Tom if he was certain, and again, despite Laura's rising giggles, he answered no. Then the hypnotist went behind Laura so he was hidden from Tom's view and pulled an object out of his pocket. He kept the object carefully concealed so that no one in the room could see it, and pressed it against the small of Laura's back. He asked Tom to identify the object. Tom leaned forward as if staring directly through Laura's stomach and said it was a watch. The hypnotist nodded and asked if Tom could read the watch's inscription. Tom squinted as if struggling to make out the writing and recited both the name of the watch's owner (which happened to be a person unknown to any of us in the room) and the message. The hypnotist then revealed that the object was indeed a watch and passed it around the room so that everyone could see that Tom had read its inscription correctly." Of course we've all heard stories of magic shows illustrating the effects of hypnotic suggestion to make people see things that aren't there, or making certain things in the room invisible to them. And most of us have offhandedly discarded the possibility of these events constituting evidence other realities, or even other levels of the same reality. But in this event that Talbot relates, the man's consciousness had to have been tuned into a reality in which his daughter reverted back to her energetic-ethereal self. It isn't just that he imagined her not being there. It's that as far as his consciousness was concerned, she truly had shifted into an ethereal level of existence, thus allowing him to read the inscription on an object behind her that he could not have been able to read otherwise. In this event, Tom's consciousness reverted back to conceiving of reality in a very plastic and holographic way, the way that it really is. Also in this story, Talbot doesn't tell us that Tom was a specially gifted individual. He refers to him as an ordinary person like you and me, meaning that the ability to tune into the True holographic nature of reality and to manipulate it as we wish is a latent ability in all of us.

Of course, this is by no means a complete scientific exploration of reality. But from this discussion I hope it is becoming more apparent to you that there are in fact many levels, aspects, and dimensions to our reality besides the mere "physical" one that you have become so accustomed to experiencing.

From the vantage point of looking at reality from both a loosely scientific perspective and from the spiritual perspective of having had some glimpses into Divine Oneness, I can tell you that the so called "unified super string field" is in fact the pure LIGHT of the Creator. One point that scientists fail to mention, is that this LIGHT is composed of intense Love, clarity and aliveness that is compassionate and peaceful all at the same time. In fact, all the energy in the Universe is really the Love energy of our Creator. It is the same energy referred to as Chi (=life force) in china, Ki in Japan, Prana in India, or RUACH CHAIM—the breath of life that God blew into Adam and Eve in the original language of the bible. Thus, our universe (and all other parallel universes) is composed of Divine Love-energy.

There are deep connecting forces between all the different levels of reality. Part of it is our consciousness, which is one continuous stream of Divinely encoded information that streams from the Divine plane of existence, through the doorways of our energetic bodies, chakras, and meridians, into our brains, internal body environment, and physical reality, and from our physical body and brain to the ethereal, and back into the higher energetic realms. So in fact, the cosmos and us are a part of one continuum, from the unmanifest Creator, to the Divine element and all of Her-His emanations, through us and the reality of our lives.

The beginning phases of Creation start with the ever so subtle shift of the Unmanifest God into a Creator, reducing (for lack of a better word) Her-Himself into pure Creative energy I call the Divine Element. It's not quite differentiated into elements yet, but is the Divine essence of all there is. Meditationally dwelling in (being Graced into) this Divine Element feels like swimming in an ocean of Light, Love, freedom, lightness, immense power, profound peace, and all the elements of Nature, all at the same time. Then the Creator's consciousness and intent to Create then shifts from the Divine Element into a stream of consciousness filled with what looks like sacred symbols, before it differentiates into the different emanations and elements of which our reality is made. These sacred symbols of Creation, although Infinite, are really all variations of the same energy. Just like a color printer can print all the color of the rainbow from little dots of black, red, yellow and blue, so can whole universes be made of different variations of the same energy. The sacred symbols of Creation really are just like wrinkles in the fabric of the Infinite-Divine, as She-He transmutes Her-Himself into these symbols that then make up all the forces and particles that make up our Universe and reality. Could these Sacred Symbols be the strings of energy that quantum physics is trying to tune into? Could be. But if so, scientists have yet to fully understand the Divine nature and intense power of these symbols. What I have seen is that our reality is really made of the Divine Element flowing into these Sacred Symbols and emanating as the different elements of Creation according to different levels of energetic density. There are higher Angelic realities in which these energetic "wrinkles" of the Divine energy do not beef up into physical form as we know it, but keep vibrating in high frequencies that remain very close to the Love-Light of the Divine. The sacred symbols are in no particular language that I could recognize. But many ancient cultures have tried to recreate these ethereal symbols of Creation with the use of sacred geometry and symbols. Thus sacred symbols and geometries of different traditions are all fractions of the complete Divine sacred symbols of Creation. But the truth is that the sacred symbols of Creation exist only on the highest vibrational level – at a level that even the most elevated Angel is not always meant to fully perceive. They translate to the Love-Light-Joy-Energy of the continuously Created world in which we live.

Different points of view perceive and define the emanations of God differently. Kabala refers to Creation as occurring in twelve emanations. Ancient traditions ranging from Native American, to Chinese medicine, to yogic tradition, and perhaps also other cultures have symbolically defined Creation as occurring from the less to more dense elements, although they slightly defer in naming these elements: ether (yogic), air, fire, water, wood (CM), earth, and metal (CM). The wider Truth is that different belief systems, divinations and manifestation are really in the consciousness of the beholder. As we have explored in Chapter 5 in the section *Belief As A Condition For co-Creation*, they work because we believe in them, love them, and rejoice in them.

I know that all of this multidimensional reality, parallel universes, and 11 dimensions of existence may sound a bit overwhelming. *But the important thing* I wanted you to get from this discussion *is that even from a scientific point of view, reality is not solid. Nor is it concrete or permanent. It is plastic and holographic, and within it – your consciousness, and therefore your desires, as parts of one continuum with your Creator's consciousness* (although physicists won't call it God) *is the one that brings reality into "physical" manifestation.* **In other words, it is your intent (free will), as an integral part of Divine consciousness that has the authority to harnesses Divine power for co-Creation.**

What Is Real?

The next question that would help us understand reality and our role as co-Creators within it is: why do we perceive ourselves as separate from each other and from God, when we know that we are not? And why does this reality seem so solid, when we know for a fact that it isn't?

Quantum physics has proven through the "entanglement principal" that every particle in the universe is in oneness with every other particle. An energy quota that was split into a particle and antiparticle pair, and then separated, retains its oneness. When exciting or manipulating one particle, its sister-particle always reacts to the manipulation simultaneously, even after the two are separated by many miles at the time of the manipulation. To conceptualize this, imagine that you are bouncing your basketball in California, and your twin brother's basketball suddenly starts bouncing in New York at the same time on its own accord. And since at the moment of the big bang all particles in the universe were one huge energy quota, the inevitable conclusion is that all particles in the universe have the same oneness connection. You might suggest that, well, maybe the two particles are somehow communicating with each other. But in order to communicate the information of the manipulation and still produce instantaneous response over such great distances, the information would have to travel faster than the speed of light. And that has been proven to be impossible by Einstein in his theory of Special Relativity. So physicists have arrived at the conclusion that all particles in the universe are "entangled" with all other particles. In other words, we are all one. So why do perceive ourselves to be separate?

Age-old wisdoms, as well as people who have visited Heaven during their near-death experiences tell us that the Truest reality is in fact the Heavenly one. This is not a new notion. Spiritual teachers and seers have been telling us that for many thousands of years. But despite the consensus that our True reality is in fact an Heavenly one, theoretical physicists and spiritual gurus alike are baffled as to what makes the illusion of this "reality" seem so solid and separate from Divinity, when in fact it is not.

The first level of exploration of this question is the consistency and consensus of the illusion - meaning how things appear to us: the ground beneath our feet, the sofa you're sitting on, and everything else in the universe, all seem very solid and tangible. Objects in your life always appear the same as you expect them to appear; the sky always seem blue (at least it does in Southern California); a daisy always appears yellow and white, and they appear so to all of us, as if by a pre-agreement to see things that way. However, keep in mind that when you and I look at the same object, we do not see the exact same object. And as it comes to the noticeable surface of our mutual reality, we may not agree, for example, on the color: you may see the color of an object as green, another person may see it as blue, and I may see it as turquoise. But despite the fact that none of us really perceive reality the exact same way, the oneness of our consciousness brings us into a consensus based on an approximation of what we see. Thus, the consistency of how we perceive things is just the way our brains are programed to perceive reality while we are here in physical form, so that we may have smooth transitions from the realities of one moment to the next, in order to facilitate complete immersion in this adventure park called Earth.

However, if consistency is what convinces us of the "physicality" of this reality and its perceived limitation, than perhaps the thing to consider is another consistency that far surpasses all fragmentation and limitations that we perceive as our reality: The sense of morality that is independent of societal standards and time, our ability to feel love, the longing for an all-encompassing unconditional Love, and the longing for a deep sense of belonging, all resonate in every fiber of our being, and are universal. Those deep-rooted feelings are much more consistent than the solidness and fragmentation of our reality. A group of people sitting around a table and having coffee may not agree on the table's color or even the type of material it's made of. But they agree on the feeling of camaraderie they share during this event. They all share the deep-seated feeling of love and Oneness, even if that Oneness is buried beneath a here-now crust of worry, animosity, hatred, aggression, or unhappiness. For the feeling of love and Oneness is the very essence of who we are as divine beings. And as you will find out when you try the meditational processes given in *Seven Stages to co-Creating Prosperity From Your Soul*, a deep enough meditation will always reveal the essence of Love and Oneness inside you, and your connection to All-There-Is.

So you may ask: How is it that our senses could be so wrong? Consider that the brain itself is like a black box. We see light even though no light actually penetrates the brain. We hear sound even though no sound actually comes into the brain. Our sensory organs perceive our reality, and report it to the brain through electrical nerve impulses. But despite the fact that our sensory organs are our forefront for the intake of stimuli, it isn't the eyes that really see; it isn't the ears that really hear; it isn't the tongue that really tastes; it isn't the nose that smells; and it isn't the skin that feels touch. All of those stimuli get converted to electrical impulses that are reassembled and interpreted to give us a meaningful sense of reality inside the black box of the brain. Thus, since none of the original stimuli from our environment actually go into the black box of the brain, we have no way of knowing if what our senses are telling us is real. Even scientific experiments must be interpreted by a human being, who by definition, perceives the experiment's results through his/her five senses, which are again subject to the same potential deception. And for that matter, we know for a fact that our five senses do deceive us, because we know from a quantum physics perspective that reality is not tangibly solid, as we perceive it. One example they give in the movie *What The Bleep—Down The Rabbit Hole* is: when you bounce a ball, the ball doesn't really touch the floor. The negative charge of the electrons on the outer layer of the floor repulse the negative charge of the electrons of the outer layer of the ball and prevent them from touching. Thus, even though the ball bounces, and your senses are telling you that it has touched the floor, it didn't! And I'll add to this that on top of it, neither the ball nor the floor are solid matters. Nor are they even composed of tangible particles. They are made of the energy. In this context, it is also interesting to note that all out-of-body and near-death experiencers report that when they were outside of the confines of the physical body, their thinking became immeasurably clearer, and their senses sharper than they've ever been. So this is further evidence that the brain distorts our perception of reality from its True nature. But why? Why are we programed this way?

Now here is the simple but profound answer to why our reality seems so tangible and solid when it isn't. Each of us is an aspect (a spark) of the Divine Creator. As such, we were each given a mandate to co-Create our free will as an aspect of the Free Will of the Whole. And each one of us has then used this mandate, to choose to come into a physical human life on Earth. In other words, we each chose to enjoy this illusion-adventure park called Earth. And as we have discussed, each of us had put a lot of thought and loving intent into co-Creating the most Ideal Lifeplan for our human life. So let's say that you've spent considerable time and money going to Universal Studios for example. Then while enjoying the rides that take you through the illusory realities of different movies, you wouldn't sit there and say, "oh, this is fake, and that's fake," would you? Even if the ride were scary, you would do your best to temporarily "buy into" the illusion, and pretend that you really are being threatened by a dinosaur, or you really are threatened by an ancient scary mummy. You would do your best to pretend that you are indeed participating in the reality of the movie, right? Why? Because coming to the illusion-park, that *is* what you spend your money on, isn't it? If you've chosen to spend your day experiencing this illusory rides, then at the end the day, they leave you with a wonderful experience that has enriched you in some way. Well in the same way, coming into an earthly life, your Soul Self has programed your here-now self's consciousness to partially forget the Oneness nature of reality, and to perceive things as separate and solid, since that was the only way you could learn certain lessons that your Soul deemed necessary for your growth at this point of your personal evolution. So the reason we all buy into this separateness and solidness illusion is simple: *because we want to!* We each *chose* to come here. We *chose* this illusion of separation from the Divine in order to enjoy this earthly amusement park and learn something from it. And in order to do so in the best way, we had to program ourselves to fully immerse in this experience.

As a quick mind exercise on what is tangible and solid, consider again the group of friends who are sitting around a table having a cup of coffee, and consider that the table is made of glass. Well, while all the friends who are sitting around this table perceive its glass as solid, classic physicists among the friends would say that glass is in fact a liquid. Then quantum physicist sitting at the table would say that it is actually made of strings of energy. And spiritualists sitting at the table would say that it is made of the energy of Divine Love. Which of these realities is true? All of these realities are simultaneously true, and it is up to you to decide which level of reality you choose to tune into. You may wish to just sit and enjoy the conversation with your friends, and ignore the table, and that would be the level of reality you tune into at that moment. Or you may wish to observe the table, but enjoy its beauty and functionality from a very here-now reality perspective, in which case the table is absolutely solid. You may, on the other hand, wish to take a microscope that allows you to observe the movement of molecules composing the structure of the glass. And in those moments, the table is absolutely liquid to you, because you would be observing its liquidness with your own eyes. You could be sitting around that same table pondering and discussing with your friends the mathematical formulas that prove that the table is made of strings of energy. And in those moments, if you close your eyes and visualize the implications of these formulas, the table absolutely could (depending on your visualization skills) revert back to strings of energy, at least in the reality of your mind. I've once talked to a guy who while meditating under the influence of LSD, had physically seen a table as composed of strings of energy in a soup of bright colors of energy. You could also sit around that table, close your eyes, and meditate deeply on the energy of the table as a part of the same Divine Oneness that you are a part of. And in those moments the table and you are absolutely made of Divine Oneness energy in the reality of your consciousness. The kicker is that all of those levels of reality exist and are true at the same time.

Now, there is a practical reason why it is so important to recognize that the solidness and fragmentation of our reality are in fact not real: *once you gain this higher perspective on the circumstances in your life, you will be able to more readily surpass the limitations imposed by the perceived solidness of your reality, and reclaim your God-given free will to co-Create the reality that you Truly want.* Because when you perceive reality as a stream of consciousness that pulls in Divine Creative energy to co-Create your life according to your True wishes, you understand that co-Creating millions of dollars is as simple as co-Creating a sprouting seed. And once you understand that, it becomes easier to embody the feeling of power and to achieve vibrational resonance with what you want—it is easier to be a successful co-Creator of your life.

Universal Travel of Choice

When it comes to co-Creation, it is important to understand that everything you deeply desire already exists in the Universe in one realm or another. Whether it is a desire that was planted there by your Soul, as part of the blueprint called your Ideal Lifeplan, or it is a desire that arose later, it has already fully manifested in this or another realm of existence at the time that the desire was born within you.

Physicists talk about level-three parallel universes as occupying the same time-space that we do, but existing on what could be simply understood as different phases. While all of those realities exist at the same time, which reality you perceive of depends on your consciousness intent to bring it forth or to merge with that reality. The realities of parallel universes are said to be on a different vibrational levels or different realms, which is why we cannot perceive them. Think of it as all the radio and TV stations that are broadcasting their programs at the same time. You need to *choose* which one to tune your receiver into.

A more metaphysical understanding of this multiple parallel universe theory explains that every time you deeply wish for something that is aligned with your True Self, you effectively give birth to a whole new reality in which the object of your desire exist. The reality in which your highest wishes are manifested has already been created for you by your Soul, when It planned your Ideal Lifeplan. And since your deepest heartfelt desires are a reflection of your Ideal Lifeplan, an existence in which they are fulfilled already exists somewhere out there in the Universe at large! And in that parallel reality, you already own the successful business you want; you already are as rich as you want to be; you already possess the health you wish for; and you already are married to your soulmate, if that is what you deeply want. All that needs to happen for you to realize your dreams in this here-now reality is: your consciousness and vibrational resonance need to merge with the reality in which your desires are manifested. I know it sounds daunting. "How do I merge my consciousness with another universe?" you might ask. But it's not as complicated as it sounds, as this sort of thing already happens all the time in your everyday life. It's just that those shifts are so subtle, that it seems like the fabric of your reality is continuous and seamless.

Even though in Divinity time doesn't really exist, it may be easier to understand it as a shifting from one universe to the next *as time goes by.* As confirmed by people who have experienced NDEs, all the moments of your life (past, present and future), as well as all of your past, present and future lifetimes exist simultaneously in all parallel existences that are in Oneness with one another. Many NDErs report that during their life reviews, they experienced all the times of their lives, as well as other lifetimes, and other worlds as if they were all happening *now.* Time didn't really exist, and all of these existences felt equally real. But it is just easier to conceptualize this universal travel if you think of time as linear. So if you think of one lifetime—a seemingly solid reality, you are the traveler that shifts from one universe to the next as you go from one moment of your life to the next, kind of like bubbles of liquid mercury that blend into each other to create a bigger bubble, and then may split apart to merge with another bubble. To illustrate, let us say that there are three possible futures for you at a given moment: future A, in which you co-Create circumstances that are in alignment with your Ideal Lifeplan; future B, in which you are totally unhappy; and future C, in which you settle for only some of what you want. Any given moment is a juncture in which a decision is made. But since time doesn't really exist, all three possibilities already exist in parallel universes. In the given moment of our example, you are inevitably going to transfer from where you are right now. The only question is: are you going to transfer to an existence that brings you closer to A or B or C, all of which already exist.

"Bohm," says Talbot, "admits to believing that the universe is all 'thought' and reality exists only in what we think…" In a private conversation with Talbot, Pribram says that he "believes a number of different potential realities exist and consciousness has a certain amount of latitude in choosing which one manifests." Talbot brings many examples of talented individuals who are able to tune into past events with startling accuracy by touching archeological artifacts, predict future events, and alter bad future events that they have tuned into because of the advent of premonitions. The classic question that Talbot asks in this regard is the same question that we have addressed in Chapter 2: how can we have free will, but also insight into the future at the same time? But when you consider that there are many different possible futures, all of which exist in parallel, it can explain how the future can be predetermined, but we can have free choice at the same time. That is, each possible outcome exists in a parallel existence, and we determine by our choice which one would manifest as our reality—which reality our aware-of-itself consciousness would travel to. Another scientists that Talbot brings to support this idea is clinical psychologist Dr. David Loye, a former member of Princeton and UCLA medical school faculties. Loye "believes that reality is a giant hologram, and in it the past, present, and future are indeed fixed, at least up to a point. The rub is that it is not the only hologram. There are many such holographic entities floating in the timeless spaceless waters of the implicate, jostling and swimming around one another like so many amoebas. 'Such holographic entities could also be visualized as parallel worlds, parallel universes,' says Loye… these holograms also occasionally swallow and engulf each other, melding and bifurcating like the protoplastmic globs of energy that they are… And when we act upon premonition and appear to alter the future, what we are really doing is leaping from one hologram to another. Loye calls these intra holographic leaps 'hololeaps' and feels that they are what provides us with our true capacity for both insight and freedom." So it appears that this idea of travelling from one universe to the next as you make choices and shift from one moment to the next in the course of your life is not solely a spiritual-metaphysical idea. Once again, scientific data supports this idea, which Light workers have known about for centuries.

Now, some seers theorize that only big decisions, which happen every number of years, trigger this reality shift. But in reality, every moment in life is a decision juncture in which you chose to go one way or the other, and all of those moment, like a collection of dots that make up a line, form the path that leads up to the big junctures that make up your Lifepath. It is true that many choices in life seem small, like the decision of whether to put butter on your toast or spray a little olive oil on a given day for example. But even this seemingly inconsequential decision determines what level of health and kindness-to-self you are resonating with at that moment. It is a one of the dots that make up the line of your Lifepath.

As I've mentioned in the last chapter, certain events in life (set up by your Soul Self) are Triggering Events—events that trigger whole other chains of events, depending on your choice.

One choice leads to a chain of events and circumstances that are far removed from your Ideal Lifeplan, while another choice leads to a chain of events and circumstances that lead you to merge you with your Ideal Lifepath. And of course there are always a whole array of choices that lead to a chain of events leading somewhere in between the worse and the ideal. As an example – All of us have experienced times when we are in a depressed foul mood, and feel like our lives are stuck. But you always have a choice. You can choose to stay in and nurse this foul mood, or you can choose to do something about it. It could be something trivial like going on a Nature Walk (See *Seven Stages to co-Creating Prosperity From Your Soul*), eat a good wholesome meal, or even just open the window and let the cool breeze bring in a certain smell that reminds you of all that is good in life. From a yogic point of view, depression is not a permanent clinical condition but a temporary condition of heavy/stuck energy, which should only last from a few minutes to a few hours at most. Just a few simple breathing exercises have the power to dissolve the stuck energy, move your chi, and therefore shift your entire energetic vibration into a positive upbeat one. So if you are depressed for longer than a few hours, it is because at some level of your consciousness, you are choosing to dwell in it and perpetuate it. From the yogic perspective, it is just as easy to snap yourself out of it by moving-shifting your energy. When you do the little things that uplift you, suddenly your whole feeling about reality shifts, and you suddenly become hopeful, happy, and peaceful. This conscious shifting of perspective is a perfect example of how your decision has propelled you into a parallel reality that is very similar to the one you were in before, but better. This process is already happening in your life moment to moment. And if you get in a habit of always choosing the highest vibrational path that uplifts you, than it becomes easy and natural for you to also make ideal choices during the triggering events of your life.

But understand that this universal travel is not really all that woo-woo or hocus-pocus. It isn't really like space travel. I say, "merge your reality" because it isn't that you go in a spaceship and physically travel to another universe. It's that your current reality *merges* with the parallel reality in a very subtle, almost imperceptible way. This is where our understanding of how fluid and holographic the universe really is comes into play. Since the universe is nothing but Divine Love-Light energy taking form according to our free will as co-Creators, it really is being Created each moment anew, kind of like blowing soap bubbles that get created each moment anew, except that in the case of the Universe, you and everyone else are not only the ones who blow-create each bubble, but also exist inside each bubble. And when you blow soap bubbles, the aware-of-itself part of your consciousness is outside each bubble at the viewing point of a creator. When you are living a human life, the aware-of-itself part of your consciousness is in one of those bubbles; then it transfers to the next bubble, and then to the next… as the moments of your life progress in what creates for us the illusion of time. These shifts happen all the time in such a subtle way that it creates the illusion of a cohesive reality of solid tangible matter in which time progresses only forward. But both the cohesiveness and the tangibility of matter is an illusion that is created by *your* own consciousness.

Pulling The Rabbit Out of the Hat

So why is it so important to understand the ethereal fluidity in which reality is co-Created, and the way we travel from one universe to the next as we go from moment to moment in our lives? Because here is how you actually bring an object into physical manifestation: First, you desire it within the depth of who you Truly are, which instantly co-Creates it in some parallel existence. Then your consciousness—not just your cognitive faculties, but your total consciousness, which includes your feelings and your energetic vibration—tunes into the reality in which the object of your desire is already manifest, and consequently shifts your energetic vibration into likeness and resonance with that object. Then, with the power of your mutual resonance with that parallel reality, you merge the two realities so that they are superimposed. And then your manifested desires crystalize from ethereal to physical, which is greatly assisted by your continued dwelling in the vibration of joy (the trust-joy of knowing that you wish has been granted) and resonance with it.

To better understand this, your consciousness travels exponentially faster than the speed of light. You might say that it travels at the speed of Light—Divine Light. And since time doesn't really exist, since you are living all of the past-present-future moments of your many lives simultaneously, your Total consciousness can obviously be in more than one place at the same time, and is the vehicle that travels from one reality to the next. If your desire is in alignment with your True Self, than there is a part of your total consciousness that has already seen and experienced your desire manifest. They say that a picture is worth a thousand words. But a first-hand experience is worth a million pictures. That is why part of your higher consciousness always knows beyond doubt that your True desire is possible for you, because it has already seen-experienced it manifested in another reality. You see, when you become aware of a true desire, it isn't just that your Soul has planted it in you and you are just responding to that implantation. On the other hand, it isn't that you are birthing that desire at the level of your here-now self and sending it up into some higher planes where your Soul resides. The reality of it is that your expanded Self is in all those planes of existence at the same time. In this case, neither the chicken nor the egg precedes one another. They happen simultaneously! A True desire is born at the inner chamber of your heart and at the level of your Soul simultaneously. And when it is born, it has all five aspects of manifestation that we discussed in Chapter 5: it has its vibrational essence, its sound vibration, its visual form, its dimensional properties, and the structure/senses/qualities that support it. At that point, the object is already co-Created. It exists.

When you tune into the inner chamber of your heart, and through it into your Higher Self, you also tune into all of the manifestations you have already co-Created with your free will, all of which already exist somewhere out there in the ethers. At present moment (before they come into physical manifestation in your "physical" reality), they express themselves in your here-now world as desires. But they are fully formed manifestations at some level. The only difference is that in your present-moment-universe, their dimensional properties are miniaturized, and their structural qualities are ethereal, with the potential to beef up into true-to-size dimensions and physical structure and qualities.

Put another way, by agreement between your Soul Self and your here-now self, your Total Self co-Creates your True desires simply by conceiving of them and wishing for them. These co-Creations at that point are energetic-ethereal in nature, and exist as parallel possible realities free-floating like bubbles in the primordial soup of possibilities from which all Creations spring. You magnetize these "bubbles" to merge with your bubble of reality when you shift your energetic vibration into a like vibration, dwell in the vibrational reality where your wishes are manifest, and maintain a mutual resonance between the two realities.

At the moment in which the reality of your manifested desires first merges with your present reality, it is still in an ethereal state, vibrationally superimposed on your present reality. Therefore, the manifestation of your desires first show up energetically as holographic figures floating in your auric field, then beef up into physical structures with true-to-size dimensions, and finally show up in your "physical" reality, only when you continuously dwell in vibrational resonance with them—shift your consciousness to dwell in the new reality.

There is some supporting evidence of holographic figures first showing up in a person's auric field before they beef up as physical manifestations. Michael Talbot relates two cases psychic readers who were able to "see" ethereal objects imbedded in people's auric field, and then verify that these objects actually manifested in their lives. The first is psychic reader Beatrice Rich, who on one reading "saw silver spoons, silver plates, and similar objects circling around a man's head. Because it was early in her exploration of psychic phenomena, the experience startled her. At first she did not know why she was seeing what she was seeing. But finally she told the man and discovered that he was in the import/export business and traded in the very objects she was seeing circling his head." The second story is of psychic reader Carol Dryer who on one reading "she saw a bunch of potatoes whirling around a woman's head. Like Rich," says Talbot, "she was at first dumbfounded but summoned her courage and asked the woman if potatoes had any special meaning for her. The woman laughed and handed Dryer her business card. 'She was from the Idaho Potato Board, or something like that,' says Dryer." And so potatoes were constantly manifesting in her life, and therefore floated as an ethereal image above her head.

There are also quite a few miraculous stories of instant manifestation, which Talbot has artfully collected in his book that are worth telling here, as they may just give you the glimpse that you need into what's possible for all of us.

The first line of evidence of manifestations that attests to the plasticity of our reality is at the subatomic level. According to Talbot, professor of aerospace sciences and dean emeritus of School of Engineering and Applied science at Princeton University Robert G Jahn, and his associate, clinical psychologist Brenda Dunne believe that "instead of discovering particles, physicists may actually be creating them. As evidence, they cite a recently discovered subatomic particle called *anomalon*, whose properties vary from laboratory to laboratory. Imagine," says Talbot, "owning a car that had a different color and different features depending on who drove it! This is very curious and seems to suggest that an anomalon's reality depends on who finds/creates it."

But in Talbot's Holographic Universe, things get even more interesting than just manifesting subatomic particles. Biologist and scientist Lyall Watson has studied the paranormal events all over the world. On a trip to a small Indonesian island called Timor-Timur, Watson encountered an impressive example of materialization. He was visiting a local family, where Alin, the unwed half-sister of the husband looked and seemed to have been treated differently than the rest of her family. "That evening during dinner in the family's grass-roofed home, Watson witnessed several startling phenomena. First, without warning, the couple's eight-year-old boy screamed and dropped his cup on the table as the back of his hand began to bleed inexplicably… As Watson was examining the wounds, the lamp flame turned blue and abruptly flared up, and in the suddenly brighter light a shower of salt began to pour down over the food until it was completely covered and inedible. 'It wasn't a sudden deluge, but a slow and deliberate action which lasted long enough for me to look up and see that it seemed to begin in midair, just about eye level, perhaps four feet over the table,' says Watson."

Talbot himself admits that he grew up in a house in which things just manifested. Although he calls initially calls it a poltergeist haunting, he admits that because the manifestations related to his moods and followed him to college, he eventually understood that they were done by him at some level of his consciousness. "The manifestations started when I was six years old," says Talbot, "and inexplicable showers of gravel rained down on our roof at night. Later it took to pelting me inside my home with small polished stones and pieces of broken glass with edges worn like the shards of drift glass one finds on the beach. On rarer occasions it materialized other objects including coins, a necklace, and several odder trifles." Talbot reportedly had he never learnt to control the manifestations, and controlling one's manifestations is what it's all about, isn't it?

Paramahansa Yogananda describes in his book "Autobiography of a Yogi" his meetings with several Hindu ascetics who would materialize out-of-season fruits, gold plates, and other objects.

But the best example of a person who could consistently (for more than fifty years) manifest objects out of thin air at will, forwarded by Talbot is Sai Baba. According to Talbot, Psychologist Erlendur Haraldsson of the University of Iceland had spent over ten years studying Sai Baba, and was impressed with the authenticity of Sai Baba's manifestation. Sai Baba was able to manifest specific rare objects upon request, gold jewelry, with diamonds and other precious stones, food, sweet delicacies, as well as the famous "sacred ash" that was almost continuously pouring out of his hands. He was also famous for "producing exotic objects such as grains of rice with tiny, perfectly craved pictures of Krishna on them, out-of-season fruit… and anomalous fruits, such as apples that, when peeled, turn out to be an apple on one side and another fruit on the other." As observed by haraldsson and his faculty members, all of these manifestations happen in mid air, and most of them were still hot to the touch when people grabbed them.

Another profound example of materialization forwarded by Talbot is of a young woman named Tia—a shaman-healer who Watson encountered on his trip to Indonesia. According to Talbot, Watson witnessed many miraculous healings that Tia performed. "But he witnessed one of Tia's most awesome displays when he accidentally stumbled upon her talking with a little girl in a shady grove of kenari trees. Even at a distance, Watson could tell from Tia's gestures that she was trying to communicate something important to the child. Although he could not hear their conversation, he could tell from her air of frustration that she was not succeeding. Finally, she appeared to get an idea and started an eerie dance. Entranced, Watson continued to watch as she gestured toward the trees, and although she scarcely seemed to move, there was something hypnotic about her subtle gesticulations. Then she did something that both shocked and dismayed Watson. She caused the entire grove of trees suddenly to blink out of existence. As Watson states, 'One moment Tia danced in a grove of shady kenari; the next she was standing alone in the hard, bright light of the sun.' A few seconds later she caused the grove to reappear, and from the way the little girl leapt to her feet and rushed around touching the trees, Watson was certain that she had shared the experience also. But Tia was not finished. She caused the grove to blink on and off several times as both she and the little girl linked hands dancing and giggling at the wonder of it all."

These stories just show you what is possible. Granted, most of us co-Create things in a much subtler way, and are not consciously able to control our manifestations in the same way that Tia or Sai Baba can. Nonetheless, if you start writing down in a journal all the everyday seemingly mundane incidents in which you thought something was going to happen (or not happen), and then it happened exactly the way you "saw" it, you too would come to the conclusion that the ability to co-Create and then materialize things from the ethereal into the physical is a latent ability in all of us. We've all had incidents in which we've seen in the eyes of our minds a rare parking space in a specific location near the door, and then it materialized just as we've seen. We've all had premonitions of somebody saying or doing something we wouldn't normally expect, which then happened just as we've seen them. I've often wondered whether in those cases I am really manifesting the parking spot by thinking about it, or if perhaps I am just intuiting to its existence before I come around the corner and physically see it. And then it came to me that in a holographic universe in which time does not really exist and all is Oneness, those two possibilities are not mutually exclusive. They are both true at the same time. At any rate, while this book may not teach you (nor does it aim to) how to miraculously materialize whole groves of trees or diamonds in mid air, it will guide you to become more aware of how and what you co-Create, so that you can better control what you manifest into your reality.

Now that we know what is possible, let's talk about how to realize that potential. As I mentioned above, as you travel from one moment to the next in this continuously forming reality, you may travel into a multitude of possible realities, good, bad, and in between. So how do you make sure you always travel your Ideal Lifepath—the path that leads to the manifestation of your desires?

Well, once you have tuned into the aspect of your consciousness that had seen-experienced the object of your desire manifest (in a parallel reality), if you can keep resonating with it as one even after you return to ordinary awakened consciousness, and if you can live your life while dwelling in the vibration (joy) of that mutual resonance, than the reality that the aware-of-itself part of your consciousness travels to will be your Ideal one. For example when you hike, if you were going to walk a straight line from B to A, ideally you would keep line-of-sight (the shortest distance between two points is a straight line) with point A, so that you don't end up at point C, D or F, right? Think of a mountain climber holding onto the rope that is attached to the top of the mountain. That rope ensures that the climber doesn't climb up to an alternate peek or slide down into the abyss. In manifesting the reality you want, you too can have a straight line to the endpoint—the result that you wish to manifest. And that straight line is your consciousness's ability to stay tuned into your Soul Self. That is why having a complete Internal Experience of what you want is so important. It literally is the line that pulls you towards the reality you wish to manifest, as you travel from one soap bubble moment of your life to the next.

A big part of pulling the rabbit out of the hat is self-validation! All of the principles of kindness, generosity, and the feeling of gratitude that we have discussed in Chapter 3 come into play here, but especially the self-validation principle. You must validate yourself every day as deserving of every good thing in order to manifest it. As explained in Chapter 3, as you give to others, it creates, and continues to activate, the vacuum that attracts (sucks in) Divine blessings through your Infinite Funnel of Abundance. It's like causing the water to flow quicker through a funnel by not only keeping the narrow end of the funnel open, but by applying suction at the narrow end of the funnel, so more water would flow in from the wide end faster. At the same time, your generosity and kindness to others create a love connection to everything and everyone in your reality, which anchors (like anchoring pegs of an erect tent) the freshly co-Created blessings into your present reality through strings of love. But the most important love connection of all—the one that facilitates all other love connections including the Divine's, is your love connection to yourself—your validation of yourself as a beloved child of God who is deserving of every good thing. Those feelings of love, kindness, gratitude, and validation go a long way to help you live your life not as a mere reflection or resonance, but as a direct energetic extension of your Soul, in oneness with all that you Truly desire.

It might make it simpler for you to grasp, if we look at changing your life towards your Ideal as changing a TV channel. And let's divide it conceptually into five steps.

The <u>first step</u> to co-Creating a better reality for yourself is being aware that something better is possible and available for you. This is kind of like knowing that there are many TV stations simultaneously broadcasting programs that are available for you to watch. The epiphany here being that you don't have to be stuck watching a program that you don't like, since there are nicer program available, and you have the capability to switch channels. This awareness is effectively what we are doing in this first book.

<u>Step two</u> is to eliminate all negativities and lower vibrational thought forms from your life, so that they do not block you from co-Creating your Ideal Lifeplan. This can be likened to cleaning the TV antenna from dust and rust, so as to eliminate static and allow you clear reception of the beautiful new program of your choice.

Once you have walked these first steps—awareness and eliminating negativity, you are ready to tune into what you truly want with every fiber of your being. So <u>step three</u> is when you tune into what you deeply desire in great detail, which helps connect your consciousness with the parallel existence in which it already exists. That brings forth your Ideal Lifeplan like enlarging a window of a computer program that was already running in the background and contains all the elements you wish for. In our TV illustration, it is like watching a preview of the new program you are now going to watch, and making sure it is indeed what you'd like to watch, prior to actually switching the channels.

<u>Step four</u>—strengthening your connection with this alternate reality to the point that it merges and is made manifest in your current life. It can be likened to actually switching the

channel and watching the new program. You can strengthen your connection with your Ideal reality and invite it to merge into your reality by meditating on the internal reality of your Ideal Life (*Seven Stages to co-Creating Prosperity From Your Soul*). Having a complete internal experience of what you want strengthens the vibrational resonance between you in your current situation, and the reality of having what you want, a resonance that works like a rubber band that springs what you want to you.

The resultant merge—step five—happens when you are able to sustain the complete internal experience of what you want, and extend it to your everyday life. To continue our TV illustration, at this point, even though the program that you wish to watch is the predominant one on your TV screen, you are still not participating in it. This is a metaphor to understand that the two realities are superimposed on one another, with your Ideal one still being ethereal. This is similar to one of those computer programs in which wear special glasses that allow you to participate in a seemingly three-dimensional holographic cyber reality that the computer projects. The program influences you but is not beefed up into having physical properties yet.

The actual proverbial "pulling the rabbit out of the hat," the sixth step, happens when you walk the walk, so to speak, and allow the new reality to "explode" from an ethereal to physical. To understand this explosion, imagine that the cyber reality of your computer program (the one you wore the special glasses to perceive) gradually become your the real reality, and your current reality become just a mere computer image, like a switch. And what gives energy to this explosion of materialization, what springs your desired co-Creation into physical manifestation, is when you are able to bring the bliss of your meditations into your everyday life, and when you can live your life in the joyous vibration of the new you.

This doesn't mean that you become delusional and suddenly start spending money that you don't have just on a whim. It means that you plan your life knowing that the money you need to bring your dreams into full manifestation is going to be there for you, and knowing that the Universe supports you in every possible way, including financial. You walk around tall and radiant, feeling and beaming the air of a winner. Trust that as long as your desires are anchored in the True vision of your Soul, than the resources to make them happen will find their way to you. Enjoy and savor every moment as a jewel, knowing that this sparkling moment is indeed leading you towards your highest Lifepath. For example, at the time of this writing, I didn't have a publisher. I didn't have the money or know the investors that were going to make my vision of Soul Path Retreat a reality. But I followed the guidance that my Soul Self gave me: I wrote these books diligently, and I wrote all the curriculums for four levels of retreat courses Soul Path Retreat was to offer. Because my vision of creating a retreat center was one of helping humanity, I believed that it was indeed anchored in the True vision of my Soul, and would therefore be fulfilled. And since you are reading these lines, we know that at least the book part of my vision has already come true, and I have already started to merge my reality with the reality in which my deepest desires have come true. And if I (who have had no writing, publishing, or any kind of business experience or knowledge) can do it, you can do it.

To summarize, the point of this section is: you already are co-Creating your reality as you read these lines. In fact you have magnetized this book to come into your hands because you were ready to change your life for the better. And quite simply, all you need do to co-Create your desires is be a bit more conscious of the process, so that you can magnetize to come to you only that which you Truly desire. Using the Joy Meter and the God Meter (chapter 7), the meditational processes offered in *Seven Stages to co-Creating Prosperity From Your Soul*, participating in RezoDance sessions (if they are offered in your area), and taking our retreat courses are all tools to help you ensure that as you make each choice moving from one moment in your life to the next, you are traveling into the best possible reality, one that is in accordance with your Ideal Lifeplan.

So in this section, we have discussed the simple energetic workings of magnetizing the reality of what you want to you. But to strengthen your confidence in your ability to co-Create your desires, let us talk a little bit about the why: Why do we have this physical existence in which we want for things that are perceivably separate from us?

If God Is Perfect, Why Did She-He Create Us?

One of the biggest questions that have been nagging at mankind since the beginning of time is: If our Souls are perfect at their inception, and if God was already a perfect being before Creating us, then why does She-He need to Create a physical universe? In other words, why did a perfect being (God) need to Create this whole "physical" universe? Why are we here?

Why is this understanding important to co-Creating the life that you want? Because understanding the awesomeness of your Creator, and understanding that there is no real separation between Heaven and Earth, and between you and your Creator, would help you understand that getting the power to co-Create the things that you want in life is never a problem. And since you are an integral part of your all-powerful Creator, it follows logically that you too have Her-His Infinite power and resources for co-Creating the highest wishes of your Soul! Before we answer the question of this section, let us first look at a few ancient traditions' *attempts* at answering it.

Jewish Kabbalah explains that God was a perfect being, and He (I narrowed it down to He, because Jewish thought does not recognize a female aspect of God. Neither does Christianity for that matter) needed to have someone to love and bestow His goodness on. So He reduced Himself from His enormity in a process of reduction ("tsimtsum"), and Created a perfect world. But since God had too much love to give, the perfect world He created could not hold all of His love, and it exploded into a gazillion pieces, leaving us with the task of putting it back together. And putting it back together, according to Jewish tradition, is through our good deeds of kindness, which form invisible strings of energy (named messiah-strings—"chevlei mashiah) that put the perfect world back together.

With all due respect to Kabbalah and to Jewish tradition, there are several holes in this theory. For one, if God is a perfect being, then why did She-He have a need to have someone to love? Perfect means perfect! You shouldn't have any needs if you're perfect. Because when you're perfect, you ARE all the love that IS. The second hole in this theory is: well, if God is a perfect being and She-He has created a perfect world, then if this first world was so perfect than why did it explode into a gazillion pieces? It obviously wasn't so perfect. And the third hole through this theory is: we know from meditational channelers and from NDE reports that God is still Whole.

She-He has not really reduced Her-Himself in any way. Even quantum physics agrees that our reality is not really fragmented, but is still a continuous flow of energy. So this whole theory of "Tsimtsum" (reduction) does not explain our existence, at least not in my mind.

Another attempt to solve the riddle of our existence comes from yogic Sikh tradition. Sikh tradition explains that God was simply bored sitting up in heaven being lofty for all of eternity, and She-He wanted to create this physical reality as a show or a play for Her-Himself… similar to how we like movies and entertainment so much. But the hole I see through this theory is very similar to the hole through the Kabbalistic story: If God is perfect She-He does not get bored! When you're perfect, you don't have need for entertainment. Perfect means perfect!

There are as many theoretical explanations to the question at hand as there are thinkers, traditions, and philosophers. But the Truth of the matter is simpler, but complex to grasp at once: our world is still whole! We are all still in oneness with each other and with the Divine right now. God hasn't shrunk Her-Himself or made Her-Himself small in any way. God still is living and breathing throughout every corner of Creation, through you, through me, through the flowers that you may have seen in your walk today, and every bit of this reality is vibrating God energy!

As you remember from our discussion of the composition of the Soul, both Yechida—singular Divine Oneness, and Chaya—the Divine life-force and Creation element that is flowing through you and throughout all of Creation, are integral parts of each Soul. That is why throughout this book I have capitalized the word Soul, because it is not just a tiny little piece of the whole that you regard as yourself. Your Soul, and the living spirit that is animating you to live and breathe and read these lines right now, is actually an integral part of God! It is true that each wave is separate and has its own characteristics, and free will. But is each wave really separate from the ocean?

Who you are is God, experiencing Her-Himself *as* you at this very moment. She-He is simply vibrating Her-Himself to shape this very universe every moment anew. It might be easier to understand if you think of it as in the next moment, God returns to unmanifest Divine One, and in the moment after that She-He pops back into our "physical" existence (in the same way that quantum physics sees particles as popping in and out of existence, and never actually traversing the distance between different energy levels). Except that this pulsation doesn't really happen. This pulsation illustration is just a way to understand that God exists on the Infinite plane of the Unmanifest Divine, as a Creator, and as this "physical" Creation all at the same time. I know this is hard to grasp. But think of it as if God is manifesting or popping Her-Himself into this physical existence every moment anew.

So let's recap here: The main intent of what your Soul wishes you to experience and learn in each lifetime is included in your Ideal Lifeplan, which your Soul has so joyously planned for you before you came into this lifetime. And since time doesn't really exist, the gifts that are to manifest as the main occurrences of your life already exist in a parallel existences, which merge into your reality as you immerse in your earthly existence in which time is perceived as linear. All of those intersections in your life are matched as a perfect mosaic with the main occurrences in the lives of all of those you cross paths with. However, all of these main intersections and themes in your life only exist as kind of a blueprint. When your Soul is in Its Heavenly state, it is beloved, content, and absolutely joyous. It wants for nothing. That is why the blueprint of your Ideal Lifeplan needs to be beefed up with human level experiences, and with all those thoughts, wants, needs, feelings, and actions that together, form the complete experience that is to serve your Soul's growth. As you might understand, this chance that you have been given to be immersed in this human experience, to forget the glory of whom you Truly are, and to want for more, serves a purpose.

The purpose is not really to deprive you in any way shape or form. God lovingly wants to give you all that you want, because you are an integral part of Her-Himself. And God wants every part of Her-Himself to be fulfilled and happy. So *each time that you make an earnest and heartfelt request, the entire Universe expands to birth whole other existences to oblige your request.* A simple but wonderful illustration of this idea was given in the movie *The Never Ending Story*. In the movie Fantasia was a beautiful fantastical world, which a little boy was able to visit as he read his book. But Fantasia was threatened by big black cracks of nothingness, which eventually caused all of Fantasia to crumble and dissolve. At the end of the movie, it was revealed that it was the little boy's task to save and restore Fantasia. As it turned out, the only way to save Fantasia was to keep making wishes, and the more fantastical and demanding these wishes were, the more wonderful the new Fantasia became. Although the movie was just a fictional story, the idea that your earnest wishes give birth to whole new realities that expand our existence is based on Truth.

Think about it: when do you really wish for something so badly, and dream about it so intently that you can almost feel its taste in your mouth? When you don't have it! And you only wish for more when you perceive yourself from within your human limitations. If we all walked around truly feeling our Oneness and the Divine bliss of our True existence, we wouldn't wish for anything more, because the Soul at Its Heavenly state is totally content. Therefore It lacks and wants for nothing! It is bathed in Divine bliss. But since wishing for more is what causes God to expand Her-Himself and Create whole new dimensions and universes to oblige our requests, then *our requests help God expand Her-Himself!*

So the reason why existence in physical form is important is because only when we are totally immersed in and accept this illusion, its limitations, and our perceived separateness within it *as real*, do we have a reason to wish for more. *And it is our desire for more that provides the conscious intent (free will) to co-Creates whole new Universes.* The most important illusion in our reality is our perceived separation and lack of love, which make us strive extra hard to co-Create more love in the world. That is the reason why God needed to Create this illusory reality of lack, fear, wars, suffering, so we can continuously do our utmost to expand Creation, and to co-Create more love in the world. This is also why it is important to co-Create things that you love and enjoy, because prosperity is more than just money. True prosperity from your Soul, which is the subject of this book, is inevitably dipped in all the love and joy the Universe has to offer. And since Love is the Divine energy from which this whole universe is made, co-Creating more love in the world really helps God expand Her-Himself, and in the process, it helps co-Create more tangible prosperity for you.

So in effect, your physical existence, and with it, your desires to co-Create blessings in your life, are the very reason why God Created this whole Universe. Once you fully wrap your mind around this, it goes without saying that wishing for more (as long as these are earnest heartfelt desires) is not being greedy. Wishing and desiring to co-Create more True blessings in your life is why you were put here to begin with, since your desires to manifest things that bring you love and joy help God expand Her-Himself! Prosperity, if it comes from a something that brings you love and joy, is just a natural extension of it.

The Sacred Sound of Creation

Many ancient traditions talk about sacred languages, mantras, and words that have a special vibrational potency when it comes to co-Creating and magnetizing things into one's life. According orthodox Jews and yogic alike, a sacred language is a language in which the vibrational essence of a word (its flavor or core feeling) is equal to its meaning. However, there is much debate as to which is the sacred language.

Yogic tradition believes that Sanskrit and Gurmuki are sacred languages, in which the sound Om represents the name of God as well as Her-His essence. Orthodox Jews believe that the original language of the bible, which is a combination of ancient Hebrew and Aramaic, is the only sacred language, and therefore should be the only language of prayer. Tibetans believe that just the sound "O," chanted deeply from one's root is in itself a tool for absolute communion with the Infinite, as the sound "O" represents Its essence. And, of course, let us not forget the Roman Catholic Church, who for hundreds of years enforced on vast areas of the world its belief that Latin was the only sacred language.

There are also many ancient, as well as New Age traditions that profess that the sacred language of creation is in fact music vibration, and that chanting harmonic overtones (which is a skill that's hard to acquire) is what brings about the vibrational essence of Creation.

Jumping up to modern times, Dr. Wayne Dyer[2] has researched the different names of God in many languages, and has arrived at a conclusion that they all predominately use the sound "Ah." He therefore believes that chanting the sound "Ah" is very potent and powerful meditation, as well as manifestation tool. Dr. Dyer actually has a meditation on YouTube[3] which involves listening to him chanting some very long deep-hearted "Ah"s, and staring at an evolving mandala, which would put you into a deep peaceful sleep every time.

I personally love to listen to wordless music, and find music with BrainSync technology like Anugama's "Shamanic Dream" perfectly soothing into a deep blissful stillness. I find that even the most soothing Mozart andante helps me sharpen my awareness and focus my brain in a very calming way, for example, if I need to not fall asleep while driving. And there are many researches that back up my feelings about Mozart's music.

But the important question for us is: do those sounds really possess healing and manifestation powers in and of their own? Or is it the subconscious memory of experiences we've had in the past listening to them, and the meaning we've imbued in them that have the healing-manifestation effect?

As you can see, there are many schools of thought on how certain sounds represent different healing affects and powers of manifestation. These theories start as early as the Theosophical Society (perhaps even earlier), and all the way to modern New Age spiritualism. And of course there is the bibles account of the world being Created in seven days by the spoken *words* (sound vibration) of God. And of course each tradition claims that its language to be the only sacred one.

But the Truth is that sounds, as well as language, are in the ears of the beholder, and in the vocal cords, or musical instrument being played to produce the sound. The reason you feel so at peace while listening to Wayne Dyer's "Ah" meditation is because when he chants it, he believes he's uttering the vibration of God. The reason you feel such a sublime peace and love when listening to Snatam Kaur singing yogic devotional music in Sanskrit and Gurmuki, is because she wholeheartedly believes that these ancient chants are devotional to God. So as she sings, her whole being is in a total devotional state to God. Her heart is open, and she becomes a pure channel for Divine Love and Peace. It is her high vibrational energy that transforms and uplifts you when listening to her sing.

So in essence, the sounds we hear are but a medium to transfer that Divine spark, through the pure hearts of the people who sing or speak them to us. And out of this state of Divine Oneness, love, and devotion, the sound of God could be "Uh," "Ih," "Eh," "Oh," "Ah," or just gibberish. It doesn't matter what language you speak, as long as your heart is pure and open. Because when your heart is with God, any language and every musical instrument becomes sacred. I remember driving once on beautiful magical night and listening to Jascha Heifetz play Bruch's Scottish Fantasy and realizing that the violin was "speaking" as if it had a Soul. I called my father (who is a professional violinist) to tell him of this profound truth I have tuned into. I said, "Dad, the violin has a Soul. It speaks like a person, and conveys complex ideas and feelings." And his reaction was, "Yes, but one have to know how to talk through it." I don't think he understood at the time how profound what he said was. Of course it wasn't the violin itself that had a Soul. It was the Soul of the musician that was able to transfer an aspect of Celestial music for us.

To further convey the idea that sacred language is in the heart of the beholder, here is a Hasidic story that says it all: Yom Kippur is the holiest of Jewish holidays. On this day, everyone (who is Hasidic) dresses in their finest white clothing that are pure without a spec, and goes to synagogue to pray and honor the holiness of the day. At the end of Yom Kippur, the rabbi of a synagogue blows a large horn, traditionally made of a hollow horn of a bull, with the belief that the sound of this horn would open up the gates of the heavens to accept the congregation's prayers. Once upon a time, on this holiest of days, a poor and ignorant boy came into the synagogue's silence of prayer, barefoot, and wearing dirty torn clothes. At that moment, a murmur of disapproval was waving all over the synagogue, as no one knew that these were the only clothes the poor boy had. The boy didn't know any of the formal prayers, didn't own a bible, and in fact was illiterate. But in his pure heart, he felt the presence of God so profoundly, and he passionately felt a desire to express his ecstasy of this communion with God, but didn't know how. Then, out of this excited feeling of the presence of God, out of the depth of his heart, the poor boy put two fingers in his mouth, and blew a couple of ear-piercing whistles into the reverent murmur of prayer that prevailed over the synagogue. This made the congregation furious with him. People started yelling and demanded that the rabbi throw him out of the synagogue. But while the congregation judged the boy by his appearance, the rabbi understood that what gave the boy the courage to overcome his shame of being poor and ignorant was his deep desire to commune with God, that it was the excitement of the True presence of God within the boy's heart that made him whistle. The rabbi also understood that it was this boy's whistles, which came out of the pureness of his heart that opened up the gates heavens to receive everyone else's prayers that year. So I ask you: in this story, which language is the sacred language of Creation? Was it Hebrew and Aramaic (the original language of the Bible)? Was it Yiddish (the spoken language of the congregation in those times)? Was it the horn blowing? Or was in in fact the ear-piercing whistle that came out of the pure heart of a little boy? Of course, the sacred language of Creation that won Divine favor for everyone in this story was the whistle of the little boy.

Further, sound, in whatever language, is a vibration—a tool to convey particular aspects of Creation. To understand the vibrational nature of Creation, we need to understand that musical notes are words too. Every music and every sound is an aspect of celestial music and Divine vibration. Sound is a purer more distilled version of words. And as sound is formless, it is vibrationally a bit closer to the un-manifest Creator than words. Thus music is another language that can serve as a tool for tapping into the Infinite funnel of Divine abundance, which we harness each time we RezoDance.

When it comes to sound as an element of Creation, the Bible describes the Creation of the world as God speaking the world into existence. Corinne D. Heline[4] writes that the Creation of the world was a musical one. Few people have been Graced into experiencing the Divine upper worlds, and claim to have heard celestial music while they were there. Others who have had a near death experience (NDE) report that the Light we go into is God's breath or Love, depending on their belief system. But while we may interpret these experiences as light or as sounds of celestial music, Creation really is a vibration. When you go beyond form, God's essence is pure energy-intelligence-love-peace that is so intense, that it feels like a musical light vibration. And I can tell you that it's satisfying beyond words. It is a Love that once you have glimpsed, you can spend a whole lifetime feeling homesick for. And the key to happiness and prosperity in your here-now life is to find a spark of it within your heart, and let it guide your path.

The difference between the afterlife and life on earth is that in your afterlife you are totally bathed in God's intense Love-Peace-Intelligence-Energy in Its purest state. And in your life on earth, your ability to feel God's energy is reduced to the subtle spark within—the spark that you must perpetuate and follow in order to manifest prosperity from your Soul. While God's Love underlies every string of Creation, in every realm, universe and dimension, our perception of it shifts. It is like looking through the lens of a camera, in which you can zoom in or out, or you can put different colored filters through which to look. In the reality of your life, you are zooming in on one aspect of the Whole— one leaf, one raindrop, one flower petal, one persona, one life (yours). And when you transition HOME, it is as if you've climbed a mountain that allows your camera lens to capture the entire bay in a 360° view, while still being intently focused on the beauty of every detail with crystal clarity at the same time.

The key to rejoining the Divine higher perspective (liberation) one day, and to indeed co-Creating a prosperous life while being zoomed in, is to thoroughly *enjoy* every moment of your seemingly small life. For God does NOT regard you as small! You and your life are an integral spark of Light, without which the beauty of the entire picture would be lost, and the whole would not be Whole.

In conclusion, it is not a specific sacred language that has the authority to co-Create. It is the rememberance of your Divine spark within that the words, music or image evoke. And it is God's Love for you that gives the power to bring your wish into manifestation, just like a mother who truly wants to give her child everything that he/she wants, as long as it's good for him/her. Our words have power to co-Create our reality because they convey (to yourself and to the Universe) that what you speak of brings you joy and love, and is therefore worth manifesting. To put it to you bluntly: you can chant "Om" every day from 4 am until the cows come home, but if you chant it angrily, and unhappily, then trust me when I say that this chanting is not going to manifest for you anything good! On the other hand, you can joyously sing to yourself "ma-fua zumzum" (gibberish words I've invented), and if those words make you smile and feel happy, then in those moments they absolutely gain the power of a sacred language! That is, in the moments that you use these gibberish syllabi happily, and allow them to help you connect with the most joyous (perhaps humorous) place within you, they absolutely gain the power to manifest good blessings into your life. You see, it isn't our words that weigh so much in the balance of manifestation. It is the feeling and vibrational essence that these words evoke in you, as a part of the Divine.

So since there isn't one particular sacred language other than the vibration of Divine Love, as you learn to shift your vibration into resonance with the reality you wish to manifest, choose thoughts and words that evoke positive feelings in your daily life. Use words that make you feel happy, positive, grateful, beloved, and empowered. And you'll find that it's a two way street: the more positive and inspiring the words that you choose, the more tuned in you are to Divine blessings; and the more in tune you are with Divine blessings, the more able you are to choose positive words.

Now, to convey just how potently powerful words can be once you have imbued them with your feelings and intent, think of the biblical command "thou shall not speak the name of the Lord in vain" from a metaphysical standpoint. Contrary to orthodox religious belief, the intent of this commandment was not that one should never speak of God. And it was not meant protect God's honor. God does not suffer from a malfunctioning male ego! The commandment was really meant to protect us. Because God's name, in any language we speak it with pure intent, is very powerful! So powerful that invoking it is a powerful manifestation tool. Whether you believe that the Ten Commandments were given by God on Mount Sinai, or you believe that they were ancient wisdoms that were intuited by the authors of the bible, this particular command was meant to protect us from co-Creating things we might regret later—things that don't serve our highest purpose. Because when you speak God's name (the Universe, Infinite, Nature, consciousness, or whatever else you wish to call Her-Him) with potent intent, you invoke all the powers of the Universe to show up. And they do. Always. Without exceptions! It's the law of the Universe that our Heavenly Creator is always compelled, by Her-His Love and Oneness with us, to be here for us, to ease our pains, and to give us whatever makes us feel happy, beloved, and joyous.

Now, why is all this Love business so important to understanding the co-Creative process of manifesting prosperity? Because if there ever was a sacred language of Creation, it is ***Love***!

The Creator blows Her-His essence of Love-Energy to become each one of us, and we in turn imbue it with our intent (free will) to co-Create. But the very essence—the "material" that makes up every energy form, each force, and every atom throughout Creation is Love energy! So the keys to successfully co-Creating your wishes, beyond knowing your Soul's wishes, and beyond understanding all the principles we have outlined, is to love your life and everything in it.

Certainly, the point is to find out what you can change in your life to make it more lovable and enjoyable for you, including manifesting more prosperity. But even from within the circumstances of your current life, finding a spark of Light, and perpetuating it brings more than just a warm fuzzy feeling. It brings the Love energy of the Divine, and harnesses it to co-Create all the abundance that resonates with it. Once you find that spark of Light that shines the brightest within you, from it stems every good thing, each blessing to come, and every brilliant idea that would co-Create more abundance in your life. Even if most of the circumstances of your life are in the midst of darkness, the spark of God-likeness is somewhere in your life. Reiki healing, whether you are a reiki practitioner, or someone else is showing you the kindness, can help crack an opening in the door to let more Light in. No doubt, there are many other tools, many of which we will explore in *Seven Stages to co-Creating Prosperity From Your Soul* and in *A Lifestyle of Prosperity From Your Soul*. But it is these kindness practices that help you tune into the spark of God-likeness within, that connect you with the Infinite funnel of Abundance.

It is this connection with the Light-Love within and all around that gives you new strength to rise above the challenges in your life, and to turn them into gifts that are about to fall into your lap. And once you are truly in a state of walking your highest Lifepath and expecting blessings, you are emitting the most potent signal that energetically resonates with the most auspicious blessings, which magnetizes them to come into manifestation in your life.

The discussions of this chapter were meant to help you tune into how fluid and changeable your reality is, in order to give you more confidence in how potent your power of co-Creation is. A good place to start being a more conscious co-Creator is just to start tuning into the Light of your Soul, to deeply know that the best manifestations of your highest wishes are already on their way to you; enjoy the expectation; love your life and every moment in it; and be prepared: what comes into manifestation may not be as exactly as you've imagined it. It will be much more auspicious than you dared to imagine! In the next chapter, I will give you some tools with which to evaluate your thoughts and desires in terms of which are superficial wants of your here-now self, and which are True desires that you wish to manifest into your life.

Chapter 7

Deciding What You Truly Want

Life is full of choices. You might ask: "what if I know I'm not happy with where I am in life, but I don't know what would make me happy and what is in my power to change?" I will guide you through the steps of deciding how you wish to co-Create your prosperity in *Seven Stages to co-Creating Prosperity From Your Soul*. In this chapter, I wish to give you some basic tools, so you can start becoming aware of the choices you make and the things you magnetize into your life on an every day basis, an awareness that can go a long way towards becoming a more conscious co-Creator of your life.

First, let us start by understanding the co-Creative implications of the Serenity Prayer: "God, please give me the serenity to accept the things I cannot change, the courage to change the things I can change, and the wisdom to know the difference." In the mosaic of your life-circumstances, the first key to constructing a favorable picture is to know which of the mosaic pieces need to change, and which of them enrich the picture just as they are. This is wisdom that you will develop in *Seven Stages to co-Creating Prosperity From Your Soul* and in *A Lifestyle of Prosperity From Your Soul*. But within this mosaic, what about the pieces that you cannot change? Accepting the things you cannot change in life can be challenging, but not if you tune into the wisdom of your Soul, see the hidden blessings and Soul-growth lessons embedded in each condition, and are able to rejoice and be grateful for these conditions. But then again, is any condition in life really permanent? Are all the challenges in your life really there to stay? Or have they already served their purpose? Indeed, conditions that have served their purpose lend themselves to your rising above them, leaving them behind, and changing the situation for the better. It boils down to love: Love yourself as a beloved child of God. Then love the circumstances of your life, or change them! If you don't love it, if you don't resonate with it in the deepest way, change it! You have the power to change everything, even if in some circumstances the only change is your attitude towards the situation. Even in situations that are seemingly here to stay, like paralysis for example, there are many examples of miraculous healing where people were determined that their positive thinking and prayers were going to bring results. And if you think about it deeply enough, most of the circumstances of your life have been brought about by your choice, and they can be changed by your choice.

Once you understand that you have the power to change any situation in life (or at least make sweet yummy thirst-quenching lemonade out of it), the bigger question becomes what to bring into your life from the vast menu of choices that the Universe offers. So we are going to spend the rest of this chapter exploring some basic tools for deciding what you wish to magnetize into your life. Of course, *Seven Stages to co-Creating Prosperity From Your Soul* includes many meditational processes that will help you tune into your specific Ideal Lifeplan, and devise a plan of action to co-Create it. Once you start the processes, you will start radiating to the Universe a vibration that resonates and attracts your desired manifestations into your life.

In this chapter, I wish to open up your awareness of where your hopes and dreams come from as the basis for their fulfillment, and to give you some basic tools to becoming aware of which of your thoughts and feelings originate from your Soul and are therefore empowered to come into manifestation in your life, and which are not.

Where Do Your Dreams & Desires Come From?

Where do you think your deepest dreams and earnest desires come from? And when I say earnest desires, I don't mean the occasional desire to smash ten cars and explode them into pieces because they cut you off in traffic, unless your Ideal Lifepath is to be a stunt man/woman. I'm talking about desires that come from the heart: like to love and be loved, or to build a career that would not only provide abundance for you, but also help better humanity or make some positive contribution to your community. For example, if you've always wanted to be a beautiful ballerina, if your desire came from your need to make your classmates green with envy or to show somebody off, than it is, most likely, not a desire that was planted there by your Soul, and therefore is not likely to be a part of your Ideal Lifeplan. If, however, your desire to be a ballerina stems from a desire to enrich and give beauty to the world, that sounds very much like the type of desire that indeed originates from your beautiful Soul, and is therefore likely to be a part of your Ideal Lifeplan. But it doesn't have to be anything glamorous. Even being an IRS auditor can provide you with an avenue to shine your Light on others through little acts of kindness, as long as that path is inspired by your deepest heartfelt yearnings.

Remember that your Soul is a direct extension and an integral part of your Creator. Therefore, by definition, any idea or dream that is a part of your Ideal Lifeplan is not only an expression of your Soul's free will and of God's free will as one. Because any idea, dream or theme that is a part of your Ideal Lifeplan is in perfect alignment with God's essence of unconditional Love, Light, compassion, and all that is good. So any idea or dream within you that is in alignment with your Soul's vision of your Ideal Lifeplan, is there because your Soul Self has put it there. And since your Soul is an integral part of with God, then by definition – any and all of your deep desires and heartfelt dreams are there because God and your Soul (as one unit) have put them there. To illustrate, if my finger decides to exercise its free will to wiggle itself, did it really decide to wiggle itself, or did I decide to wiggle my finger? Is there a difference? Is my finger not an integral part of me?

And of course God didn't put those ideas, dreams, and desires there in order to tease you with a desire that would never be fulfilled. God put those ideas, thoughts, desires and dreams in you because She-He has already fulfilled those dreams for you. You just have to rise up to whatever challenges are on your way, and reclaim that victory, but it was always meant to be yours. Because your highest Lifeplan, which reflects the fulfillment of your mission on Earth, is guaranteed success!

Those deepest core hopes, dreams and desires were planted there by your Soul to guide you along your Ideal Lifeplan, and help you fulfill your mission on Earth. We have seen in Chapter 5 how much stronger and more powerful your Soul's Will is, compared to the will of your here-now self. And now, knowing that your deepest dreams and earnest desires were actually planted there by your Soul Self makes it even clearer just how important it is to concentrate your co-Creative efforts on things that are in alignment with your Soul's Will, and not waste efforts on low vibrational endeavors that would not lead to success or happiness.

The next challenge becomes differentiating which of your wishes originates from your Soul, and which of them originates from the lower part of your here-now self. Making that distinction, and living every moment of your life by the radiant guidance of one's Soul is an art form that can take a lifetime to perfect. But in this chapter, I've gathered some tools to help you begin to be conscious of your choices, and examine each of them in light of your Soul's perspective. It's kind of like an introductory lesson to help you get to know your Soul more intimately.

Joy—Your Buoyancy Control Device

When it comes to co-Creating True prosperity and bringing it into manifestation in your life, the lighter you are in spirit, the more adaptable you are to changes as you travel from one universe to the next with each passing moment of your life. This adaptability and lightness "unsticks" the affinity to the "old slipper" misery, and helps us move into happiness, freedom and prosperity. It helps us connect with the Divine Source of prosperity. Now let's ask the obvious question: How does one achieve that lightness of spirit and at the same time stay present in the moment of one's life? How does one achieve that perfect balance between the connection with the Soul Self and being grounded into the physical reality of one's life?

So let's analyze for a moment misery versus joy-happiness. Why do people stay in a rut or a miserable situation, despite knowing that it is not serving them, and despite sometimes even knowing what they have to do to change things? Well, to a certain degree, society has programed us to accept pain and discomfort as part of the human condition. And so we put up with it because it is familiar, like the old beat up slipper, which if you think about it, could be easily replaced by a more comfortable new slipper. True, part of any stuck situation is fear of the unknown, fear of taking a step and failing, and sometimes even fear of success. Many times, staying in a miserable or painful situation is a desperate way to ground oneself (pain can wake up in a great big hurry!) into the denseness of this reality. But as we all know, and as we'll find out in *Seven Stages to co-Creating Prosperity From Your Soul* (Nature Healing and Nature Walk), there are better ways to ground and achieve balance.

And as you already know, contrary to how society might have programed us, suffering is **not** the natural state of our human condition! For our original natural state is one perfect health, joy, happiness and prosperity. That is how come our inner compass always drives us to change things when we are unhappy, and why we always strive for health, joy, happiness and prosperity, because we are *of* them, and they are *of* us.

So how do we begin to bridge our current state to our Ideal, and how do we achieve and maintain the perfect balance between dwelling in the blissful reality of your Soul-Self, and being grounded into the physical reality of your life? Well, the short answer to that is that in order to achieve that balance – you must live every moment with joy.

But to fully understand that statement, and to understand the important role that joy plays in deciding what you want to co-Create in your life, let's understand joy a little deeper.

As mentioned earlier, joy and love are one of the chief reasons God has Created you in the first place. She-He wanted to experience Her-Himself *as you* in this physical reality. And since this reality is God's adventure park, experiencing Love and Joy is the common thread through all levels of reality. Recall from our discussion of the aspects of your Soul that the immeasurably greater part of your Soul still lives in Heaven right now, and that only a small part of yourself is grounded into your here-now self that interacts with this reality. So since the greatest part of your essence is of Love-Joy-Bliss, Joy is the one thing that connects you to your immortal Soul, and helps you truly experience the aspect of yourself that still live in Heaven.

Remember from Chapter 5 our debate on what would happen if your Higher Self pulls you one way, and your here-now self pulls you the other way? Well, the good news is that there is one thing they both agree on—Joy! Thus experiencing deep joy in everything you think, feel, and do in this physical reality serves to ensure that what your here-now self thinks it wants, is indeed in line with what your Soul really wants. This makes joy immensely important for the successful manifestation of your desires. And here's why:

Dwelling in the ethereal essence of your Soul can bring wonderful visions and great foresight. But walking through life in a dreamlike state of the memory of your angelic High Self without grounding any of it to reality could make you an aloof dreamer, and a poor co-Creator of your reality. Aloof dreamers are seldom successful in their manifestation efforts, because their Souls are often ones who had spent considerable time in more advanced realms in which manifestation is instant and happens with the power of thought. These people are therefore not accustomed to the demands of taking an active part in this physical reality. Further, they are not accustomed to the need to have things manifest as physical reality. And they are often very satisfied just having an ethereal dream. You might say that these people live in the in-between the higher meditative states and this physical reality, and therefore physical co-Creation of the object of their dreams holds no joy for them!

On the other end of the spectrum, walking through life's reality without the connection to your Soul Self can get one very lost in a life that's devoid of the understanding of the bigger picture, in the physicality of this reality, and in the jungle of the scars and disappointments of life. This can manifest as stress, fear, lack, illness, war, or unhappiness to name just a few examples. So where is the balance?

To illustrate, let's think of life as a diving experience. Think of yourself as a happy vacationer going on the boat with the dive master for a dive in a beautiful Caribbean island with turquoise-blue ocean around. Think of the gorgeous and colorful reef below the surface, to be explored and enjoyed on your dive. Planning your dive to best enjoy the experience and explore the reef correlates to your Soul's planning of your Ideal Lifeplan before coming into this life, in which It plans a roadmap for touring through the reefs of life such that you would be able to get the best experience from it.

In diving, one of the first important things you'd learn is to control your buoyancy. If you have too much air in your vest (your buoyancy control device or BCD) or carry too much air in your lungs, you'd float up too much and would not be able to enjoy the beauty of the reef (allegorical to the aloof dreamer). If you put in too much air too quickly in your BCD, you would bolt up to the surface very quickly, which is dangerous because it could rapture your ears, damage your lungs, or give you the bends, and needles to say that the dive is over (allegorical to death). On the other hand, if you keep too little air in your BCD or you take too many weights with you, you would sink down to the bottom too much, and could get scratched by the reef and bottom rocks (allegorical to the person who is weighed down by the scars of life and have allowed pain/fear to cut them off from the Infinite funnel of abundance). In diving as in life, the best situation is one where you have just enough air in your vest, so that you could float-glide just above the reef, but stay submerged deep enough to enjoy the beauty and colors of it all.

In life, what is the perfect Buoyancy Control Device that can help us immerse ourselves in this reality deeply enough to successfully ground-co-Creator our wishes, but at the same time stay in touch with our magnificent Soul and the Infinite Funnel of Abundance? Joy! Besides being the very purpose of life, experiencing love and joy is also the one thing that both your Soul-Self and your here-now self agree on.

So what happens when your here-now self wants something that is conflicted with the Will of the Soul? The resulting delay in manifestation could be understood by our diving illustration. It's like going on a dive with air filling up your BCD or not enough weights, but at the same time continuously exerting effort with your muscles to go into the depth of the dive; or like to having too much weight on and not enough air in your BCD, so that you would have to continuously exert effort to stay above the scratching rocks. You can also think of it as swimming against a powerful current. In all those examples your muscles will work extremely hard to help you get somewhere that is contrary to Nature, i.e., your here-now self tries to pull you in a direction that is contrary to the natural tendency of your Soul's Will.

But again, joy and love are the things that both your Soul and your here-now self agree on. Your feelings are a barometer to gage whether a particular moment in life, an intent, or a course of action are in alignment with the will of the Soul. If you feel bad, sad, and burdened by life, it isn't, and you need to do something to unveil what the True Will of the Soul is.

Your joy buoyancy control device can indeed help you find that perfect balance in your life: being connected to your sixth sense can give you insight into infinite dimensions of your Soul's wisdom; while being connected to your body temple means that the flow of Spirit within it is free and uninhibited. The balance is being grounded enough to produce the youthful vitality and true feeling of joy that your senses communicate to you in every point in your body (that's called being in your body), but at the same time being readily connected to the Divine nature of your Soul and Its wisdom, Love, Light, and joy. From a vibrational energy standpoint, joy is the thread that connects all parts of you harmoniously.

There are many ways to achieve such balance. The seven stages of co-Creation outlined in the Level 1 Prosperity From Your Soul Course will take you step-by-step to unveil what the True Will of your Soul is, and take action to navigate your life towards that more auspicious destiny. And of course, attending RezoDance sessions daily, practicing the meditational practices outlined in *Seven Stages to co-Creating Prosperity From Your Soul*, and the lifestyle choices recommended in *A Lifestyle of Prosperity From Your Soul* are all tools to help your manifestation process, as they will help you stay in a vibration of living a healthy, joyous, abundant life—a vibration that is resonates with and attracts all that you wish to co-Create.

The Joy Meter

To be clear, True joy is different than instant gratification. Here-now level instant gratification enjoyments could be short lived. And some of them, like drugs, violence in any form, and other low-vibrational habits, can enslave the Spirit and obscure its Light inside a dark non-see-through crust. In comparison True joy is Divine. It is joy that echoes throughout our entire beings and makes our hearts sing. It is long lasting, and gives freedom for the full radiance of your Soul to shine through. As a result, when we experience True joy, there is never any doubt that this moment, this choice, this feeling, was meant to be. It just *feels right* in the most profound sense. Being guided by this feeling is the real stuff of co-Creation. It is what brings Heaven to Earth, and reclaims your highest most auspicious Lifeplan into manifestation in this here-now reality.

The question becomes: how do you know whether something you enjoy is just a momentary enjoyment of the low vibrational kind, or a True joy that is the serves your Soul-Self? For example, some people enjoy taking various recreational drugs, or using and abusing other people. And yet we all intuitively know that these are destructive habits that do <u>not</u> serve anyone's Higher Self in any way, not even their own. Momentary enjoyment could come out of an impulse, force of habit, revenge, mean streak, or any other lower motivation. These are things that your here-now self pushes you to say or do because at a certain moment of disconnection from your Soul, it is the only way your lower-self remembers how to fend for itself. But these are not things that satisfy you on all levels. In fact, quite often, we feel regret after having said something mean to a co-worker, even if it was witty and gave us the upper hand in a particular situation; we quite often regret going down on a one-pound hamburger with oil-soaked French fries and a sugary milk shake, because it is only a particular aspect of us, usually our primal, instinctual Nefesh, that is temporarily satisfied by these behaviors, not the Ruach (spirit), and definitely not our Neshama (Higher Self).

True joy, on the other hand, is an experience that is more deeply satisfying. For it originates from your Soul, and by extension, your heart and your here-now self are also joyous. All parts of you are in alignment and balanced with regards to this decision or action. And the result is a feeling of joy that's at the core of your heart and throughout your entire being. It's when something just feels so very right and so good that you secretly start wiggling your toes in joy! Do you see the difference?

If you experiment with this awareness in your everyday life, and you'll most often see that choices you make that are directed by True joy suddenly lead you to a position of advantage and good fortune, without even having to think hard to get there.

The God Meter

To give you a meter that could actively and more precisely help you ascertain whether a certain thought, behavior or choice is a bad habit that needs to be eradicated, or if it does in fact originate from your Soul Self, I've summarized the above Truth into this shorter meter I call "The God Meter." It gives you specific questions you can ask yourself, to find out what level of yourself the thought, behavior or choice comes from, which in turn will help you decide what to do with it:

<u>Decisions That Originate From Your Soul-Self Would Produce A "Yes" Answer To All Or At Least The Majority Of These Questions:</u>

- ☯ Does this thought/behavior/choice promote your health and wellbeing?
- ☯ Does it enhance your overall state of being?
- ☯ Does it support your highest good in the greater sense?
- ☯ Will you still be happy about this decision/behavior/choice later… tomorrow… next week… next year?
- ☯ Is this behavior/choice pro-life?
- ☯ Does it satisfy you deep – to the core?
- ☯ Is it pro-happiness? Does it make your heart sing?
- ☯ Does this choice/behavior make you feel light hearted and happy?
- ☯ Is this a loving decision that would promote peace and harmony and a win-win situation for everyone involved in the long run?
- ☯ Does it create more love in your life, in the lives of those around you, and in the world?
- ☯ Does it support the good of mankind?
- ☯ Will this behavior/choice produce long lasting happiness?

If you answered no to most or all of the questions above, then consider that this decision or thought probably does not originate from the highest part of you, and may be the result of some limiting condition originating from your here-now self.

<u>To confirm that a behavior/choice comes from your lower here-now self, ask yourself:</u>

- ☯ Does this behavior/choice produce only short-term gratification, but is destructive in the long term?
- ☯ Does this behavior/choice hurt anyone else?
- ☯ Is it fear driven? Is it driven by hate or vengeance?
- ☯ Is it a "to spite" reaction, to show off, or scare other people into respecting you?

- Is this decision imposed by your boss/family/friend?
- Does it make a deep part of you unhappy? Does it make your heart close up and feel numb like a dark room that hasn't seen Light for a long time?
- Do you feel heavy-hearted with this decision?
- Does this choice/behavior give you a knot in the pit of your stomach?

If you answered "yes" to <u>any</u> of these questions, it indicates that this choice or behavior driven by fear or an otherwise low aspect of your here-now self. In that case, the best course of action that would serve your Soul is to eradicate this thought/feeling/behavior, and meditate on how to alter your path (the choices that you make) towards one that would be pro-life, pro-happiness, and pro all-inclusive health and prosperity. The meditational processes in *Seven Stages to co-Creating Prosperity From Your Soul* will help you eradicate all negativities and stress from your life, so that you can be free to tune into and co-Create your Ideal Lifepath.

But you see, the behaviors/thoughts/actions that originate from the lower self (which resonate with the second list) produce the opposite of joy, and therefore shift your energetic vibration into likeness and resonance with all that you don't want to magnetize into your life—that which is the opposite of prosperity. On the other hand, the thoughts/feelings/decisions/actions that originate from your Soul (which resonate with the first list) produce a True joy, which is synonymous with the Love, Light, kindness, gratitude and all the highest vibrations that shift you into resonance with the Infinite funnel of abundance of All-That-Is. Therefore dwelling in the supreme True joy that comes from acting, living, and making decisions that are inspired by your Soul is the real stuff of co-Creating prosperity from your Soul.

The metaphysical understandings that you've acquired in Chapters 1-6 are important. They lay the groundwork for the internal shifts that are about to happen on your path to becoming a conscious co-Creator of your life. But beyond metaphysical understandings, this "God Meter" is the first real tool I've given you towards becoming a more conscious co-Creator. Indeed, within the process of knowing what you wish to attract into your life, becoming aware of which thoughts, behaviors and themes attract all-inclusive prosperity into your life, and which do not, is a first step. Of course, having a clear picture of the details of the Lifepath that you Truly wish to co-Create is the real key to manifesting it. We will go through a detailed step-by-step process of helping you zero in on your Ideal Lifepath in *Seven Stages to co-Creating Prosperity From Your Soul*.

But at least now you have some tools with which to monitor your progress of becoming a conscious co-Creator. So from now on, start sounding everything you go through in your everyday life against your internal God Meter: how does it make you feel? Feelings, not capricious sensations but deep feelings of your heart, are the barometer of your Soul, and are therefore barometers of close the current moment in your life to your Ideal Lifepath of health, happiness and prosperity.

In the next chapter, we will address and dissolve certain fears, which have been plaguing humanity for far too long, which you can no longer afford to let stand in your way of fully reclaiming your most prosperous life. We will also take a look at money from a metaphysical perspective, as a form of energy that should be flowing abundantly into your life.

Chapter 8

Death & Money – Taboo Or Not Taboo?

So let's actually talk about money. How do we start bringing the Infinite energetic abundance of your Soul into your here-now reality?

To be clear, I am not a financial guru of any kind. When you get to the point when you've had a crystal clear Ideal Life Meditation, a profound Ideal Daily Routine Internal Experience, and have gotten some great ideas on a plan of action for co-Creating your Ideal Lifepath of prosperity (all of which will happen when you go through the meditations taught in *Seven Stages to co-Creating Prosperity From Your Soul*), then you may need to do some research in the here-now world to anchor your meditational ideas into reality. As part of that research, you will probably need some specific financial information. And when that time comes… when you are ready to start taking action in the here-now level of your reality, there are whole libraries, written by real financial experts that could offer you all the specific financial/business information you'll need. The only aspects of money that I wish to talk about in this chapter are: if money is just another form of co-Created energy (in the same way that all matter is just "frozen" energy), than where does it fit in with all the highly metaphysical principles we've discussed in previous chapters? In other words, which concepts and beliefs about money do you need to shift, if any, to magnetize more money into your life? What do you need to actually do, to co-Create the strong and steady resonance with money that would continually manifest it in your life? And the biggest question is: How do you reconcile the Ideal and the now? Meaning: *how do you start shifting the current reality of your life into your Ideal Lifepath?* That is the first subject of this chapter.

The second part of this chapter deals with dissolving the unconscious fear of death, in order to enhance your ability to co-Create abundance in your life. And how is fear of death relevant to co-Creating prosperity? Simple: as shown by surveys[1] done on hundreds of NDE survivors, one of the most common results of the near death experience is an elimination of the fear of death. And following the experience—without the fear of death—most NDEers go on to have meaningful and **prosperous lives**, which points to a direct correlation between the elimination of the fear of death and prosperity. Indeed, only when one no longer lives in fear—of death or anything else, can one live every moment of life with joy. Lacking fear of death gives you the ability to boldly go forward and fully live every moment of life with zest. It is a vibration that connects you with the Love-Joy energy of the Infinite Funnel of Abundance. As you already know, living in the vibration of "I'm afraid of what would happen if…" shifts your energetic vibration to resonate with, and therefore attract, all that you do *not* wish to co-Create into your life; whereas living in a vibration of love-joy and zesty aliveness changes your energetic vibration into likeness and resonance with the prosperity of the Divine, and magnetizes it into manifestation in your life.

Our Preconceptions About Money

As you already know, prosperity in the financial sense, as well as in all Divine senses, is created by a mutual vibrational resonance between you and the Divine Source of all abundance. In order to manifest as money in your physical reality, that mutual resonance has to have an anchor in your heart center. However, beneath the surface of your consciousness, any unhealthy preconceptions about money can create energetic debris in your Mental Body, which restrict the flow of your co-Creations from the ethereal into the physical, like a clogged filter that restricts the flow of fresh living water from pouring into your cup. Thus, the first step to attracting more money into your life is to change any unhealthy subconscious beliefs—clear your Mental Body from debris, and uproot all thought patterns that do not serve your highest wellbeing as a conscious co-Creator of your life. So let's examine some of the preconceived ideas about money that may be floating in there, beneath the surface of your consciousness.

 The first belief that we must uproot is that money is somehow not spiritual. While on a conscious level everyone agrees that money is good, unconsciously our society has wrongfully programed us to believe that money is bad. History has deeply ingrained in us old religions beliefs that "sin crouches in every doorstep," that money leads to temptation, and is therefore the root of all evil. Now from an aware perspective, one starts to wonder about the motivations of the church and other leaders who have, throughout history, made the masses believe that money was bad.

 As all misconceptions go, this misconception too stems from a twisting around of truths. So let's separate the wheat from the moss: It is true that a thirst for money that ignores (forgets) the Infinite resources of your Soul; a hunger for money which comes from pure greed (driven by fear); and a willingness to do anything to obtain money, including lie, step on others, steel, and ignore the highly moral character of one's Soul, are all unhealthy. They are feelings and actions that go against the True nature of the Soul, and therefore shut off one's connection with It. The results of this disconnect is a dimming of the Light in one's heart—the human anchor for Soul's Light—making the heart a dark and miserable place, all of which effectively cut one off from the Infinite Funnel of Abundance. However, what is bad in all of those behaviors is not the money itself, but that they are contrary to the True nature of the Soul. The money itself is just another form of manifested energy, and is therefore neither good nor bad. Just like poppy seed flowers are neither good nor bad. Imagine yourself putting poppy seeds in the ground, and giving them water and sun. A few months down the line, beautiful poppy flowers bloom. Now whether the poppy flowers are good or bad depends on you—the grower: Are you going to make opium from those seeds, and sell it to unsuspecting teenagers? Or are you going to bake from them delicious poppy seed pies imbued with all your love, and donate them to feed hungry children? You see, the flowers themselves haven't done anything wrong. In the same way, money-energy is neither good nor bad. It's what you do with that manifested energy – your intent, and the flavor of your essence that's imbued in the manifestation, which make that energy-form (money in this case) good, bad or indifferent.

And here is where money becomes highly spiritual: when you live your life in a heart-centered way that resonates harmoniously throughout your entire being, you are following your Soul's directives. And your Soul's directives would never do anything to harm or take advantage of others. Your Soul's directives are always pure, benevolent, and considerate of everyone's highest-best good at the same time. Your Soul would always direct you to adhere to Its high moral character of honesty and integrity. Moreover, your Soul always remembers the Infinite resources available to you from the Divine, and therefore has no need to be greedy or fear lack. As it relates to manifestation of money, your Soul's directives would also always lead you towards your Ideal Lifepath, which *is designed to be financially auspicious!*

But it isn't that you chase money and then stumble across some good way of making it. It's that first, you seek to merge your current lifepath with your Ideal Lifepath, and then the money is just an inevitable natural outcome. Beethoven and Chopin did not write music because they were greedy or wanted to get rich. They wrote music because they couldn't help *but* write music. It came out of the truest place inside them (a dictation from the Divine?). Thus, the financial prosperity that they enjoyed (in the form of rich baronesses who sponsored their lives) was just a natural byproduct of living their bliss. Because this financial abundance was the result of listening to (and writing) the purest music of the Divine within them, there was nothing wrong and everything right with it. Soul's directive always directs people towards the kindest channels for use of their newfound wealth, which enable them to do great things for themselves, for people around them, and sometimes for humanity. So since you are now in the process of merging your lifepath with your Ideal one (in which you're going to do lots of good for yourself and for the people around you), the money that should start now precipitating into your life is a fabulous and very spiritual thing. Put that in your pipe and smoke it!

A second type of subconscious programing that might be restricting the flow of abundance is how worthy of it we feel. We've talked about kindness-to-self and self-validation in Chapter 3. But realize just how important this feeling of self-worthiness is to co-Creating prosperity: subconsciously feeling unworthy acts like a huge clogged filter that limits the flow of Universal Abundance into your life. And unfortunately, a subconscious feeling of unworthiness is not all that uncommon: Most of us have been told at one point of our childhood or another, "Bad boy/girl! You should have minded me. Now you don't deserve your allowance this week," which planted seeds of subconsciously feeling that we are bad and therefore do not deserve to have money. Some of us have also heard statements like, "Don't boast. Be modest. You should never take credit for yourself," which leads to the creation of a subconscious program that makes us never take credit for ourselves (even in our own eyes), and eventually start putting ourselves down. I was even told, "Your grandmother loves you too much, and you don't come to see her often enough. You are bad! You don't deserve being loved like that!" And while I now understand that in her own twisted way, my mother was just trying to teach me to be more respectful of other people's feelings, the seed of negative programing that stemmed from that statement grew into such a huge baobab tree that I had to later do extensive meditations and self-healing to uproot it and reprogram a more positive belief system. In most cases, our parents' intents were probably benevolent: to discipline and make us better people. But these things that they had offhandedly told us, in many cases, have become seeds for a subconscious belief that we are not deserving of credit and not worthy of receiving love, money, or whatever the case may be. As we grow up, that program keeps going on in the back of our mind like a tape. And every time something goes wrong, we reinforce that negative belief by telling ourselves, "of course it went wrong, because I'm not worthy of receiving money, (success, love...)." But that inner feeling of unworthiness is <u>not</u> based on Truth. Far from it. In fact, even the parent, who had at one point said those things, does not really think that you're bad. And I'm sure if you ask your parents today whether you have ever been really bad, they would say 'no'. And I'm sure that the parent who had blurted out these statements so many years ago believes that you are very worthy of every good thing. It is only your young child's mind that had taken these statements literally and has internalized them as "truth." The Truth is that your claim to fame, love, abundance—your worthiness does not stem from anything you did or didn't do. Your worthiness comes from *just being you!* Because who you are, is a beloved child of God. You are the unique expression through whom God chooses to experience Her-Himself in this lifetime. And that is something nobody else can do but you. It is something that no one can take away from you! So of course you are worthy of every good thing—including money. In the last chapter of *Seven Stages to co-Creating Prosperity From Your Soul*, I will introduce a practice that can help you uproot all of those unhealthy subconscious beliefs about money, and reprogram healthy ones. But one simple practice that you should probably adopt right away is: when encountering a less-than-ideal situation on your path to prosperity, say to yourself, "this is only a minor setback, directing me to learn something, better my strategy, and situate me to receive greater success and prosperity very soon." And when something good happens, you should say to yourself softly and lovingly, "Of course! Of course this good thing happened to me, because I deserve it!"

<u>The third</u> preconception about money that must be changed in order to co-Create it is our perception of how much effort is going to be required to manifest financial wealth. Most people are convinced that we must work hard in order to make money, again, because we have been preconditioned to believe so. In the course of growing up, most children have heard from their parents at one point or another, "What, do you think money just grows in trees? Your father/mother and I work very hard for that money... You'll find out when you grow up how hard it is to make money." The parents saying those things are just trying to avoid superfluous spending at that moment, and perhaps teach their child to be responsible with money. The same goes for "save your pennies for a rainy day." The parent is just trying to teach the kid to be responsible with money. But these statements plant a seed in a young child's subconscious, from which a whole belief system stems, that money is difficult to make.

And most of the time we are completely unaware of those <u>un</u>conscious belief systems. But since we magnetize into our lives that which vibrationally-energetically resonates with our deep beliefs and feelings, these pre-conceived ideas work as a self-fulfilling prophecy. So the belief that we must work hard to make money puts restrictions on the Universal free flow of Abundance into our lives, like that clogged filter through which Light-Abundance energy must pass before it can manifest. And here again is major misconception, which must be uprooted before Universal prosperity can flow into your life easily and abundantly. The Truth is that you do not necessarily have to work hard for every dollar you make. There are countless examples of people who just blink and they make money, usually capitalizing on their natural gifts and passions. Why couldn't you become one of them? You absolutely can, especially if you co-Create your Ideal Lifepath.

The fourth misconception about money is our preconceived ideas of exactly how the money is to appear in our individual lives. All my life I thought that hard work was my only option of making money (a belief that my father had programed in me), and that I was going to do so by becoming an airline pilot. In my long career path as an airline pilot, money wasn't manifesting easily or abundantly for me. Imagine my surprise when money started manifesting more easily and abundantly from practicing reiki and teaching spiritual retreats (in retrospect, I say "of course, reiki and teaching spiritual retreats were my True calling"). The point is, you never know. You may have thought that you'd have to work as an engineer all your life, when suddenly a brilliant idea sparks in your mind… Yesterday, I met a retired electronics engineer who, until 25 years ago, was just a simple engineer, working for a small Israeli company, making humble wages. Then at one point during a visit to the US, he and his wife were having dinner with some friends, who introduced him to some NASA engineers. At dinner, the NASA engineers were telling him about a technical problem with the mirror of their space telescope, when suddenly, an idea of how to solve it sparked in his mind, a solution that would improve process of the telescope's calibration once it got into space, as well as lower NASA's cost of manufacturing the telescope. I didn't quite understand all the technical details, but it sounded like it was one of those simple-but-brilliant ideas. The man left Israel, opened an independent engineering company, and through his new dinner connections, got a contract with NASA to develop an application of his solution for their space telescope. As was evident by the man's dress, grooming, and the type of car he drove, it sure did look like his idea has made him and his wife very wealthy. And if you analyze what it was that allowed this humble-wage engineer to become a wealthy man, it was that he didn't mentally box himself into one particular avenue through which the money was going to come. When you are locked into only one source of income, and you think of it as the only avenue through which the Universe may bring prosperity into your life, you are effectively limiting the channels through which the Universe can now bring you prosperity. And the truth is that you never know.

You need to open your mind and allow room in it—conceptually and energetically—for the Universe to surprise you – to bring you prosperity through other avenues than the ones that your limited here-now consciousness can perceive. We are going to do some meditations in *Seven Stages to co-Creating Prosperity From Your Soul* to help you tune into your Soul's specific plans for manifesting prosperity for you. But for now, the first step is to just let go of preconceived notions, and be mentally-emotionally open to new avenues, opportunities and surprises that the Universe has in store for you.

The fifth concept that needs to be changed in order to free our minds, and thus make us more conscious co-Creators, is our preconceived notion that it is more difficult to manifest money than love, thought, and other ethereal energies. We need to free our minds and allow for the possibility of grand things to happen to us. Miracles can and do happen every day! Because the Truth is that love-energy is not much different than money energy when it comes to Divine manifestation. It's true that Love-energy is of the lowest-density (highest-vibration), and therefore can move and change very faster. In comparison, money is a higher density energy, which moves so slowly that it appears, from our human perspective, to be "frozen" solid. But in light of what we've discussed in Chapter 6, realize that the only difference between them is only the density of the energy being co-Created. Love (and here I'm talking about Divine Love, not human love) is Creative energy in its purest form, which moves and vibrates faster than anything else in the Universe. The next, slightly denser type of energy is thought and consciousness energy, which still moves/vibrates pretty darn fast... but slower than Divine-Love energy. Feelings (human emotions, which includes human love) move even slower than thought-energy since their energies are heavier and denser, but still faster than actions and tangible manifestations. Human actions vibrate slower than feelings, and are thus already happening at a level we can perceive from our human perspective. But they still vibrate and change at a faster rate than physical objects. The heaviest densest energy we know is that of physical objects, which move, vibrate and change at the slowest rate. To illustrate, envision a helium balloon tied to a heavy marble (through a hole in the marble). While the balloon travels a larger distance forward (or from side to side), the marble only roles a smidge. But once you get the balloon (your thoughts and feelings) to move in the right direction, the marble (the financial circumstances of your life) will move in that same positive direction as well.

However, the slowness of change in our physical reality is <u>not</u> indicative of any difficulty in co-Creating it, not for a God that Creates whole universes every moment anew! Your awesome Creator is just as capable of manifesting a flower as She-He is of manifesting a hundred million dollars, in a blink of an eye. The only condition for manifesting more money in your life is: It has to fit in with what your Soul Self Truly wants (Free Will), in perfect harmony with the mosaic of your life; and every blessing has to fall into your lap at the most opportune moment from the higher perspective of your Soul, as you walk your Ideal Lifepath and enjoy the treasure hunt of your life.

But the purpose of this section is not to dwell in all these unhealthy preconceptions, but to help you develop an awareness of the clogged filters that were until now limiting the Universal flow of abundance to you, and to empower you with the understanding that these clogged filters do not have to stay with you throughout your life. You aren't married to them! By the power of your free will, you can and will let them go. The last chapter of *Seven Stages to co-Creating Prosperity From Your Soul* has a section that explains how to simply stop any non-serving internal monologue, and reprogram your mind with the positive beliefs of your choosing, and by that – allow yourself to open up all your channels for receiving easily flowing abundance from the Infinite.

Manifestation Of Money As Divine Guidance

So leaving behind all of our unconscious preconceptions about money, money is not only good and spiritual, but its very appearance in your life can actually be a sign that you're on the right track, as far as your Soul Self is concerned. Manifestation of unexpected favor, including financial prosperity, in your life can be a great barometer of how close your current vision is to your Soul's Ideal Lifeplan, and where you stand in relation to its co-Creation as you start walking the new path. Money and auspicious synchronistic events, which are showered on you as a result of a particular choice that you've made, are positive feedback from the Universe that your choice was in accordance with your Ideal Lifeplan, and you are on the right track to co-Creating it. In other words, money can be a telltale of if you're getting it right. Now, if you are co-Creating money as a result of the meditational practices in this book, or of your participation in Level 1 Prosperity From Your Soul Course, than you can trust that the prosperity being precipitated upon you is rightfully yours to keep. Because this program is geared towards connecting you to your Soul and Its highest Lifeplan for you.

So let's say that you meditationally formulate a vision of your Ideal Life (as you'll learn how to do in *Seven Stages to co-Creating Prosperity From Your Soul*). And since you are new to this type of meditational exercise, you are not sure whether this vision really originates from your Soul's Ideal Lifeplan, or if it's just wishful thinking. One sign that your vision is based on your Soul's Truth is the feelings of peace and elation you'll get during the meditation. That profound peace and stillness usually means that you are tuned into your Soul's consciousness. Another positive sign is if your vision deeply resonates with every fiber of your being. But let's say that you still are not sure whether you've just had a good meditation or have really tuned into your Soul's vision for your life. A sure way to tell is to pay attention to the signs the Universe is giving you as you start walking the path of your vision: If you start walking the path of your new vision, and every difficulty mounts your way, then you'll know that this new vision wasn't really in accordance with your life's mission, at least not this particular version of it. It may be the wrong timing, the wrong location, the wrong business partners, or maybe the concept just needs tweaking. There may be a missing element in it, which the Universe intends to synchronistically send you so you can complete the concept. In any case, you would need to meditate deeper, and either fine-tune this vision, or be open to a totally different vision that *would* be in accordance with your Ideal Lifeplan. Conversely, when you start walking the path of your new vision, and Universal gifts just start falling into your lap, that's a pretty sure telltale that your vision is indeed based on your Soul's Ideal Lifeplan.

For example, good friends of mine have always dreamed of opening a Kolache bakery. But for many years, they didn't have the money to do it, and doubted that the Universe would opportune them the money to open this business. Through the years, they worked in the hotel industry for a while, struggling to make ends meet; they managed someone else's franchise business; opened a partnership with an investor to sell inexpensive fuel services for business jets. But all of these business endeavors were unsuccessful. Then came the maturity of understanding that their Kolache bakery dream was part of their Ideal Lifepath. They understood that it was meant to be. Just then, the money that afforded making this dream a reality showed up miraculously through a good friend who suddenly received a large disability settlement, and was willing to invest it in their dream. This wasn't by any means the end of the auspicious synchronicities. One night, when looking for a restaurant in which to celebrate their anniversary, they found out that the restaurant was closing and looking to sell them their kitchen equipment inexpensively. So they were able to buy most of the kitchen equipment required to make their dream come true for only $3,000, instead of the $20,000 it would have otherwise cost. But the Universe wasn't finished with the auspicious synchronicities. That same week, they found the perfect location, which the landlord was willing to rent to them for a fraction of the normal cost, if they would do some required improvement themselves. Then, shortly after the new bakery was opened, the city came and asked their permission to turn the bakery's parking lot into a park and an official meeting place for the city. Not long after that, through no efforts of their own, a national television show asked if they could do a news story about the bakery, and success just snowballed from there. This is a perfect example of how the Universe communicates to you that you're on the right path through synchronistic events. Now, I don't know why specifically opening a Kolache bakery was important enough to make it someone's life-mission. Maybe because my friends imbue their baked goods with loving intent and reiki energy, and serve everyone with a kind smile? Or maybe it's the bakery's quaint dining room, which my friends have created as a loving oasis for people to relax, shed off all the worries of their day, and just feel nurtured. The point is that all those auspicious synchronicities made it clear to them that this bakery was a part of their Ideal Lifepath, it was as if God and Her-His Angels were just waiting for my friends to choose (exercise their free will) the right path in order to precipitate abundance on them.

So throughout your new path, it is important that you know how to interpret the signs that the Universe is giving you. This goes back to what we talked about in the introduction: you have infinite free choice in your life. One of those choices is inevitably the path that is your Ideal Lifeplan, which is guaranteed success, health, happiness, and prosperity.

Once you are able to live your life as an integral part of your Soul Self, and are directed by Its wisdom, money is simply another form of energy that flows freely and abundantly to you. When you find your bliss, an abundance of money is inevitable! It is the law of the Universe, because when you live your bliss, it means that your here-now self is connected to your Soul in an unobstructed way; and your Soul is in turn is an integral part of God. Therefore, when you live your life according to your Soul's wisdom, you are inevitably hooked up to God's Infinite Funnel of Abundance, which inevitably provides Light, health, abundance, love, happiness, freedom, radiance, beauty, Grace, and joy.

The Ideal & The Now

So we know that money is a good thing if anchored into the right vision, and we know that its unexpected manifestation in your life can be a Universal sign that you are on the right track. But the biggest question that we've asked in the beginning of this chapter was: "How do I reconcile the now to the Ideal? How can I start merging the current reality of my life with my Ideal Lifepath?" Before I answer that, first a little joke:

Rabbi Moshe was a perfect rabbi. He prayed a lot, and was always busy doing good deeds and helping others. But he had one prayer for himself: "Dear God, let me win the grand prize in the lottery," which he prayed daily. So one day, God called Archangel Gabriel and told him, "Hey

Gabe, you see Rabbi Moshe down there?" "Yes, Sir" nodded the Archangel. "Well," continued God, "go down there and arrange for him to win the lottery. I'm tired of hearing his lottery prayer over and over again. Just go down, and let him win already!" The Archangel then hesitantly pulled on God's sleeve and said, "Well, sir, there is only one problem." "What do you mean there is a problem?" God roared, "Are you defying My word—the Lord of the Universe?" to which Archangel Gabriel replied, "No Sir. But if Rabbi Moshe would only meet You half way—if he would only buy a lottery ticket."

This story brings up an interesting question: What exactly is half way? Although each situation is different, it is always a fine line: doing too much means you don't really trust the Divine plan to work *for you*, and you're not leaving enough room for Universal abundance to flow in effortlessly. Knowing that the Universe may bring you the blessings through a different avenue or in a different form than what you have originally expected is important. And so is trusting that the final manifestation, in accordance with your highest Lifeplan, will always be better, in the greater sense, than just what you have originally perceived. And so your adherence to the visions that come to you needs to be a loose one that allows the magnificence of God's Love to show you favor in an unexpected way.

On the other hand, doing too little means you are not really meeting God halfway. It also means that you're not yet ready to take your vision to the bank, so to speak. Sitting on a mountaintop and envisioning that you are co-Creating things does not actually manifest them in your reality. And while meditating and bringing yourself into vibrational resonance with what you want are important keys, all of these internal energies must come into play through actions— you must live your life and *act* on those soulful internal knowings. Because if dwelling in your Soul's blissful essence was the only thing that was important, you would not have come here to have a physical life on Earth. You would have stayed in your blissful Heavenly state. Coming into a physical life on Earth, the growth that you do here happens through harnessing the blissful essence of your Soul into actions, which along with your powerful consciousness and energetic vibration, help shape your physical reality.

So where is this "halfway" point in which you meet God to co-Create prosperity? Before I give you the simple answer on how to reconcile the ideal and the now, I would like to relate to you some of the answers given by some thinkers that I appreciate.

A few years ago, I accidentally went to the festive world premier of the movie "The Moses Code" at Agape. I was following the directions to meet a group of friends, and when I got to the location, it turned out to be Agape church, and the event turned out to be the world premier event. After the showing of the movie, there was a panel of the producers, directors and creators of the movie to answer questions. And one guy asked the very question we are addressing in this chapter: "How do you reconcile what you want with what is?" In his answer, Reverend Michael Bernard Beckwith talked about the two extreme. He said (I'm paraphrasing) that if you only have a vision that you just keep in your head without doing anything about it, than it is just a dream. On the other hand, if you don't have a vision, and you just do-do-do without direction, than it is chaos—your efforts are scattered cannot amount to anything. Manifestation, says Beckwith, occurs in the midpoint between your vision and the actions you are taking. And I have to say that this answer comes pretty close to the Truth, although Beckwith did not specify exactly *how* you are to jive the two realities—of the Ideal and the now—together.

Jack Canfield once wrote[2]: "Meditating and visualizing that which we want to create is simply not enough. To get results, in any area of our lives, we have to commit – in spirit, in mind, and in body. This means action… [and] unless you are in action… you do not yet believe… Because belief without action is really not belief." This is a good point. Although Canfield doesn't explain it in the same way as I've channeled it, in light of all that we've understood it in Chapters 5 and 6, action shifts your body's energy in a most profound way, which shifts your emotions, which in turn shift your energetic vibration. And if the shift is harmonious with your Soul's essence and with your Ideal Lifepath, than that action helps to more actively shift you into likeness and resonance with your desired co-Creation, which in turn speeds up its manifestation in your life. But again, Canfield does not specify what kind of action is required.

Lao Tsu said five thousand years ago: "A journey of a thousand miles starts with one step." I'll humbly add to that, your journey of a thousand miles can actually start with a tiny little baby step.

Yogic philosophy talks about manifestation of money as an outcome of the interactions between a person's Light Bodies. Yogic philosophy talks about our energetic bodies in terms of ten energetic bodies, each relating to a different aspect of the Self, three of which are aspects of the mind (not the brain, but the mind aspect of your expanded self), called the Negative Mind Body, the Positive Mind Body, and the Neutral Mind Body. According to yogic belief, the Negative Mind is the part of you that protects you against danger, gives you discernment, and gives you the ability to see yourself as separate from other people and things, thereby giving you an individual identity with which to experience this physical incarnation (ego). As it relates to co-Creation of prosperity, when the Negative Mind body is out of balance, it could create manifestation problems. For example, if your Negative Mind is underdeveloped, then you may tend to jump into unsafe situations, make rash decisions or unsound investments, which could be detrimental to walking the balanced path of your Ideal Lifepath. On the other hand, if this body is overdeveloped, it can make you gun-shy about taking a step forward. I mean, you could be sitting on a perfectly perfect vision that is truly inspired by your Soul, but just be scared to move forward. From a yogic perspective, this happens because your Negative Mind is overdeveloped.

The Positive Mind is what I call the "Yi Ha" factor! It is that part of you that wants you to open up, grab life by the balls, and say "here I am life!" It is your strong will to achieve, and be playful and optimistic. It makes you outgoing. And as it relates to co-Creating prosperity, it allows the Divine energy to pour into your individual self and manifest prosperity. However, this body can get out of balance too. A week positive body may cause one to be depressed and overly influenced by the negative mind. On the other hand, an overly active Positive Mind can make a person take unnecessary risks (investment-risks, job-risks, etc.) that are not based on a reality check, or to be overly hungry for physical possessions and therefore splurge unwisely.

The Neutral Mind is your meditative mind, which balances the positive and negative and finds the neutral center. It is also the mind that helps you tune into the perspective of your Soul.

So from this perspective, even if you discard the idea that we each have three separate Mind Bodies, there is some logic in the idea of finding a balance. If you constantly ask yourself "What if there is not enough?" and "Will this hurt me?" it may indeed shelter you from making mistakes, but it will also prevent you from seizing opportunity, and restrict or shut your connection to your Infinite Funnel of Abundance. On the other hand, if you are constantly in a "Yi Ha" mode, you are likely to take too many risks, splurge, and lose your sense of purpose, as well as your connection with the your Soul Self. True prosperity comes from dwelling in the balance between the two, and following the directives of your Soul, always directing you to reclaim your Ideal Lifepath, which inevitably leads to prosperity.

Notice, though, that all of these wise thinkers and inspirational leaders have only given us a general idea that there is a bridge between the dream/vision of your Ideal and actions in your current reality. But none of them have given us a description of that bridge.

Your Ideal Lifework:

Before I describe the bridge that would take you from your "now" point to merge your Ideal Lifepath, let's first explore the vehicle with which you get to and across that bridge. That is, within your Ideal Lifepath, what are the channels through which Universal, all-inclusive prosperity can flow to you? Because "work" in the traditional sense is not the only avenue through which the Universe can bring you prosperity, I've used the word lifework to talk about your Ideal line of work that would not only bring you income/wealth, but also the thing that you're most proud of—your passion—the thing that gives you a feeling of fulfillment. It could very well be a traditional job, but only if that job is a True passion—and we will expand on what that means throughout this section. It could just as well be a business, a sideline turned into a moneymaking thing, managing your investments, or even being a fulltime mom (in which case your husband is likely the source of the financial aspect of your prosperity). As you can see, your Ideal lifework is at this point a pretty elusive concept, and we need to sharpen our understanding of it. What exactly would your Ideal lifework have to be in order to help you co-Create the True prosperity from your Soul? What are the characteristics of your Ideal line of work? How do you know that you've picked the right one? And why did I say that you don't have to work hard to make money?

The first characteristics of your Ideal line of work is that it produces joy, to the point that joy is what actually drives you to that work to begin with, and every day anew. Because the work that is in accordance with your most Ideal Lifeplan is one that resonates with the very essence of who you are, joy is an expected outcome, and the reason why your Soul has chosen this kind of work for you to begin with. So you can use joy as one of the first telltales that a particular line of work is in accordance with your most prosperous Lifepath.

It is true that working long hours or physically hard is not necessary to produce prosperity from your Soul. But when you find your bliss—your dream job or endeavor, *even if* you do work from the crack of dawn until nightfall, you will derive so much joy, and feel so fulfilled from it that you won't even notice you are working, that it would seem like you are playing your favorite sport, or engaging in your favorite pastime. For example, my friends who own the bakery. Although they wake up at 4am and work until about 5pm on most days (because their business is still in its growing stage), they don't really feel the hours going by as they work. He enjoys talking and schmoozing with people all day, drawing them out, making people feel at ease, radiating kindness and love energy to all who come into the bakery; and she enjoys baking things with wholesome ingredients and imbuing them with all of her love and reiki energy, while exerting kindness, and coaching their employees. So at the end of the day, even though it is a long one, they both feel very fulfilled and happy.

My friends both told me that if they had won the grand prize in the lottery, they would continue to work at the bakery, which brings us to the second telltale that a particular endeavor is in accordance with your True life-mission: you feel so passionate about it, and you enjoy it so much, that you would do it even if you won the grand lottery prize. I always knew that if I win several millions of dollars in the lottery, I wouldn't just live on the money and do nothing. I would invest that money in creating a retreat that would teach people to connect with their Higher Selves, and live happy, healthy and abundant lives, a retreat that would also do nonprofit work to help at-risk youth. Now financially this idea seems illogical. It is more logical to just enjoy the money. But for me, I would enjoy life more if I not only had enough money to do everything I want, but if I had an opportunity to help uplift people to reclaim all that they were always designed to be and have. You see, all-inclusive prosperity also includes feeling happy and fulfilled in the deeper sense. So your Ideal lifework is indeed something that gives you so much joy and satisfaction that you cannot imagine not doing it. For example, my father is a professional violinist who was the concertmaster of the Israel Philharmonic orchestra for thirty years, and then the concertmaster of the Houston Symphony for another eighteen years. He has also recorded many CDs with his trio over the years. But although dad is now retired, and although he has reached financial success to the point that he doesn't have to worry about money, do you think he has stopped playing? Of course not! Playing the violin is the deepest expression of whom he is. It is an integral part of his Truest identity, and he will continue to play music until his last day. My father still derives the same joy from playing the violin today as he did many years ago as a teenager going to Julliard School of Music. And that is another question you can ask yourself as part of this second telltale: Can you see yourself deriving joy from your chosen lifework many years down the line, even after you've reached financial success? In other words, if you built from it a financial empire that can continue to bring you income even in your absence (retire), would you still crave engaging in this activity you've chosen as your Ideal lifework.

The third telltale is: because your Ideal line of work resonates with the very essence of who you are, it is inevitably something you have profound natural talents in—something you've always been good at, even if you never paid much attention to this talent, or didn't think you could capitalize on it. When it comes to capitalizing on your natural talents, your Ideal profession capitalizes not necessarily on learnt skills that were acquired through college or other training, but on your innate gifts that you were born with. If you are lucky, your professional training brings out and enhances your natural talents, the way my father's education at Julliard School of Music had enhanced his innate gift for playing the violin and allowed him to make a *successful* lifelong career out of doing exactly what he loves. But even if you haven't yet been lucky enough to match your professional training with your Truest talents, there is still plenty of time to shift your focus, and to pursue a path that brings out your Truest talents and capitalizes on them. For example, the famous pianist Arthur Rubinstein says in the book about his life that he only got serious about playing the piano at age fifty. Of course, Rubinstein's natural musical talent was revealed at a very young age. But it took him until age fifty to get serious about practicing techniques, which accentuated his talent, and helped him become one of the greatest pianists of all times, not to mention rich and famous. Another example is Colonel Harland Sanders, the founder of Kentucky Fried Chicken (today a multi-million dollar empire), who started his chicken franchising business at age sixty-five[3]. His passion and natural gift of cooking actually started when he was six years old, and had to cook and care for his younger siblings after his father died. Most of his life, he cooked chicken and served it out of his back yard. It took him until age sixty-five to tune into the fact that cooking was his natural gift, and turn them into a financial success.

That's not to say that you are necessarily in the wrong line of work. Just like the engineer in the example of the previous section – you could very well be in the line of work that is Ideal for you, but just haven't tweaked it into the particular avenue that's meant to bring you prosperity… In that example, the man was already an engineer, which was his Ideal lifework. He just had to change whom he was working for, and which project within his chosen profession was to bring him the prosperity he was destined for. The clearest visions of how your Soul essence translates into an Ideal line of work (within your Ideal Life) will come into clarity when you do the meditations of Chapter 6 of *Seven Stages to co-Creating Prosperity From Your Soul*. And in Chapter 7 of *Seven Stages to co-Creating Prosperity From Your Soul,* we will use a creative thinking/meditating process to focus your Ideal Life into a cohesive plan that would lead you to the all-inclusive prosperity that was meant for you. The purpose of this subsection is just to give you some pointers that would help you recognize your Ideal lifework when the vision does come.

Now, here is the reason why you need to consult your Soul on business decisions, as well as in all other important decisions: Many times, we get a cognitive idea in our heads, of the business endeavor we think we want, and we gather so many emotions around it that we kind of get stuck on that idea. But as fantastic a researcher, and as business savvy as you may be, here-now logic can never have all the pieces of the puzzle. And investing, or going into business, shouldn't be an emotional thing, because the market may not bear your idea; it may be the wrong time or the wrong location for it; the investors you had in mind may not be on the level; and there could be a million other nuances hidden underneath the surface. Your Ideal Lifework, though, is guaranteed success, as long as you listen to your Soul, and consult It on the "when," "where," "with whom," etc. Your Soul's advice can help you get unflustered. Since the language that your Soul uses is one of feelings, visions—essentially an ethereal language, you may need to research some data, to anchor those clues into real knowledge that can help your here-now self then take specific action. But since your Soul is in cahoots with God, It can give you foresight on business endeavors too. Your first clues as to what your Ideal Lifework should be are your passion and your natural talents for it. We will do some extensive meditations in Chapters 6 and 7 of *Seven Stages to co-Creating Prosperity From Your Soul,* to help you zoom in on exactly what your Ideal Lifework is.

Next comes the question of the actual bridge from the "now" to the Ideal: How do you reconcile your here-now reality with your Ideal? How do you make the leap from your "now" reality, to what it's going to be when you bring your Ideal into manifestation? And what is the first step that you should take towards co-Creating your Ideal Lifepath to prosperity?

The A-B-C Bridge:

Let me preface the answer by saying that the only one who is *Truly* qualified to answer these questions *for you* is your own Soul Self. In *Seven Stages to co-Creating Prosperity From Your Soul*, we will go together through a seven-stage process aimed to help you become a more successful co-Creator of your life. In steps four, five and six of this process, you will meditate to tune into the details of your Ideal Lifeplan. During (and after) those meditations, you'll have an inflow of ideas, wisdoms, and vision from your Soul that will make clear the best way *for you* to start navigating your life from its current state towards the True and all-inclusive prosperity that is part of your Ideal Lifepath. You see, your Ideal Lifeplan is a "for-your-eyes-only" kind of a thing. It is meant *for you and only you*. My Ideal Lifepath is different from your Ideal Lifepath, which is in turn different from anyone else's. Thus, it is not for me or anyone else to taint or influence the vision and directives of your Soul in any way. All I or anybody else could offer is to prepare you for your journey: help you understand the metaphysical principles of being a conscious co-Creator; give you some guidelines on what the path from A to Z should feel like; guide you to tune into your Soul's directives and visions; give you some pointers on healthy body-mind-spirit practices that would facilitate receiving the new abundance; and perhaps give you a few examples of how this bridge between the now and the Ideal has worked for others (all of which I humbly hope I've done for you in this book). The rest is up to you – to craft your life in accordance with the highest free choices you can make.

The meditations of *Seven Stages to co-Creating Prosperity From Your Soul* usually lead people to unique ideas that drive them to capitalize on their gifts and passions. In many cases, people have then decided to open a business that, because it was based on ideas that came from their Soul Selves, found niches in the market that no-one else could, which in turn brought them financial success. However, not everyone has to be an independent business owner. I'm not condemning ascending the corporate ladder to success, if that is where your True passion lies. I'm not going to evoke the cliché "make sure you have time in your life for your family and loved ones," but if you devote all of your time and efforts to ascending the corporate ladder, make sure you're doing it *for you*, because this job is something you deeply enjoy, and not because society expects it of you. There is also nothing wrong with being someone else's employee, or a housewife. You can be a clerk, a factory worker, or even a street sweeper, and still enjoy prosperity from your Soul. Just make sure you are following your True calling and deepest passion.

So for example, you may be a simple factory worker who has been struggling to make ends meet. But you have a talent of making unique little wooden dolls conveying different expressions of life that people can resonate with. You may have never thought that anybody would be interested in these dolls, until you meditated on it, tuned into your Soul, and then found a way to trademark, outsource their manufacturing, and sell bigger quantities of these dolls, perhaps even through the very factory you work in. Eventually you start mass producing these dolls and selling them online and to select stores, enjoying much financial abundance doing the very thing you were always passionate about.

Or maybe you are a stay-at-home-mom who loves to bake delicious pies for her family, and you have some unique recipes that came out of your creativity and your love for your family. My accountant recently told me that his best friend's wife used to be such "bored housewife" who always baked wonderful cakes for every occasion. He said that she had recently trademarked names for her unique cakes, patented the recipes, found a factory to outsource their production to, and has started selling them through a William Sonoma. He said that her cakes are selling like hot potatoes, and she is doing very well financially. The key in both of these examples is that these people capitalized on their true passion and gift.

If your True calling involves helping others, than the Universe will always help you in a profound way. You'll be in awe of the synchronistic gifts the Universe showers on you when your focus is on service to others. For example, you may be a simple receptionist whose struggling to make ends meet, but you happen to have a knack for putting people at ease and counseling them in times of need. When you truly embrace that your highest calling involves your ability to comfort others with your compassion, the Universe will opportune you gifts that will show you the way to financial prosperity. Perhaps it's in the form of a possibility to go to college on a full scholarship, and become a counselor or a social worker, or perhaps you "accidently" bump into a reiki master, who offers you free training to become a reiki practitioner, after which you become a full-time healer and counselor. There is no telling just how many auspicious gifts the Universe will opportune you when your focus is on service to others.

Now in all of those examples, *the shift happens* after you meditate to at least embrace your True gifts and passions, and in most cases, after you have had a vision of your Ideal Life (*Seven Stages to co-Creating Prosperity From Your Soul*). However, and this is the real bridge that we're talking about, don't expect the plan that you meditationally come up with to be perfect. Your plan will most likely have gaps. And that is how it should be, because *you aren't meant to go it alone!* You are meant to assert your free will by showing initiative. Taking the first inspired steps towards your Ideal Lifepath asserts your trust in your Ideal Lifeplan, and shows the Universe that you are ready to co-Create it. But you aren't *the* Creator. You are a <u>co</u>-Creator. This means that *the Universe (God) has the obligation to meet you more than half way!*

If we equate the stages of your lifepath to the alphabet, then after the meditational planning of Chapter 6 of *Seven Stages to co-Creating Prosperity From Your Soul*, you will absolutely know what parts U through Z (your Ideal Life) look like. And after the planning you'll do in Chapter 7 of *Seven Stages to co-Creating Prosperity From Your Soul*, you will have a good idea of how to start walking from point A (where you are right now) to points B, C, D, E and maybe even F of your plan. But more than likely, you will have no idea how to get from point F to point U. And that's ok. Once you get to point E and F, points G, H and I will unfold for you, doors will open, and you will just happen to synchronistically meet the right people who share a common goal, give you ideas on how to make your plan come true, and are ready to help you along your path. The Universe will continue to show you the way and unfold your path for you at each step. And as you start walking your Ideal Lifepath, you will get so immersed in the joy of it, that when you get to about point Q, nonchalantly lifting up your eyes and catching a glimpse of points U and V coming up on the on your horizon will almost catch you by surprise.

If you think of life as a mountain hike, then throughout your hike, depending on visibility that day, you will only be able to see the next hundred yards (or the next mile) along your trail. But you will, most likely, not have full view of the entire trail. That's why it would be most helpful for you to have some idea of where you want your trail to end up ("I'm going to hike to that peak over there so that I could look at the beautiful view"—destination and motivation/a reason), and a map of the trail, in the same way that it is most helpful to meditationally tune into your Ideal Lifeplan before making major life decisions and choosing your path. Once you've chosen a destination and the trail that you wish to hike (your Ideal Lifeplan), then with the help of your map (the plan of action that you've made based on that Ideal Life), you'll be able to navigate to the trailhead, and you'll know that you're looking for certain guideposts along your way. Some of the guideposts of kindness, generosity, gratitude, love, and joy you already know to look for – you'll be constantly checking everything you experience along your trail against the God-Meter and the Joy Meter (Chapter 7) to keep you on track and ensure that you don't get lost in the haze of mundane life. As you continue to hike your trail, you'll see more guideposts in the form of auspicious synchronicities assuring you that you are on the right track, and helping you trust that the next hundred yards of your trail will come into view as you progress on your path. In life, just because the path is a Universal energetic imprint doesn't make it any less real. It is only stored as an energetic potentiality in order to give you more chances to assert your free will. But you can rest assured that as long as this path is along your Ideal Lifepath, the next few steps will show themselves to you in time.

Now what constitutes steps along your trail? Steps that lead you towards your Ideal Lifepath of prosperity are not necessarily along the lines of climbing Mount Everest. Even meditation is an action towards co-Creating your vision. Certainly some of the simple lifestyle steps that are outlined in *A Lifestyle of Prosperity From Your Soul* are considered taking action, even if they do not seem directly related to prosperity. They are steps to shift your vibrational resonance and your physical lifestyle towards the auspicious meeting between your here-now reality and your Ideal Lifepath. Once you've finished the meditational processes of *Seven Stages to co-Creating Prosperity From Your Soul*, you'll have a clear vision of where your life is going; and when you introduce the kindness practices the outlined in *A Lifestyle of Prosperity From Your Soul* into your lifestyle, you will have shifted not only your energetic vibration into lightness, freedom, health, zesty aliveness and joy that resonates with the all-inclusive prosperity that was always meant to be yours. But you will have also anchored that higher energetic vibration into your physical. At that point, you will be walking the path of a conscious co-Creator, and you'll be ready to implement some of the steps that *you* have decided on in *Seven Stages to co-Creating Prosperity From Your Soul*.

But to give a simple answer to the question of how to bridge the "now" to your Ideal: you don't actually create the bridge; you just walk on it. The Universe is the one that Creates the bridge enabling you to transfer your "now" reality into the Ideal. In our alphabet illustration, you assert your free will by meditating and perceiving points U-Z (Ideal), and you increase your resonant connection with that Ideal reality by starting to walk steps A-F of your plan. But it is the auspicious synchronistic flow of the Universe that actually carries you smoothly from F to U, where you are merged with your prosperous Ideal Lifepath.

Practical Tips For Vibrationally Connecting To Prosperity

In this section, I give you some financial practices that, *from a metaphysical standpoint,* can help you attract more prosperity. The idea is to engage in everyday financial habits that would foster an internal reality of prosperity, and by that, strengthen your energetic-vibrational resonance with the riches that are to come.

Streamline Your Finances:

A number of years ago, I was a struggling first officer in a regional airline. I was making about $1,200 a month in the first year, and struggling to make ends meet. Even after 8 years of seniority with the airline, I was still making only $1,800 a month. As I was by then living in Southern California by the beach, you can imagine that when monthly bills came around, I was always stressed, worried and upset. And because I was always worried about making ends meet, I was always in a vibration of lack, and thus I was emitting into the Universe an energetic vibration that only resonated with, and therefore perpetuated lack. I knew I had to do something different! I started doing a lot of reiki healing on myself and on my finances, and meditationally dissolving energetic blocks.

As my reiki-meditations continued, the first insight I got was that I needed to consolidate debt, and simplify my payment structure, so that my consciousness is not constantly revolved around lack. So I consolidated all of my (humungous) credit card debts into one loan, and set up the monthly payments of that loan and of all my other bills to automatically withdraw from my account each month. Of course, this consolidation of debt and automatic payment arrangement did not yet change my upside-down income-to-expense balance, but it changed the energy of the game. Because I wasn't spending so much time and energy thinking about bills, I wasn't preoccupied with lack anymore, and wasn't sending out that vibration into the Universe. Whenever I did receive a bill, it wasn't a bill anymore; it was just a statement. So it became easier to emotionally detach from its burden and to feel like this was a monopoly game. I decided to treat bank reconciliations as a monopoly game. I made it a point to catch myself whenever I allowed myself to get stressed out about money, and to antidote financial stress by meditationally tuning into Universal abundance. At the same time, my daily reiki self-healings helped me feel Divine favor within my heart, which connected me to the joy I was supposed to be feeling all along—it helped raise my energetic vibration to resonate with prosperity.

This being said, I'm not advocating any particular bank program. In the here-now world, you need to research the bank programs that are going to fit your situation. But whether that's automatic bill payment, consolidating debt, or any other program, it would behoove you to organize your finances in a way that would allow you to not worry about them and live in joy. Because when you worry about it, your aura shrinks, your energetic vibration shifts into likeness and resonance with more bills and more lack, and you magnetize more financial trouble into your life. Conversely, putting debt/bills out of your mind allows you to concentrate your thoughts, feelings and daily activity on your Ideal Lifepath and internally experience the natural abundance that stems from it. This adjusts your vibrational essence into likeness and resonance with financial abundance and blessings, which magnetizes them into manifestation in your life.

I'm also not advocating any particular external level of lifestyle, just one that allows your internal reality to dwell in whom you Truly are, and therefore allows you to resonate with and attract prosperity into your life. All I'm saying is: simplify and streamline your financial structure, so that the reins that this reality holds you in can loosen up some, giving you *freedom* to bring about positive changes leading to grander, more long-lasting prosperity. In terms of financial action, this is just a first step.

Shifting Your Financial Balance:

While putting bills off my mind was a good start, I knew that to permanently shift my vibrational resonance out of lack and into prosperity, I had to start making more money that I spent even before I got to co-Create my Ideal reality. I have always had a passion for healing. I have been fascinated with the ability to heal ever since I was a little girl. So I decided to combine my passion for healing with the need to make more money. I was already a level-2 reiki practitioner at that point. But at the time, I was only doing reiki on myself, and for friends and family. I didn't really know that I could make money from practicing reiki. After meditationally tuning into my Soul Self, I decided to go to massage therapy school, so that I could use massage as a vehicle for bringing reiki to more people. Sometime during massage therapy school I received my reiki mastership, which made it all the more clear that reiki and spiritual teaching were my life-mission. Following my passion for healing, I soon began to work a second job at a lucrative spa, which manifested much more prosperity for me. And soon after that, as I continued to hold my vision and feeling of prosperity at heart, I was awarded an opportunity to upgrade to a captain's position at the airline I worked for, and my salary tripled. But since healing is my True life-mission, I did not stop working at the spa just because I was now making more money in my airline job. Reiki is who I am… it is part of the very essence of my Soul, and I will continue to do reiki until my last day on earth (and possibly beyond). So I continued to work at the spa, enjoying the difference I made in people's lives, even after I no longer needed the money, until I was guided to devote my time to receiving and transcribing the information in this book.

And the necessity to have a balance budget holds true for everyone; I don't care how financially savvy you are, or how good your financial advisors are. Your income and expenses have to be at least balanced in order to not drill yourself into a hole both in your physical reality, and spiritually-vibrationally. Now, that's not to say that you slave your ass off doing a job that you hate. It doesn't mean that your level of income is always going to be as limited as it may be today. And it certainly does not mean that you give up on your dreams. It just means that to have peace-of-mind to pursue your long-term goal of True, all-inclusive, long-lasting prosperity, you need to think creatively and find a way to earn more or equal to what you spend even in the now. This is because if you are spending more than you earn, you are continuously creating for yourself situations in which you'd be stressed about money, and thus perpetuating a vibration of lack. And if that is your case, you need to either let go of some assets for which you are paying dearly, let go of some of the extravagant lifestyle choices that you don't really need, or make small shifts in your life that would allow you to make more money now. This is not just financial commonsense. It is Universal law that all energy is balanced: Creation and destruction, yin and yang, positive and negative, and income and expense. Also, an income-to-expense imbalance in your "now" reality may be there to drive you to make big moves. Perhaps selling the big house that you hate anyway, and temporarily moving to a smaller apartment, will not only balance your income-to-expense ratio. Perhaps that situation was put there by your Soul to drive you to move to a place where synchronistic opportunities could lead you to find your bliss. Or perhaps a low-income situation was there to drive you to find your Ideal line of work that is more in line with your Ideal Lifeplan.

It is absolutely true that once you start shifting your life towards your Ideal Lifepath, your level of income will increase. But living in a vibration of prosperity doesn't mean splurging beyond your means. So if part of your Ideal Lifeplan includes living in a beautiful big house in Malibu for example, you wouldn't go right away and buy that house by borrowing money for the down-payment, and taking on a mortgage you can't afford, as that would only dig you deeper into a hole of despair, having to put in many extra hours at a job you hate in order to make payments, which would leave you feeling more and more like a failure – a vibration that resonates with and magnetize the opposite of prosperity. In comparison, living in a vibrational resonance that attracts True prosperity into your life means that you feel rich even if you rent a small studio apartment. To continue the Malibu example, if Malibu is what you want, you could take pictures of beautiful houses in Malibu and hang it in your house to remind you of your goal; you could go to Malibu often and do an Internal Reality meditation, envisioning yourself in your big house there… until the opportunity to live in the Malibu house of your dream synchronistically shows up in your life. Because when you *feel* the vibrational abundance of the Divine within you, and you know with every ounce of your being that Her-His abundance is already on its way to you, then you know that when you do buy your dream house, it'll be from money that is rightfully yours—money that was awarded to you through your Infinite Funnel of Abundance, living your bliss!

And let's think for a moment about what it is that makes people splurge beyond their means and engage in "retail therapy." Buying new things <u>*that you don't need*</u> (we're not talking about charging groceries to feed your family, but only about buying things that you <u>don't</u> really need) comes from a certain insatiable inner hunger. It's your inner self saying: "I'm running out of ki energy; I feel unsatisfied with myself and my life; I don't feel like I am enough; I feel cut off from the Infinite Funnel of Abundance, and therefore I am now going to artificially bring into my surrounding some new things to make me feel better." From a yogic point of view, this is caused by a weak or shrunk aura, making you feel temporarily small. A good look into the depth of the situation reveals that this tendency to engage in retail therapy beyond one's current means and needs stems from feeling cut off from the wealth of all that you Truly are—your Soul.

Now that's not to say that taking a business loan for implementing a well thought out and well meditated-on Ideal Lifeplan, or that taking a student loan to better develop your Ideal lifework are bad ideas. But those are different from continuously depleting your resources by living an extravagant but shallow lifestyle without regards to happiness or fulfillment. Taking a student or business loans to fulfill your dreams are calculated risks (expenses) you take when you are deeply sure that the path you have chosen is indeed in accordance with your Ideal most auspicious Lifepath.

Also, it may not always be possible to immediately shift your income-to-expense ratio into a balanced one before implementing your Ideal Lifeplan, as you may already work hard to feed a large family and keep roof over their heads. In those cases, you would need to put a timeline on your plan. Richard Bach, the author of "Jonathan Livingston Seagull," "Illusions," and other wonderful books, have once written: "the difference between a dream and a vision is a deadline." And the idea of a deadline plugs beautifully into this scenario. Let's say that your current budget is $500 in the hole each month, but you have already had a profound Ideal Life meditation, and have already come up with a specific plan of action shift your current reality into the Ideal Life (all of which you'll do in Chapters 6 and 7 of *Seven Stages to co-Creating Prosperity From Your Soul*) that would manifest easily flowing financial prosperity into your life, engaging in your Ideal lifework. And let's say that you estimate that it would take you a year and a half to make it happen. So if you give yourself up to two years (including fudge-factor) to make it happen, you'd need to creatively think of where to borrow $12,000 ($600 x24 months) from. But in that case, since you have set up a deadline for yourself to co-Create your Ideal Lifepath of prosperity, the $500 of monthly deficit is not really considered an upside-down budget, but an investment in your future – it is an investment in the time that you are giving yourself to leisurely reach your long-term goal, and a Lifepath that would bring you a lifetime of happiness and prosperity.

Now, with all this talk about a balanced budget, it is important to remember that cutting expense in the "now" does not in any way constitute conforming to a reality of lack. You are *not* accepting a reality of lack! On the contrary: You are balancing your income and expenses in your "now" reality, so that you can shift your energetic vibration from a consciousness of lack and stress about money into a consciousness of peace that you'd always have enough money. And you are doing so with the understanding that any tightening of the belt you might be doing in the now is only temporary, because as you start implementing the steps of your Ideal Lifeplan, your income will increase, and then you'll be able to spend more money from a position of power—without depleting your resources.

Fake It Till You Make It:

At the same time, don't get stuck in an "I'm too poor, I'll never be able to afford this" type of internal reality. While you may be *temporarily* on a tight budget, you are not poor! So instead of getting yourself wrapped out in these limiting vibrations, get busy reclaiming your Ideal Lifepath, and the prosperity that comes with it. If you've already meditated to figure out your specific plan of action (*Seven Stages to co-Creating Prosperity From Your Soul*), you should be busy doing some here-now research and creative thinking to figure out all the ways that would lead you to bring your Ideal plan into manifestation, which in turn will lead you to a situation in which you *can* afford everything you Truly desire.

One of the most important financial practices which magnetize prosperity into your life is *feeling* abundant and successful <u>now</u>. Because as you already know, shifting your internal reality into a consciousness of abundance shifts your energetic vibration to into likeness and resonance with the prosperity you seek, and therefore magnetizes it to you. And feelings are the major force that shifts your energetic vibration into that resonance. The idea is that in order to attract prosperity into your life, you have to feel rich and successful before you actually are. So how can you start feeling prosperous and successful on the one hand, while maintaining your temporarily tight cash flow balance?

One of the most basic methods of tuning into feeling wealthy is to tap into the consciousness of your Soul and have an Internal Experience meditation. You can even do a Zohar Breath Meditation (*Seven Stages to co-Creating Prosperity From Your Soul*) and ask your Soul to show you your abundance potential. Tapping into the vibration and higher vision of your Soul can help you *feel* that you are already rich beyond your current physical resources, that everything you need is absolutely going to be provided, and that you'll always be cared for. More than that, it can help you deeply know-feel that all that you Truly desire will be given easily, abundantly, and joyously. The only trick to magnetizing all of that into your life is keeping your Infinite Funnel of Abundance open, which requires matching the vibration of your Internal Reality with that of abundance you seek. And you do that by *feeling* abundant and rich in the now. I call it "fake it till you make it." But the kind of "fake it till you make it" that we are talking about is not about overspending what you don't have and acquiring what you don't need, just because. It's about your internal reality dwelling in the richness of possibilities that your Soul is soon going to precipitate upon you.

Now to draw again from my own experience, at the point that I was making much more money than I needed – working as both an airline captain and a spa therapist, I didn't jump into an extravagant spending lifestyle just because I was now making more money. To tell you the truth, before I embraced my spiritual gifts, I used to have holes in my hands—money used to just slip through my fingers. I was doing "retail-therapy" to mask every inadequacy and drown every sorrow in my life. But once on my spiritual path, I didn't need to keep buying frivolous things to make me feel worthy and happy. I started to feel worthy and fulfilled just being me, spending a lot less money. It's true that at that point, I hadn't yet fulfilled my ultimate life-mission, and I hadn't yet co-Created the huge prosperity that's to come. But I was cruising along comfortably, not too worried about money, yet not overspending it; looking forward for the bigger prosperity that I knew was coming, yet at the same time enjoying every moment of the 'now'. And that is a good place to be as you start walking the steps to make your Ideal Lifepath a reality.

One practice that can boost up your "I'm fabulous, life is fabulous" feelings, and remind you of the riches that are to come is including a special expense category in your new balanced budget called: "Rewards For Just Being Me" or "Just Because I'm Fabulous!" This expense category should include periodic (monthly? Weekly?) gifts that you should pamper yourself with, to remind you of how fabulous and special you really are; that you deserve every good thing; and that a much vaster flow of abundance is already on its way to you. And it doesn't matter how big or small these gifts are. They should be something that makes you feel special, abundant, and like everything is going to be ok. For example, if you have achy feet, buying yourself a monthly pedicure that includes 10 extra minutes of foot massage usually costs no more than $25. And it's an "I'm Fabulous" gift that could make you feel like king/queen of the world. Or let's say that all the high-paid executives in your office always go to a sophisticated restaurant with a very trendy atmosphere and interesting looking dishes. And you too want to go to this restaurant because you think it would make you feel pampered and rich, but you think you can't currently afford it. Well if you think that going to that restaurant would make you feel all that, than that's exactly the type of expense that your "I'm Fabulous" expenses should go towards. You don't really have to order a four-course meal to dine there. You can even go there after eating a little snack at home beforehand, so you won't be wolf-hungry, and when you get there, order something small that fits your budget. But make it a festive evening: spruce up, put on your best clothes and cologne one evening, and go dine at that restaurant. Enjoy your evening. Take your time to eat slowly and festively savor the flavors. Soak up the atmosphere; allow yourself to feel as rich everyone there; and enjoy the preview of what you'll be able to afford (on a more regular basis), once you co-Create your Ideal Lifepath.

Your "I'm Fabulous Just Because I'm Me" expenses should go towards things that make you feel deserving and worthy, specific things that you've always wanted to be able to afford. If your budget is very tight, it may take some creative thinking to find the money for those expenses. But remember that this doesn't have to be more than $25 a month. Mind you – some "I'm fabulous" practices don't require monetary investment at all. For example, window-shopping at Rodeo Drive, playing pretend with yourself doesn't cost you a penny. And if you play the game right, it can make you feel oh-so-rich. Doing a beach walk and enjoying beautiful sunsets in a place you love could be one of those practices. You can take with you a $4.99 bottle of wine you bought at Trader Joe's, with fabulous wine glasses you got at the 99-cent store, and sit on a beach bench with a friend (or a lover) to enjoy the sunset and celebrate life. That "I'm Fabulous, Life's Fabulous" practice made you feel rich, but only cost you $7. And those are exactly the type of practices that, because they help you *feel* the richness of life, shift your energetic vibration into likeness and resonance that in turn attract more financial abundance into your life.

Be Grateful for The Flow:

One thing that helps shift your energetic vibration into resonance with prosperity in a profound way is being grateful for the flow. Be grateful for the income that you *do* have, even if you currently don't think it's enough. The trick here is to get yourself to see the full half of the cup, and the positive aspects of what you do have, which aligns your energetic vibration with more of it.

I know it is sometimes hard to see everything as blessings, especially at times when you are struggling to make ends meet. But you can start by being grateful for the opportunity to pay your bills, knowing that as money flows out of you, it opens up channel for more money to flow in through your Infinite Funnel of Abundance. The metaphysical principle is the same as the water flowing through the Infinite Funnel (hose) as a result of being generous with others. If you open up the hose on both ends, fresh living energy can flow through it endlessly and abundantly. You can even set the intent that for every dollar you spend three dollars will flow back in.

As you pay for bills and things you decide buy, be light about it. Be grateful for the Universal abundance that IS flowing through you and allowing you to have the apartment, the telephone service, the electrical service that you pay for, the groceries that you spend money on... because these are all services and things that you enjoy, which the Universe is affording you. When you buy yourself something, imbue it with the feeling of "I'm fabulous." I mean, even if you buy something at a thrift store, you can still have an air of "I'm fabulous" about you as you do it. And that connects you to the vibration of Divine abundance, because you really are fabulous! Use this as a time to validate yourself as a beloved radiant child of God—a God that wants you to be happy and abundant. Use the time that you pay for the things that make your life comfortable and enjoyable as a time to shift your energetic vibration into resonance with the Infinite Source of all gifts and all abundance, and you will magnetize into your life an increased ability to pay for more services, more goods, and more of what you Truly want.

Rejoicing in the Riches of Others:

The next concept about the flow of money, which is a bit more difficult for most people to grasp, is based on knowing that we are all One at some level. If you can truly connect with the feeling of Oneness with all, then you know that when paying or giving money, you are not really paying the money to someone else; you are paying it to another aspect of your expanded Self. Once you realize that the other person really is a part of you in the grandest scheme of things, it becomes easier to feel joy for other people's riches. This realization that you are paying the money into another aspect of your extended Self can help you tune into what abundance feels like, "my money... your money... our money... swimming in an ever abundant pool of money (energy) that is flowing abundantly for all."

But there is another, more practical, aspect to feeing joy for other people's riches and success. If you suddenly start bumping into one rich person after another, it means that you're emitting the right frequency into the Universe. Your energetic vibration is indeed resonating with, and therefore starting to magnetize riches to your immediate surrounding. Therefore, you are not only on the right track, but you're very close to the manifestation of riches in your own life. First the manifestation takes the form of other people having the prosperity, perhaps showing you the way. But pretty soon, if you continue resonating with the high vibration of your Soul Self, the riches will start showing up in your own pocket. Don't worry about how the riches are going to come into your pocket. Concentrate only on manifesting your Ideal Lifepath. The riches will follow! By the way, the same goes for bumping into many people who are in love, healthy, and/or happy. You are magnetizing into your life those things that are in line with your new vibration. It means that your reality is shifting to reflect the new Internal Experience that you've been practicing, and it is only a matter of time before those blessings manifest *for you*.

On an even more practical level, being happy for other's riches means you are identifying with them as we identify and feel kinship with friends that we care about. When your friend feels sad, you empathically feel sad for-with him/her; when your friend feels rich, you resonate with them and feel rich with them. Not because you're expecting financial favor from them, but because they are in your heart, and your kinship with them makes you feel like you're in their shoes. It's kind of like watching *Sex and The City* makes me (and apparently millions of other women around the world) feel rich, and pretty—like a liberated woman of the world. But guess what? Identifying with your new rich friends to the extent of genuinely feeling happy for-with them *helps you vibrationally and energetically resonate with prosperity, which helps you attract it into your own life.*

All of these above are just what I called them: practical tips for vibrationally connecting with prosperity. Now if you are financially savvier than me (and that is not very hard to do), you might think of even better financial tips to help vibrationally connect you with prosperity. But the idea is simple: whatever financial practices you use, they should be ones that help you feel abundant, give you enough peace of mind (not worrying about money) to leisurely plan how you're going to join your Ideal Lifepath, and help you continuously dwell in an internal reality that strengthens mutual resonance with prosperity.

That is the story about money. It is not the root of all-evil. Nor is it all that's important in life. It is just a tool of energy exchange (reciprocity) between people—just one of the many forms of energy coming through your Infinite Funnel of Abundance. And it will start flowing freely and abundantly into your life just as soon as you start walking the Lifepath that honors all that you Truly are, and leads to the fulfillment of your life-mission. And it will keep flowing freely and abundantly into your life as long as you keep your energetic vibration resonating with the Joy-Love-Light of the True Source for all Abundance.

Your Life Is Eternal

When it comes to joyously walking your Ideal Lifepath with zesty aliveness in every moment, there is real value in lifting and dissolving our underlying, perhaps subconscious fear of death. Fear in any form is not of God, and does not serve your purpose of co-Creating True prosperity. But even if not conscious, fear of death runs deeper in our society, and affects each of us much more than any of us care to admit. Now, it is natural to be concerned about the unknown. I'm also not saying that you should take unnecessary risks – go bungee jumping, drag racing, jumping off of cliffs and the like. It is always a good idea to involve your highest judgment when making life decisions. But since our civilization has divorced itself from spirituality to the point that it has become socially acceptable to believe only in "scientifically proven facts," our fear of death has deepened. Moving past this fear is important for our evolution as sentient beings, so that we can live life more fully. *For only when you can fully grasp that this reality is not the only reality in which you exist, that you go on forever, and that this human reality is but a tiny piece of the vastness and eternalness of all that you are, only then can you fully live the life you were meant to live, and experience every moment with zest, radiance and joy!* And it is this zest, radiance and joy that energetically bring you into the vibrational likeness and resonance with all positive forms of abundance.

Afterlife in Theology:

Now it is not just a cliché that death is <u>not</u> the end, but only the beginning! Virtually *all* religions throughout the history of mankind believe in an afterlife, meaning that our essence or Soul lives on after the physical body dies. However there are many philosophies on what happens in the afterlife. The philosophies and traditions that explain the afterlife can be divided into two main categories: those that believe in Heaven and hell, and those that believe in reincarnation, although within each of those categories, religions, and even different sects within the same religion, differ in their take on what exactly happen in the afterlife. As you read through the summary below, ask yourself: could all religions that mankind has ever known be so very wrong?

Mainstream Judaism and Christianity believe in a heaven and hell. And without getting into any "resurrection" issues here, there are many sects within each of these religions that explain differently the exact steps that the Soul goes through in the afterlife, as well as the conditions leading to each. Surprisingly, early Christians, Rosicrucian, and the Kabbalistic sect of Judaism also have an extensive belief in reincarnation. As controversial as reincarnation may seem at first glance, it is believed by Kabbalists, early Christians, about 10% of modern Christians, Rosicrucians, Wiccans, Hindus (800 million), Sikhs, Buddhists (300-million), Jains, New Age believers (at least a million)[4], all of whom amount to at least a quarter of the world population—a higher number of believers than one might have thought.

Both Hindu and Buddhist traditions talk at length about the many steps that our Soul takes after exiting the body and on its way to either another incarnation or to liberation in the Light. An interesting, if somewhat cumbersome, account is detailed in the Tibetan Book Of The Dead from which it becomes clear that each Soul's next destination is up to the free will of each individual Soul. Dr. Raymond Moody mentions in his pioneering book about near death experiences[5] that the steps that the Soul goes through according to the Tibetan Book Of The Dead match exactly the ones that NDEers report, despite the fact that an English translation of the Tibetan book was not yet available at the time that the NDE data was collected. Many other Hindu and Buddhist texts verify their belief that each Soul chooses Its next destination, whether it is another human incarnation, or liberation in eternal bliss and Light.

According to Sikh belief, we each have ten energetic bodies, each relating to a different aspect of our being: the Soul Body, Negative Mind, Positive Mind, Neutral Mind, Physical Body, Arcline Body, Auric Body, Pranic Body, Subtle Body, and Radiant Body. There is also an eleventh energetic body—the eleventh Embodiment, which has the ability to oversee this human life from the perspective of the Soul. According to Sikh belief, just before the moment of transition (death), our breath slows down and our Pranic Body becomes weaker and weaker until at the moment of death it dissolves. At that point, the Soul, enwrapped in Subtle Body, goes up into the Divine ethers. There are five ethers to which the Soul can elevate: The first and second ethers are the ones where the famous life review occurs. Sikh tradition maintains that there are a few questions that are asked of the Soul on the first 30-60 seconds after transition, which seems to agree with NDE accounts. Those questions have to do with self-assessment. NDEers have described these questions (although non verbal) as translating to something along the lines of: "Are you satisfied with your life? Do you feel that you have expressed enough love? Do you feel that you have acquired enough wisdom?" It is up to each individual Soul to judge its here-now persona. From this we understand that the first ticket to move up in the ethers (towards liberation) is indeed kindness and love towards oneself and others. According to Sikh belief, it takes a total of fourteen days between death and reincarnation, although I personally have seen it take much longer (a year). After the Soul's visit at the first and second ethers, it either chooses another incarnation (or in the case of NDE it chooses to go back into the same incarnation) or moves on to the third ether. If a Soul moves up to the third ether and chooses to stay there, It has chosen to be in service to humanity through the Angelic realm. Some Souls "graduate" and move up to the fourth ether, where they are totally liberated in Divine everlasting bliss. Dwelling in the fourth ether also allows the Soul freedom to travel at leisure through all other ethers and realms. As part of that freedom, they can also choose to wait there for loved ones to complete their earthly cycles, periodically help humanity, or just do as they please. However, once a Soul moves up to the fourth ether, it can no longer choose to reincarnate as a human again. The fifth ether means total Divine Oneness and eternal Bliss[6].

New Age thinking talks about various "dimensions" of consciousness, which seems to agree with Sikh's idea of the different ethers, albeit the New Age thinkers talk about much more than just five "dimensions," and have different definitions of what characterizes each level. The consensus seems to be that the Soul goes on after termination of physical life, and that there is free choice, meaning that it is up to each Soul where and how high to go.

Shattering Some Old Beliefs That No Longer Serve:

Now, let's go beyond the collective unconscious compiled by our past belief systems, and understand a simpler layer of Truth: As I have already clarified in Chapter 2, there is *no* devil, and there is *no* hell! It is true that if the circumstances of deaths are traumatic, undue, or happen unusually fast, some Souls become temporarily confused and earthbound as "ghosts" for a while. If the Soul judges itself too harshly, doesn't think it deserves to go into the Light, perceives that its work on earth is not done, or for some reason decides to carry with it the scars and entanglements that were weighing it down during life, it can become lost in realms that are removed from the Light of God. Some people have experienced these realms during their near death experience, but it is very rare (1%). However, the good news is that the Love-Light of God never denies anyone salvation. Virtually <u>all</u> of those who have experienced dark realms said that even one thought of love, the slightest yearning for God's Light, or simply calling out any of the names of God (in any language or tradition) <u>automatically</u> pulled them out of these scary realms, and brought them either into the Light, or back to their physical bodies[7].

So rest assured that whatever you think you may or may not have done during this lifetime, whomever you may have disappointed, God loves you anyway. And as you already know, choosing a life path that is guided by the Light of your beautiful Soul is not only about avoiding those scary dark realm in the afterlife. It is also the key to co-Creating prosperity, health and happiness while you are living <u>this</u> life. So in the afterlife, as well as in your here-now reality, all you need do in dark moments is forgive yourself, internally dwell in all that is joyous and beloved, and walk a path that honors your True Light, and Divine favor, love and abundance will find you.

Scientific Proof Of The Afterlife:

The technological advances of the twentieth and twenty-first centuries have enabled us to scientifically obtain some proof of the afterlife. The simplest line of research that points to the existence of an afterlife are the many scientists that are researching the nature of our human consciousness, as discussed in Chapter 6. In the movie *What The Bleep, Down The Rabbit Hole (Quantum Edition)*, Dr. Hameroff—a physician researching the nature of consciousness—explains that consciousness is not localized in the brain, but is an etheric substance that seeps out into the Universe and lives on. And I ask you: if our consciousness seeps out into the Universe and continues to exist, does that not constitute proof that there we continue to live after our bodies die?

A phenomenon that verifies that our essence exists outside of the human brain is out of body experiences (OOBE). And there many reports, documented by medical doctors, of people who have had an OOBE (with or without an NDE), and were able to give verifiable testimony of things and events that they witnessed while out of their physical body. One extraordinary account, detailed in his fascinating books "Journey Out Of The Body" and "Far Journey", is brought to us by Robert A. Monroe, a business man from Virginia who started his journey as a total non-believer. One fine Sunday, Mr. Monroe found his whole being buzzing with a strange unexplainable, which he couldn't control. After a few times experiencing this vibration, one night Mr. Monroe found himself floating at the ceiling of his bedroom looking down on his physical body and his wife sleeping peacefully next to it. Because he was a non-believer, he initially assumed that something was wrong with him, and so he underwent a series of medical exams and psychiatric evaluations (all of which found him to be in perfect health), until one open minded psychologist-friend suggested that he might be having an OOBE. What is unique about Monroe's account is that he eventually learnt to control the phenomena so well, that he not only learnt to have out of body experiences at will. He also participated in extensive research about the subject, done under strict scientific scrutiny, and eventually established his own research institute. In his years of OOBE research, Mr. Monroe took many OOBE trips into other physical locales, which he was able to describe in details that were verified as correct later.

Another, more direct verification of life after death comes from people who, under hypnosis, are able to recall details of their past life and verify them later. In his wonderful book "Many Lives Many Masters," Dr. Brian L. Weiss tells the true story of how he stumbled across the existence of reincarnation and the afterlife quite by accident. Dr. Weiss started his path as an internal medicine doctor, the son of a long line of medical doctors who did not believe in anything "unscientific." He later converted his specialty to psychiatry. After a long period of treating of a woman he names Catherine (to protect her identity) with hypnosis therapy with no significant improvement, during one particular treatment, Dr. Weiss gives Catherine a hypnotic suggestion to go back in consciousness to the root of her issue—the moment that instigated her phobia. To his surprise, this simple-minded woman responded by recounting her past life in ancient Egypt. Because of his scientific and atheistic background, throughout the book, Dr. Weiss continuously tried to disprove the evidence of reincarnation that was unfolding before him. But the scientifically conclusive evidence that supported reincarnation (and an afterlife) was too overwhelming. Towards the end of his book, he was compelled by the evidence to shift his beliefs, and become a believer. Dr.

Weiss went on to published a total of eight books about the subject, and in his book "Messages From The Masters" he described many past life regressions that he has performed for his patients, and the messages they have received from their Angelic spiritual masters during intervals between lifetimes, during what I interpret as their Heavenly basking in the Light that happens between lifetimes.

As I've mentioned, with our ability to resuscitate people and bring them back to life after a period of complete death (i.e., no breath, no pulse and <u>no brain-waves</u>), came the most profound evidence of the afterlife, which completely dissolves all fear of death: people who had died, have gone into the Light, and were subsequently resuscitated and lived to tell about their wonderful-beyond-words experience. The first most complete research into the subject was done by Dr. Raymond Moody, and is detailed in his book called "Life After Life." Dr. Moody collected a large number (over 150 cases) of impressive accounts from people who have had a Near Death Experiences (NDE), which he analyzed scientifically. Another fascinating evidence of the afterlife is detailed in a BBC documentary (available on YouTube) "The Day I died"[8]. In these accounts people of all walks of life (believers as well as former atheists) recount their death experience as a loving wonderful experience. And there are many more books and accounts of people who have died, and came back to life to tell about it. Over 3,400 NDE accounts from real people who have experienced heaven and lived to tell about it are available on the Near Death Experience Research Foundation's website.[10, 11]

Despite this overwhelming evidence, for many years, doctors have excused away NDE's as residual brainwaves that remain in the brain for a few minutes after the heart and breath stop. But this excuse is no longer valid. In a recent book, Jeffery Long MD and Paul Perry[11] use the scientific method to disprove the residual brainwave explanation, and prove that near death experiences are in fact very real.

There has been one famous NDE case[9, 10] of a woman who was undergoing an innovative new brain surgery where all brain activities were stopped for the purpose of the surgery. The woman was connected to an EEG machine, documenting that there were no brain waves. And yet after the experience, the woman accurately described what was going on in the operating room during the time she was supposedly "dead", and surgical instruments that were used, of which she had no knowledge before the experience. There have also been many cases of NDE when the person was clinically dead for longer than the maximum amount of time in which any residual brain waves are thought (by doctors) to exist after death. And yet in all those cases people describe things they viewed while they blissfully floated above this reality, which were later verified as accurate. One woman described that she had floated up to the roof of the hospital, which appeared to have not been attended in many years. Her observation of the roof included a description of an old beat up red tennis shoe lying there, before she went on into the Light. This observation was later found to be correct after the woman was resuscitated.

My own meditational experiences verify NDErs accounts. And no verbal account can fully describe the essence of the Light, the beauty, the profound peace, the sense of belonging, and the nurturing of Divine unconditional Love. The experience is way beyond words. Indeed, all thought forms, words, actions, and manifestations in our "physical" universe are but a fraction—an aspect of Divine Whole. Even without the profound meditational experience that I've been Graced into, despite the fact that most of us rely on other people's NDE experiences for verification of our eternalness, those reports are so wonderful and so genuine that they are enough to dissolve the fear of death, and restore our ability to live this life with full zest. They also give us an idea of just how real the Divine Light (from which all prosperity comes) IS.

Although not everyone experienced each stage, most NDE accounts are strikingly similar, despite the fact that their experiencers come from different cultures and different belief systems, and despite never having met each other. According to these NDEs, the first short stage after death of being confused and not fully understanding that one has passed. Shortly after this brief period of confusion, people usually find themselves floating above their physical bodies (OOBE) and witnessing the events of their resuscitation. They feel a lightness and freedom that they had never felt before, and they realize that all of their physical afflictions are gone. Next, most people experience being in a dark tunnel, shortly after which they begin to observe a point of Light. Then, as if automatically, they begin advancing rapidly towards the brilliant and beautiful Light. At this point, most people are greeted by Angels and loved ones who have passed before them and who have come to greet them and accompany them into the Light. People defer on what they call the Light, depending on their belief system. Most people (including former atheists) understood the Light as either the breath of God, or the Love of God. But all people were unanimous describing the Light as endless unconditional love, joy, freedom, and happiness. And they have all come to understand this Heavenly realm as their truest existence, and a HOME that they never wanted to leave. So much so, that one woman[9] said that she had never forgiven her teacher, who greeted her in the afterlife, for shoving her back into her physical body. She wanted to stay in that Light forever.

Although many NDEers become saddened after coming back into their human body because they felt that their true HOME was in the Light, the grand majority of them acknowledge that the choice to come back was their own. Despite how happy they were in the Light, all of them were compelled by strong reasons to come back and finish their mission on Earth. And all NDE experiencers go on to have zestfully happy, loving, healthy, and successful lives, filled with the joy of living every moment to the fullest.

However, with all the wonderful things that can be said about making the transition into Heaven, Dr. Moody notes at the end of his book that taking one's own life is not the solution, as the Soul doesn't end up anywhere near the Light. And I'll second that. As much as I myself am HOME-sick for God's Light-Love, there is much joy to be experienced while we are here in our human existence, and many lessons for the Soul to learn on this joyride called Earth. And let's face it, we each have come here for a particular learning experience—a mission, which if we don't complete, we'll come back here again and again, kind of like in the movie *Groundhog Day*, until we "get it right!"

Mellen Thomas Benedict is the man that has experienced the longest near death experience recorded in history. He was clinically dead for several hours, and when he came back, his fully metastasized cancer was completely cured, and he lived to tell about his fascinating journey to the Creation of the world and back. Mr. Benedict has given many interviews, some of which are available on YouTube. One of the interesting wisdoms he received in the Light that he shared during one interview was his impression that you start your next incarnation where you left off in this one. In other words, if for example, you had an inclination towards depression and self-pity, and you killed yourself because of it in this life, than the first obstacle you'd have to overcome in the next lifetime is depression and self-pity. And that agrees with the information that I have received: Whatever the lessons you haven't mastered in this lifetime, you will (by your own choice) take with you into the next one. So we may as well get it right this time around, and enjoy our earthly experience while we're at it. Besides, after we've gained the earthly experiences that would propel our Souls to the next level of growth, our experience of the Light (Heaven) will be so much sweeter, since our new vibrational resonance will afford us the ability to go to a higher realms within Heaven, gain more freedom, and to stay there to enjoy as long as we want, not to mention enjoy our new Lighter being.

The bottom line is: the whole journey into this physical existence is in order to perpetuate, amplify, and co-Create more love and joy in the world. So it isn't that this world is just an unimportant narrow bridge into the afterlife, as some old religions would have you believe. On the other hand, it isn't that only the here-now is important, and the afterlife unimportant. Both realities harmoniously feed and complete each other. But while we are here living this physical existence, letting go of the fear of death helps to better ground our Soul's essence into every moment of this physical existence, which helps both realms of existence: it helps your Soul, fed by Its earthly experiences, propel into a higher level of growth, and at the same time, harnesses the Light of your Soul to make your stay here on earth more enjoyable—full of radiant joy, love, Light, beauty, and True prosperity.

Now, it is interesting to note that in all cases, the NDE experience have completely dissolved the person's fear of death. Most people went through a period of adjustment to accept the fact that they now have to deal with this four-dimensional reality and all of its time-space limitations again. They all have had to accept the fact that they would have to wait some years before they reunite with the Light again. But while the feeling of being homesick for the Light never really goes away, one thing that characterizes NDEers after their recovery period is their zest for life: *Virtually all NDEers have reported that their whole attitude towards life has changed as their fear of death dissolved. They were able to enjoy every moment, see more beauty in everything, love more freely, let go of fear, and follow their passions! And following your passion (your Ideal Lifepath) is indeed the very thing that helps you co-Create prosperity from your Soul!*

Grieving

Knowing what you know now about what happens after physical death, and how blissful and wonderful the experience of reuniting with HOME is, you may be already starting to understand that grieving for deceased loved ones is not really a grieving for them. It's OK to send them prayers and good intents to help their Soul elevate to the highest level. But the sorrow of grieving is really just our sorrow of the separation perceived from our perspective—sorrow for ourselves. Although there is not a day in my life in which I don't ache the separation from my beloved grandmother,

I know that she has ascended to the highest level of existence, and is blissfully in Oneness with God. And so I understand that my sorrow really is for myself. Before she died, I attuned my grandma into all three levels of reiki, so she became empowered as a reiki master. And to this day, I sometimes feel the warmth of my grandma's reiki hand hovering over mine during her occasional spiritual visitations. Since she has now become one of my spirit guides, during her visitations, grandma's message is that she does not feel the separation from me, and her energy is always one of pure Love and bliss. The message that I keep receiving is that our departed loved ones never truly depart. In her inspiring book "Dying To Be Me," Anita Moorjani describes her journey from cancer, to near death and merging with Oneness consciousness, and back to a life of complete health and happiness. During her NDE, Anita was reunited with her departed father and with her best friend. And from that meeting came her deep realization that her loved ones never felt and never were really separated from her. This is a firsthand experience of the Beyond, which verifies that the separation is only perceived by us—the ones who stay behind here in this human earthly realm.

As human, we mostly understand reality through the perception of our five senses. And so we perceive our loved ones, whom we can no longer touch and hug in a physical sense, as gone forever. But our deep feeling of grief—those times in which even years after our loved ones have transitioned, we still feel a deep sense of loss, when we cry and we cry, and then sob some more, really are just our experience of the love we shared with them, at the core of our hearts. For the departed never really departs. Let me explain that:

As mentioned in previous chapters, there is a very real integral part of you that is eternally living in Divine bliss in Heaven even at this moment. This is the aspects of your Soul we have named Chaya—the Divine element of Creation within all living things, and Yechida—pure Divine Oneness. Even Neshama is only partially here (as an ambassador), and partially in the upper worlds. And since your Neshama, Chaya and Yechida always dwell in the essence of God—a "place" where all Souls are One, all Souls are always in Oneness with you. You connect with them through the core of Oneness, accessible through the depth of your heart and upper chakras, which your tools for tuning into the Divine. You are especially equipped to connect with the Souls of your loved ones, through your love connection with them. So in a very real way, your heart center is the doorway through which you can tap not only into the Light of your Soul, the Divine Her-Himself, and countless Infinite wisdom and Truth. It is also the center through which you connect to all Souls with whom you have a love connection (subject to their free will).

So in those times that you sob and feel the loss deeply, where are all those tears suddenly coming from? To answer that, we need to understand that during our everyday lives we mostly dwell in this "physical" reality, and are accustomed to feeling mostly human-level emotions. And don't take this the wrong way, but even when we love, we do not fully experience the untainted intensity of pure Divine Love. There are infinite ways to tune into your Soul, a few of which are given in *Seven Stages to co-Creating Prosperity From Your Soul* (especially Zohar Breath Meditation). But when you dare to not only tune into your Soul's vision, but also to allow yourself to fully experience Its essence, the intensity of Love can be overwhelming! So during those times (even years after passing) in which we suddenly feel the loss deeply, what's truly happening is that we are receiving visitations from our ascended loved ones. During those visitations, it is the intense feeling of Love (Divine Love, which is immeasurably more intense than human love) that overwhelms us and makes us sob so deeply. Because our ascended loved ones have ascended into a realm of pure Divine Love, they are able to bring some of that intense Love with them during their visitations. And through our love connection to them, we connect with them heart-to-heart, even if we don't recognize with our five senses that they are here visiting us. Their visitations bring us a piece of the Love of HOME. And those feelings of Divine Love are so intense, that our human psyche is just not equipped to handle them. And so it comes out as a profound overload of our proverbial hearts, and deep sobbing tears start Niagara-falling out of our eyes.

With that in mind, don't be afraid of feeling things deeply or even crying. Don't be afraid of having an evening of melancholy once in a blue moon, knowing that tomorrow, you will rise anew with a fresh start and a zest of happiness. Those evening of melancholy and feeling things deeply can provide a healthy catharsis—a purging of negative emotions and stress. They provide a way to experience your Soul more fully. But mostly, dwelling in the love that you shared with the departed can help you experience the Light-Love of the Divine, which can help you reconnect with the Infinite and Her-His funnel of Abundance, Love, health, happiness, and all that is good.

However, know that it is possible to experience the profound Love and Light of your Soul meditationally, through Divine Grace. My first experience of the vastness of my Soul Self was during Kundalini yoga teacher training, which was an intense twenty-eight-day retreat-style course. During one afternoon's class we were learning about the naad—sound vibration. Our teacher was leading us through the most intense yoga-set, followed by a very deep meditation. During the meditation, she sang a mantra song. But it wasn't the mantra that sent me soaring as much as it was her voice, which embodied a certain purity and Divine power and Light. Soon after she started singing, I stopped experiencing myself as me. My consciousness merged with the breath of every person in the room (and there were fifty five people there). I was each leaf outside. I was the summer breeze, every bird chirping, the teacher singing… and soon, my consciousness expanded to be all that God has created. My physical body couldn't move, for I could not associate myself with it. I was all of Creation at once. There was a feeling of timelessness. I couldn't tell how much time has passed, whether it's been minutes, or days or years, and I was in state of absolute peace and Angelic beauty. When the meditation was over, it wasn't until the rest of my classmates snapped out of their meditation that I descended back to here-now consciousness, and slowly started to move. This was an indescribably profound experience, which you too can experience meditationally, if you choose to. And if you do, an experience like that can be treasured, so that at the most hectic moments of your life, you can "pull out" its memory from your internal pouch of treasures, and be reminded of the peace, love and beauty of whom you Truly are.

As it relates to the intense feeling of Love that are similar to those that you experience when grieving, let me tell you about my first time in which I actually experienced the intensity of Divine Love-Light within my own heart. Until then, while I had profound meditational experiences, the deep feeling of being beloved had been an elusive thing that I was always yearning for, but never internal experienced. On one Kundalini yoga workshop, during the last meditation of the day, it happened: During a meditation of the heart chakra, suddenly a feeling of intense Divine

Love came into my own heart, as if it were descending into me, or like it was just given to me by Grace. The feeling was so indescribably intense, that I started crying so deeply that it was like the Hoover Dam had broken loose. There was no way to stop it. And I didn't want to, because these were not tears of sorrow. These were tears of Joy! Since that day, I have had many experiences of Divine Love within me. A good way to experience it on a regular basis (minus the tears) is to participate in RezoDance, during which one can experience Light-Love-peace-joy, but at the same time, ground them into a balanced aliveness. There are many other ways to ground within you the feeling of Divine Love that is necessary to assure you that you are beloved, and you are worthy of all the blessings that you Truly wish for.

But within all the forms of tuning into Divine Love, one of the most potent ways is to allow yourself to remember and feel the love that you shared with an ascended loved one. Whenever I want to tune into the pure essence of the highest Love, I call upon the spirit of my grandmother to come and visit me. And through her love, I can feel God's Love internally flooding into my own heart. Although I cry when that happens, I now recognize that these are not necessarily tears of sorrow, but tears of joy of her spiritual presence— joy of the gift of having known her, and the tears of the profound Love that her visitations bring into my heart every time. And I noticed that after I allow myself to fully feel these visitations, I always wake up the next morning with a freshness of a new dawn of hope, and a feeling of imminently new blessings arriving into my life… it's as if my whole life path has been freshly blessed with additional Light and Love.

I earnestly hope that you can move past the grief of your perceived separation from your loved ones, rejoice in their freedom and ascension, and appreciate the blessing that their presence in your life has been to you. Know that you carry their love and strength in your heart, and that makes you stronger, more radiant, and more ready to reclaim all the happiness, love, and prosperity that are meant to be yours.

In this chapter, we have learnt to see money as just another form of energy, and to shift your subconscious attitudes about money from unhealthy to healthy. We have also discussed the important bridge that is to bring you from your "now" reality to your Ideal Lifepath.

Whatever the source through which money appears to be coming into your here-now level of reality (a job, a business, family wealth, a creative endeavor, an investment…), the True Source of all-inclusive prosperity, which includes not only a free inflow of money, but also of health, happiness, joy, and love, is the Infinite Divine! Dissolving your fear of death, and letting go of the sadness of grieving, are but some of the tools that can give you the courage to live your life fearlessly, with a passion that charges forward to reclaim your Ideal Lifepath, and bring forth Infinite prosperity from Source.

In the next chapter, we will discuss True communications as a way to harmonize and facilitate your path to True prosperity, and the people in your life that help pave your way to your most auspicious Lifepath, and the completion of your life mission.

Chapter 9

Soul Communications & Soulmates

We all have some idea of what communication is. But what is Soul Communication from a metaphysical standpoint, and how does it relate to co-Creating prosperity? More to the point, how can we employ this type of communication to facilitate our goal of co-Creating more prosperous lives for ourselves? And what do Soulmates have to do with co-Creating prosperity? To give you the "reader's digest" version of the answer: both Soul Communications and True Soulmate relationships complete our transition to always living by the Light of our Soul, and making choices in our everyday lives that keep us on our Ideal Lifepath, which ensures long lasting all-inclusive Prosperity. But of course, we need to understand these concepts more deeply in order to be able to harness them as tools to facilitate our paths as conscious co-Creators.

Before we get to Soul Communication, let's just agree that in an ideal world, it would be nice if all of your communications were calm, peaceful, compassionate, and yet at the same time clear, direct, and reflect your True passions and convictions. I mean, wouldn't it be nice if you could always express your deepest convictions clearly and with confidence, and still communicate them in a peaceful, kind way? And wouldn't it also be nice if everyone around you communicated in a way that takes into account not only their own best interest, but your best interest as well? Well, through Soul Communications, there is a way to achieve that level of communication in your life, and incidentally, that is also the type of communications that best facilitates the co-Creation of True prosperity.

On a very here-now level, any basic business management class would tell you that good communication promotes harmony and productivity in the workplace, which I agree – promotes a certain aspect of prosperity. But the level of prosperity that we have been talking about in this book is way beyond just harmony in the workplace and financial success for your boss, isn't it? We have been talking about all-inclusive prosperity—including financial abundance—*for you*. And the level of communication that constitutes Soul Communications is also beyond that. The communication that I'm talking about that is clear, direct, truth-to-yourSelf, yet peaceful, kind, and takes into account everyone's highest-best interest is called Soul Communication or True Communication. True Communication inevitably includes communication with your own Soul, draws on Its wisdom, and at the same time communicates with another person. And we'll spend a considerable part of this chapter understanding how.

The second subject of this chapter is Soulmates and Soul groups. As you have come to know, the easiest way to tap into the Infinite funnel of Abundance is to connect to your Soul Self, and live a life that is inspired by Its Light, and blessed by Its co-Creative powers. True soulmates are people who connect with you deeply on both the here-now level and the Soul level, and therefore help you better tap into your Soul Light, and by that, they help you magnetizes more of Its prosperity into your life. They are the people in your life who bring out the best in you, inspire you, and thus help you stay connected to your Higher Self and achieve your Truest life mission, from which easily flowing abundance comes. Thus, Soulmates who walk this Lifepath alongside you help you tap into your Infinite funnel of Abundance in a very real way, while you help them do the same.

But also remember that True prosperity is beyond just financial prosperity. Sure, it includes financial abundance. But True prosperity is all-inclusive, which means that it includes happiness. And the highest level of happiness, the highest level of self-actualization, and the richest joy you can ever know is to walk this lifepath alongside your True Soulmates, nurtured by the love that you share with them.

What Is Communication?

Before we get into Soul communications, let's first understand why communication so important to health, happiness and prosperity. Consider a medical condition known as "failure to thrive." It is a condition developed by infants, mostly orphans, who are not held, touched and loved. These babies are provided with the right food, medications, temperature, clothing, and changings—all the physiological conditions that should seemingly be enough to sustain their lives and help them develop. And yet, without the touch and love of another human being, they don't grow, and most of them die. Even adults are not meant to live in a vacuum. Think of how good you feel after receiving a hug from a friend. Is that hug a form of communication?

Consider a scenario: two people sitting at a restaurant, waiting for their lunch to be served, and each of them is engrossed in his smart-phone, texting, emailing, or writing notes. Was that email so urgent that it warranted missing the opportunity to visit with the person they are sharing lunch with? Keep in mind that to communicate, it wouldn't have been necessary for those two people to divulge any part of themselves that they do not wish to. Nor would it have been necessary for each of them to interrogate the other about their lives. All it takes is having the desire to look the other person in the eye and project peace and kindness towards them… Does that look of kindness constitute communication? What exactly is communications?

According to Wikipedia, the word communication comes from the Latin word commūnicāre, which means "to share." On the simplest here-now level, communication is "the activity of conveying information through the exchange of thoughts, messages, or information, as by speech, visuals, signals, writing, or behavior… It is the meaningful exchange of information between two or a group of living creatures."[1] The effectiveness of communication is measured in the similarity between the message transmitted and the message received, as evidenced by the feedback of the receiver. And the feedback could be verbal or behavioral. For example, if the communication is a teaching event, than the effectiveness of the communication is measured by the changed in behavior (learning is defined as a change of behavior as a result of experience) displayed by the student. If you're in a board meeting, you may reflect on the how accurately the message was received by the reactions you get, verbal or non-verbal. But communications is much more than that.

Communication doesn't have to be verbal. In fact, psychic communication is the most direct form of communication. Through some profound meditational experiences, as well as from NDEs[2], we know that our Soul Selves are capable of communicating by direct transfer of thought that is crystal clear beyond anything words could ever describe. And those communications are at the same time always benevolent and loving. In fact, that direct non-verbal transfer of thought is the most natural form of communications in existence, which retains our Soul-level Truth. But as ideas (to be communicated) filter through to our here-now level of reality, it is first filtered through any debris or imbalances within our Light-Bodies-chakras-nadi apparatus that most people carry around as a result of their human conditionings and scars, which distorts the original intent of the thought from its purity at the Soul level. Then, the now humanized (fogged) thought gets processed by our brains, and translated into language, which is by definition a fragmentation of the Whole. The very use of language takes into account that you take an idea away from its pure-Whole essence, and break it down into syllables, words, and sentences, according to the rule of that language's grammatical form. Thus all languages take away from the integrity and clarity of the message being communicated. Add to that the fact that your human here-now self is most often controlled by the lower Nefesh (which may harbor fear and survival instinct), and more rarely by your higher Neshama, and you begin to understand the forces that most often distorts our communications with our human agendas and biases, and cause them to loses their authenticity.

In light of that, looking into another person eyes, and radiating peace and kindness is actually a form of communication that is closer to True communication than lecturing for example. The Aquarian Age—also referred to as the Age of Enlightenment—is going to be all about open communications leading to a spiritual revolution, world-peace, and a brotherhood of man. Although my intuition tells me that it's going to take us another three hundreds of years before we actually get to the peace on Earth part, the Aquarian Age will bring much happiness and abundance for all who dwell in it. But as we have discussed in Chapter 4, all of this spiritual evolution and world-peace begin with each of us communicating truthfully both with our own Soul and with others.

In its True essence, *communication is a direct transfer of thoughts-ideas in the energetic original form of their True essence—a vibrational resonance*—either between different aspects of a person, between people, between a person and Nature, or between a person and God. So for example, when you do Your Ideal Daily Routine Internal Experience meditation (Chapter 7 of *Seven Stages to co-Creating Prosperity From Your Soul*), you are communicating with your own Soul and with the Universe, and co-Create a mutual vibrational resonance with the life that you wish to manifest. That is a form of communication too – one that fosters co-Creating abundance in your life.

In its purest form, communication is a multi-dimensional energy exchange between two Souls, which could filter into many levels of our "physical" reality, starting with a vibrational-energetic exchange (direct non-verbal communications, which could be expressed through mutual prayer, meditation, performing healing on another person…), a mental exchange (verbal, visual presentation of ideas, or telepathy), an emotional exchange (an emotional conversation, a deep look into each other's eyes, a kiss…), or a physical exchange (touch, an embrace, a massage…). Communication could simply be a subtle awareness of the other person in the room, and a subconscious attunement with their breath and state of being. Whether we are aware of it or not, we all are in tune with other people around us energetically-biorhythmically. Think of how many times you have had a stressful day, and then a kind and radiant person then crossed your path and completely uplifted you, and made your whole day better. The Institute of Heartmath has conducted some scientific studies[2] proving that "when people touch or are in proximity, a transference of the electromagnetic energy produced by the heart occurs."

An example of this energetic-biorhythmic attunement can be drawn from a technique I use when I teach the Rezossage. To demonstrating this technique to my students, as the client/student gets comfortable on the treatment table, I take some relaxing deep breaths just as I establish contact with the client/student. And in most cases, the person automatically begins to deep-breathe and relax just as a reaction to my deep breathing. The effect of relaxation of my own body is even more profound… During the demonstration, I perform the same massage move twice, once with a tense body, and the second time while relaxing my own body with Zohar Kindness Movement (see *A Lifestyle of Prosperity From Your Soul*). And the results are surprising: despite the fact that the receiver's eyes are closed, when my own body is tense, client's muscles also tense up, whereas when my body is relaxed, the client's muscles immediately melt down like butter under my hands, and a big sigh of relief usually echoes throughout the room. This attunement of a client's body to their therapist's state of relaxation is merely as a result of the higher-level attunement that always occurs between the Etheric Bodies (auric electromagnetic fields) of people who are in close proximity. It is true that during a massage, this biorhythmic attunement is perhaps more profound than, say- in a board meeting. But this kind of reaction to how others are thinking, feeling, and acting, happens all the time. We pick up on other people's breath rhythms, and stress or relaxation level. And we are affected by it even if we are not fully conscious of it. This energetic-biorhythmic attunement with others is simply a remnant of our Divine oneness filtering through to our everyday consciousness.

If you look at this energetic attunement from the yogic perspective – the aura of a healthy person should extend to nine feet in every direction from their physical body. And from the discussion of Chapter 1, we know that the aura is more than just one's protective electromagnetic field. It contains the person's Light Bodies—the essence of their thoughts (Mind Body), feelings (Astral Body), and energetic vibration (Etheric Body). So any time two people are closer than eighteen feet apart (9'+9'), their auric fields are temporarily interpenetrating. So of course we are affected by each other's "physical" presence. For example, what happens when you take a taxi, and your cab driver is stressed out and starts yelling and cursing at other drivers? To physically distance yourself from his low vibration, you would have to be at least eighteen feet away, which is impossible in a regular cab, as it is impossible in many other situations in life when you are sitting in close proximity of just a few feet from another person. So unless you have employed some specific meditational techniques to strengthen your auric protection, you are going to be affected by the other person's energy, which may or may not deter you from the steps you were going to take towards your most auspicious Lifepath that day.

Now, it is true that you cannot control other people's free choices in how they think, feel, or act towards you. But when you allow the Light of your Soul to guide your own thoughts, feelings, and communications, you are being true to yourSelf, which at a subtle level, inspires others to follow suit, even if the results are is not always immediately apparent.

As we've discussed in Chapter 4, different people play different roles in your life, not all of them warm and fuzzy. So given this energetic-biorhythmic attunement that you inevitably share with people who cross your path every day, the only way to stay centered on your Ideal Lifepath without being weighed down by others is to dwell in the wisdom of your Soul, employ Its radiant protection, and allow your communications with others to stem from that higher consciousness— True communications. Once you have learnt to dwell and bring forth your Soul's Light, your aura becomes radiant and strong. And when you can keep tuned into your Soul Light during your everyday interactions with others, you not only stay strong in your own Ideal Lifepath, but also inspire others. You become the Light-ball that dissolves negativities around you, which means that in your energetic-biorhythmic attunement with others, instead of letting them drag you down, you become the person who uplifts everyone around them. And that's a fabulous thing because that magnetizes buckets of happiness and prosperity for yourself in the process. And the meditational processes of *Seven Stages to co-Creating Prosperity From Your Soul* will help you do that.

But here is the most advantageous aspect of True communications: As you put together all parts of this multidimensional exchange called communication, at the level of the Soul, we are all One. And the reason this oneness is so important is because our Oneness at the Soul level can give us insight on how *to communicate with each other in each situation towards a solution in which everyone wins!* This is because at the Oneness level—the hub of all spokes—there is only one Truth, a Truth that takes into account the perfect mosaic of everyone's lives, through a stretch of time. That Truth may translate into opposing points of view and conflicting agendas, when it gets stepped down into the human level of awareness. But consulting with your Soul will give you a glimpse at this core Truth. It is not exactly like spying on enemy camp, but close. It may not tell you the private details of what's going on in your opponent's life, since your Soul will not violate your opponent's choice of privacy. But in order to facilitate a solution that takes into account everyone highest-best interest, It will base Its advise to you on knowledge of those details, available at the core Truth of the Oneness level.

The Roles We Play

So how do we deal with less than harmonious communicators in our lives? How do we communicate with people whose vibration is low and just plain angry? After all, (and I mean no disrespect) True communication is not about turning the other cheek again and again and letting others beat us endlessly, and it's not about being a martyr. In Chapter 4, I have given you some thought-tools to deal with the energy thieves in your life. But not everyone whose vibration is low is there to stay in your life, and not everyone is an energy thief. Some people are just plain old grumpy, because that is the persona they have chosen to indulge in at this moment in their lives. To really know how to deal with those, from a True communications perspective, let us discuss again the roles that different people play in our lives.

When Native Americans bless "Oh Mctaquia," which literally means "to all of my relations," they are really blessing and *thanking* all of them: the sun, the trees, all the elements of Nature as reflections of Great Spirit (God), Great Spirit Itself, and the spirits of their wise ancestors, which for us may correlate to blessing our Angels and ascended loved ones. But in that saying, they are also blessing all of one's human relations, making no distinction between friend and foe. The People's wisdom understood long ago that one should thank one's antagonists, as well as one's friends, for affording one the lessons and opportunities for growth.

As we have discussed in chapters 2 and 4, we all have many different kinds of relationships in our lives, each of them helping us to externalize or connect with a different theme of our personality, all of which serve our Soul growth. In the here-now reality, even if you don't absolutely love every person that stands in front of you in line in the supermarket, and you love even less each person that cuts you off in traffic, understanding the roles they all play in your life may help you tune into the real reason you have magnetized these people into your life, can help you graduate from uncomfortable lessons, and move on to the more joyous experiences in your life. Also remember that not all of your relations were meant to stay in your life forever. Some were meant to teach you (while you teach them) a brief lesson, and move on.

We come into each other's lives for all kinds of purposes, ideally serving the highest good of all. Sometimes your best teachers are your antagonizers that challenge you to become the best version of yourself. We all cross paths with many people who doubt us and challenge us, which gives us an opportunity to gracefully stand up for what we deeply believe, in a way that honors whom we Truly are. And those are valuable opportunities for your Soul's growth. Our many relationships give us a chance to resolve karma on our path to reclaiming our True freedom and radiance.

While the true role of each person in your life can only be illuminated by your own Soul Self, here are some examples: a person who cuts you off in traffic may be there to teach you patience, and help you reclaim your ability to stay heart-centered and unaffected by small annoyances in life; a difficult situation can teach you your own strength and perseverance, and give you feelings of self-actualization once you surmounted the difficulty; an antagonistic person can teach you to set healthy boundaries while being kind (as we've discussed in Chapter 4); a needy person in your life can help train you to find balance between giving and receiving; a nagging busybody neighbor can teach you tolerance and respect for other people, and how graceful you *can* be, or the lesson could be about setting healthy boundaries again. Needless to say that finding your grace and peaceful strength amidst all of these less-than-harmonious relationships is a real triumph that would help you stay centered on your Ideal Lifeplan of co-Creating prosperity in a harmonious free-flowing way.

As it relates more directly to co-Creating prosperity, the key is that you don't have to become a martyr to attain Soul growth. To satisfy karma with another person, you don't necessarily have to suffer at their hands. Remember that karma is not a punishment! Karma is nothing more than a pre-agreed upon opportunity for two people to play different roles to gain an experience that completes each of them. Inevitably, both you and your antagonist have moved onto a higher level of Soul growth since you encountered each other in your last mutual incarnation. So you don't necessarily have to suffer just because you were the antagonist in the previous lifetime. You have the free choice to satisfy your karma by helping your opponent rather than suffering at their hands. And if you prayerfully set that intent, I guarantee that it will work every time. Think about it: if you were the antagonist of person-X in a previous lifetime, the only purpose that a role-reversal serves in this lifetime (which is why you pre-agreed to it) is *for you* to learn unconditional love and compassion, by way of learning to love this person despite your differences in vibrational essence. So if, despite everything this person may have done to you (which you have no cognitive memory, but a vibrational-energetic memory), you start feeling and showing them love and compassion out of a position of peaceful strength, then you demonstrate that you have graduated the lesson—you've learnt unconditional love and compassion. Therefore there is no more need for you to be antagonized by this person any more. Lesson's over! And that is why showing kindness to your opponent cancels any karma you may have had with them. However, this needs to be love and compassion that come out of peaceful-graceful <u>strength</u>, not from a position of weakness. This is just one example. In general, the more open you are to learning your karmic lessons (which stems from deeply knowing that they were set up by You to serve your highest good), the more harmoniously you will experience them, and the quicker you'd be able to move on to the prosperous joyful part of your human adventure.

All that being said, there is a delicate balance between being grateful for all of your relations in their many colors and fragrances, and knowing that some of them are not meant to walk alongside you your Ideal Lifepath. So while your own God consciousness will guide you to know that love is at the core of all relationships, It will also guide you to be kind to yourself first. As we've discussed in Chapter 4, in some relationships it is necessary for you to love and respect someone at a distance, pull away from the people who habitually doubt you and put you down, keep at arm's distance the people who are always negative, and keep your respectful distance from ill-meaning people. And in all of these decisions, there is no judgment on your part, just a knowing that those low-vibrational people are not in harmony with your Ideal Lifepath, and are on their own path. Being guided by the Light of your Soul will allow you to comfortably hold space for them to evolve on their own path and at their own timing, wish them well from the bottom of your heart, while staying heart-centered on *your* Ideal Lifepath.

Of course, the most pleasing of the roles we play in each other's lives is that of True Soulmates. But we'll talk about those later in this chapter.

Seeing Other People

Before we define the "lofty" endeavor of Soul Communications, let us first discuss some of its elements, so that you can get the feel of it, and see that Soul Communications is actually not such a lofty or unreachable goal, but is actually the way we were always designed to communicate.

So the first thing we should discuss is what happens before we communicate, before we form the sometimes-intricate relationships that we have with the people in our lives. Of course, before we communicate, we first look at the other person, and do a mini little assessment of who he or she is, kind of like we are trying to categorize in which box in our minds we are to fit this person into. So when walking over to great a new person in our lives, what is it that we are really seeing?

Well, whether looking at a new person in our lives or at someone we already have a long and intricate relationship with, we may think that what we are seeing is his/her outside physical appearance. But since this "physical" reality is really a hologram made of energy, when you look at anyone, you really are seeing what he/she radiates—the energy fields around them. Now it's true that a person's energy-fields do come together in our limited human perception as the person's physical body and appearance. But what reconstitutes a person's body on a moment-to-moment basis is in fact their spiritual essence. And this is not as far fetched as you may think. How many times have you asked a friend if she/he has lost weight, or if she/he has started a new exercise regime, just because they feel radiantly happy that day? I have seen many students of RezoDance with a radiant face that looks like they've either just had the most luxurious facial, or they just got laid… Many times, I have also seen men look at a woman who was not particularly pretty as if she were the most beautiful thing in the world, and completely ignore a classy and beautiful woman passing by. This is because the woman that attracted their attention had an aura of confidence and radiance about her that magnetized their attention (and I'm not talking about trashy or overtly sexual dress). When we communicate with others, verbally or non-verbally, it is more than just our words that we communicate. It is more than even how we are dressed, carry ourselves, or even our body language. We all communicate with each other energetically first, whether we are aware of it or not.

Consider again the fact that we are all part of the same Divine Oneness. At the level of our Divine Oneness, each of the people who cross your path in life is a reflection of your own consciousness. You have magnetized them into your life by the state of your consciousness, to serve a purpose.

The Prosperity in Non-Judgment:

As you already understand after the previous chapters, we are each on a path of our own to fully experience life, get Soul growth, and ultimately expand Creation by increasing the amount of Love-Joy in the Universe. And throughout this journey, each of us is endowed with infinite free choice. Within this infinite free choice, there are three levels of benefits to non-judgment, as it relates to co-Creating prosperity from your Soul.

But before we get to the benefits, let's tune into the higher Truth here for a moment: Just as no one can walk your lifepath for you, so too, within the Lifepath that your neighbor, co-worker, friend, foe, or boss, has chosen, they are the only ones who have insight on the path that is Ultimately right for them. Even if their path is erred in your eyes (and it may very well be erred), even if it is low-vibrational, and even if their choices fail to serve their own higher purpose, it is still their free choice to make. And since all paths lead to the same Destination (eternal bliss and liberation in Heavenly Oneness), you must trust that their erred path too would *eventually* lead these people to ultimate enlightenment. You cannot walk that path for them, as they cannot walk, or even be privy to yours. You can offer high-vibrational advice and help if they ask for it. But you cannot otherwise coerce them into doing it your way, especially not if you're only manipulating them for your monetary benefit. That is not the way to Prosperity from your Soul! Moreover, you shouldn't judge or gossip about people who, in your view, are making bad choices. Perhaps your neighbor's use of profanities and throwing of temper tantrums is his way of getting unhappiness to the extreme, so that he may (at some point) recognize it, let the negativity go, and eventually reconnect with his Soul Self. Perhaps the homeless bag lady who crossed your path had been a queen trapped in the riches of her palace in a previous incarnation, and her life as a homeless woman in this incarnation is her way of not conforming to societal rules and experiencing her freedom. Perhaps your boss is only tough because she/he has had a rough childhood, and is trying to excel in the business world. There can be many more examples. The point is that you never know the full multidimensional reality behind a person's choices, and it is not your place to judge.

That being said, gossip and judgment of others are self-preservation mechanisms we all unknowingly engage in to a greater or lesser degree. So do not judge yourself for the judgment you had passed upon others in the past. Respect and honor your here-now self for protecting you. But at the same time, know that it is safe to let go of those defenses, because the Light of your Soul can protect you and keep you in the flow of God's Grace better than any here-now level defense mechanism, if you let It.

Beyond right and wrong, non-judgment of yourself and others has three layers of benefits – the first relating to practicing kindness to yourself and to others (as discussed in Chapter 3), as one of the pillars of Prosperity. Think about it: if you're judging others or yourself harshly, you're not really being kind are you?

The second benefit of non-judgment is that it allows you to devote your resources (time and energy) to co-Creating *your* Ideal Lifepath, instead of wasting them dilly-dallying with judging, gossiping, moaning, griping or complaining about what others do. You are now in a critical time in your life, one of exciting positive changes, and of reclaiming the radiance, health, happiness and prosperity that you were always meant to have. And on your new exciting path, there is a lot to be done. There are meditational processes (detailed in *Seven Stages to co-Creating Prosperity From Your Soul*) that you should do to zero in on your most auspicious Lifeplan; there are physical-lifestyle changes you should be making (detailed in *A Lifestyle of Prosperity From Your Soul*) to vibrationally start taking your life towards your unique path of Prosperity; and then there are, of course, the steps that you should be taking—as guided by your Soul—to actually bring the new prosperity-path into manifestation in your physical reality. All of these activities should make you a pretty busy bee… vibrating the whole while with joy and vitality. You don't have time to judge others, or to sit around griping, moaning and complaining about what they do. You have an Ideal Lifepath of prosperity to manifest!

The third benefit of non-judgment has to do with resonating with your new prosperous path. You see, negatively judging and gossiping on others keep you in a loop of expecting a continued lower vibrational behavior from other people around you. But more than that, by slandering someone else, you are collapsing your own natural high vibration into a lower one, and perpetuating a negative vibration that can only magnetize into your life more of the very negativity you are condemning. I'm not saying that you should sit around and wait for others' negative behavior to affect you adversely. But now that you know how powerful your intents and words are in co-Creating the mutual reality you share with others in your life, it would be more beneficial for you to turn the wheel around.

The first step to letting go of the behavior and restoring your natural high vibration is to forgive yourself, and recognize that your need to gossip and judge others may come out of fear, jealousy, or a need to feel superior and therefore good about yourself. But here are some antidotes to those old thought forms: If we look at fear, knowing what you know now, you understand that gossiping about the instigator of your fear would only magnify its effect in your life. The proper way to deal with fear is to eradicate its roots from your psyche and from your life. You already know that if you walk your highest Lifepath, and gracefully stand up for what you Truly believe in, there is no need to fear others, since your Truth is anchored in Soul Truth, which inevitably promotes the most harmonious situations, as well as puts you in a powerful protective Light. Looking at jealousy – you also already know that our Universe is all about vibrational resonance, and therefore there is also no need to be jealous of other's success, since being happy for other's success makes you resonate with that success, which actually magnetizes the same kind of success into your own life. But most importantly, if you need feel better about yourself, there is no need for gossip or judgment of others. All you need do is see yourself for whom you Truly are—a beloved child of God! That should give you enough inner peace to know that the Universe supports all of your thoughts, feelings and actions that are True to the very core of whom you are.

You may wonder: "Then how do I predict my opponent's moves in order to strategize my own moves?" The simple answer is: you don't! Your life is not a game of monopoly! Your Soul has already done all the strategizing that needs to be done. And It has done so keeping in mind the biggest picture of all! Remember that your Soul is in cahoots with God. So the most auspicious way to make decisions in your life is to let them be guided by the wisdom of your Soul. This means listen and be in tune with your innermost convictions – the thoughts, feelings, behaviors and decisions that resonate most harmoniously in every fiber of your being. For when you act on the superior guidance of your Soul, every moment and aspect of your life falls into place perfectly and in your favor.

All that being said, talking and thinking about someone with concern, compassion, and love are different than gossip. Indeed the first step in turning the wheel around is being compassionate towards any unhappiness in the lives of others. From that compassion, you will find the resources within you to hold space for those people to become the radiant wonderful people that are no-doubt hidden inside them.

Listening To Others:

Caring enough about others to listen to them attentively is an important aspect of every communication, whether the exchange is balanced or imbalanced. And listening is an art that many of us are lacking in.

It is especially critical to listen attentively when the communication is unbalanced. And here is why: Among the many people who cross your path every day, you may encounter some dense-communicators—people who like to talk a lot and dominate the conversation. And many times, these people pontificate views that are diametrically opposed to yours, not letting you squeeze a word in between, and get angry if you try to interject. Although this is an extreme example, most of us have had encounters such as these, at one point or another. So how should we communicate Truthfully with those people who are clearly not open to two-way Soul Communications?

As disharmonious as the situation in this example seems, understand first that the intensity of these people's communications really stems from their desperate plea to be heard. Granted, something is unbalanced in them. Perhaps they are lonely. Perhaps their self-esteem is lacking and they are trying to ensure that their opinion is heard, despite the fact that they can't defend their position logically and in a calm way. Perhaps this person is nice otherwise, but is just very anxious about a particular issue. Whatever the situation may be, this is a person that desperately wants to be heard. And the best thing you can do for both of you is to listen to them attentively and kindly.

But here is a revolutionary thought: *attentively listening to someone does not mean agreeing with them! And it certainly does not mean complying with what they say!* It just means that you respect that that's their opinion, you respect the inner feelings underlying their opinions, and you care enough to listen. For example, if you are an animal lover, and the person you are attentively listening to yells "we should kill all stray dogs," when you say "aha," it does not mean that you agree with him/her; and it absolutely does not mean that you're going to pick up a shotgun and join them in a street hunt of stray dogs. It just means that you acknowledge that this is how they feel, and you empathize with the pain and fear inside them, which are making them harbor such hateful feelings.

The reason that listening attentively is in your favor is that most times, just listening attentively, and showing that you empathize with the inner pain someone must be feeling, drains the potency of the person's feeling, and calms them down. But again, you are empathizing, not agreeing, and only with the cause of the person's low-vibrational behavior, not with the behavior or negative opinions themselves. But in the inner world of this dense-communicator, being listened to is a lot! It takes the sting out of their feeling of never being heard, not mattering, not being important. Now that this dense-communicator knows someone cares enough about their feelings and opinions to listen, nine times out of ten, they'll be off their high-horse, and you'll get the chance to express your opinion, peacefully, kindly, yet directly and honestly. At the end of the conversation, the two of you may not agree on the main points. But you will probably agree on something, even if it's just your agreement to respectfully disagree, and end the communication on a high note

For example, I recently had a phone conversation with the dense-communicator of my family. My Dense-Communicator accused her daughter-in-law of being a kleptomaniac and stealing her table-runner. Before this conversation, Dense-Communicator had been making the same accusations for a couple of weeks, and there was no way to convince her that she had probably just misplaced the table-runner in the same way that she always misplaces things and later finds them. On that particular conversation though, I decided to experiment with this theory of attentive listening. I let her talk and talk and spin her theories about kleptomaniacs, and express her feelings of being violated and trespassed against. Through her long pontification, I gave her an occasional "Aha." Now, my "aha" was not an agreement with her opinion, but simply an acknowledgement that I acknowledge her opinion, even if it's different than mine, and that I respect her *feelings*. After a long while in which I felt the potency of her emotions draining, I quietly, kindly, yet clearly, acknowledged that I knew there were a lot of hurt feelings between Dense-Communicator and her daughter-in-law, but pointed out that those disharmonious feelings went both ways, and started many years before the missing table-runner. I gently asked my Dense-Communicator if she thought it might be possible that she was psychologically projecting all of her heavy feelings surrounding her relationship with her daughter-in-law on one stupid table-runner. My remark, acknowledging the existence of hurt feelings in her relationship with her daughter-in-law seemed to calm her down some. But then she went on, "But it's missing, and I've looked everywhere! Who else could have taken it?!" I listened some more, and let her drain more of her emotions without interjecting, until she was quiet. Then, quietly, peacefully, yet clearly, I made two points: first was that her daughter-in-law is a close friend of mine, and has never taken anything from *my* house; and the second was that directly after visiting Dense-Communicator, the daughter-in-law also came to visit me, during which time we unpacked and cleaned her suitcase, and the table-runner was not there. I reminded my Dense-Communicator that this table-runner is only a material possession. It was insignificant. And then I directed her attention to the fact that her True spirit is bigger than that. I talked about her good inner qualities of being a nurturing mother, a quality that no one can ever take away from her. By the end of the conversation, she had forgotten all about the table-runner, and felt elated.

But in this example, saying all the things I wanted to say to my dense communicator only became possible after listening to her attentively for a while. For I tried to say all the same things to her in numerous conversations before, with no success. What was so different in this conversation was that I took the time to attentively listen to her first. I let her drain her emotions. I made her *feel* that someone cares enough to listen. And I made her feel that someone cares about how she *feels* even if I didn't agree with her opinion. And only then I respectfully, clearly, and simply spoke my opinion. Listening opened up the lines of communications even with the person in my life that's always been the toughest for me to communicate with. And it didn't diminish my self-expression. On the contrary: It forced me to take some deep breaths, and draw power and wisdom from my Soul Self, which allowed me to direct the conversation into the high vibration that resonates with my new path of Prosperity from my Soul.

Loving Others:

Given the highly spiritual tone of this whole book, I don't know if it even needs mentioning, but loving others does not mean sleeping around, sixties style. It means opening your heart to love people as they are, even if they are not as evolved as you are, not as smart as you are, or not as kind as you are. It means accepting who they are in the present moment of their personal evolution, while holding space for them to step into who they can become (even if you have to do it at arms length in some cases). It means rejoicing in all of your communications, and brining your True radiance into them. And it means seeing all people as your brothers and sisters to the human race.

The Dalai Lama comments in his book "In My Own Words" that he never gets lonely despite the fact that he spends much time in meditational solitude, despite his celibacy, and despite not having a family. His concept is that the whole human race is his family, so why should he feel lonely?

While communicating with others non-judgmentally, attentively listening to them, and even loving others for whom they are now, are some of the aspects of True communications, we still haven't quite defined what Soul communication is, and how we achieve it. But we are beginning to get the feel of what it is. Before we delve into a deeper exploration of Soul Communication, let's first talk about why most of us do not communicate Truthfully on an everyday basis.

What's Been Keeping Us From True Communications?

One of the things that keep people from True communications is the fear that their listeners would be bored, or disagree with them about the content of the communication. It is entirely possible that your audience has a different take on things, different realm of interest; they could be edgy or stressed out; they could have a lot on their minds; or it is entirely possible that they are just not in the same open space to deeply listen and resonate with your highest Truth. But that's ok. It is where they are at this point in *their* personal evolution. And it is very possible that in this here-now reality, your listeners' opinions on the subject at hand are conflicting with yours. And that's OK too. Each of the conflicting opinions is a part of the Wholeness of Divine Truth. But the thing about True communications is that your infinitely wise Soul already knows which part of your core truth your opponent/listener is ready to hear. Therefore your Soul is the only one who is qualified to guide you on what to say, how much to say, and how to say it in the most harmonious way that resonates with your listeners, but still adheres to your core Truth.

Another fear that often keeps people from true communications, beyond generally fearing their listeners' response, is the fear of exposing themselves, being vulnerable, or revealing their imperfections when speaking their Truth. Fear can certainly mask one's clarity, and hinder their ability to tune into their higher Truth. But remember that your Soul Self is in on bigger picture, and can wisely guide you on which parts of your core Truth is appropriate to expose at each point of the communications. Harmoniously communicating your core Truth, and showing kindness to yourself and others are not a sign of weakness, but a sign of strength and courage. Any authentic relationship with people in your life should not come out forceful strength, but out of the angelic-peaceful strength of the inner convictions of your True Self.

In case you are wondering about business/work situations, it is true that you don't have to talk about your hemorrhoids or your marital problems in a business meeting. But if you have a choice between letting your logical brain guide your strategic thinking, or letting your Soul guide you, your Soul's wisdom is far superior in Its wisdom to any strategic thinking courses you may have taken in business school. That's not to say that you shouldn't allow basic hard facts to support your Soul's guidance. For example, on your new path of Prosperity, let's say that you're about to decide whether to go get another degree or open up a business. Well, your Soul already knows which way leads to your Ideal Lifepath of Prosperity. But in order for you to be able to accept your meditational Truth, and ground it into a cognitive understanding of what to do, you may have to dig up some facts, like: "what would the added earnings of the additional degree amount to?" "What are the earning capacities of this new business you are endeavoring to open?" etc. Then, you're going to leave the facts aside, and meditate to have a complete Internal Experience of each one of those paths (in *Seven Stages to co-Creating Prosperity From Your Soul*), and consult your Soul about the decision. Because when there is a conflict your here-now self and your Soul Self, remember that your Soul has inside information on your opponent's intents. It is looking at things from the highest perspective possible. Your Soul Self is privy to pieces of the information about your opponent's side, which are hidden from your logical mind. Plus, your Soul is not limited to this "now" time. It has foresight on how certain decisions are going to play out. So your Soul Self is exponentially more capable of guiding your communication strategies than your logic alone ever could. And It can do so in a way that is clear, direct, effective, yet kind and peaceful all at the same time.

As an example, let's say that you are an advertising executive who is working on an important presentation for an advertising campaign. And for some reason, your company's client has distinctly said not to use the color red. But two days before the important presentation, you meditate late at night, and Divine inspiration comes upon you and brings you a wealth of free flowing ideas that resonate with you deeply, all of which involving the red colors. You suddenly get a very vivid vision of the whole campaign (which avoids the dangers because of which the client wanted to avoid red in the first place) and every picture in it. You allow yourself to indulge in this late evening vision, and get a deep feeling that this should earn you a promotion to head the project. As you draw your visions into a new presentation, you notice that it's making you feel very whole, complete, good to the core! You decide to go with this idea, and two days later you present it to your boss, your colleagues, and the client. You of course start the presentation by acknowledging that you respect your client's cautions about red, explaining that you had another presentation not involving red, but you beg everyone indulgence for a few minutes, because you feel that your new idea could result in the breakthrough the client was looking for. Your enthusiasm and positive energy is catchy, and the client agrees to see your new idea. As you proceed to deliver your presentation, you feel tuned into your higher-level Truth, upbeat, positive, and full of life. Through the presentation, you notice that the boss is feeling edgy and glancing at the client every five seconds, but you stay heart-centered, and you animate passionately your idea and why you think it would be a success. Despite the boss's apprehension, and much to your surprise, you notice that the client has completely lets go of all of his/her old notions about red, is extremely happy with your ideas, and is insisting that you head the project! This is an illustration of the Light of your Soul shining on others as it relates to the business world.

And this is not just a "too-good-to-be-true" Hollywood-style idea. Any idea that makes you feel so very complete, whole, good to the core, and resonates favorably with every fiber of your being, is most likely anchored in a True vision from your Soul. You cannot go wrong by expressing it, even if your listener doesn't agree with you. As long as you are communicating from the respectful and loving place of your Higher Self, the conversation will not be an argument or a confrontation, but a pleasant exchange that enriches both.

Soul Communications

Here we come to the meat of the chapter—Soul-level communications, which is the key to staying on your Ideal Lifepath without being weighed down by others. So, let's ask the inevitable question: What *exactly* is True or Soul communication?

So far, we know that it is a form of taking the higher road, so to speak. But as we've discussed in Chapter 4, taking the high road certainly does not mean letting others walk all over you. On the other hand, it does not mean that your communications with others become blunt without regard for whom you hurt in the process. Simply defined – True/Soul communication means that you speak or communicate your Soul Truth – the highest-level of Truth that you are most passionate about, in an untainted way. And there are three parts to this Soul Communication: First, you (your here-now persona) must communicate with your Soul Self, tap into Its higher-level wisdom, and merge (through your consciousness and feelings) with the biggest picture. Secondly, you must stay tuned into your Soul-level Truth, trust the solutions It gives you, and let It guide your words and actions. The last part of Soul Communication is actually expressing your higher-level Truth to the receiver(s) in a peaceful yet confident way. Another way to look at it is: you—your here-now persona—is only a vessel, a hose if you will, through which the wisdom of your Soul pours out. In this illustration, the faucet delivering the Clear water is your Soul; the hose itself is you, staying debris-free (agenda-free) in order to keep delivering clear water; the Clear water itself is the Truth being delivered; and the outlet where the water nourishes the flowers is your Truth being received by your listeners.

So Soul communication happens when the words/actions of one person (transmitter) are so inspired and driven by their Soul level of consciousness, that they create a favorable vibrational-resonance within the other person (receiver), sometimes despite the receiver's opposing point of view. Whether that takes the form of verbal communication, a look in the eye, a touch of the hand, a deep breath of relief, or simply a resonant silence, in this communications it is clear that there is a harmonious resonance felt at the core of both the listener and the speaker. This heart-to-heart resonance can only be possible if the speaker (and preferably the receiver too) communicates from a Soul level of consciousness—tuning to their Soul wisdom, hence the term

Soul Communications. Now, I know that this level of communication can seem too idealistic, but it isn't. This level of communication is perfectly achievable in your everyday life.

Think of a situation in which you have a discussion with someone, who is advocating a belief system that is diametrically opposed to yours. There are several ways in which this discussion can go: If this person is operating out of non-Truth, meaning that the person's communications originate only in his/her want for gain, and are not based on Soul-level Truth, then they'll either employ sales tactics or otherwise push their opinion on you in a way that disrespects your convictions. This tends to irritate most people, and may make you bunker deeper into your opinion. If, on the other hand, this person is respectfully relating to you their earnest understanding of the Truth, meaning that they respect who you are, and that your opinion is different, but they truly believe that what they are saying could have a positive affect on your life, than your reaction to their opinion will usually be a peaceful one.

As an example, not long ago, while attempting to help a friend of mine, I had the occasion to sit across the dinner table from a guy she was dating, whose opinions about everything in life were diametrically opposed to mine. I'm a peace lover, and a spiritual person who advocates love, peace and trust between all people. In contrast, my friend's date was an angry militant guy who believes in forcefully staking out his territory, and shooting at everything that crosses him. You could say that I should have given him some of the wisdoms in this book. But this guy wasn't ready or receptive to any of it. He was angry at life and everyone in it. And he was interested only in displaying his superiority, not in being taught a new way of life. To make things worse, he was drunk and getting drunker by the minute. My friend was eating her dinner, and quietly contemplating whether to continue dating this guy. Obviously, I could not have a two-way Soul Communication with this guy. Arguing with him, or justifying my different belief system would have been fruitless, and would have only dragged me down into his lower vibration, which was undesirable. But I did communicate *to* him via Soul Communications. On a physical level, all I did was actively listen to him. On an energetic level, I took a few deep Zohar Breaths, envisioned a bubble of Light around the three of us, and prayed for help being my most radiant self. This instilled supreme peace in me, which helped me stay within the Truth of who I am. It helped me not only not getting sucked into an argument at his energy level, but also beam kindness, peace, and healing energy to this poor restless guy. I don't know if it was my active listening, my staying heart-centered on my most radiant Self, sending the guy active prayers, or visualizing the three of us in a bubble of Light, but whatever I did, it seemed to put all three of us in a state of peace and Grace, at least for that evening. In this example, I humbly believe that I was communicating at the level of Soul Communication.

So what makes you effective in achieving Soul-level communications? The key is being in touch with your own Soul Self. The more in touch you are with your own Soul Self, the more capable you are of Soul Communication. Being in constant contact with your Soul allows you to communicate from the core of who you are, and at the same time, also ensures that you respect yourself and your listeners, meaning no tricks, no lies, no deceptions, and no cheep shots. Just plain truth that honors who you Truly are. In this fashion, two people whose opinions are diametrically opposed can have a mutually enriching discussion and still respect each other in the morning, so to speak. I mean there is much honor and respect even in agreeing to disagree. Remember: the argument between two holy people whose opinions are diametrically opposed is a silent one. In this high vibrational resonance silence, each of them recognizes the importance of God having given to their opponent a different aspect of the Whole Truth that completes their own.

Again, what's so great about communicating at the level of the Soul? Envision that you have a unique helium balloon soaring up to great heights (several hundred feet). Installed on this unique balloon is an extremely very powerful camera that is able to pick up every little detail through a large radius under it (around you). This camera also has x-ray capability and is able to see through solid objects. And through a wireless transmission into your heart chakra, the camera of this fantastic balloon reports to you all of its findings on a moment-by-moment basis. Now envision that each of us has their very own helium balloon that transmits higher-level of information into their heart chakra throughout their lifetime. And all of these fantastic high-level balloons never bump into each other or cause discomfort to each other, because at an even higher level, they are all tied into and monitored by a central Loving Intelligence. So the balloons themselves are always in harmony with one another. Now wouldn't it be great if we can all listen to information coming from this high perspective that has a birds-eye view on everything that's happening in our lives? And when it comes to communications and relationships, we all have some relationships that are strained. If we knew in advance that our personal upper-level balloon has the inside view on our opponent (because of Its birds-eye view, and through its harmonious Oneness with the opponent's balloon at the highest level), wouldn't it behoove us to consult and listen to the information coming from that balloon? Well, our Souls are not exactly balloons, but they do access the biggest picture in the same way. The information is very subtle. But at the same time, it is information that takes into account everyone's position as seen from the highest perspective, and over a span of time.

Now, the reason that Soul-level Truth reverberates so profoundly within you is that it comes from your own Soul. It is almost like this higher level Truth brings into your heart a little piece of your Divine Home. That is also how you know whether a vision/idea that has popped into your mind comes from your Soul's perspective, or from your cognitive here-now self. So given how wonderful it feels to communicate with your own Soul, what if you could simultaneously listen to your Soul's higher information, enjoy its nurturing resonance within you, and communicate this higher-level Truth to others... kind of like a professional simultaneous translator? Then you'd be engaging in Soul Communication.

In Soul communication, since it is the most angelic aspect of you that is expressing itself through you, the communication is inevitably kind, loving, anchored in True wisdom, and represents of the highest good of all involved, because your Soul is an integral part of the Divine. Therefore at the highest level, your Soul is in touch with the Soul of your counterpart in the communication, just like two spokes of the same wheel that are connected at the hub. It is only the here-now persona that forgets the oneness and can get centered on the narrowest low vibrational perspective of things. Soul-level communication is neither selfish nor selfless. Since at the Divine level we are all One, Soul Communications comes from a level of Truth that takes into account everyone's best interest, even if the highest interests of some of those involved is not immediately apparent.

Low-level communication can be weighed down by heavy emotions (which could be masked), anchored in lower self (ego), inhibited, or reflect fear. So if someone is communicating to you and posing like a performance, or trying too hard, they are <u>not</u> engaging in Soul Communications. Soul Communication is effortless, and allows the Light of your Soul to shine through you. It is an ideal communication that reflects clear integrity, vitality, adherence to your core Truth, yet at the same time it is neutral, open, compassion, and uplifting for both giver and receiver.

How To Communicate With Your Own Soul

So as the first component of Soul Communication is communicating with your own Soul Self, let us ask: How does one communicate with his/her Soul?

Communications with your own Soul and with the Divine comes from stillness within. In simple terms (as simply as I can put it), just clearing your mind of the busy "brain-fucking" noise—discarding all worries, agendas, stresses, and low-level vibrations of your here-now self, and listening to the stillness that remains within, will help you achieve a level of peace that then allows the wisdom of your Soul to come through. God is already there – inside you. Setting your intents for the meditation certainly helps achieve mental and energetic openness to communicate with that highest part of you. But you don't have to climb Mount Everest to reach God. You don't really have to do anything but invite Her-Him to dwell within you, and be open for the blessings. Of course, in our hectic modern lives, there is always much energetic debris, stress, worries, and everyday life issues to be thought of. So it is not always so easy to achieve that stillness of peace that allows listening to your Soul. So in *Seven Stages to co-Creating Prosperity From Your Soul*, I will give you many techniques, the most profound of which is Zohar Breath Meditation, to help you achieve communications with your Soul Self. In fact, it is those meditational communications with your Soul Self that, by the end of *Seven Stages to co-Creating Prosperity From Your Soul*, will help you formulate your Ideal Lifeplan for success.

Short of the profound meditations of *Seven Stages to co-Creating Prosperity From Your Soul*, throughout your everyday life, there is much wisdom in being able to differentiate between thoughts that are part of the everlasting "brain-fucking" noise, and those that are indeed communications from your Soul. Generally speaking, you know that you are listening to your Soul when there is a period of stillness before any messages come. I.e., the "brain-fucking" has stopped, and a pleasant, nurturing feeling washes over you. Then, when messages come, they are crystal clear, sometimes to the point that putting it in words (through a process of automatic writing) proves difficult, and you get the feeling that words would limit the vastness and clarity of the message. That is a definite sign that the messages are coming from your Soul. But the ultimate clue that you are receiving Creator wisdom is that you are basking in such peace and Light, that you simply *don't want to move*, even if you're hungry or thirsty. This peace is so pampering that you just want to stay there indefinitely. This is when you have meditationally tuned into your Soul's wisdom. And you'll certainly get a chance to do that in *Seven Stages to co-Creating Prosperity From Your Soul*, when we learn Zohar Breath Meditation.

However, I know that during the course of your hectic everyday life, you don't always have the time to go into a deep meditation for every decision you make. You certainly don't have time to do extensive meditations for every communication you engage in during your everyday life. Thankfully, there are always clues that can help you decide which choice or idea is more in line with your Soul Self. In general, you can use The God Meter (Chapter 7) to check the vibrational quality of the choices you have (which, as it pertains to communications, also include the choices you have of what to say, how to say it, how much to say, etc.).

But in the smallest moments of your everyday life, listening to the joyful resonance within can help you distinguishes Truth in an instant. There is always one choice that reverberates within you more favorably than the other. There is always one story that just doesn't feel right, and another which reverberates deeply with every part of you like celestial music. You can always do Zohar Breath Meditation later, at the end of the day, to gain a more comprehensive perspective on the situation. But in the small moments of your life, use the God Meter, and attentively listen to yourself: which choice reverberates within you most harmoniously, like the most beautiful symphony? Which choice rings all of your joy-bells so profoundly, that you secretly want to wiggle your toes in pleasure?

Achieving Soul-Level Communications

As lofty as Soul Communications may sound, they are innate to all human beings. They are the way that our original-Selves were always designed to communicate. However, due to social conditioning, and the long treacherous path through which mankind has walked before ending up at its present state of consciousness, achieving Soul Communication may require some re-training, depending on your personal level of evolution. This retraining involves relearning how to tune into our Soul-level Truth, and overcoming any fear or doubt about communicating it to others.

Once you become proficient at tuning into your wise and Angelic Soul Self (through use of Zohar Breath Meditation), you begin to be comfortable dwelling in your Soul Light, and living a life that is guided by Its wisdom. As you get in a habit of weighing all your choices by how musically harmoniously they resonate with the inner fiber of your being, you entire vibration begins to shift, and you begin to realize your natural affinity to making choices that are in alignment with your Soul. As you'll find out, it is intoxicating to make choices that are inspired by the Soul, because those choices lead you onto a path that dwells in joy. They bring you into a high—a rush, if you will (kind of like the rush you feel when you help someone), from which you wouldn't want to come down, and you shouldn't have to. Because incidentally, the path onto which those Soul-inspired choices takes you, is also your Ideal Lifepath of prosperity.

Once you've nurtured your relationship with your Soul to the point that Its presence makes you feel intoxicatingly vivacious, alive, peaceful, and fabulous, your communications too inevitably begin to come *through you directly from your Soul Self*. This results in communications that are calm, heart-centered, radiant, innocent, kind, loving, and at the same time firmly adhere to your core Truth and your deepest convictions.

For example, if your best friend tells you the details of her last argument with her husband. Maybe your here-now self wants to tell her: "He's an ass-hole! Divorce him!" Or conversely: "Sorry dear, but you were a bitch to him in this incident!" neither of which promote peace, love, and understanding. Then you take a few deep Zohar Breaths, and tune into your Soul's wisdom, which gives you a higher-vibrational solution. You may then find yourself instructing your friend to take some Zohar Breaths of her own, and see the situation from the perspective of her own Soul Self. You may then hear yourself helping her see her husband's reasoning behind his behavior, finding a peaceful perspective on the situation, and contemplating the steps that she could do to bring more peace into her home. Whatever solution your Soul shows you, you will find yourself planting more seeds of love and peace into any situation when you communicate from your core of Truth.

Once you get the hang of it, you will find that allowing your Soul to communicate through you is effortless, for you are just letting the truest part of yourself flow through you freely. And in doing so, you captures your audience much more, simply because the Truth is always more powerful than any fraction or twists of it. It is kind of like: would you rather eat a chemical imitation of chocolate? Or would you rather eat pure chocolate made from the best organic cacao beans?

Truth Speaking Techniques

There are many meditational techniques detailed in *Seven Stages to co-Creating Prosperity From Your Soul* to help you connect and stay connected to your Soul. And the more proficient you become in those meditations, the more comfortable you'll get at dwelling in the consciousness of your Soul Self and living a life of auspiciously receiving your Soul's blessings. And as I've mentioned above, that continuous pampered dwelling in your Soul Light will inevitably carry over to your communications, and naturally enable you to engage in Soul Communication.

However, because at this point, Soul Communications is a dormant skill in most of us, which needs to be relearnt, it never hurts to have a few simple techniques, which help facilitate the transference of your Soul's Truth into your here-now persona. While from a here-now business perspective, there may be many other techniques to help you become a better communicator and a better speaker. The techniques presented here facilitate True Communications from an energetic-metaphysical standpoint. And the idea behind them is to open up your chakra and energetic apparatus as you speak your Truth, and to get the full power of your clear energy powerhouses (chakras) behind the speech that's coming out of your vocal cords. As with everything else, I invite you to experiment with them, and choose only the ones you find helpful—the ones that you feel are right to you in the greater sense.

A Few Zohar Breaths:

It is true that the full Zohar Breath meditation, as outlined in *Seven Stages to co-Creating Prosperity From Your Soul,* involves an extensive cleansing and blessing of your space, as well as a process of speaking your intents, which must be done before the meditation in order for it to be effective. And needless to say that you will not have the time to do all that before every conversation with your boss, for instance. But taking a few Zohar Breaths is not the same as doing the full meditation. After you've done the full Zohar Breath Meditation as outlined in *Seven Stages to co-Creating Prosperity From Your Soul* a number of times, you'll become proficient in it, and it will then become easier for you to just consciously take two or three deep Zohar Breaths in a casual way to help you out throughout your day.

Taking a few Zohar Breaths before you speak will help you achieve a relative level of peace and attunement with your Soul. You can then set your intent to keep your consciousness anchored into your Soul-level Truth throughout your communication. It is not quite like speaking out of a trans-like meditative state. But it will give you a level of peace, and comfort that facilitate Soul Truth pouring through you, and very importantly – it will also set up sort of an energetic filter of Truth within you as you speak. So you'll suddenly hear yourself say things in a clearer, more concise, kinder, and more peaceful way than you cognitively thought you were capable of. And I've tried it many times. It works!

Kindness Is Always Well-Received:

As long as you are setting out to do Soul level of communications, your state of mind with regards to how the information will be received should be very relaxed. And we've talked about why above. Remind yourself not to worry about how other people will accept your Truth. Remind yourself that your Soul is now in charge of selecting how much and which aspects of your overall Truth are in your highest-best interest to communicate, and how to deliver the information in the best way. So just let go of all worry and stress, relax, and let your highest Truth come through you. All you need do is keep speaking while monitoring that the truth you speak is really Truth, meaning that it makes you feel empowered, yet at the same time resonates peacefully and joyfully within. Make sure you keep feeling the harmony as you speak.

However, remember that speaking your Truth does not mean being blunt. For example, the Truth about a fat coworker is not that she looks like a cow. That may be the lower level truth. The higher-level Truth is probably that she has a beautiful face, or that she is a lovely person, If you find that her overweight keeps coming into your consciousness, the reason may be that you were the person who was meant to helps her get into shape, or maybe her situation was meant to help you reach some type of an internal understanding for your personal growth. Whatever the case may be, there is always a kinder aspect to the truth, which your heart can help you find.

But there is a fine line between finding the kind aspect of the Truth, and twisting the truth for ulterior motives. And at this level of your personal evolution, twisting the Truth or lying just to make good with the boss, or to sweet-talk your way through something for example, would be detrimental to your Soul growth, and would definitely lengthen your path to prosperity, as well as make it more treacherous. The kinder aspect of the Truth that your audience is receptive to already exists, and so does the aspect of Truth that is the harmonious common denominator between you and your audience. You are not inventing things. You are simply *tuning into* those peace-enhancing aspects of Truth, along with which aspects of Truth are in your best interest to communicate now, and the best way to communicate them in the clearest, most peaceful way.

On an energetic level, setting your mind frame with this ease that comes from trusting your Soul's wisdom goes a long way to keep your Mind Body and Astral Body clear of any heaviness or energetic blockages, so that the powerful energy of your Soul's ideas can pour freely into your physical level of reality. When you speak out of the relaxed peaceful strength of your Soul, your audience cannot help but palpate the positive energy radiating from your communication.

Grounding The Truth:

Just before you speak, envision roots of Light extending from your navel, through your legs, and out from the soles of your feet, into the center of the earth. As you breathe in and out, envision orange-earthly energy coming in and out of you, grounding and balancing you. This way, you are not only connected to your Soul's Truth in an ethereal way that's floating out there. You are also grounded, and able to anchor this Truth into this reality in a harmonious way, which allows your truth to come out in the right words and proportion that this here-now reality is ready to withstand.

Relaxing Your Physical Speaking Apparatus:

As you speak, relax your whole body. In particular, pay special attention to relaxation of your shoulders, throat, and face muscles. Think about the fact that the expression of truth that you deeply know and believe does not require effort to convey.

This relaxation helps prevent any energetic blockages in your throat chakra – in charge of communications.

Getting Your Echoing Box Behind Your Strings:

Singers and professional speakers alike are trained to make sure that the sound does not just come from the throat, but amplified by the big echoing-box of their full lungs, like the body of a cello amplifying the sound of the strings. Likewise, taking a full (deep) breath of air before you speak helps, get the echoing-box of your lungs behind the strings of your vocal cords, and makes the sound of your speech sound fuller, deeper, and more convincing. However, from a metaphysical standpoint, uttering the sounds of your words with the air escaping from your full lungs on exhalation does much more than just that.

On the first level of exploration, breath brings in more Heavenly Ki to circulate throughout your energetic apparatus, which empowers you with more zest of life at the moments that you need them, and puts your harmonious feelings behind your convictions, which on a subtle level, radiates them out to your audience more convincingly.

But empowering your speech with fresh breath does more than just make a subtle difference: Taking a deep belly breath (which we'll also learn in *Seven Stages to co-Creating Prosperity From Your Soul*), makes the sound of your voice originate from your belly center, called the Hara in India, the lower Dan-Tien in Chinese medicine, and the Tanden in Japan, which is the area where your Heavenly Ki mixes with your Innate Ki, as discussed in Chapter 1. This echoing full-breath speech harnesses the powers of your second, third and heart chakras to stand behind your throat chakra, and therefore empower your communications. These are the chakras that hold your energies of relationships, personal power, and Divine connection, respectively. So bringing your innate capabilities of harmonious relationships (second chakra), personal power (third chakra), and Divine connection (fourth chakra) to support your communication makes the communication more potent and powerful. Your audience may not cognitively know all that. But they will feel the power of your convictions, and your communications will resonate well with them.

Now, why is it so important to get all of your chakras, including your heart chakra behind your communications? One line of proof comes to us through the Institute of Heartmath, whose research has concluded that: "The heart's electrical field is about 60 times greater in amplitude than the electrical activity generated by the brain. This field, measured in the form of an electrocardiogram (ECG), can be detected anywhere on the surface of the body. Furthermore, the magnetic field produced by the heart is more than 5,000 times greater in strength than the field generated by the brain, and can be detected a number of feet away from the body, in all directions, using SQUID-based magnetometers."[3] This is interesting because the key to communicating with our own Soul Self, which is the basis of Soul Communication, is through the heart chakra.

Now in case you are wondering if it's better to communicate through your head or your heart, the answer is: both. What has the greatest effect on your listeners and communicates the power of your conviction in the most effective way is when your head and your heart are one, when all aspects of you resonate in a perfect harmony with your Soul Self, and with your listener. That effectively melts even the fiercest opponent, and instills harmony in the communication.

Third-Eye Projection:

It is said that the eyes are the mirrors of the soul. Keeping eye contact with your listeners will not only let them know that you are honest. It establishes a connection that is deeper than that. You might say that not every business meeting needs a teary-eyed heart-to-heart. But True Communication doesn't have to be teary-eyed or a meltdown at all. On a here-now level, keeping eye contact helps you gauge at your receiver's mindsets, emotional reactions, the overall flow of your communications, and it helps your audience know your sincerity. But it is much more than that.

Remember that even if your audience is a rival, on a Soul level, we are all One. So energetically speaking, keeping eye contact helps re-establish the connection between the Souls on a mirror-to-mirror (Soul-to-Soul) level, on an extremely subtle level. But again, metaphysically, there is much more to eye contact than that.

Ancient yogic theorized that when we communicate, the majority of our communication actually takes place not at the level of the throat chakra that speaks our words, but at the third-eye level, which projects out the energetic essence of our True vision. When the projection is strong, the audience will receive the communication loud and clear. They will understand it deeply. Keeping eye contact also helps you keep line-of-sight between your forehead—the location of your sixth chakra—and the person you are projecting psychically to.

However, your projection is only as good as the level of Truth that stands behind them. So to powerfully project Truth, the wisdom has to come from your Soul-level Truth, then resonate harmoniously within your body (nervous and endocrine systems) to evoke harmonious emotions (which shifts your energetic vibration favorably), and only then be vibrationally projected to your receiver through your third-eye (sixth) chakra. Have you ever seen the movie *Meet Joe Black?* In the movie, the Angel takes on a human form for about a week, in order to experience life as a human. However, even in this human form, the Angel is able to communicate complex ideas through a deep look in someone's eyes. And in the reality of the movie, those ideas are perfectly understood, even though the receivers were ordinary humans. The movie, of course, was an over dramatization of a fundamental Truth. OK, so not all of us communicate quite at that level. But all of us communicate energetically by projecting through our sixth chakra. This energetic communication underlies all other communications, including verbal. This is why we can all tune into what's true and what's not even when we don't know what exactly triggered the notion. A woman can say and even convince herself that she wants a man, but until she projects that vibe through her third-eye chakra, the man would not respond to her or oblige her. You could tell your boss that you are enthusiastic about heading a certain project. But if your energetic sixth chakra projection is saying: "I'm apprehensive, and I have a lot going on at home," than what comes out is the confusion of mixed messages, which are neither effective nor productive. This is why it is so important to consult your Soul on the things that you communicate.

So better than any technique I can give you, the best advise I can give you on True Communications is simply to stay in touch with the highest level of your Soul Truth while you communicate with others. Even if your view is controversial, if it originates from the Light of your Soul, it is a Truth that needs to be heard, because it serves everyone's highest-best interest. For example, Albert Einstein did not speak until the age of four, could not read until he was seven years old, which caused his parents and teachers to think he was retarded. Einstein was also expelled from school, which necessitated his parents to get private tutoring for him. Even after he became a well know scientist, his scientific truths were controversial[4] for a long time, before they finally gained worldwide acceptance (and a Nobel Prize). But both you and I are benefiting daily from the fact that Einstein had enough courage to publish his then controversial theories of Relativity, not to mention that Einstein's truth did eventually win him worldwide recognition, and enabled him to co-Create True prosperity for himself. Henry Ford's first five businesses failed, before he founded the successful Ford Motor Company; Walt Disney was initially fired by a newspaper editor who said that, "he lacked imagination and had no good ideas,"[4] which is hilarious when you think about it now. But needless to say that Walt Disney died a very wealthy man. And these are just a few examples of people whose truth were initially unacceptable to others, but who eventually gained much recognition and wealth as a result of speaking their Truth.

Soulmates

I am sure you intuitively already know that the highest level of self-actualization, and the most joyous life you can have, is a life of love, walking side by side with your Soulmates. But Soulmates are more than that. Soulmates also help you bring forth the best version of yourself—help you stay connected to your Soul Self, and thus help you co-Create your most auspicious Lifepath. Since Soulmates are so important in your path of prosperity, let's talk about what they are, and how their role in your life helps you co-Create prosperity.

At the highest level of reality, all of us are Soulmates. That is because all Souls come from God. This is a fact! So if at a Divine level we are all One, then what exactly constitutes a soulmate? The short answer is - a soulmate is someone with whom we have a close affinity – an instant connection that is felt by both parties. These are the people who understand you and sometimes even feel what you feel without having to say a word. And there is a reason why I talk about soulmate**s** pluralistically. And we are going to explore that reason. But first, let us explore the concept of soulmates a little more.

Akashic Records:

You may have heard the term "the Akashic records" before, but didn't quite understand what it was. Since the understanding of the Akashic records is relevant to understanding soulmates, let's devote a moment to understanding what the Akashic records are.

The word "Akasha" in Sanskrit means "sky," "space," or "ethers," referring to the spiritual realm of the Divine. According to ancient beliefs (Hindu, Sikh and Buddhism), all Universal knowledge, as well as the history of each Soul as an aspect of the Divine, are stored in a non-physical ethereal "library," called the Akashic Records. According to this belief, all of who you were in this or parallel pasts, as well as all possibilities of who you are going to become in all realms of existence, all of your incarnations, and all realities, in all times within any particular lifetime, are all stored in your Akashic Records. This means that all of your possible futures (recall our discussion of "Universal Travel of Choice," Chapter 6), including your Ideal Lifeplan, are also contained in this Akashic Records library. However, the Akashic Records is not really a physical library but an ethereal heavenly existence of this information.

While not locked under lock and key in the sense that we understand it from our human perspective, access to the Akashic Records is restricted, and could be accessed only by the person the information is relating to. This means that your powers of Free Will can grant you access only to the records pertaining to you, and only to the extent that it serves your Soul Self. You can access information about other people in your life only to the extent that this information pertains to you… For example, "what is in my highest-best interest to give my best friend for her birthday?" or, "what should I say to my friend to best console him in his time of trouble?" These are questions that relate to other people, but they revolve around action that you should do or not do with regards to the highest-best interest of both of you.

There is some proof that the existence of the Akashic Records: People who have had near death experiences[5] describe that during their life review they were shown scenes not only from the past of their present lifetime, but also from the future, as well as scenes from other lifetimes and other worlds relating to the issues at hand. They report that they had a crystal clear perception of all other lifetimes, and all moments in each lifetime existing simultaneously, such that past-present-future are all real at the same time. It seems that during their NDE, they were privy to their Akashic records, as they also said that all the wisdom of the Universe suddenly became available and crystal clear to them while they were in the Light. In his book "Messages From The Light," Christopher Copper documents many cases in which NDErs were able to accurately predict future events based on their experiences. What is interesting in NDEs as it relates to prosperity, is that virtually all NDErs were compelled to come back to earthly life when they understood the importance of their Earthly mission. They were all also assured that if they came back to Earthly life to complete their life mission (i.e., Ideal Lifepath), they will be granted Divine favor, health, Grace, Love, and abundance.

Soulmates Across Cultures:

In Western civilization, the first person to talk about soulmates and twin-flames was Plato. Plato wrote a symposium in which he had Aristophanes present his theory, which postulated that God originally had created humans to be androgynous, and have four arms, four legs, and two faces. According to his theory, Zeus feared the power of these humans and split them in half, "condemning them to spend their lives searching for the other half to complete them."[6] But of course, as you know by now, each of us is a complete Soul and an integral aspect of God. So saying that we are but a fraction of ourselves does not really reflect who we Truly are. For our Creator has more than enough Creative energy. She-He doesn't need to split anything in half!

Hindu and Buddhist traditions profess that we each have many soulmates, some of them karmic soulmates and others dharmic soulmates. According to those philosophies, not all soulmates are meant to become romantic relations. Karmic soulmates are souls with whom we have walked a path together many times before, but with whom we have unresolved issued— unfinished karmic lessons to still teach each other during this lifetime. Dharmic soulmates are those people that give you the immediate warm-fuzzy feeling. Those are the people with whom you have completed your karmic lessons long ago, and have agreed to come together again to support and love one another during this lifetime.

It is interesting to note that Sikh religion does not believe in soulmates, as it believes that since all Souls come from God, we are *all* soulmates.

Traditional mainstream Judaism believes in "bashert," which in Yiddish means, "meant to be." The concept is that all matches are made in Heaven by the Divine. But this tradition does not talk about the reasoning for coming together, like many people think of Soulmates as fitting perfectly like lock and key, but simply states that God decides who is to come together and who is not. Ouch, that sounds a bit arbitrary and cold, doesn't it?

Both Kabbalah and Sikh traditions postulate that Souls are only attracted to other Souls that remind them of their own True essence of HOME. So that the closer you are to living in the pure Light of your Soul, the more you will attract your soulmate, like a bright beacon that allows the ships to find the harbor at night. This concept is closest to the Truth.

Karmic & Dharmic Soulmates:

An interesting explanation of what Hindu and Buddhists term "karmic soulmates" is offered by Rasha in her book called *Oneness*. According to this explanation, most often, soulmates can help us externalize our sharp edges, so we can smooth them out, and make our personality more balanced and cohesive, which in turn does a high service to our Souls. By this explanation, a soulmates can be the people in your life who get under your skin the deepest, and push our buttons the most annoyingly. Are those really Soulmates?

An example of a "karmic soulmate" is my mother: My mother is an atheist, and the least spiritual person I know. She is a good woman, but her viewpoints and personality are diametrically opposed to mine. And despite all of her good intents, she can skillfully drive me insane in a matter of minutes. However, there is a strong mother-daughter bond between us. Because of all the qualities I described above, my mother had been a force in my life that had created the necessity for me to learn greater spiritual Truths. Talk about smoothing out sharp edges within myself, my mother's ability to push my buttons had created in me the need to find meditational tools, which enabled me to find a level of inner peace that cannot be thrown off. Whether her character is the result of negative conditioning of her own past, or pushing me by negative motivation was her pre-agreed upon role in this lifetime, is irrelevant. In retrospect, the skills that she pushed me to develop—the ability to find inner peace was a necessary step to finding my True calling in life. Is she one of my karmic-soulmates? Are karmic soulmates really Soulmates? I don't know. Perhaps we can all agree that these souls, considered karmic-soulmates, are souls with whom we've walked a path before, and for whatever reason, we have agreed to teach each other lessons again. Whether or not they are True soulmates is a matter of definition.

I personally don't believe in Karmic Soulmates. And I absolutely do not believe in negative motivations. But whether you believe that we have karmic soulmates or not, it is important to be aware of the forces at work here: It is true that some people you can walk away from. But some people are in your life to stay, like members of your immediate family, for example. And you cannot force them to live a more high-vibrational life, because violate their free will. In many of these cases, you have actually usually chosen these people's presence in your life on a Soul level in order to teach you something. The two things you can do, now that these people are in your life, is choose how you perceive these relationship, and what you can do to correct the disharmony between you.

First, it would be wise for you to ask your Soul Self what the lesson embedded in the disharmony is, and whether it is still valid at present time. Perhaps the two of you have already learnt the lessons you were intended to teach each other, and you can move onto more harmonious relationship. For example, now that I am no longer impatient and have already learnt to meditationally find my center, I do not need for my mother to push my buttons in order to propel me to learn those skills. So in recent years, I've started gently but firmly set boundaries, as we have learnt to do in Chapter 4, and I have found that our communications have become more harmonious. So of course you can choose to look at the people in your life with whom you have strained relationships as nuisances. And the result will be that you would continue to get annoyed by their presence in your life, and detracted from following your Ideal Lifepath. On the other hand, you can choose to look at them as karmic soulmates, who have come to help you learn something about yourself, and push you to be the best version of yourself, even if it was by negative motivation. That does not mean that karmic soulmates are True Soulmates. It just means that you are choosing to look at the bright side of things, in order to move past these lessons, and enable yourself to co-Create True prosperity in your life.

The Truest Soulmates are the ones that Hindu and Buddhist traditions have named "dharmic soulmates." These *are the people in your life with whom you have an instant deep kinship, who give you a wonderful warm fuzzy feeling, who always uplift you, who always believe in you and support your greatness, who inspire you, and who always bring out the best in you by their mutual resonance with that goodness in you.* They will always tell you the Truth constructively in order to help you reclaim your greatness, even if it's not pleasant to hear at that moment. But they'll do so with such love and grace that it'll be music to your ears because you know that you are loved. They are the people that support your goals, believe you can achieve anything you set your mind to achieve, and see the Divine spark in you even when you cannot. And these soulmates are the only kinds of people that should be in your inner circle.

For example, the truest soulmate in my life, without whom all of my spiritual understandings, and the totality of whom I am would not have been possible, was my grandmother. My grandmother has bathed me with unconditional love throughout my life (and even after her passing), always saw the spark of God-likeness in me, inspired me to be pure-hearted, giving, loving, and the best version of myself. My grandmother led by example—she always saw nothing but good in every person she has met. She gave more than she could afford, and she was the epitome of motherly love for all the people who knew her. And after 93 blessed years on this earth, hundreds of people wept at her funeral. Because she only saw the beauty and Divine spark in every person, she couldn't help but pour out love for the good she saw in people. It is those people in your life, like my grandmother, that are your truest soulmates. Soulmates are those people you'll always remember, and will always have place in your heart (and visa-versa), even if you only lay eyes on one another for a brief moment in life.

Soul Groups

The Truth is that we have many soulmates. Some are indeed romantic soulmates, while others could be siblings, best friends, parents, children, teachers, and many other relationships. These are the people with whom we have an instant and effortless deep bond of supporting one another, inspiring each other to be the best version of ourselves, having deep conversations about making the world better, and understanding one another sometimes even without a word spoken. Those true soulmates are all core members of your Soul group. And through many lifetimes and existences, your Soul has achieved much growth and mastered many lessons with the help of these Souls.

According to Linda Howe, an expert on reading the Akashic Records, and the author of the book *How To Read The Akashic Records*, Souls really move in circles or groups she calls your spiritual ancestry. Soul groups come together through many incarnations in many different roles, usually for a mutual purpose in addition to creating more Love in the world, which is the overall purpose of every Soul in existence. According to Linda Howe, your spiritual ancestry comprises of not necessarily of your biological family, but could also be comprised of those warm-fuzzy-feeling Souls with whom you have a close kinship, and I can attest to that. Soul groups may include blood relatives as well as Soul brothers and sisters who are not really related to you in the traditional sense of the word. For example, I have at least three friends whom I trust more than I trust any of my living blood relatives, and feel that they are my True family. And by the way, none of those three Souls are romantic soulmates. They are friends that I know, beyond the shadow of doubt, I'll be seeing even after this lifetime, when I go HOME. Linda Howe's theory is based on her many years of experience in conducting Akashic records readings for many people. And she is not alone in this Soul group theory.

Thanks to Dr. Raymond Moody[7] and Dr. Jeffrey Long[8, 9, 10], we now have an accurate, verifiable method of tuning into Truth from its Heavenly perspective. NDEers reported that during their experience, they met with relatives and loved ones who have died before them, as well as by Souls that they did not know during their current life, but with whom they had such an instant deep kinship and Love bond, that they knew that they have known these Souls forever. Also, there are many NDE stories that report meeting relatives that they had never met during this lifetime, in most cases because they were relatives who died before they were born. Moreover, in many of those reports, the NDEer never knew about these deceased relatives until their NDE. But once they came back into physical life, they asked their living relatives, who confirmed (and were astonished) the existence of the relatives met in the afterlife. Whether the Soulmates were deceased relatives, or other Souls, all NDEers said that they knew these Souls had a deep commitment to them which has spanned over eons of time, and they felt such a love connection with them, that that they never wanted to part with them. This is strong evidence that indeed we do move in groups of Souls that support one another, and propel one another to thrive according to each of our highest Lifeplan.

When it comes to co-Creating your Ideal Lifepath, there are a few reasons why it is important to be aware of Soul groups. One is the deep empathic connection we have with the members of our Soul group. I cannot count how many times I have woken up with an unexplained left wrist pain, only to find out later that my father was having a wrist pain (1,500 miles away) at the same time. And in all of those times, as soon as I sent him reiki distant healing to heal his wrist pain, and did a Cord Cutting Meditation (see Chapter 4 of *Seven Stages to co-Creating Prosperity From Your Soul*), my own wrist pain also disappeared. This is an example of empathic pain, and how to make it go away. For we are supposed to uplift one another, not drag each other down. Besides empathic pain, many of your beliefs, attitudes, and behavior patterns are shared with the members of your Soul group on a deep subconscious level. And of course, belief systems and behavior patterns that are not in alignment with your highest purpose can block or postpone your successful co-Creation of prosperity in life.

To be clear, you may feel empathy and share life circumstances with many people in your life, not all of whom are members of your Soul group. And with those, doing Cord Cutting Meditation (*Seven Stages to co-Creating Prosperity From Your Soul*) will always help the relationships become more harmonious. What distinguishes the members of your Soul group is the strength of your heart-to-heart connection with them. The love and empathic connections we share with members of our Soul group is so enormous, that it makes it difficult to cut cords, because your purpose of co-Creating love, joy, health, prosperity, and harmony in life is shared with the closest members of your Soul group who are incarnate with you at the same time.

To better understand this, envision yourself in a big energetic balloon, in which you and some members of your Soul group are striving to go up, or in a particular direction, kind of like a bunch of flies inside a balloon striving to drive the balloon in a particular direction. But in that mutual effort, some members' pre-agreed upon job is to balance the balloon horizontally, some to give it weight and ground it, and yet others' job is to provide an uplifting force. So in order to ascend or navigate the balloon to its destination, even if you are one of the main up-driving forces, the balloon is more beautifully inflated because of all of its members, and its movement is smoother towards the mutual destination when all of its members are at their best. So this explains why it is helpful to cleanse the balloon from influences that do not drive it to the proper mutual destination, i.e., to rid it of people who are not true members of this balloon, metaphorically speaking.

What this means to you, as it relates to co-Creating prosperity, is that it is beneficial to nurture your strong bonds with the True members of your Soul group as it is most likely that your Ideal Lifepath is closely related to the Ideal Lifepaths of the close members of your Soul group—intertwined. You walk hand in hand as you fulfill your respective most auspicious Lifeplans: you bounce ideas off of each other; you hold each other's vision in the Light of your prayerful intent; and you empower each other in supportive ways. If the members of your Soul group are stuck in a vibration of worry, fear, and negativity, this could delay the manifestation of your own auspicious Lifeplan. For this reason, every time my father tells me how much he worries about me, I implore him to stop worrying and direct his consciousness to his positive hopes and dreams about me. Although his motivation is loving, I do not want the negative vibration of his fear and worry to stand in my way of manifesting my Ideal Lifepath. Everyone becomes more empowered to fulfill their most Ideal Lifeplans when the members of their Soul group are in a positive vibration. So don't worry or be fearful about the members of your Soul group. Be optimistic! Be encouraging. Hold their highest vision in a bright Light of your belief. And ask them to do the same for you.

If one of the members of your Soul group is having an issue, better than worry, do the Lightening Bold Meditation, detailed in Chapter 4 of *Seven Stages to co-Creating Prosperity From Your Soul*, to powerfully cleanse any negative-heavy elements from your entire Soul group in one fell swoop. It is a meditation that helps you use your Divinely given free will to send healing energy to automatically rid all the members of your Soul group of the particular negative themes, and instill healing Divine energy in its stead.

Romantic Twin-Flame

Some of the core members of our Soul group can become romantic partners, with whom we can have a long lasting strong marriage. That is why some people can be married more than once, and have a strong Soulmate connection with each of their spouses. But there is that one perfect Soulmate—your "twin-flame" or "essence-twin." This twin is a Soul that has been carved out of Divine Oneness at the same time with you, out of the same Divine spark. It therefore is of the same vibrational essence as your Soul, and fits with you perfectly like a key to a lock. However, despite being carved out of the same Divine spark, each of the twin-flame Souls is complete and perfect within Itself—a Soul that is Whole.

Now, contrary to what you may think, a twin-flame rarely reincarnates with you at the same time. You may have occasional lifetimes with your twin-flame. But most of your romantic partners, with whom you have had a deep Soulmate connection, are core members of your Soul group. As each Soul's task is to grow and become more radiant, in most lifetimes, your twin-flame serves as your guardian Angel while you are incarnate, and you serve as his/her guardian Angel while he/she is incarnate. This is the closest most efficient way to more fully support one another throughout a lifetime, and not just during your adult marrying ages. However, as your Souls become more complete and mature, as your mastered lessons include bringing the Light of your Soul into your earthly lives, and as you near the end of your life cycles, you and your twin-flame will once again be reunited to have a human incarnation together.

For reasons of not violating your twin's free choice, a twin-flame is the one thing you cannot just manifest. Your twin-flame already exists, and is always living in the same world with you (as opposed to other worlds in which you may have existed together). You travel in and out of worlds *together*. If you are incarnated in the same lifetime together, the only variable is when you are going to show up in each other's lives, which depends on how closely to the Light of your Souls you have both evolved according to your Ideal Lifeplan. Also, twin-flames tend to have an incarnation together when they have a mutual mission, relating to spiritually elevating and otherwise serving the good of others on this planet. For this reason, more and more twin-flames are being reunited in our times, in order to help the changes on Earth and bring about the new age of enlightenment.

But a twin-flame relationship is not always an easy one. The reunification with a twin-flame is intense beyond words. In other relationships, intensity is really just neediness. But in a twin-flame relationship, it is a positive spiritual intensity that drives the emotional and physical intensities. The intensity and completeness of twin-flame union also means that nothing can stand in its way. If you and/or your twin-flame have emotional or mental baggage, it will be brought to the surface to be purged out, because nothing stands in the way of your closeness with your twin-flame. So in order to have a lasting and successful union with your twin-flame, the union must be delayed until both Souls are evolved enough, and until both persons are ready to live *only* by the Light of their Souls. In fact, it is said that all of your earthly relationships are a preparation for the one with your twin-flame, which inevitably enhances the spirituality of the entire planet. The intensity and raw honesty of your relationship with your twin-flame is worth the preparation work for the moment of reunion, because whole worlds of spiritual esoteric knowledge, and a bright Light of unseconded spiritual awakening come through this union. It is a union whose Light shines exponentially brighter than the sum of its parts, and a profound feeling of HOME.

Magnetizing a Soulmate Into Our Lives

In a way, soulmates are really a part of us. Rumi wrote in one of his poems: "The minutes I heard my first love story, I started looking for you, not knowing how blind that was. Lovers don't finally meet somewhere; they're in each other all along."

An interesting point of view, shared by most NDEers, is that soulmates connections are not always instantaneously obvious to both people. The recognition of a soulmate depends on both people's openness of heart, and how connected they each are to their own Souls. What is always obvious is our level of caring about the other person. But if either (or sometimes both) person has a thick layer of dark crust (stress, fear, preconditioning…) around their bright spark of Godlikeness, and are therefore not in touch with their Soul Self, than it could take both people time to recognize that this is a soulmate relationship, and the relationship could take time to develop. Perhaps now that you know you have many soulmates, it would be easier to connect to people on a Soul level, as you'll know that opening up to one soulmate does not preclude you from opening up to another.

The key to magnetizing soulmates into your life is, as you might have guessed: the closer you get to your own Soul, the more you'll magnetize soulmates into your life. To deeply understand this, it is helpful to recall the hub and spoke illustration of our connection to God. If you think of soulmates as the adjacent spokes of a wheel, than all Souls connect at the heart of the Divine— the hub of all the spokes. So naturally, the closer along each spoke you get to the hub, in terms of our consciousness and energetic vibration, the closer two spokes actually are. This is an over simplification, of course. But principally, the connection between soulmates follows the same reasoning: the closer we get to grounding and living by the Light of our own Soul Self, the closer it'll bring us to the Core where we and our Soulmates are One.

Energetically speaking also, the more you dwell in the radiant Light of your Soul, and the more of Its Light you ground into your every day reality, the more you'll radiate that Light like a beacon of Light that your soulmate can see, and find you. Or if you think of two Soulmates like two sides of a magnetized zipper closing downward, than the more radiant you are with your Soul's Light, the stronger the magnet that you apply to close the zipper, and magnetize your Soulmate to you.

Another aspect of this is: Your two Souls are really the ones orchestrating the meeting between the two of you. And they are able to orchestrate this perfect meeting because they connect with each other at the Core. But essentially, your Soul is your matchmaker! So the more inspired every moment of your life is your Soul's guidance, the better chances you have of not missing the "blind-date" that your Soul has set you up on. Of course, free choice is still given to each one of you at every step of the way. Thus, there may be choices that you've made on a Soul level, which your here-now self is not quite aware of, such as things you have set out to do before reuniting with your soulmate. There may also be things that your soulmate has set out (on a Soul level) for him/herself to do before meeting you.

And since there is a perfect and most auspicious timing for every piece in the mosaic of your life, the timing for the reunification with your soulmate may or may not be now. All you can really do to eliminate delay in meeting your romantic Soulmate is to make life choices that are inspired by the wisdom of your Soul, and to live a life that is lit by Its Light. And as we've been discussing throughout this part, your connection with your Soul Self is also what keeps you on your Ideal Lifeplan, and magnetizes easy, free flowing, True, and all-inclusive prosperity to you.

☯   ☯

☯

You and I have walked a long path together, as we delved deeply into understanding the metaphysical principles that govern your co-Creation of prosperity into your life. Understanding all that you have understood throughout this first book is no small feat. And whether or not you acknowledge it at this point, you have evolved much as you read each concept and contemplated its effects on your life. And for those achievements, I would like to congratulate you, and deeply bow to your Soul. More than my salute, now that you understand all these principles of co-Creation, you have inevitably become more conscious of what it is that you co-Create into your life everyday, and therefore better able to tweak your thought forms, feelings, and actions into ones that are more inline with your Ideal Lifeplan, which in the weeks to come, will enable you to subtly shift your vibrational resonance into one that magnetizes prosperity.

But all these understandings and subtle tweaking are only the first steps. The more profound path that you and I are to walk together is one of bringing all these understandings into real action in the reality of your life. And we will do so in two steps:

In *Seven Stages to co-Creating Prosperity From Your Soul*, we will engage in a very powerful seven-stage meditational process, which will help you bring into focus the specific details of your Ideal Lifeplan, and devise a specific plan of action to bring its prosperity into physical manifestation.

In *A Lifestyle of Prosperity From Your Soul*, I will give you many powerful tools to prepare the physical foundation of your body-temple and life for grounding the enhanced amounts of Creative energy that's to come through your Infinite Funnel of Abundance now. Whereas *Seven Stages to co-Creating Prosperity From Your Soul* is mostly a meditational introspective phase designed to help you attain knowledge of the exact details of *your* specific Ideal Lifeplan, *A Lifestyle of Prosperity From Your Soul* is about actually starting to walk the path of a conscious co-Creator. It is about choosing to live a lifestyle of health and happiness in your everyday life, therefore allowing the visions of your meditations to beef up with the Creative energy necessary to translate them into real blessings in the physical reality of your life.

As we go into all these processes, the understandings that you have developed in this book will begin to click even more profoundly as they are anchored into actual experiences. But by the same token, after you've had some meditational and experiential "Aha" moments, going back and re-reading any subjects of this book that might have seemed esoteric the first time will reinforce your understanding of how the subjects relate to you specifically, and how they might be relevant in your life.

Know that even though I am not physically with you to hold your hand through this process, I am very much with you in my prayers, holding space for your success. I hope that the loving members of your Soul group are also with you on your journey, holding your hand, and giving you their love and support. But the most powerful support of all is that of your Soul Self, who is with you always, rooting for your co-Creation of a magnificent life, full of the most radiant health, blissful happiness, and True and all-inclusive prosperity. I pray with everything that I am that you will come to know your Soul Self intimately, that you will live every moment of your life bathed in Its Light, and that you will enjoy a life filled with the highest blessings that only your Soul could precipitate on you.

I look forward to helping you tune into your specific Ideal Lifeplan in *Seven Stages to co-Creating Prosperity From Your Soul.*

Bibliography

Introduction:

[1] TASLAMAN, Caner Ph.D. "Entropy and God." *Author's own website.* Aug. 2012. July 2013. <http://photochemistry.epfl.ch/ERC/ENTROPY_and_GOD.pdf>

[2] Penrose, Roger *The Emperor's New Mind.* Translated by Tekin Dereli, Tübitak Popüler Bilim Kitapları. Ankara: 2003, p. 50.

Chapter 1:

[1] Nirvair Singh Khalsa. *Kundalini Yoga For Grace And Prosperity.* Produced, filmed & directed by Nirvair Singh Khalsa. Year of release unknown. Film.

[2] Moody, Raymond, MD. *Life After Life.* San Francisco, CA: Harper Collins, 1975.

[3] Long, Jeffery M.D. and Perry, Paul. *Evidence Of The Afterlife, The Science of Near-Death Experiences.* New York, NY: HarperCollins, 2010.

[4] Gerber, Richard MD. *Vibrational Medicine.* Rochester, Vermont: Bear & Company, 2001

[5] Hameroff, Stuart MD. "Quantum consciousness." *YouTube videos.* Nov 2007. June 2013. <http://www.youtube.com/watch?v=OEpUIcOodnM> & Oct 2007. Jan 2013 <http://youtu.be/y4y8mTRqXAo> & also Nov 2007. June 2013. <http://youtu.be/OEpUIcOodnM>

[6] Yogi Bhajan, PhD. *The Aquarian Teacher.* KRI International Teacher Training in Kundalini Yoga as taught by Yogi Bhajan. Santa Cruz, NM: Kundalini Research Institute, 2007.

[7] McCarty, Rollin. Articles of the Heart. Institute of Heartmath. Oct. 2012. Jan 2013. <http://www.heartmath.org/templates/ihm/e-newsletter/article/2010/summer/energetic-heart-is-unfolding.php>

Chapter 2

[1] *What The Bleep!? Down The Rabbit Hole (The Quantum Edition).* Dir. William Arnts, Mark Vicente, Betsy Chasse. Samuel Goldwyn/Roadside Attractions, 2005. Film.

[2] Coppers, Christopher. *Messages From The Light.* Pompton Plains, NJ: Career Press, 2011.

[3] Private conversation of my parents with Mr. Perlman

Chapter 3

[1] Bohm, David. *Wholeness In The Implicate Order.* First published in 1980. New York, NY: Routledge Classics, 2006.

2   *What The Bleep!? Down The Rabbit Hole (The Quantum Edition)*. Dir. William Arnts, Mark Vicente, Betsy Chasse. Samuel Goldwyn/Roadside Attractions, 2005. Film.

Chapter 5

1   Hameroff, Stuart MD. "Quantum consciousness." *YouTube videos*. Nov 2007. June 2013. <http://www.youtube.com/watch?v=OEpUIcOodnM> & Oct 2007. Jan 2013 <http://youtu.be/y4y8mTRqXAo> & also Nov 2007. June 2013. <http://youtu.be/OEpUIcOodnM>

Chapter 6

1   Hameroff, Stuart MD. "Quantum consciousness." *YouTube videos*. Nov 2007. June 2013. <http://www.youtube.com/watch?v=OEpUIcOodnM> & Oct 2007. Jan 2013 <http://youtu.be/y4y8mTRqXAo> & also Nov 2007. June 2013. <http://youtu.be/OEpUIcOodnM>

2   Dyer, Wayne. Manifest Your Destiny: The Nine Spiritual Principles for Getting Everything You Want. New York, NY: HarperCollins, 1998

3   Dyer, Wayne. "Ah meditations." *YouTube Video*. Oct 2011. Mar. 2013. <http://youtu.be/0PwVJOiRcl8>

4   Heline, Corinne D. Healing and Regeneration Through Music. Santa Barbara, CA.: J. F. Rowny Press, 1945.

Chapter 8

1   Long, Jeffery MD. "Current NDERF Individual NDE Experiences" & "Archives Main Page." *Near Death Experience Research Foundation*. Dec. 2013. Jan. 2014. <www.NDERF.org>

2   Canfield, Jack, and Ford, Ariel. *The Soulmate Secret*. Book written by Ariel Ford, Afterwards by Jack Canfield. New York, NY: HarperCollins, 2009.

3   Author unknown, KFC Corporation. *KFC's website*. Publication date unknown. July 2013. <http://colonelsanders.com>

4   "Afterlife." Wikipedia. Jan. 2014. Jan 2013. <http://en.wikipedia.org/wiki/Afterlife>

5   Moody, Raymond, MD. *Life After Life*. San Francisco, CA: Harper Collins, 1975.

6   Yogi Bhajan, and Guru Terath Kaur Khalsa. "Dying Into Life, The Yoga of Death, Loss & Transformation." Espanola, NM: Guru Ram Das Books, 2006.

7   Coppers, Christopher. *Messages From The Light*. Pompton Plains, NJ: Career Press, 2011.

8   BBC. "The Day I Died," YouTube. May 2010. June 2013. <http://youtu.be/u1vWoUoiaP4>

9   Long, Jeffery MD. "Current NDERF Individual NDE Experiences" & "Archives Main Page." *Near Death Experience Research Foundation*. Dec. 2013. Jan. 2014. <www.NDERF.org>

10   Entire website of: *International Association For Near Death Studies. 1996. 2013.* <www.IANDS.org>

11   Long, Jeffery M.D. and Perry, Paul. *Evidence Of The Afterlife, The Science of Near-Death Experiences*. New York, NY: HarperCollins, 2010.

Chapter 9

1   "Communication." *Wikipedia*. Jan. 2014. Jan. 2014. <http://en.wikipedia.org/wiki/Communication>

2   Moody, Raymond, MD. *Life After Life*. San Francisco, CA: Harper Collins, 1975.

3   McCarty, Rollin. Articles of the Heart. Institute of Heartmath. Oct. 2012. Jan 2013. <http://www.heartmath.org/templates/ihm/e-newsletter/article/2010/summer/energetic-heart-is-unfolding.php>

4   "50 Famously Successful People Who Failed At First." Online College. Jan 2014. Jan 2014. <http://www.onlinecollege.org/2010/02/16/50-famously-successful-people-who-failed-at-first/>

5   Coppers, Christopher. *Messages From The Light*. Pompton Plains, NJ: Career Press, 2011.

6   "Soulmate." Wikipedia. Dec. 2013. Jan 2014. <http://en.wikipedia.org/wiki/Soul_mate>

7   Moody, Raymond, MD. *Life After Life*. San Francisco, CA: Harper Collins, 1975.

8   Long, Jeffery M.D. and Perry, Paul. *Evidence Of The Afterlife, The Science of Near-Death Experiences*. New York, NY: HarperCollins, 2010.

9   Long, Jeffery MD. "Current NDERF Individual NDE Experiences" & "Archives Main Page." *Near Death Experience Research Foundation*. Dec. 2013. Jan. 2014. <www.NDERF.org>

10   Entire website: *International Association For Near Death Studies. 1996. 2013.* <www.IANDS.org>